It a great and good man
who is one of my
intellectual heroes. Thanks
very much for everything!

John Allen

POLITICS AND CAPITAL

Politics and Capital

AUCTIONING THE AMERICAN DREAM

John Attanasio

OXFORD
UNIVERSITY PRESS

OXFORD
UNIVERSITY PRESS

Oxford University Press is a department of the University of Oxford. It furthers the University's
objective of excellence in research, scholarship, and education by publishing worldwide. Oxford is
a registered trademark of Oxford University Press in the UK and certain other countries.

Published in the United States of America by Oxford University Press
198 Madison Avenue, New York, NY 10016, United States of America.

Library of Congress Cataloging-in-Publication Data
Names: Attanasio, John, author.
Title: Politics and capital : auctioning the American dream / John Attanasio.
Description: New York : Oxford University Press, 2018. | Includes bibliographical references and index.
Identifiers: LCCN 2017041361 | ISBN 9780190847029 ((hardback) : alk. paper)
Subjects: LCSH: Law—Economic aspects—United States. | Law—Political aspects—United States. |
Campaign funds—Law and legislation—United States. | Law and economics. | Libertarianism. |
Distributive justice.
Classification: LCC KF380 .A88 2018 | DDC 342.73/078—dc23
LC record available at https://lccn.loc.gov/2017041361

9 8 7 6 5 4 3 2 1

Printed by Edwards Brothers Malloy, United States of America

Note to Readers

This publication is designed to provide accurate and authoritative information in regard to the subject
matter covered. It is based upon sources believed to be accurate and reliable and is intended to be current
as of the time it was written. It is sold with the understanding that the publisher is not engaged in rendering
legal, accounting, or other professional services. If legal advice or other expert assistance is required, the
services of a competent professional person should be sought. Also, to confirm that the information has
not been affected or changed by recent developments, traditional legal research techniques should be
used, including checking primary sources where appropriate.

*(Based on the Declaration of Principles jointly adopted by a Committee of the
American Bar Association and a Committee of Publishers and Associations.)*

You may order this or any other Oxford University Press publication
by visiting the Oxford University Press website at www.oup.com.

For my wonderful wife, Kathy; and my loving family

Contents

Preface

IMAGINE YOU'RE PLAYING a Monopoly game.[1] You're winning but you run into a fix. Because you have the most money of any player, you decide to spend some of your money to get out of the difficult situation or to take advantage of a perceived opportunity. But rather than buy property, or houses, or hotels, you buy a rule change. That doesn't seem fair. Indeed that isn't possible under the rules of Monopoly. But it is possible in a game that is a bit more consequential than Monopoly. This game is called Democracy. And now, if you run into serious problems, and have money, you buy a rule change. That is what the rules—the *constitutional rules*—of campaign finance permit, indeed protect. Maybe this game's name should be changed. Monopoly now has many versions. At some level, this book is about a new version called Election Monopoly.

This book begins with campaign finance—the titanic challenge to the American epic. But the analysis doesn't end there. The problems plaguing elections and campaign finance illuminate a new philosophical approach called distributive autonomy.

Autonomy theory has been engulfed by modern libertarian theory. Modern libertarianism has drifted far from its original moorings of autonomy and liberty constructed by Immanuel Kant and John Stuart Mill. The analysis demonstrates the fallacies in highly individualistic modern libertarianism. Instead, it proposes a new philosophical idea called the principle of distributive autonomy.

Chapter 1 involves a fairly broad brush examination of the long-standing collision between traditional philosophical conceptions of liberty and equality, of how the campaign finance cases exemplify this collision, and how the principle of distributive autonomy avoids it. Chapter 2 engages in a fairly extensive analysis to discern what a principle of distributive autonomy might look like without actually stating much more than early approximations of the principle. The next few chapters examine the libertarian/property rights enterprise of American constitutional jurisprudence in the early twentieth century, the departure from this model in the middle of the century, and the return to a highly individualistic libertarian/property rights approach in the campaign finance cases. The critique further illuminates what the notion of distributive autonomy is about and what a more refined principle of distributive autonomy might look like.

Chapter 7 explores analytical problems with the campaign finance cases and several egalitarian critiques of those cases. After exploring the libertarian analysis of Robert Nozick and the attempt to reconcile liberty and equality by John Rawls, Chapter 8 presents the principle of distributive autonomy. Chapter 9 applies the principle in various ways, including constitutional arguments of how the campaign finance cases violate numerous constitutional provisions. The last two chapters demonstrate the economic dangers that highly individualistic libertarian notions have catalyzed. Chapter 10 talks about the astonishing correlation between the rise of economic inequality in America chronicled by Thomas Piketty and the 1976 decision of *Buckley v. Valeo*, the first of the campaign finance cases. Chapter 11 examines the potentially calamitous implications of this grossly unequal distribution of wealth and income for the demand curve and consequently for the *entire* economy.

One need not be focused on campaign finance reform to enjoy this book. One can easily skip over the legal chapters, particularly Chapters 5 and 6. They provide a concise but elaborate account of the major campaign finance cases. A large part of the constitutional case law is relegated to the endnotes so that readers will not get bogged down. Someone keenly interested in campaign finance reform can study the detailed endnotes in Chapters 5 and 6.

Even for someone who likes the current campaign finance regime, this book illuminates the scope of the philosophical, political, economic, sociological, etc. problems that it has spawned. It is at first blush surprising but upon reflection completely logical that campaign finance law would exert great impact. After all, elections constitute the *government*.

A constitution, and many other laws are almost like instructions in an Erector Set as to how people should go about constructing a government. So when one deals with something as important as election speech, there will be huge implications for the system. This is only natural, as voting and speaking are the two principal ways that the United States, and for that matter other democracies, form a government. If one changes people's participation ratios in these *constitutive* processes of speaking and voting—based on a variable of say, wealth or income—then there will be predictable skewing in the behavior of elected officials and the resulting regulatory structure that they fashion. Even if many of the same people would have been elected or appointed anyway, their behaviors would have varied dramatically as their incentives to gain election or re-election will have changed.

This chasm between popular representation and representation according to donations has precipitated the worrisome, perhaps dire, problems described in Chapters 10 and 11. The tremendous inequalities in political influence predictably have triggered immense inequalities in public policy, primarily but not exclusively expressed in the economy. They are also expressed in such non-economic policies as "three strikes you're out," which has helped generate a burgeoning prison population.

Elections matter. . . . In essence, what we are talking about here is whether we remain a capitalist democracy, or continue on our path toward an oligopolistic oligarchy. "In an oligarchy, as Isocrates wrote, even the citizens are really resident aliens."[2]

Notes

1. MONOPOLY © 2017 Hasbro.
2. Michael Walzer, Spheres of Justice: A Defense of pluralism and equality 61 (Basic Books, 1983).

Acknowledgments

I BEGAN THIS project over thirty years ago. Many people have been extremely helpful at various stages in its development. I would like to thank Norman Redlich—my Dean, co-author, and mentor; Judith Thompson, Terry Checki, Burt Neuborne, Jack Greenberg, Walter Murphy, Mary Ann Glendon, Jim Jacobs, Donald Kommers, Robert Post, Barry Cushman, Daryl Levinson, and Arthur Miller for their insights, wisdom, combativeness and disagreements at various stages of this project.

In particular, there are several individuals to whom I owe a truly great debt. First and foremost must be Guido Calabresi. One of the founders of Law and Economics, he advised me through early versions of the ideas contained in this volume. I have been most fortunate to have Guido as a teacher; he is such a generous mentor. He is brilliant, warm, wondrous, and wonderful. Most of all, he's hugely patient. William Nelson, one of the great legal historians of our time, labored through many different drafts a number of times, helping me immensely to elucidate the argument and make it cohere. Donald Elliott, one of the great figures in environmental law and risk analysis, offered deep insights and helped shepherd me through complex concepts of risk analysis that were vital to correlating the campaign finance cases and the inequalities chronicled by Thomas Piketty. Michael Walzer, one of the most profound thinkers of our time, provided important insights on Chapter 8, which proposes the principle of distributive autonomy, and on other matters. Bruce Ackerman, who has written so many important books in so many areas including this one, gave me sage advice on the publication process.

Louis Lusky, Justice Stone's law clerk when the famous *Carolene Products* footnote was drafted, generously provided me with personal insight into the process of drafting footnote four.

My editor, Jamie Berezin, was magnanimous with his time, and provided magnificent support and keen guidance. My editorial assistants, Alden Domizio and David Lipp, shepherded me through the publication process.

My most discerning critic is my wife, Kathy. I wish to thank her for her many invaluable comments and criticisms. My son Thomas also supplied abundant deep insights. My son Michael forced me to think clearly. I dedicate the book to my wife and my entire family.

I Challenges to Modern Libertarianism

For if liberty and equality, as is thought by some, are chiefly to be found in democracy, they will be best attained when all persons alike share in the government to the utmost.
Aristotle, *The Politics*[1]

... the principle of the sovereignty of the people governs the whole political system of the Anglo Americans. Every page of this book will afford new applications of that same doctrine. In the nations by which the sovereignty of the people is recognized, every individual has an equal share of power, and participates equally in the government of the state.
Alexis de Tocqueville, *Democracy in America*[2]

Notes

1. 98 (Stephen Everson ed., Cambridge Univ. Press, 1996).
2. 80 (Francis Bowen ed., Cambridge Univ. Press, 1863).

1 Distributive Autonomy and the Foundational Problem of Campaign Finance

A. The Idea of Distributive Autonomy

The great philosophy contest of the twentieth and twenty-first centuries has featured the values of liberty and equality. Some commentators have tried to exalt one over the other; some have claimed that only one or the other matters at all; a smaller group has labored to achieve some reconciliation.

This book proposes a new philosophical principle called "distributive autonomy." The principle of distributive autonomy aims to achieve some congruence, fusion—perhaps even some synthesis—between the two core constitutional values of liberty and equality in the touchy realm of first-order rights.[1] The eminent twentieth century philosopher John Rawls treats equal liberty as a first-order right, hierarchically ranked above his second-order right of equal opportunity and his third-order right of minimal resource equity propounded in his famous difference principle. However, Rawls never gives a systematic account of his first-order principle of equal liberty.

The principle of distributive autonomy seeks to elaborate what a confluence of liberty and equality might look like. It also articulates a version of liberty that does not violate equality. I contend that distributive autonomy represents authentic autonomy because it respects the autonomy of all.

Unlike Rawls's principle of equal liberty, the principle of distributive autonomy is sketched exclusively using autonomy values. Its main egalitarian quality is being

Politics and Capital. John Attanasio.

concerned with the distribution of autonomy. At core, Rawls's claim appears to be that liberty has to be allocated equally in a significantly unspecified way. A committed modern libertarian could easily dismiss this claim by arguing that it reduces to equality trumping liberty. The committed modern libertarian can simply reject the superiority of the equality claim in this or other contexts. Unlike the principle of equal liberty, however, the principle of distributive autonomy plays strictly with autonomy marbles. Consequently, the committed modern libertarian has difficulty simply dismissing distributive autonomy with the rhetorical flourish that liberty is more valuable than equality, or that equality is a pernicious value or simply doesn't matter at all.

B. The Lens of Campaign Finance

This volume endeavors to achieve some harmonization of the values of autonomy and equality with regard to first-order rights using perhaps the key first-order right of free speech.[2] The crucible for this attempted harmonization is the realm of democracy, free speech and campaign finance jurisprudence, where the tension between liberty and equality could not be more raw.

But why use campaign finance to illuminate a new philosophical principle? Campaign finance provides a penetrating, crystalline window through which to discern what a theory of distributive autonomy might look like. It comprehends and profoundly shapes autonomy, democracy, and the distribution—egalitarian or otherwise—of both power and wealth. Campaign finance has been a subject of intense debate in American politics and law for many years, as well it should. Elections are the heart of the American governmental process. Political campaigns erect the entire edifice of government, and government passes laws that routinely infringe on the autonomy of some and enhance the autonomy of others. Law affects such first-order rights as political influence and freedom from imprisonment, and lower-order rights involving the distribution of wealth.

So the nature of political campaigns goes to the heart of what the democratic state is about. As we shall see, elections go to the core of what autonomy and political theory are all about. At least insofar as the modern American polity goes, elections are among the most fertile areas in which constitutional law informs political philosophy and political philosophy informs constitutional law. In his second book, *Political Liberalism*,[3] Rawls himself, in an almost lawyer-like fashion, uses the U.S. Supreme Court's campaign finance cases as perhaps the key examples of deep violations of his principle of equal liberty.

Since the infamous Watergate episode, Congress has made stout efforts to circumscribe the role of money in politics. Constricting the sway of campaigning for dollars (rather than votes) has a long and respectable pedigree in American history.[4] However, in 1976, the Supreme Court of the United States emerged as the dominant player in the fray by striking down sweeping congressional reform of campaign financing as a violation of the First Amendment right of freedom of speech.

As I will elaborate, the campaign finance cases violate virtually any conception of a fair distribution of autonomy rights. Indeed in deciding these cases, the Supreme Court itself has repeatedly emphasized that displaying any concern with equalizing speech rights violates the Constitution. Consequently, the case law has generated a starkly disparate distribution in the autonomy to influence political elections. Predictably, the resultant disparities in the autonomy to choose representatives have dramatically skewed the formation of public policy. Elections choose representatives who make laws. Laws inherently draw lines that restrict the autonomy of many individuals and frequently enhance the autonomy of others. Ironically, the case law professing to protect autonomy actually infringes it.

Buckley v. Valeo[5] fundamentally altered the path of American constitutional jurisprudence and shattered the already dominant and then ascendant constitutional paradigm of participatory democracy, which nurtured distributive autonomy. The *Buckley* decision was an inflection point, leading the transformation of the prevailing paradigm from somewhat "*equalish*" participation to radically unequal participation in governance. Its new model of free speech jurisprudence connected access to the marketplace of ideas to personal and institutional wealth.[6] That case law does not rest on an affinity toward property interests or even toward laissez-faire economics, but on a construction of the Constitution premised on contemporary libertarian values. If the theory of distributive autonomy is correct, it scuppers the philosophical foundations on which the campaign finance cases rest.

Incongruously, the campaign finance cases ignore the democratic values on which the Constitution was erected. After all, the concept of individual liberty was primarily introduced in the Amendments, specifically, in the Bill of Rights. The original Constitution features a number of structural, instrumental values to advance liberty, the primary ones being divided power and democracy. As we shall see, the campaign finance cases consolidate rather than divide power and subvert democracy by guaranteeing government of the few rather than the many.

C. Property Interests v. Participatory Democracy

As elementary democratic theory would suggest, control of the political process translates into control over law. (Even many judges are elected). Predictably, a few short years after *Buckley* was decided, legislative policy began to turn sharply toward property interests as evidenced by the astonishing and temporally correlated rise in income share of the top 0.1 percent, to levels not seen since the Great Depression.[7] By "property interests," I simply mean persons who own substantial property of any kind. The focus here is on those who own mammoth amounts of property. In an October 2014 speech at the Federal Reserve Bank of Boston, Federal Reserve chair Janet Yellen remarked:

The past several decades have seen the most sustained rise in inequality since the 19th century after more than 40 years of narrowing inequality following the Great Depression. By some estimates, income and wealth inequality are near their highest levels in the past hundred years, much higher than the average during that time span and probably higher than for much of American history before then. It is no secret that the past few decades of widening inequality can be summed up as significant income and wealth gains for those at the very top and stagnant living standards for the majority. I think it is appropriate to ask whether this trend is compatible with values rooted in our nation's history, among them the high value Americans have traditionally placed on equality of opportunity.[8]

As Chair Yellen observed, things were not always this way. In fact, *Buckley* is nothing less than a metamorphosis not only of the American electoral system, but also of the American polity and our long-standing commitments to participatory democracy, individual autonomy, and equal opportunity.

The Supreme Court has the final word in construing the fairly general language of the comparatively succinct American Constitution. Consequently, the Court exerts tremendous influence in shaping what the American conception of democracy might be.

For almost forty years before *Buckley*, the famous "footnote four" in the Court's decision in *United States v. Carolene Products* had defined much of the American constitutional landscape.[9] As I shall outline, the *Carolene Products* decision was a reaction to, indeed a retreat from, a line of cases typified by *Lochner v. New York*. For the first third of the twentieth century, the Supreme Court protected property rights against economic regulation by striking down many democratically enacted laws, including maximum hours laws, minimum wage laws, child labor laws, protections for labor unions, etc.[10]

In 1938, *Carolene Products* proposed a constitutional settlement between the judiciary and the elected branches of government. In its simplest form, *Carolene Products* relinquishes judicial power to determine the distribution of societal resources and other social policies, devolving nearly all of these decisions on the democratic process.[11] The case refocused much judicial constitutional energy on ensuring the fairness of the democratic process to advance true majoritarianism.[12] Amplifying participation, footnote four safeguards the rights of citizens to influence this distribution of societal resources by speaking, associating in groups, and voting.[13] The footnote also protects those whose participation in the political process has been marginalized, viz. discrete and insular minorities who have repeatedly lost the political games.

Constructing a conception of democracy on the blueprint of *Carolene Products*, the Court gradually elaborated its core idea of participatory democracy. The Court did not originate this idea. As the quote from Alexis de Tocqueville's *Democracy in America* that begins this chapter suggests, this conception of democracy dates back to the original understanding of the Constitution; and, as the quote from Aristotle attests, long before.

American participatory democracy was at its apex at the end of the Warren Court era when myriad Supreme Court cases moved toward fashioning an egalitarian, in the sense of majoritarian, theory of participatory democracy focused on the rights to speak and vote.[14] This work of the Court may even have influenced the theory of "equal liberty" of

John Rawls, who published *A Theory of Justice* in 1971—two years after Chief Justice Earl Warren retired.[15] But the theme of participatory democracy, in the sense of majoritarianism, has dominated American political discourse. For example, over thirty years after the Warren Court, Justice Breyer said that courts should pay more attention to "participatory democratic self-government."[16]

Five cases in the free speech area, decided strikingly within seven years of Earl Warren's retirement, rekindled the same libertarian ideas that underpinned the *Lochner* line of cases. These new cases dismantled the participatory democracy essence of the *Carolene Products* settlement by reconstituting strong libertarian constitutional rights for property interests. The Court used libertarian values to amplify the public policy voices of property interests under the First Amendment. Chronologically, first, *Columbia Broadcasting System, Inc. v. Democratic National Committee* (1973)[17] foreclosed a general right of access to the media, free or paid. Then, *Lehman v. City of Shaker Heights* (1974)[18] began a sustained process of dramatically narrowing a right to speak for free on government property, including parks, streets, and sidewalks. *Lehman* curtailed places where one can speak for free, thereby dramatically constricting access to the marketplace of ideas for the less advantaged.

Hudgens v. NLRB (1976)[19] foreclosed a right of speech access to shopping centers, which for many people are the modern day equivalent of parks. *Virginia State Board of Pharmacy v. Virginia Citizens Consumer Council, Inc.* (1976)[20] extended free speech protection to commercial advertisements—which, by definition, advance economic or property interests. *Buckley v. Valeo* was actually decided slightly before *Hudgens* and *Virginia Pharmacy*, and ironically, all three of these cases were decided during the first six months of the Bicentennial Celebration of 1976. The Court decided these cases during the seven years following Earl Warren's retirement. During this time, five new justices came to the Court—Chief Justice Warren Burger (1969), Harry Blackmun (1970), William Rehnquist (1972), Lewis Powell (1972), and John Paul Stevens (1975).

Each of these five cases described above was the first in a cluster of cases. Some of these clusters contain more cases than others. If you multiply numbers of cases by number of pages per case, the campaign finance cluster may have more pages than all the other clusters combined.

Although the *Buckley* line of cases is not the only one driving the strong libertarian paradigm, this line is easily the most important. Hence the book focuses on them. Because the *Buckley* line involves elections, these cases most directly undercut the participatory democracy model of American governance. The *Buckley* case, and the many subsequent Supreme Court decisions on campaign financing that followed it, did not directly undercut electoral participation by using such libertarian doctrines as freedom of contract. Nonetheless, *Buckley* led the transformation of the electoral paradigm from increasingly "*equalish*" participation, to staggeringly, and increasingly, unequal participation based on a citizen's wealth. Indeed, the new paradigm of free speech jurisprudence connected access to the marketplace of ideas with personal and institutional wealth.[21]

During the heyday of the participatory democracy regime, free speech protection focused on content neutrality, that is, on allowing each individual the right to say whatever she wants to say.[22] This ensured that all ideas gained access to the marketplace of ideas in that government could not exclude ideas it did not like. I term this approach the "weak libertarian paradigm of free speech jurisprudence." The weak libertarian paradigm forbade government from denying access to the marketplace of ideas based on the idea's content. It also required government to permit broad access to speech on government property and allowed government to require at least some access to the broadcast media. In striving to afford access to all ideas on an equal basis, the weak libertarian paradigm of free speech jurisprudence was a crucial part of the Court's central project of advancing majoritarian participatory democracy.[23]

However, *Buckley* and its progeny protect[24] not only an individual's ability to say whatever she wants to say, but also her ability to use whatever resources she has *at her disposal* to express her ideas. This critical addition underpins what I call the "strong libertarian paradigm of free speech jurisprudence." By effectively incorporating the differential distribution of societal wealth into the marketplace of ideas,[25] the strong libertarian paradigm tremendously empowers property interests to amplify their voices, allowing a very few to crowd out—and effectively mute—the voices of the overwhelming majority of others. As previously noted, several of these lines of cases also limit places where one can speak without cost.

Economic theory would predict that property interests, shaped by their immense holdings and their tiny percentage of the population, will differ markedly from those who hold little property. As this text demonstrates, the ability of the mega wealthy to advance their interests in the marketplace of ideas eclipses the ability of those with lesser means.

Several front-page articles in the *New York Times* starkly depict the scope of the problem. According to an article published at the beginning of the 2016 political season: "Fewer than four hundred families are responsible for almost half the money raised in the 2016 presidential campaign."[26] Another article began:

With nearly $400 million raised during the first half of 2015, this has been the fastest start to a presidential contest. In a stark departure from previous elections, most of the money is flowing not into the campaigns, but into outside groups like "super PACs" and other political organizations that are allowed to raise unlimited amounts of money from wealthy individuals, labor unions, and corporations.[27]

Despite the onslaught of criticism, the role of money has grown ever larger. In the 2012 presidential election year, Barack Obama and Mitt Romney raised a total of $2,065,100,000.[28] Campaign finance has been among the biggest growth industries in the United States. In the 1992 presidential race, George Bush and Bill Clinton raised $185,000,000.[29] So the amount has skyrocketed by a factor of eleven in twenty years. To give an idea of the growth, a June 20, 2017, special election for a congressional House seat, which was admittedly off-cycle, raised over $50 million.[30] Adding to the disparities, in February 2016, the Internal Revenue Service awarded nonprofit tax-exempt status to an organization that looks and acts a lot like a PAC.[31]

D. The Discourse

Chapter 2 introduces the idea of distributive autonomy. It begins by offering some foundational ruminations about what comprises liberty and why it is valuable. The chapter explores notions of baseline autonomy and bounded autonomy. Baseline autonomy emerges from the idea that if autonomy is a universal value, it is valuable for all. Consequently, there are duties on the part of those who are autonomous actors in a society to ensure that some baseline of autonomy exists for all. This entails the controversial idea of imposing some minimal upper boundaries on autonomy in at least some instances. Specifically, these are instances in which imposing some upper boundaries is absolutely necessary to preserve some elemental level of baseline autonomy for all.

Chapter 3 discusses the Supreme Court's first espousing strong libertarian conceptions. In this first embrace, the Court focused on directly protecting liberty of contract and property by striking down laws that restrict those liberties. The chapter briefly sketches the Court's strong protection for property rights epitomized by *Lochner v. New York*.[32] The *Lochner* line of cases began near the turn of the twentieth century and reached its apex during the Great Depression of the 1930s.

Chapter 4 outlines what I call the *Carolene Products* constitutional settlement, which effectively was a peace treaty resolving a political war or crisis between the judiciary and the elected or political branches of government, particularly President Franklin Roosevelt. The crisis revolved around whether libertarian constitutional rights interpreted or invented by the Supreme Court played an important role in determining the regulation and distribution of societal resources in the United States, or whether the elected branches of government carried out that role. Chapter 4 describes how the *Carolene Products* constitutional settlement left the distribution of societal resources exclusively to the legislative and executive elected branches of government. The Court's primary role was to ensure that electoral and other political processes followed a fair framework for participatory democracy based on the core constitutional values of liberty and equality. The Court's focus on protecting the specific guarantees of the Bill of Rights primarily involves procedural protections for those accused of crimes. Closer to the concerns of this book, the *Carolene Products* footnote also focused on protecting the key democratic fulcrums of speaking, associating, and voting, and those minority groups who repeatedly have lost in the democratic games.

Chapter 5 chronicles the rise of the strong libertarian paradigm of free speech jurisprudence starting with *Buckley v. Valeo. Buckley* initiates a long line of cases that underwrite wildly disparate levels of participation in the democratic process. Specifically, it bestows on property interests strong and disproportionate rights through the electoral process to protect and enhance their already advantaged economic positions. In affording property interests a strongly disparate ability to legislate property protections, or rights, *Buckley* and its progeny share important parallels with *Lochner's* direct judicial constitutional protection of property rights.

Chapter 5 begins by recounting the absolutist speech protection positions of Justices Hugo Black and William Douglas. The first section shows how their absolutist positions laid the groundwork for the weak libertarian paradigm of free speech jurisprudence. It also demonstrates how their theories sowed the seeds of the strong libertarian paradigm. The second section of Chapter 5 examines *Buckley* and the early campaign finance cases, which play a central role in building the strong libertarian paradigm of free speech jurisprudence. These cases most overtly parallel the extreme libertarian, property rights thinking that undergirded *Lochner*.

Buckley and its progeny most directly undercut the *Carolene Products* paradigm. More than any other line of cases, this one paved the way for systematically incorporating the wealth inequalities in American society into the marketplace of ideas and consequently, into our democratic process.[33] The phrase "marketplace of ideas" derives from the dissenting opinion of Justice Oliver Wendell Holmes Jr. in *Abrams v. United States*.[34] Ironically, Holmes, whose classic *Lochner* dissent objected that the Constitution did not embody any particular economic theory, "uncritically accepted the view that constitutional status should be given to a free market theory in the realm of ideas."[35]

The third section of Chapter 5 describes the countertrend of decisions in the campaign finance area that for a short time exhibited sensitivity to the distribution of autonomy. During this countertrend, the Court reined in the strong libertarian paradigm to accommodate broader participation in electoral speech.

As Chapter 6 outlines, the strong libertarian paradigm quickly roared back and has reached a crescendo in *Citizens United v. Federal Election Commission*[36] and *McCutcheon v. Federal Election Commission*.[37] *Citizens United* protected electoral expenditures by corporations, and *McCutcheon* struck down limitations on aggregate campaign contributions, which *Buckley* had specifically upheld.

The 2014 *McCutcheon* decision represents the strong libertarian paradigm on steroids. Essentially, it empowers very few individuals to sway not only individual races but entire election cycles. It thereby enables those with resources essentially to purchase public policy. In this way, it goes further than any previous campaign financing decision. As political science would predict, the changes in the structural rules of the game have fueled even greater disparities in the distribution of wealth.[38] After all, campaign speech influences elections, which in turn influence public policy.

Chapter 7 begins with a political theory critique of how the campaign finance cases have jumped the tracks. It questions the extremely tight connection that the Supreme Court has posited between spending money on speech, and speaking.

The chapter probes some political theory approaches for cabining in the vastly undemocratic implications of the strong libertarian paradigm. It outlines some ideas of several influential egalitarian theorists. Their philosophical approaches have sought to curb the immense disparities in electoral influence spawned by the strong libertarian paradigm of free speech jurisprudence. To do so, they invoke—and arguably prioritize—equality.[39]

With the backdrop of the campaign finance cases, Chapter 8 formulates the principle of distributive autonomy. It begins by critiquing the robust individualistic libertarian theory of Robert Nozick. The chapter shows how far modern libertarianism has strayed away from the mother lode fashioned by John Stuart Mill's views on liberty and Immanuel Kant's conception of autonomy. It then examines John Rawls's principle of equal liberty. Rawls explains his concept of equal liberty partly through his critiques of constitutional (primarily free speech) cases.

Essentially, distributive autonomy injects allocative considerations into first-order autonomy rights. Distributive autonomy urges that if one takes autonomy seriously, one must be concerned about the autonomy of all, not just the autonomy of the few who have the resources to self-actualize their own liberty in an unbridled way.

Chapter 9 applies the principle of distributive autonomy to the campaign finance cases. Distributive autonomy subdues the anti-autonomy aspects of the virulent strong libertarian paradigm of free speech jurisprudence, while preserving the content-neutrality ideal of the weak libertarian paradigm. The chapter first applies the distributive autonomy principle, demonstrating how it would reverse the *Buckley* line of cases. It then uses the principle to scrutinize the work of two premier free speech theorists, Alexander Meiklejohn and Thomas Emerson. Both were heavily cited by the Supreme Court and as such helped to construct modern free speech jurisprudence. The theories of Meiklejohn are more congruent with the principle of distributive autonomy than those of Emerson.

The chapter then contrasts the sharply differential treatment that the Court has afforded voting rights, which has been heavily egalitarian, with its treatment of campaign financing rights, which has been deeply inegalitarian. What renders the incongruity more striking is that speaking and voting are the key fulcrums for influencing public policy in the United States.

Chapter 10 demonstrates some of the immense impact that the strong libertarian paradigm has had in recasting public policy in favor of property interests. First, the chapter gives some data about the impact that the *Buckley* campaign financing regime has had on the behavior of elected officials and public policy, particularly in taxation.

Relying on the work of Thomas Piketty and other distinguished economists, Chapter 10 demonstrates astonishing time correlations between *Buckley* and its progeny, and the geometric rise in income inequality in the United States. Uncanny time correlations exist connecting *Buckley* and subsequent campaign finance cases, with Piketty's charting the steep ascent of income inequality. These repeated temporal correlations suggest that the core source of the problems Piketty so assiduously and astutely depicts is a flawed Supreme Court jurisprudence. In sharp contrast with distributive autonomy, this jurisprudence is predicated on a philosophically incoherent individualistic libertarianism. This malaise has skewed the American system of participatory democracy and with it public policy. This conclusion is buttressed by evidence that the problem of wealth and income inequality has been uniquely amplified in the United States by post-*Buckley* taxation laws and other policies that strongly favor property interests.

Chapter 11 begins by discussing the dramatic contraction of the U.S. middle class post-*Buckley*. The chapter examines the problematical, potentially dire, consequences that the skewed distributions of income and wealth have had on the demand curve for goods and services. If the ballooning poor and dramatically shrinking middle class have less and less income, their purchasing power will contract once these consumers are loaded down with debt. Demand and supply could contract in a synergistic downward spiral. The chapter briefly shows how the 2016 election continues these dangerous trends. It also discusses the tax cuts candidate Trump campaigned on, and how they would exacerbate the already worrisome U.S. debt-to-GDP ratio to its highest point since the Second World War. The chapter also correlates the steep rise in the national debt with *Buckley*. This is predictable, as the tax cuts, which also correlate with *Buckley*, decreased government revenues, which increased debt.

Nobel laureate economist Milton Friedman thought that capitalism was necessary for freedom. By freedom, Friedman means narrow individualistic libertarianism. In contrast, the logical implication of this work is that democracy may be necessary to do, or at least to sustain, capitalism.[40] If political power becomes concentrated in the hands of a few, then it is unsurprising that economic power will become concentrated in the hands of a few. That is, oligarchy will lead to oligopoly. This is only natural as those in political power will deploy their political power to increase their wealth and economic power.

The concept of distributive autonomy contradicts Milton Friedman's core claim that individualistic libertarianism is necessary for capitalism, which is necessary for political freedom. Instead, the analysis suggests that distributive autonomy will provide more robust, perhaps essential, and deeply synergistic sustenance to capitalism, freedom, and democracy.

If this analysis is correct, this problem in political theory could have vital economic implications for all. Elections matter. . . .

Notes

1. JOHN RAWLS, A THEORY OF JUSTICE 179 (Harvard University Press, 1971, rev. ed. 1999). This work builds on earlier articles treating the distribution of autonomy for lower-order rights. John Attanasio, *The Principle of Aggregate Autonomy and the Calabresian Approach to Products Liability*, 74 VA. L. REV. 677 (1988); John Attanasio, *Aggregate Autonomy, the Difference Principle, and the Calabresian Approach to Products Liability*, in PHILOSOPHICAL FOUNDATIONS OF TORT LAW 299 (David G. Owen ed., Clarendon Press, 1995).

2. Justices and scholars have discussed the "preferred position" of First Amendment rights. "Freedom of press, freedom of speech, freedom of religion are in a preferred position." Murdock v. Pennsylvania, 319 U.S. 105, 115 (1943). Justice Douglas wrote the majority opinion. Justice Black also took this position. See HOWARD BALL, HUGO L. BLACK: COLD STEEL WARRIOR,

Chapter 8, *Commitment to "Our Federalism" and to the Primacy of Freedom of Expression*, esp. 188 et seq (Oxford University Press, 1996); Edmond Cahn, *The Firstness of the First Amendment*, 65 YALE L. J. 464, 474 (1956); Jack M. Balkan, *Some Realism about Pluralism: Legal Realist Approaches to the First Amendment*, 1990 DUKE L.J. 375, 392 & n.39. For a good summary of the preferred position doctrine in the case law, *see* Kovacs v. Cooper, 336 U.S. 77, 89 (1949) (Frankfurter, J., concurring). While the preferred position doctrine was never formally adopted by a majority of the Supreme Court, it has exerted great influence on the Court and effectively the Court treats the First Amendment in a preferred position.

3. JOHN RAWLS, POLITICAL LIBERALISM (Columbia University Press, 1993).

4. *See* ROBERT E. MUTCH, BUYING THE VOTE: A HISTORY OF CAMPAIGN FINANCE REFORM (Oxford University Press, 2014).

5. 424 U.S. 1 (1976). *Cf.* Richard H. Pildes, *Romanticizing Democracy, Political Fragmentation, and the Decline of American Government*, 124 YALE L.J. 804 (2014) (romanticized rights-oriented approaches including freedom of association and political equality have failed to consider adverse institutional consequences).

6. *See* John Attanasio, *Personal Rights and Economic Liberties: American Judicial Policy*, in GERMANY AND ITS BASIC LAW, 14 SERIES DRÄGER FOUNDATION 221 (Paul Kirchoff & Donald Kommers eds., Nomos Verlagsgesellschaft, 1993).

7. *See infra* chart accompanying notes 78–80, Chapter 10.

8. Janet L. Yellen, *Perspectives on Inequality and Opportunity from the Survey of Consumer Finances* (2014) http://www.federalreserve.gov/newsevents/speech/yellen20141017a.htm.

9. 304 U.S. 144 (1938). One notable exception is substantive due process jurisprudence; see Attanasio, *Economic Liberties*, *supra* note 6, at 236. Indeed, *Carolene Products* itself specifically rejects a substantive due process challenge. I have written about *Carolene Products* myself. *See* John Attanasio, *Everyman's Constitutional Law: A Theory of the Power of Judicial Review*, 72 GEO. L.J. 1665 (1984).

10. *See generally* notes Chapter 3.

11. *See* Attanasio, *Economic Liberties*, *supra* note 6. *See also infra* text accompanying notes 32–61, Chapter 4.

12. *See* JOHN HART ELY, DEMOCRACY AND DISTRUST: A THEORY OF JUDICIAL REVIEW 76–77 (Harvard University Press, 1980); Attanasio, *Judicial Review*, *supra* note 9, at 1680–81. Considerable judicial constitutional energy was also refocused on protecting the rights of the criminally accused, as the *Carolene Products* footnote itself proposed.

13. *See infra* text accompanying note 34, Chapter 2 and notes 8–10, Chapter 3. For a wonderful description of how democracy is the key value driving the American constitutional structure, see BURT NEUBORNE, MADISON'S MUSIC: ON READING THE FIRST AMENDMENT (New Press, 2015). Philosophically, democracy is predicated on the more fundamental values of autonomy and equality.

14. *See* ELY, DEMOCRACY, *supra* note 12, at 114–16 (characterizing the free speech jurisprudence of the Warren Court as helping those typically excluded from or disadvantaged in the marketplace of ideas).

15. *See* RAWLS, THEORY, *supra* note 1, at 194.

16. Stephen Breyer, *Madison Lecture: Our Democratic Constitution*, 77 N.Y.U. L. REV. 245, 248 (2002).

17. 412 U.S. 94 (1973).

18. 418 U.S. 298 (1974). Two subsequent key cases signal just how dramatically the Court would allow speech to be curtailed in the public forum. Perry Education Association (PEA) v. Perry Local Educators' Association (PLEA), 460 U.S. 37 (1983); Cornelius v. NAACP Legal Defense & Educ. Fund, 473 U.S. 788 (1985).

19. 424 U.S. 507 (1976).

20. 425 U.S. 748 (1976).

21. *See generally* Attanasio, *Economic Liberties, supra* note 6 (maintaining that modern free speech jurisprudence protects property interests); Norman Dorsen & Joel Gora, *Free Speech, Property, and the Burger Court: Old Values, New Balances,* 1982 Sup. Ct. Rev. 195, 240 (maintaining that the Burger Court prioritized both private and governmental property rights when they conflicted with speech rights); Frank I. Michelman, *Possession vs. Distribution in the Constitutional Idea of Property,* 72 Iowa L. Rev. 1319 (1987) (arguing that contemporary free speech jurisprudence exalts possession over distribution of property concerns).

22. *See* Geoffrey R. Stone, *Content-Neutral Restrictions,* 54 U. Chi. L. Rev. 46 (1987). *See generally* Norman Redlich, John Attanasio & Joel Goldstein, Constitutional Law ch. 12–15 (LexisNexis, 5th ed., 2008). For an interesting critique of certain aspects of the content-neutrality approach of the weak libertarian paradigm of free speech jurisprudence, see Jeremy Waldron, The Harm in Hate Speech (Oliver Wendell Holmes Lectures) (Harvard University Press, 2012).

23. Other parts of the Warren Court's free speech jurisprudence also advanced the overall project of participatory democracy. Notably, the Court's public forum jurisprudence ensuring that people could speak for free on streets, parks, and sidewalks also nurtured participatory democracy. *See, e.g.,* Cox v. Louisiana, 379 U.S. 536 (1965).

24. *See infra* notes 2–24, Chapter 5 & Chapters 5, 6.

25. *See generally,* Owen M. Fiss, *Free Speech and Social Structure,* 71 Iowa L. Rev. 1405, 1411–13 (1986).

26. Nicholas Confessore, Sarah Cohen & Karen Yourish, *Small Pool of Rich Donors Dominate Election Giving,* N.Y. Times, Aug. 2, 2015, at A1.

27. *Million-Dollar Donors in the 2016 Presidential Race,* N.Y. Times, Aug. 2, 2015, at A1. *See also* Phillip Elliott, *Power Brokers Recharge,* Time, Aug. 17, 2015, at 28 (chronicling political financial activities of the Koch brothers).

28. https://www.nytimes.com/elections/2012/campaign-finance.html.

29. https://theawl.com/how-much-more-money-do-presidential-candidates-raise-today-8bfcbcdd8960.

30. http://www.cnn.com/2017/06/20/politics/georgia-house-results-ossoff-handel/index.html.

31. Editorial, *How the IRS Just Made Political Dark Money even Darker,* Dallas Morn. News, Feb. 17, 2016, at https://www.dallasnews.com/opinion/editorials/2016/02/17/editorial-how-the-irs-just-made-political-dark-money-even-darker ("Karl Rove's conservative group Crossroads GPS").

32. 198 U.S. 45 (1905).

33. *See, e.g.,* Stanley Ingber, *The Marketplace of Ideas: A Legitimizing Myth,* 1984 Duke L.J. 1. Ingber notes problems with the market in economic theory, and also the flaws of extending the market metaphor to the context of protecting speech. *Id.* at 5, 15–17. *See also* Paul H. Brietzke, *How and Why the Marketplace of Ideas Fails,* 31 Val. U. L. Rev. 951 (1997).

34. 250 U.S. 616, 630 (1919).

35. *See* Jerome A. Barron, *Access to the Press—A New First Amendment Right*, 80 HARV. L. REV. 1641, 1643 (1967).

36. 558 U.S. 310 (2010).

37. 134 S. Ct. 1434 (2014).

38. *See infra* text accompanying notes 14-15, and notes 94 & 111-113, Chapter 5.

39. For the most part, these commentators seek to preserve the content neutrality of the weak libertarian paradigm, the traditional core of constitutional protection for free speech.

40. MILTON FRIEDMAN, CAPITALISM AND FREEDOM (University of Chicago Press, 1962).

2 Distributive Autonomy
AN INTRODUCTORY ESSAY

A. What Is Liberty? What Is Autonomy? And Why Do They Matter?

As the campaign finance cases are built on the value of liberty, this chapter seeks to place the case law into some philosophical context. The argument starts with some basic concepts of autonomy and liberty and describes why they are important. If autonomy or liberty is valuable, then they are valuable for everyone. Proceeding from this point, this chapter first explores the logical imperative that autonomy is valuable for all. If this is the case, there must be rights for each person to at least some baseline of this value. This baseline imposes duties on all in society to do their part, including giving up some of one's own autonomy to make a minimal amount of autonomy available to all. But once one accepts these duties, one accepts some kind of theory of bounded rather than unfettered individual liberty. As we shall see, even the most committed libertarians do not accept actual unfettered individual liberty.

The theory of bounded autonomy is more of a justification for the principle of distributive autonomy rather than a principle itself. This chapter only articulates a first approximation of the principle of distributive autonomy. This first approximation will provide a context for discussing the campaign finance cases in subsequent chapters.

To further sketch the initial contours of the principle, the discussion shifts to how key autonomy and liberty theorists have approached this problem. Butting the principle of distributive autonomy up against competing approaches is not intended to refine the

Politics and Capital. John Attanasio.
© John Attanasio 2018. Published 2018 by Oxford University Press.

principle but only contextualize it to enhance understanding. Even a first approximation will allow readers to glimpse how far the principle is from modern libertarian notions and from the campaign finance case law. Refining and sharpening the principle comes in Chapters 7, 8, and 9.

With this, we can begin the argument. Let's start with an important caution. It is commonplace to regard liberty and autonomy as cognate terms, to equate them, to consider them just different words to describe the same concepts or phenomena. This is a misconception. But let's start by assuming for the time being that they are the same thing. What are liberty and autonomy? And why are they valuable? A first approximation at an answer might begin with what they are not. Slavery and imprisonment constitute clear conditions in which liberty and autonomy are absent. One could take a first approximation of a definition for liberty or autonomy as free choice—or more metaphysically—free will. Conditions of slavery or imprisonment largely vanquish conditions of free choice or free will.

Of course, prisons can be onerous or *more* onerous. Take, for example, the prison depicted in the novel *The Count of Monte Cristo*, which sought to almost completely obliterate any notion of free will, or for that matter, any rudimentary notion of meaningful human existence, even identity. The same can be said for conditions of slavery. Some slaves were allowed to exercise at least a little choice whereas others were whipped, or otherwise harshly punished if they dared exercise any choice at all. Still, even under the best of circumstances, no account of imprisonment or slavery that I can imagine would satisfy even the most rudimentary conditions for what might be described as an autonomous state of being.

So to begin, let's agree that autonomy or liberty entails some minimal threshold of free choice, below which an actor's state of being cannot be meaningfully, realistically, or reasonably described as autonomous. The reason is that below that threshold the actor is not really behaving autonomously. Instead, the will of someone, or something, other than the actor is really at work. The choice is no longer the actor's, but really that of some other force or power external to the actor that trumps, overcomes, or supervenes the actor's free choice or free will.

For the present, I will not carefully distinguish between free choice and free will. Suffice it to say for now that free choice operates more in the short run as a kind of exercise of power over individual decisions on individual issues. In contrast, free will might be thought of as a kind of aggregation of truly, or at least minimally, free choices. Once one reaches that threshold, however defined, the actor's will could be accurately described as "free" in the sense of her existence being largely the product of her own choices. Precisely or even approximately how "free" each choice must be or roughly how many choices must be in some sense, "free," is something we could debate about endlessly.

As a first approximation, nearly everyone would agree that if we posit a being whose every choice is totally unconstrained by circumstances or by the choices of other beings, that being has something that might be described as almost a platonic type of ideal free will. But such a being only exists in theological or philosophical texts. To start, such a being would have to be omnipotent against all external forces, including all forces of nature.

For the sake of practical realities, let us assume that we are talking about human beings whose behavior is constricted in the countless ways that normal human beings are. Although it is interesting to speculate about the extent to which forces of nature can constrict autonomy and the extent to which those forces are divine, natural, or chance, let us put to one side debates that are more the stuff of theology, or metaphysics.

For purposes of determining autonomy violations, then, let us start by setting to one side forces of nature and to narrow constrictions on free choice or free will to those imposed by some human beings on others. Obviously, human beings could use natural forces to assist them in creating these conditions of constraint. For example, one could use a wild animal to help impose conditions of imprisonment. But still there is a human mover behind the constriction. So to start, let us define free will more narrowly as that state of being in which one's actions are totally unconstricted by the actions of other human beings. Much later in the argument we will deal with what obligations autonomy theory might impose on those who have had their autonomy decimated by nonhuman agents such as tornadoes or earthquakes.[1]

But at this point we must define what counts as an action by another human being. For starters, we should count only actions that are volitional. But what actions are truly volitional? Suppose I move forward and slip, falling headlong into another human being. Suppose the fall causes harm to that other human being. Is that harm volitional?

Suppose the fall was negligent, that is, that I was careless in not observing where I was going and thereby stubbed my foot on a curb, which caused my fall, which caused the other person's harm. Is that volitional? Certainly if I harm another individual intentionally, for example, by punching him in the face with my fist, that must be counted as a volitional act that constrains the other person's autonomy and liberty. Again, for now, I am not differentiating between liberty and autonomy.

But what about the negligent act? At least the law would count that as a volitional act because it has some element of volition and the actor exercised that volition negligently. Under those circumstances, the law would clearly consider me liable because my negligent act, which had at least some elements of volition, caused harm to another.[2]

Suppose instead that while I am moving forward, I am struck by lightning, which forces me into the other individual, thereby injuring her. Is my behavior volitional? The law would not count such circumstances to be the product of a volitional act, but rather as the intervention of a force of nature over which the actor had no control. But why would it not count that act as volitional? After all, the other person is truly harmed. I suppose the law would not count that act as volitional because doing so would supervene the autonomy of the person struck by lightning as the person struck had nothing to do with the injury.

In that case, I might as well have been a tree branch struck by lightning that fell onto the other individual. My own actions had about as much volition as did the tree branch to fall on the other individual. One would consider it absurd to hold the tree branch liable for the other individual's injury. Like the tree branch, I was just an object that the lightning propelled into another individual. So, just as the tree branch is neither volitional nor responsible, neither am I.

But there is a very important difference between holding me liable and holding the tree branch liable. Holding the tree branch liable poses no adverse consequences for the tree branch. First of all, it cannot pay or otherwise make recompense. Second, it is an object, which definitionally has no autonomy. In sharp contrast, holding me liable under these circumstances infringes on my autonomy. I am being forced to pay or otherwise make recompense in a situation where I am not at fault—indeed in which I have done no volitional act at all. Holding me liable under such circumstances infringes upon my autonomy or free choice.

Under the circumstances it would be not only unfair, but a violation of my autonomy, to hold me liable for the injury because I really did nothing to violate the other person's autonomy. But what if that person is still a victim and that person's autonomy has been infringed? If one accepts a baseline of autonomy for all in the society, then society has an obligation to aid, or rescue if you will, the person who, by pure accident has fallen below the baseline minimum. However, the way autonomy is remedied in this case should not be by individual compensation, but rather by societal compensation. Assuming that someone has fallen below the baseline of minimal autonomy, then society, usually acting through government, has an obligation to bring that person back above the baseline, however defined.

But that immediately begs the tantalizing question: Does the imposition of a small monetary exaction comprise an autonomy infringement? What about a large monetary exaction? How do we define small or large? Is the definition the same for a rich person as for a poor person? After all, exacting $10,000 would not meaningfully constrict the long-term or short-term choices available to an individual worth $100 million.

Let's start with the question of whether a monetary exaction imposed through taxation—rather than an outright taking of property—can comprise an autonomy infringement. Some committed libertarians would answer yes, as the individualistic libertarian would count property infringements as equal to, or at least in a moral sense equivalent to, infringements on one's person. As we shall see, this moral equivalence has generated considerable controversy in philosophical discourse and in constitutional jurisprudence. I will use the campaign finance cases as a clear lens through which to glimpse this controversy. The campaign finance cases provide a useful lens because they stand at the intersection of property rights and free speech rights.

Almost any account of rights considers free speech rights first-order rights, whereas modern American constitutional jurisprudence only counts a very narrow set of property rights as first-order claims. Essentially, the Supreme Court has narrowed these to outright takings of property.[3]

Strictly speaking, holding the extraction of money as morally equivalent to putting a person in shackles is the position embraced by punctilious libertarians. This is a core controversy that I will discuss in these pages. Just as restrictions against unjustified imprisonment protect first-order rights, so does protection for speech. At bottom, the campaign financing cases equate spending money for speaking with actually articulating ideas. But is that the proper approach? Can these really count as moral equivalents, or even as rough moral equivalents?

Let's start by considering the obverse situation. Suppose there is no connection between taking another's property and infringing on her autonomy. In that instance, we might lack a satisfactory moral account of how to stop one individual from taking the property of another individual. Many would agree that this is an intolerable situation.

However, the lack of autonomy rationales to stop taking property does not exhaust the possibilities in moral theory. An alternative adequate rationale might be couched in utilitarian terms. Simply put, a utilitarian seeks to attain the greatest good or happiness for the greatest number in the society. In order to achieve such a state of affairs, we obviously want people to work to produce goods and services that benefit all. Incentives for people to work commonly take the form of monetary compensation. Consequently, we could fashion a strong argument against taking property based strictly on utilitarian rationales of incentivizing work. After all, if one could just take another's property, willy-nilly, there would be no incentives to accumulate property through hard work or otherwise.

Alternatively, as renowned libertarian Robert Nozick hypothesizes, lacking laws against individuals simply taking property or otherwise infringing on rights, people would be strongly incentivized to form what Nozick calls protective associations. These are almost like tribes, in which people band together to protect each other against autonomy infringements, including against their property.[4] Nozick depicts protective associations as perhaps the key step in the formation of the state. Protective associations are a particularly convenient step in his formulation of his minimalist account of the state, which is his night watchman theory of the state. I shall discuss this account later in the text.

Although one might stick strictly to utilitarian reasons to defend property rights, one can readily imagine libertarian ones. Property frequently represents an accumulation of work through which compensation allows the owner to amass this property. One has made the "free" choice of working rather than enjoying leisure activities. That free choice was made on the basis of and entered into as a trade to receive property in exchange for the work. In this way property, including money, could be thought of as representing accumulated freely selected choices, over time, to forgo pleasurable activities, and work in order to accumulate property. These could be thought of as a kind of freely chosen, delayed gratification. In this way, simply taking property could be counted as an autonomy infringement: one had constrained one's autonomy in order to amass property and now that property is being taken away against one's free will.

Now the choices of forgoing leisure or other pleasurable activities in order to work were in many instances choices to constrain one's own autonomy. In many of these circumstances, the worker would have chosen a different activity and elected work solely or primarily to realize compensation. I don't mean to characterize work as strictly drudgery, as many people enjoy working, but if people worked primarily for self-gratification, compensation would become largely unnecessary. To admit that individuals pursue work partly for compensation only strengthens the libertarian's claims for property rights on what one has earned.

One problem with such liberty-based property claims is that they can lead to precluding nearly all takings of property of any kind, even taxation. Some committed libertarians do not describe this as a problem at all. Libertarians tend to encounter severe difficulties here as even the most committed libertarians adhere to the night watchman vision of the state in which the state provides fire and police protection. Of course, someone's got to pay for these services, usually through some form of taxation.[5] Formulations such as Nozick's protective associations are designed to get around such problems. Justifications for treating all infringements of property rights as autonomy infringements become stretched at that point. Aren't avoiding violence and maintaining some sort of order more fundamental autonomy interests than are takings of property?

Inherently Nozick's concept of a protective association is an admission that avoiding violence and maintaining some kind of order in the protection of one's property allows invasion of absolute property rights. Of course Nozick would resist the admission on the basis that the protective association has been voluntarily entered into. I don't resist this notion entirely. To have a robust notion of autonomy or to have anything like a free enterprise system, most contracts must be presumed valid and voluntarily entered into.

Even if the choice to enter into a protective association was authentic when the association was first formed, it is difficult to defend these choices as free many generations later. Of course, a third-generation member could elect to leave the association. But this might be unrealistic, as it might put one's life at risk particularly if other protective associations have the right not to accept new members. Hence one's choice is constricted by compelling payment to remain a member of a protective association one doesn't like. So implicit in Nozick's defense of a protective association is the idea that some infringement on property rights must be permitted—such as imposing taxes to pay for the protective association—to preserve a certain amount of order so that people can exercise autonomy. Inevitably, there is an admission that without a certain amount of order, authentic autonomy cannot exist. At this point, committed libertarians are on a continuum having to defend how much order is necessary to preserve autonomy. Their traditional dichotomous claim that the state, and for that matter any other actor, can do nothing to restrict one's autonomy becomes virtually impossible to defend. The device of a protective association is brilliant rhetorically but forces the committed libertarian into a debate as to how much in the way of restrictions liberty will permit. The basic claim that it permits no restrictions at all is relinquished. What forces this abandonment is the reasonable fear of anarchy.

B. Baseline Autonomy

As one can imagine, and as we shall see in greater detail in Chapter 8, extreme libertarian visions of the state can quickly descend into something scarily similar to anarchy. Even committed libertarians quite reasonably tend to oppose anarchy. Usually, they implicitly recognize that there has to be some order to permit the authentic exercise of liberty. Under conditions of anarchy, there is a kind of chaos, a condition in which no one has any liberty. So even committed libertarians often fashion complex theories and arguments to avoid anarchic situations.

This anarchic position has been roundly rejected by virtually all nation-states (except arguably failed states sui generis), and certainly all large modern, prosperous economies. Far from the anarchic position, all large modern, prosperous economies, as far as I am aware, embrace (at least nominally) moderate to aggressive systems of progressive taxation of property interests and social safety nets of varying densities to protect the poor and others. Consequently, some redistribution of property seems to be a widespread idea accepted by governments around the world from authoritarian to aristocratic to republican to radically democratic.

Of course, widespread acceptance does not entail philosophical justification. So let us see if we can find the beginnings of a philosophical justification in a concept that I shall call baseline liberty. I am not proposing baseline liberty as a philosophical principle to guide or regulate behavior. Instead, I offer it as the beginnings of a justification for the principle of distributive autonomy.

To start the argument, let us agree that any essential or elemental understanding of autonomy or liberty entails some minimal threshold of free choice. Below that threshold, the behavior of the actor cannot be meaningfully, realistically, reasonably, or authentically characterized as autonomous. Instead, the will of someone, or something, other than the actor is really at work.

It is difficult for a committed libertarian to avoid this position. Avoiding it necessarily entails some unsavory and, in my view, incoherent stances. However, this position carries with it a dangerous concession for the committed libertarian. Specifically, if one refuses to admit some minimal baseline, then a libertarian can justify slavery if the "choice" of slavery was somehow "freely" entered into. Actually, communists made similar arguments initially saying that they had been democratically put in power, and then using this allegedly democratic empowerment by the people as an everlasting basis to destroy the people's freedom and democracy. The unfortunate realities spawned by this argument turned out to be a sardonic contradiction in terms. That is, the so-called democratic empowerment allegedly exercised autonomously by the citizenry was used as a basis to wipe out democracy and autonomy.

As another mystifying incongruity that we shall see later in the argument, Robert Nozick in *Philosophical Explanations* pretty much spells out a justification for slavery in autonomy theory.[6] I believe this position is virtually impossible to defend for fairly obvious reasons: a libertarian, a person professedly strongly committed to freedom, has real difficulty justifying the massive deprivation of freedom that slavery entails.

Like many arguments that seem irrational, however, this one is not altogether so. Nozick is forced to defend this difficult if not incoherent position because the alternative is far worse from a Nozickian standpoint. The alternative of rejecting theories of slavery leads naturally to the "subversive position" of adopting some minimal baseline of liberty in order to coherently and legitimately describe the person's status as autonomous. Slavery inherently violates such a baseline. But once slavery violates liberty, what else does? At this point, we are on a dangerous slippery slope. (Again, I am generally using liberty and autonomy interchangeably in this chapter; I will later distinguish the two.)

C. Bounded Autonomy?

Another way of thinking about this minimal baseline is as a lower boundary protecting an elemental amount of autonomy. But once one accepts a minimal baseline of autonomy for all, that becomes a moral injunction, which the entire society and every individual in it has a duty to defend.

This duty leads to vexing dilemmas for libertarian theory. For example, what does one do about people who lack any resources so that they can basically not formulate any autonomous life plans? Suppose they can only barely survive? Or perhaps they cannot even achieve the minimal amount of sustenance to survive? These situations obviously describe declining levels of what might be characterized as minimal or baseline autonomy. Whatever the lower boundary might be, logically, it is difficult to maintain that a person who has died from starvation, lack of medicine, or other resource deficiencies has any authentic autonomy—at least not in this world. We could debate at great length as to what the correct lower boundary might be both in terms of what rights exist and how much protection supports those rights. However, it seems extremely problematic (arguably hypocritical) for one who values autonomy to maintain that no baseline, or lower boundary of minimal autonomy, exists at all. It is also quite difficult to differentiate this position from one of slavery. The only way to do this is to argue that, unlike the slave, the starving (dying) person has no master or subjugator. But this defense invites causality thickets of why this person is starving to death. Causality becomes even more tricky if she is starving to death in a land of plenty. Moreover, from the point of view of someone starving to death, her situation might even be worse than slavery. And it is the reasonable point of view of the starving person that counts because that person's moral claim to some baseline of the intrinsic value of autonomy has been violated. Without life, autonomous existence is impossible in this world.

In a curious and ironic way, maintaining that the individual who lacks adequate sustenance to live should simply be cast adrift is inconsistent with the committed libertarian's rejection of anarchy. Inescapably, rejecting anarchy entails embracing the position that autonomy can be restricted. The kind of weight that one must place on choosing to belong to a protective association in order to avoid this problem is simply unsustainable. As previously stated, the argument that its members at one time consented to it is similar to the one that Soviet Communists once made. So the claim that the initial formulation of a protective association binds future generations is similarly unsustainable. As we shall see, so is the Nozickian device of claiming that an initially equal distribution of property gives moral justification for gross inequalities millennia later.

The claim that initial consent in a kind of state of nature to a protective association is rendered even more difficult generations later, as once one is born into a protective association that has lasted for generations, one is born into a milieu in which thousands if not millions of expectations—contractual and more casual—have been generated that will likely render extricating oneself from that association intolerably expensive in property and other terms. This further constricts the autonomy justification of a protective association as having been freely entered into.

At the end of the day, the only reason to reject anarchy is to preserve some meaningful baseline of autonomy for all. The same rationale can be applied to justify some taxation to avoid people falling below some minimal level of sustenance. After all, what is the difference? As far as I can see, there are only two ways to reconcile these contradictory positions. One is to place this unsustainable weight on the initial choice to enter into a protective association even generations later. The other alternative is to suggest that entering into a protective association benefits many if not all who enter into it whereas maintaining a lower boundary of sustenance benefits fewer people. Of course, the committed libertarian would resist this alternative as heresy as it reduces to a greatest good for the greatest number argument, which they consider starkly utilitarian. Paradoxically, the argument to maintain some baseline of individual liberty for all—at least sustenance—is very much one articulated in individualistic autonomy terms rather than societal ones.

Once one embraces a theory of bounded autonomy, though, one must provide for those people who lack any resources to survive without the social safety net that many libertarian theorists so deplore. Consequently, recognizing some minimal baseline of autonomy, as I urged toward the beginning of this chapter, is a heretical move for the committed libertarian. One alternative is Nozick's odious but immense and intellectually honest concession of defending even slavery, which is antithetical to any coherent account of an autonomous state of being. My own suspicion is that Nozick makes this concession because not making it risks undercutting the highly individualistic libertarian conception that he formulates.

Again, once one admits to any minimal baseline of liberty for all, one accepts a moral injunction to defend that baseline. Only the state through such periodic "heretical, anti-autonomy" moves as redistributive taxation can defend or enforce the baseline. So once one accepts the fundamental value of autonomy, he inevitably marches toward providing the basis for defending some baseline, or minimal level of autonomy for all.

If one recognizes some baseline of minimal autonomy for all, then one introduces egalitarian notions into autonomy theory. But what does that mean? In his article, "The Empty Idea of Equality,"[7] Peter Westen argues that equality is an empty vessel because it inherently begs the question, "equal as to what?" Once one recognizes autonomy as a universal value, a very coherent answer that autonomy theory provides is "equal as to autonomy."

Of course, as I will discuss in greater detail, trying to achieve total equality in the distribution of autonomy has frequently produced draconian governments put in place to effectuate a harsh leveling of people regardless of their work, talents, risk-taking, etc. This kind of egalitarianism clearly violates Aristotle's concept of equality, which requires treating likes alike and consequently taking disparate work, talents, and risk-taking into consideration in any just reward structure. John Rawls pushed back on these ideas somewhat maintaining that one's talents including one's ability to engage in hard work are largely a matter of luck. Pursuing this debate at this point takes us far afield. My value commitments are probably somewhere between the two, but probably closer to Aristotle's.

But the professed radically egalitarian regime is an easier position to evaluate and reject. Paradoxically, the regimes that have professed radical equality have produced radical inequality. Witness the examples of communist systems, which far from being egalitarian, tended to be radically hierarchical to the point of being not just authoritarian but totalitarian. They also produced oligarchies of elites whose resource positions, although frequently mediocre, eclipsed those of non-elites. Instead of the draconian leveling of radical egalitarianism in any distribution including the distribution of autonomy, a far more attractive approach would appear to be some sort of bounded equality in the distribution of autonomy. Thus far, we have only outlined the rationale for lower boundaries. So to describe the argument to this point, we might refer to it as seeking to establish a kind of "baseline autonomy."

At this juncture the debate shifts to what generally is entailed by this minimal autonomy for all. A common move is to segregate economic resources and property from more fundamental rights such as the right against unjust imprisonment or other unjust punishment. But segregating out all economic resources becomes difficult for the following simple reason: it is quite difficult to argue the position that one has any meaningful, authentic autonomy without having some minimal level of resources.[8] Taken to its logical conclusion, a human being without any resources, including food and water, dies. It is difficult to argue that a dead person is autonomous in any sense of the word.[9] Of course, the modern individualistic libertarian punctiliously believes in protecting property rights. Now the move that she is forced to make is to prefer her autonomy over her property as more important than another individual's autonomy to live.

Now to say that authentic autonomy entails some minimal level of resources does not elaborate a comprehensive baseline theory of autonomy. Without making any pretense of formulating an exhaustive account, candidates for possible rights that might be measured against this baseline might include: a right to free speech and thought, and to one's religious beliefs and practices; a right to participate in decisions that restrict one's autonomy such as laws or judicial process, and some right to authentically and actually influence those decisions; a right not to be tortured, which includes having to endure unnecessarily harsh conditions of imprisonment; certain protections in a criminal trial including a right against self-incrimination, a right to counsel, and a right to confront one's accusers; a right not to be discriminated against based on certain arbitrary criteria such as religion, race, ethnicity, nationality, or gender rather than one's ability or performance including some entitlement to recompense for past discrimination; a right to have laws solely focused on future behavior; a right not to have criminal laws, particularly legislation, targeting specific individual persons; rights to privacy in one's home and some rights in certain personal matters concerning the family, reputation, and sexuality; a right not to have one's property expropriated qualified by the government's power to tax; perhaps some right to education and certainly some baseline right of sustenance; and a right not to have one's choices manipulated by deception, misrepresentation, trickery, or traps such as police entrapment.

This account of first-order rights is neither meant to be exhaustive nor even consequential but merely hypothetical based largely on what some constitutions, legislatures, courts, and the academy have said. Even those bodies frequently disagree about parts of this inventory. Spelling out an account of baseline autonomy, even one only involving first-order rights, travels far beyond the thrust of this work. Even in this preliminary account of baseline autonomy, restrictions on campaign finance engage many autonomy interests. These include free speech, and fair process in passing laws that commonly restrict or enhance autonomy.

Moreover, the preliminary autonomy baseline I have sketched out does not even engage lower-order autonomy interests, such as the density of protection offered by a social safety net. As I have suggested the *complete* absence of such a net would appear to rise to the level of violating first-order autonomy rights. But these are complex questions for another day.

Like many accounts of autonomy, mine is built on reciprocity. Some highly individualistic libertarians may deny autonomy's essential reciprocal nature. Virtually all conceptions of autonomy forbid harm, but generally this means harm to others. What counts as harm can sometimes be quite vague. The predominant modern libertarian conception of Robert Nozick defines harm as any direct incursion on the person or property of another. In Nozick's thought, the concept of harm comprehends even slight incursions.[10] My theory modifies and expands the concept of harm to include not infringing on the autonomy of others. Baseline autonomy broadens the concept to include not only direct harms caused by another human being but indirect harms however caused. From the perspective of the person below a minimum level of baseline autonomy, it doesn't matter very much whether his harm was caused, directly or indirectly, or whether it was caused by another human being or some force of nature. All that matters is that he has fallen below this baseline, not the lack of a direct human incursion. The same should be the case from the perspective of moral theory. After all, to pursue my earlier example, why should the person upon whom a tree has fallen receive compensation if I negligently cut the tree down but not if the wind blew the tree down on him? What is the moral difference? The "luck" that one mishap was caused by a human agent? If one's baseline autonomy is valuable, it remains valuable whether or not it has been infringed directly or indirectly by some human force, or directly or indirectly by some nonhuman force. Once baseline autonomy is restored, there may be differences in compensation—for example, for reasons of deterrence if a human actor is culpable—but these are complex questions.

Nozick would argue that even the small wealth assessments exacted to bring others above the baseline violate autonomy by infringing on property rights. However, unlike Nozick and like Rawls and most nation-states, I view the infringement on property through taxation as a lower-order right to be legislatively determined whereas falling below a minimum baseline of autonomy involves first-order rights. Logically, it seems much more fundamental to my autonomy whether I have the ability to eat tomorrow than whether I can travel to Italy for pleasure tomorrow.

Obviously, brought to its logical extremes, my expanded view of harm could be profoundly constricting. Much, perhaps most, behavior indirectly constricts the autonomy of others. However, this more expansive view of harm is more congruent with the human condition. It's a give-and-take world as we try to live on this ever smaller planet together, as there are more and more of us. If there is one bathroom on a plane and I want to use it, does that infringe on your liberty? Technically yes. My behavior constrains you from doing what you want to do. But does this behavior rise to the level of a violation of the other person's autonomy in moral theory? Surely not.[11] If merely one person's using the bathroom when two people want to use it counts as an autonomy violation in moral theory, then paradoxically no one would have autonomy: everyone's autonomy would get constricted, or gridlocked, by the autonomy of others.

Hence, the attraction of a minimal baseline of autonomy. One's behavior does not violate first-order autonomy rights (or in the case of the bathroom example, any autonomy rights) unless one's behavior causes the autonomy of someone else to fall below a certain level.

Once one accepts some minimal baseline of autonomy, one has embraced this as a moral injunction and consequently, one accepts commitments to enforce that moral injunction. The moral injunction must entail some protection against the constrictions on any individual's liberty that bring her liberty below a certain minimal level. Logically then, once one accepts an injunction of baseline autonomy, one must accept some concept of bounded autonomy to protect baseline autonomy. That is, baseline autonomy entails bounded autonomy. This is what the controversy is all about. In a world of infinite resources where protecting baseline autonomy would literally come from the sky, no one would object. There would be no moral predicate for the objection. Where the controversy comes in is that my resources have to be used to guarantee some baseline level of resources for you.

Now we approach a first formulation of a principle of distributive autonomy. In order to coherently propagate a society in which liberty matters, and certainly one in which liberty counts as one of the most fundamental values, one must defend some minimal level of liberty for all. Sometimes, as far as I can see, the only way possible to do this is to impose some relatively weak upper boundaries on the autonomy of the more privileged. Hence the term "bounded autonomy."

I purposely use the words "more privileged" as a dodge. It allows me not to spell out with precision who occupies the more privileged group. Who are the more privileged, and how much can their autonomy be constricted for the sake of preserving this minimal level of autonomy for all? These are very difficult questions usually answered democratically by societies in significantly different ways, through systems of redistributive taxation and social welfare, through systems of regulation, through conceptions of property rights, and most solemnly through conceptions of criminal law. Different societies express their values by counting different acts as criminal or not. For example, the debate currently rages in America about the criminalization of the medical use of marijuana: the federal government forbids it whereas a majority of states permit it. Arriving at answers to these complex questions in conceptions of criminal law, which could involve imprisonment or even execution, matters tremendously. Democratic societies put much of this weight on the legislative process. That is one reason the fairness of the electoral process matters so much.

But this only begs further questions. For example, what is the content of first-order rights to be protected by this baseline? Does the baseline adjust with the nature of the first-order right so that there are actually multiple baselines? For example, is the baseline of minimal protection higher for a protection against torture (in the sense of banning virtually all torture) than it is for some baseline level of nourishment for all? In that case, are some rights so fundamental to autonomy that they are excluded from the legislative process by being codified in constitutions that are difficult to amend?

Again, if autonomy is a fundamental moral value, then everyone would appear entitled to some minimal amount of it. Many committed libertarians profess that liberty is not only a value, but the most important value. If this is the case, it is very difficult—selfish or hypocritical, or incoherent, or all three—to defend the position that some people have tremendous amounts of autonomy while other people have none. In fact, as evidenced by the abhorrent embrace of slavery itself, some committed libertarians will defend the libertarian right of some people to enslave others if those others "freely" enter into the transaction of selling themselves into slavery. It generates some logical conundrums to defend liberty as universally valuable if it is not universally protected to some minimalist level.

Preserving some lower boundary or baseline of a minimal level of autonomy requires certain upper boundaries on autonomy. One logically entails the other. Committed libertarian theorists absolutely shun upper boundaries. But once one espouses some minimal level of autonomy for all, there is no logical alternative except to be able to infringe on the absolute liberty of the more privileged. As we shall see, other approaches could be used that are more hydraulic than the term upper boundaries would suggest.

D. Distributive Autonomy: A First Approximation

I offer the notion of bounded autonomy not as a principle but rather as a rationale or partial justification for the principle of distributive autonomy. Among other difficulties, offering the idea of bounded autonomy as a principle is too rigid. The notion of boundary lines itself implies rigidity along those lines. Consequently, one could theoretically allow very large autonomy incursions against the autonomy-advantaged without demanding any moral justification beyond that of preserving some ill-defined minimal baseline for the autonomy-disadvantaged. In contrast, as we shall see in Chapter 8, the principle of distributive autonomy is paradoxically both more flexible and more constrained. For example, it focuses on certain actions that "unduly constrict" the autonomy of others. Implicit in the concept of "undue constriction," there is at least some moral responsibility, or at least causality, for the unacceptably diminished state of autonomy for those whose autonomy falls below a certain minimal baseline.

Fashioning a minimum autonomy baseline just exposes another problem with bounded autonomy. Any attempt to fashion bounded autonomy as a principle would necessarily entail defining a minimal level of autonomy for all. Specifying what an appropriate baseline might look like is a daunting prospect. One could say that democracies leave many of these questions to the elected branches of government and ultimately to the people. This is not a trivial response. As I will elaborate in the next two chapters, U.S. constitutional law devolves many of those decisions to the majoritarian branches of government. By majoritarian, I simply mean the branches of government that are elected by a majority of their defined constituencies—for example, senators from Iowa being elected by a majority of Iowans who voted. But the campaign finance cases changed all that.

Even if majoritarianism supplies some of the answer, it does not completely eliminate the problem of morally justifying a particular baseline. A school of legal philosophy called positivism maintains that law is whatever the legislature (or other lawmaking institutions) says it is. However, even the most committed positivist accepts external moral critiques of majoritarian legislative judgments.[12]

Of course, even the principle of distributive autonomy requires the difficult determination of what amounts to an undue constriction of another person's autonomy. In some ways, trying to work out what comprises an "undue constriction" offers problems similar to divining what might be an appropriate baseline of autonomy for all. But undue constriction has some parallels with the traditional autonomy mantra of harm. Avoiding undue constrictions is also a more fluid and dynamic enterprise than is determining and maintaining what an appropriate minimal baseline of autonomy for all might be. A minimal baseline implies some sort of entitlement, which might be more difficult to discern or define.

As one might expect, autonomy and libertarian theorists have always had great difficulty working out precisely what constitutes harm. But determining what constitutes harm still has several great advantages over establishing a baseline. First, harm is contextual to the particular situation or facts at hand whereas a baseline or boundary line is painted with a broad brush. Moreover, establishing harm can be somewhat backward-looking. Its contextual nature necessarily entails looking at facts in retrospect. In contrast, establishing a baseline is usually forward-looking or prospective.

Despite these practical problems, establishing some minimal baseline of autonomy for all in and of itself seems conceptually uncontroversial. As previously discussed, what introduces controversy is the notion of having to infringe on someone else's autonomy in order to attain that baseline. Thus, we moved quickly from the idea of baseline autonomy to bounded autonomy. Here's where the controversy lies: How much can one infringe on the autonomy of the more privileged to satisfy some minimal baseline of autonomy for all?

Nozick and committed individualistic libertarians would say not at all, as taking even minimal amounts of property from some to help others uses those from whom these exactions are made as means in violation of the categorical imperative of Immanuel Kant. This is ironic because Kant himself, as Chapter 8 elaborates, would respond that true autonomy entails extensive duties toward others. This idea fundamentally impairs Kantian support for Nozick's position.

A first approximation at answering the question of how much one can infringe upon the autonomy of the autonomy-privileged to achieve any minimal baseline must start with what is the minimal extent possible to preserve some basic level of autonomy for all in the society. At the outset, at least two kinds of constrictions on the autonomy-advantaged are probably necessary to preserve some minimal level of autonomy for all. First, one must have outright strong prohibitions of the more privileged totally stripping the less privileged of all autonomy or even of considerable autonomy. A good legal example is the prohibition against slavery codified in the Thirteenth Amendment of the U.S. Constitution. Another, more controversial example, would be antitrust laws, which seek to avoid undue constrictions on one's autonomy to enter a business. Perhaps because these restrictions on autonomy are less direct, more difficult to perceive, and (rightly or wrongly) somewhat controversial, antitrust laws are not enforced nearly as stringently as antislavery laws. More important, the moral implications of slave systems are much more intuitively disgusting as they inherently, and very directly, entail immense autonomy incursions.

Just because many societies count slavery and monopolistic behavior as autonomy infringements does not mean that societies treat the two behaviors as commensurate. Societies tend to treat slavery as a serious constitutional violation, whereas monopolistic behavior is frequently only prohibited by statute.[13] Moreover, enforcement of slavery prohibitions has tended to be quite vigorous whereas antitrust enforcement has varied considerably over time. Descriptively, the laws of many countries have approached antitrust rights as lower-order and antislavery proscriptions as first-order rights.

The principal topic of this book concerns another kind of serious autonomy infringement. This one involves the power of great wealth to overwhelm the ideas and votes of the majority of the society. By disproportionately influencing the campaign process, the very wealthy can elect an enormously unequal number of representatives keen to advance their interests. Through these representatives, property interests can refashion public policy to broadly enhance their autonomy and conversely to broadly constrict the autonomy of the overwhelming majority.

But why does this behavior engage first-order rights? After all, the political branches commonly make decisions about the distribution of wealth, which for the most part entails lower-order rights. But to say decisions about the distribution of wealth generally involve only economic rights does not mean they are unimportant. It is also important to distinguish economic rights from the autonomy to participate in deciding the distribution of economic rights. The principal thrust of this book involves the decision-making process that entails first-order rights such as speaking and voting, rather than the actual distribution of economic resources, which generally do not. However, as vital as the distribution of economic resources are, the political branches decide so much more. To take an easy example, the political branches decide what is a crime and what punishment that crime engages, including imprisonment—and in many societies—even death. In many societies, convictions of serious crimes eliminate many opportunities, including employment, and even participation in the body politic such as voting and running for many public offices.

Overwhelmingly, laws draw lines. Those lines commonly comprise prohibitions that frequently restrict the autonomy of some while advancing the autonomy of others. A very important moral justification for such autonomy restrictions and enhancements is the ability of all those whose autonomy may suffer constraints to have at least a roughly equal voice in what those constraints shall be.

Modern individualistic libertarians have vociferously argued that, for example, infringing in any way on one's right to influence elections profoundly impairs autonomy. Even if one accepts the position, the principle of distributive autonomy recasts it, maintaining that unfettered choice to influence elections allows some people to deeply infringe the autonomy of others. Notions of baseline autonomy help to illuminate this reality.

The ability to influence elections in a grossly disproportionate way entails a special, fundamental kind of autonomy infringement. It allows some people to virtually take over the processes by which public policy is made. For many, this kind of autonomy infringement generates a downward spiral of lower-order and even first-order autonomy rights. That is, affording some people a grossly disproportionate voice in fashioning public policy allows them to enact laws that will further artificially enlarge the disparities in resources that inherently populate any free market economy. By resources, I am talking about more than material wealth and would include such other goods as education, safety, health, freedom from unjust imprisonment, etc.

Once the ability of economic wealth to influence public policy becomes legally protected, those with money will have the ability to influence public policy in such a way as to further increase their overall resources including wealth. This increase in resources will give them further potential to enhance their ability to shape additional public policy to further enhance their resources, including wealth. In turn, their wealth and other resources can be used to further skew public policy in their favor. And so on. . . .

Thus, this ability to disproportionately influence elections generates the power to unfairly grow one's autonomy that can be used, or really abused, to further diminish the autonomy of others. Viewed from this more complete rather than myopic lens, the *Buckley v. Valeo* line of cases does not protect the liberty of some to spend as much money as they please to influence elections. Instead, these cases entail one of the most far-reaching infringements on autonomy in the history of American constitutionalism.

So, in order to critically examine these cases, let's begin with a first approximation of a principle of distributive autonomy. Let's posit a principle that at least prohibits someone from unduly constricting the autonomy of someone else. Undue constriction is key to distributive autonomy, and attention to the distribution of autonomy is a moral injunction for anyone who takes autonomy seriously.

The concept of bounded liberty seems somehow counterintuitive. After all, the theoretical idea animating liberty is to free individuals of boundaries. Indeed, the unrealizable ambition is to free the individual of all boundaries. Rather than posit some Platonic ideal type that is beyond reach (at least given the realities of this world), the committed libertarian wants this fanciful state of being to exist now and strives mightily toward it.

This ceaseless striving creates severe difficulties. Let's take the example of an individual in Africa in a drought-stricken country who cannot feed his children. Facile reactions might say that this is due to a lack of prosperity in the country, which is due to a lack of freedom and free markets. But suppose this condition is owing to drought? Certainly this is a realistic assumption. I suppose the committed libertarian would then say that the theory cannot account for natural causes and that within the limits imposed by nature, maximizing the ability of the individual to be free still produces the best society. But once one accepts limits imposed by nature, one has admitted to the idea of boundaries, indeed to the many boundaries that nature imposes. Again, the committed libertarian would say that we accept the world as we find it, and that the best way to live in this world is to maximize the freedom of the individual.

But let's explore this very realistic hypothetical a bit further. Suppose the individual is a father who cannot feed his children. Suppose further that his deepest desire, his first and most important free choice, is to feed his children. How much liberty does this man have? Again, the committed libertarian would respond that he can still be given the most liberty that he can exercise given his circumstances. This extreme disconnection of liberty from resources that supply the foundations for any ability to exercise freedom in any meaningful way is highly unrealistic to the point of being ideological. I do not use the term "ideological" in the modern pejorative sense. In its strict sense, being ideological may be noble. It entails the pursuit of an ideal. One characteristic that distinguishes the ideologue, however, is that the ideologue pursues that ideal in ways that are unrealistic in the sense of being disconnected from reality.

The ideologue may say that pursuit of this ideal will reshape present reality in ways that will curb if not eliminate the problem. But tell that to the father who cannot feed his children. Ideologies disconnected from reality have been proven to be pernicious. Take communism. The Marxian ideal of "from each according to his abilities to each according to his needs" seems quite noble. But it was totally disconnected from many realities, including human nature. Consequently, it failed miserably and turned out to be complete nihilism, ravaging freedom, equality, and the human spirit.

Let's push the analogy about the father who can't feed his children a bit further. Suppose that out of desperation to feed his dying children, the father sells himself into slavery. In *Philosophical Explanations*, Nozick justifies slavery provided that the transaction was freely entered into.[14] Now, one might argue that selling oneself into slavery under these conditions was not a freely entered into transaction. Once one makes that move, however, many, many transactions become subject to challenge. Nozick is intellectually honest in not offering an account that would challenge this transaction. His notion of freely entered into transactions is thin, amounting to an assumption that virtually all transactions are freely entered into.

However, Nozick goes even further and independently justifies slavery: it may enable the freedom of some to pursue transcendent meaning or being. This is a foreseeable, perhaps inevitable, consequence of his theory. But again, it seems at best tortured to use libertarian theory to justify a condition of slavery.

Consequently, some conception of bounded autonomy seems inescapable, if one is to take autonomy seriously. Moreover, I have carefully avoided scenarios in which human actors have played some role in infringing the autonomy of the hapless African father. Human intervention makes the case somewhat easier in terms of drawing close to the concepts of human culpability (in autonomy terms) and undue infringement.

Once one takes some concept of bounded autonomy seriously, the boundaries must be set realistically and very carefully, particularly in the area of fundamental rights, if one is to avoid the tragic steamrolling of humanity that was the essence of the Communist world.

To be serviceable, philosophical theories must be consonant with the real world in which they exist. They must serve humankind rather than some ideological fantasy disconnected from the realities in which we live. They cannot be extreme, however, as extremism frequently degenerates into ideology. This classic contrast in philosophy dates back to ancient times. For example, Plato posited the concept of an ideal. In fact, we call it a Platonic ideal. Pursuing this ideal led to his formulating a society that has certain hierarchical, authoritarian characteristics. More realistically, Plato's student Aristotle posited a theory of moderation epitomized by the golden mean. Aristotle has influenced so many cultures throughout the ages, precisely because the golden mean is more congruent with the realities of the human condition than are Platonic ideals.[15]

Let's take this idea of bounded liberty a bit further. Suppose we have a gardener who is advanced in years and performing manual labor, which is dangerous to him physically. He does not have the resources to stop doing this gardening work even though he would prefer to stop. The person for whom he works is similarly advanced in years and has similar maladies. However, he has the economic resources to watch the gardener and devote himself to doing philosophy. Meanwhile, the philosopher pays the gardener appropriately and treats him with fairness and decency.

Has the gardener freely entered into this transaction? Does the property owner somehow infringe on the autonomy of the gardener? After all, he is enjoying a cold drink reading Aristotle rather than laboring outside in 100° heat. Let's suppose further that the philosopher is doing exactly what he wishes to do in terms of his free will and the gardener would much rather be inside reading the newspaper and having a cold drink.

Has the philosopher violated the liberty of the gardener? A committed communist would say "yes." A committed individualistic libertarian would say "no." In the sense that I am using bounded liberty, I would also say no, but for reasons very different from the committed libertarian. The example given is well within the thresholds of bounded liberty—at least in the conception of it that I am propounding. To be bounded liberty, the parameters have to be somewhat flexible and the behaviors permitted before a boundary line is violated have to be fairly broad, so as not to be repressive of human freedom and counter to the human condition. Perhaps some state of perfect or even true freedom for all exists in some heaven or in some other metaphysical condition. But we must take the world as we find it and seek to reshape it in ways that respect the freedom of all.

If the boundaries of bounded liberty are broad, then approximately what are they? A concept of bounded liberty has some lower and upper constraints. Although both are constraints, they are not the same kinds of constraints. The lower boundary is much more stringent because the lower boundary is driven by paramount first-order moral concerns. Establishing an upper boundary is really driven or justified by moral concerns of respecting the lower boundary. That is why the lower boundary concerns are paramount.

Establishing an upper boundary is, however, an infringement on the immediate freedom of action of the more privileged. However, it is a smaller infringement of the liberty of the more privileged. What do I mean by that? Again, I return to the point that if one takes autonomy seriously, if one truly affords it the place of a fundamental value, then one must respect the autonomy of all. So there must be some minimal amount of autonomy that each individual is morally entitled to. If that is the case, to violate that minimal level of autonomy is an immoral act. But in the area of first-order rights, breaching the immediate liberty of the more privileged must count as a prima facie violation of their first-order rights. Under such circumstances, restraining the short-term liberty of the autonomy advantaged is justified as a moral act only if: (1) it does not rise to an infringement of their baseline autonomy, and (2) it is the minimum infringement necessary to respect first-order rights, the baseline autonomy of the less privileged. Otherwise, the latter are deprived of any meaningful sense of autonomy at all.

A more compelling justification that I have hinted about also often exists if the actions of the more privileged have helped to cause the less privileged to fall below the autonomy baseline. As heuristically this entails complex questions of causality, I am being purposely coy about what actions of the more privileged count as having helped cause the autonomy-disadvantaged to fall below whatever an appropriate baseline might be. But a fairly easy one might be if some autonomy-privileged donors usurped the election process by essentially buying it, and then fashioned public policy to further constrict the autonomy of the less advantaged or enrich their own autonomy—for example, through taxation and regulatory law. Although the campaign finance cases present a fairly easy question for distributive autonomy, more complex issues exist. Such questions are important to distributive autonomy because it purports to be a general principle rather than merely a focused critique of the campaign finance cases. I explore such questions at greater length in Chapter 8, which propounds the principle.

For autonomy to count as a moral theory, there must be moral injunctions—Kant would say duties—of avoiding immoral acts that violate the autonomy of others. Hence there is the necessity for some upper boundary. The human reality of tremendously disparate resources may be to some extent inevitable. However, meaningful theories of autonomy may at times exacerbate those disparities but cannot exacerbate them in a way that breaches the essential autonomy minimum that is the essence of being human. Theories that do become difficult to defend as moral theories.

The committed libertarian counts violation of the unfettered free choice of the privileged—even those tremendously above any minimalist baseline—as an autonomy violation commensurate in moral reprehensibility with a violation of whatever unfettered free choice someone below the baseline genuinely has. Surely this is counterintuitive and counterfactual. Taking the last bit of food away from a beggar must count as a greater autonomy infringement than taking away a lobster claw from a well-off banker or lawyer. One could say that they are both equally reprehensible as they are both theft. But suppose each of these commodities is taken away through a system of legal taxation? Intuitively, most of us would recoil against effectively taking the bit of food away from the beggar and few people would begrudge effectively taking away the extra lobster claw. Why? Because intuitively we count certain restrictions of the unfettered free choice of someone well above the baseline as a lower or second-order autonomy infringement, less serious than taking away the vital necessities of someone below the baseline without which they cannot act, or perhaps even exist. Don't believe me. Just look at laws enacted across many parts of the world.

Some would say that taking the last bit of food away from the beggar, through for example, taxation, would be considered by many to be a violation of first-order rights, whereas taking the extra lobster claw away (through taxation) would not. However, what about taking away from the beggar any ability for him to influence who makes laws for him? Isn't that a fundamental breach of the beggar's first-order rights? Is it the same as taking away 1/1,000,000, or one-half of the influence that the tremendously privileged individual might seek to exercise over the same election? Keep in mind that even this diminished influence of the more privileged may still be 1,000 times (conservatively) the influence that the beggar can exert.

Theories that do not respect this lower boundary are anti-autonomy rather than in the service of autonomy. For the committed libertarian, it is difficult to demand that others respect her liberty if she does not respect some minimum baseline liberty for others. She could assert a negative right not to have her liberty taken away, whereas the beggar asserts the positive right to have his autonomy brought to a baseline. First, that perspective will be difficult for even the most sophisticated beggar to grasp, let alone agree with. Second, any such distinction hinges on complex questions of causality in an interconnected, complex society. Even if these causality claims do not rise to the level of responsibility, they must entail not taking autonomy seriously, or at least not counting it as a moral claim entailing rights and duties. One can argue that one has the liberty to be selfish and the liberty to ignore the autonomy of others. This is a thin argument, which is also one step removed from absolute selfishness. It is tricky to denominate a theory that has strong elements of selfishness "a moral theory."

The committed libertarian could claim that others must respect the liberty to be selfish. But the committed libertarian can then also claim for herself the right to be selfish. Neither baseline autonomy nor distributive autonomy masquerades as a comprehensive theory of the good. Neither represents a good life although both baseline and distributive autonomy might get you a bit closer than a commitment to personal selfishness. But as we shall see, the theory of distributive autonomy allows for an individual to be selfish so long as her selfishness does not invade the baseline autonomy of another. So the theory allows capped or bounded selfishness. Of course it does not recommend such behavior, but autonomy theory in the sense that I'm using it does not pretend to be a complete account of the moral life. It does afford the possibility of using other virtues to attain a moral life.

Moreover, moral theories have an inherent taste-shaping effect. That is in part because moral theories also serve as moral justifications for the behaviors they protect or require. So if I have the right to be selfish, perhaps I should be selfish. To his credit, Nozick recognizes this problem and deals with it forthrightly. He supplies an attractive rationale for liberty, which is to achieve a kind of transcendent being. This is a noble purpose. Moreover, it makes his defense of liberty far more muscular. If I am interfering with your liberty, I may be interfering with your right, or even your ability, to attain transcendent being.

But the same old problem of reciprocity raises its relentless head. If we jettison reciprocity, libertarianism becomes narcissistic. It is difficult to denominate a set of ideas a moral theory if they lack the element of reciprocity: What about my right to attain transcendent being? The committed libertarian can respond that I cannot invade your liberty and you can't invade mine. But this position doesn't take autonomy seriously. If I don't have minimal autonomy, what is my opportunity to achieve transcendent being? Is it obvious that the beggar has less potential to achieve transcendent being than the highly successful doctor, or philosopher? Careful before you answer as some of our most revered religious figures (across a broad swath of religions) lived as something akin to beggars.

One can modify the argument a bit to avoid these problems by asking: Who is anyone to judge what behavior is selfish and what behavior is not selfish? In addition to being baby steps removed from stark self-regarding arguments, this move has other problems. The "who am I to judge argument" undercuts the possibility of making moral choices. If accurate, this inability would also seem to infect any ability to judge *any* invasions of autonomy inappropriate. Of course, suggesting that certain behavior is selfish does not indicate what consequences should or should not attach to the behavior. That is a separate complicated question that the book addresses with respect to certain issues, particularly campaign finance, but not more generally. I am asserting the ability to make moral judgments here primarily to give one the ability, perhaps the duty, to judge one's own actions.

Claiming the liberty to be selfish more or less entails admitting that one does not have any obligations to respect the liberty of others. Apart from the moral mendacity of this argument, it is infected with deep conflicts of interest. After all, for me to argue that "I have liberty and you don't" is not only selfish but utterly self-serving. It also will diminish overall societal autonomy, which one would think the committed libertarian would seek to at least advance if not maximize. If one does not think growing or nurturing overall societal autonomy should matter at all, one cannot genuinely value autonomy.

Up to this point, we had successfully avoided the dreaded "M" word. Once we introduce the concept of maximizing liberty, the committed libertarian can assert that this theory of bounded liberty reduces it to a kind of nouvelle utilitarian quest to maximize not happiness but the overall amount of liberty in society. This does not follow from the argument I have articulated thus far. The goal here is not to maximize societal autonomy but to maximize the number of individuals who have some meaningful minimal level of autonomy. Even the committed libertarian would admit that this is a noble quest. Nozick states that without liberty people lack dignity and become mere "playthings of external forces."[16] If this is the case, maximizing, or at least increasing, the number of individuals who have some baseline level of liberty would appear congruent with libertarian theory.

But again, once one accepts this autonomy baseline in moral theory, it becomes a moral duty to try to achieve it. Consequently, fulfilling this moral duty imposes moral obligations on all societal actors to try to effectuate such a baseline for every individual. Again, the committed individualistic libertarian would dismiss such obligations as infringements on her own liberty. But such rejections are infected with the same moral mendacity, self-regarding objections articulated above. Reciprocity is a hard idea to get around. Old school philosophy put forward stronger notions such as universalizability. Reciprocity is a kind of little brother to this larger claim. Both provide routes for acceptance as a moral theory. In simplistic terms, they proclaim: "What's good for the goose must be good for the gander." Sexism aside, this notion is deeply embedded in the human psyche.

The committed individualistic libertarian might reply: (1) my liberty gives me the right not to nurture or even respect yours as long as I don't inflict on you a narrow set of harms such as punching you in the nose; (2) liberty entails a lack of reciprocity as liberty is mine. Both of these arguments are incongruent with the human condition; they are suited for a Robinson Crusoe existence on a desert island rather than for life among other humans where one's actions inevitability affect others. The problem authentic autonomy theory must face is how to provide as clear paths as possible to pursue one's own life, while letting others pursue theirs. Reciprocity is difficult to suppress. Why should you respect my freedom of action if I don't respect yours? The committed individualistic libertarian might concede minimal reciprocity, insisting that she just does what she likes and that doesn't interfere with me. This anemic reciprocity returns to problems of causation and a Robinson Crusoe-like existence.

In a world of limited resources, doesn't it blink reality to suggest that I can consume as much as I like and not affect you? The campaign finance context presents a particularly easy case. Why would I spend a lot of money to control our government, *except* to affect you? Again, the committed libertarian could return to the hackneyed counterfactual that I'm doing this to benefit me and it doesn't harm you. Chapters 10 and 11 are replete with regressive redistributions of wealth and income that prove this position counterfactual. Even if this claim were true, is a starving person or a person barely making it going to care about the distinction? This question hints at the practical side of reciprocity; it is the fabric that weaves societies together and holds revolutions in check. The alternative check is government suppression, even massacres, but that also frequently leads to revolution.

Affirmative duties to bring persons above the baseline would only extend to societal actors who themselves are above the baseline. Those below it probably have some duties to cooperate with others who endeavor to bring them above the baseline—viz., to seek meaningful work, or to conserve resources shared with them rather than to squander these on gambling or other wasteful activities. Although a few such activities should not vitiate the overriding duty to help those below the baseline, a sufficient number of these activities would seem to at least moderate the duty.

As another clarification, those whose autonomy falls below this baseline would not have first-order moral obligations to bring anyone else to the baseline. They would, however, have duties to avoid actions that would bring someone above the baseline down to the baseline and to keep someone else below the baseline from rising above it.

E. What Counts as an Infringement of Distributive Autonomy?

But what counts as a deprivation? Surely, a human act that maximizes one's own already abundant autonomy to the deprivation of some minimal state of autonomy of one or more others would appear to count as an autonomy infringement. The act would be more reprehensible if intentional, but should count as an autonomy infringement even if the act is unintentional. Recall that the people who have had their elemental autonomy rights supervened are those below the baseline. It is from their perspective, or at least from an objective perspective displayed by a reasonable person who is below the baseline, that we must view and assess the infringement. However, people above the baseline also have rights. At least with respect to first-order rights, the autonomy of those above the baseline should not be infringed except to the extent necessary to bring people below the baseline up to this minimal level of autonomy.

As long as they comply with this basic idea, people above the baseline can exercise their autonomy with respect to first-order rights however they please. In this sense, the theory I am propounding should not be called bounded liberty but instead more closely approximates a circumscribed version of baseline autonomy.

But this begs the further question of what counts as an autonomy deprivation of first-order rights. We have already addressed the question of a regressively redistributive autonomy infringement. This is an infringement that decreases the fundamental, first-order autonomy of persons at or below the baseline to increase the autonomy of people above the baseline. This is the easiest case to impose some moral obligations of redress. After all, some are benefiting by further impairing the autonomy of those who already lack even a minimal level for basic human dignity. Moderating the advantages of those beneficiaries to help those below the baseline to become less deprived seems to satisfy even the most rudimentary notions of justice or fairness.

The easiest case to justify is when the autonomy-advantaged person gains the advantage intentionally. There only needs to be some element of intentionality. To take the example of campaign financing, there could be intentionality in making immense expenditures to sway elections to certain offices and then influencing those officials to enact regulations which benefit those who provided the large amount of campaign largess. Intentionality would survive whether or not one understands the disadvantages one is inflicting on others, as general intent frequently only requires intent to do the act that causes the harm. Some laws state that general intent must be purposeful, knowing, *or* reckless.[17] Even if a showing of knowing intent is required, knowledge of a result harmful to others exists if the person is practically certain that the result will ensue. Knowledge of facts is imputed if there is a high probability of their existence. Recklessness only requires conscious disregard of "a substantial and unjustifiable risk." Even if the speech context required a tougher intent test to justify capping campaign expenditures, the much graver harm and intent runs to those whose speech the few big spenders have drowned out. For those spending huge sums on political campaigns, the intent to dominate the elections and resultant public policy will necessarily diminish the autonomy of everyone else—even property interests who do not make such expenditures. The data in Chapters 10 and 11 indicate this.

In discussing intent, I have not commented on what should be the legal standard but only on moral theory. I only use these legal concepts to discern how the United States and other societies have approached the ethical question.

Campaign finance presents a fertile area for autonomy infringements. Although autonomy is not a zero-sum game, in the context of campaign finance, autonomy may take on aspects of such a game. Hence there are winners and losers of government power. The potential for autonomy infringements is immense. Elections by their nature have aspects of zero-sum games as only one candidate wins and the rest lose. Moreover, from the voter's perspective, the amount of time that any voter can devote to political campaigns is limited. As Chapter 10 suggests, the empirical data strongly correlates election results and the constitutionally-enforced autonomy to spend or receive large amounts of money to influence political campaigns.

But what about acts that infringe the autonomy of those below the baseline of first-order autonomy rights yet do not advantage the autonomy of those above it? This presents a more difficult case. Persons who have intentionally or unintentionally benefited by shrinking the autonomy of others below a minimal baseline of autonomy can be more readily subjected to moral claims to redress this baseline autonomy deficit. This claim grows even easier to make against those who have very high levels of autonomy, as suggested by their bounteous resources. Depriving them of a certain amount of autonomy to achieve a baseline of minimal autonomy for others would appear, under the circumstances, to be just and fair.

It may even be incorrect to call depriving those above the baseline of the nearly unlimited ability to use their monetary resources to influence elections an autonomy infringement. After all, their fundamental autonomy is unimpaired. They still have the freedom to exercise their will in nearly all ways they desire. In campaign finance, their liberty to turn entire elections—to the extent that that is really an unlimited right under a democratic social contract at all—may be more constrained depending on what the expenditure limits might be. But remember what is being limited is the power of some people to purchase autonomy enhancements for themselves and constrictions on others, enabling them to make policies further advantaging their autonomy and further contracting that of others.

However, what about the more difficult case where those above the autonomy baseline have done nothing to cause those below the baseline to be there? Even in this instance, autonomy theory would appear to impose duties on those above the line to help those below it to achieve some minimal level of autonomy. If autonomy is a moral value, it imposes duties to help all members of society to attain some minimal baseline of autonomy. The common membership in a particular society would appear to attract moral duties to address the autonomy deficit of those below the baseline of a meaningful level of autonomy.

Even if the persons above the line have done nothing and have not benefited at all from the plight of the people below the autonomy baseline (a somewhat strained and unusual situation particularly in the zero-sum game context of elections), those above the line still have moral duties to bring those below the line to some minimum level of autonomy. Recall the essential nature of the claim. If autonomy is valuable, then all are entitled to a baseline minimum amount of autonomy.

But what about resource inequalities that exist independent of any human actions? What about the earthquake victim who has lost everything and has no insurance? Does society have any obligations to bring that individual back to some meaningful level of autonomy? This is the toughest case as no human behavior, intentional or unintentional, has in any way caused the autonomy infringement. Why should I, who have been more fortunate, have any obligations in moral theory to help correct misfortunes caused by the forces of nature or other nonhuman causes? Autonomy rights are predicated on the idea that autonomy has immense value. This value is universal for all human beings and consequently should be universalized. If autonomy counts as one of the most fundamental values, one must try to provide a baseline for all. Moreover, as previously stated, the person above the line should not have his fundamental autonomy impaired by helping those below the line.

I have circumscribed autonomy claims to those who exist within a particular society. Let us simply describe a society as a nation-state. This assumption avoids the tricky issue of what one does with global deprivation of first-order rights owing to extreme poverty and other circumstances.

After all, the story of the father who cannot feed his children more probabilistically applies to certain parts of Africa, South America, and Asia than it does to Europe or the United States. However, as we have previously agreed, autonomy's value is universal. How can we justify not defining the community as the global community rather than the national community? Is there any basis in moral theory to do that? One can fall back, I suppose, on precedent: most philosophers focus their theories on a particular society rather than the global society.[18]

For whatever reasons, the nation-state is much more descriptive of the way we realistically treat societies than is the global society. There is comparatively little supranational law. Instead, law tends to be a national construct.[19] Generally speaking, one needs law arguably to impose and certainly to enforce duties. Consequently, it is at least not unreasonable to circumscribe any theory of distributive autonomy to the nation-state. If we want duties that are legally enforceable, then we must circumscribe duties to the nation-state or to entities with similar legal attributes to the nation-state.

The tantalizing question of what to do beyond the nation-state I will leave for another time. Humanity has at least considered this problem in institutions such as the United Nations, the World Bank, and the International Monetary Fund. The continuing magnitude of this problem is illustrated by the large migrations to the more wealthy nations and the attendant controversies sparked by those migrations.

All this begs the question of what rises to the level of a meaningful or proper baseline. Should, for example, the baseline be set differently in a rich society in which depriving the autonomy-advantaged of some resources would not be sorely missed? But what about the society in which the vast majority are poor, so that achieving a similar baseline would be nearly impossible without bankrupting that society, to the detriment of all? Societal resource limitations must also comprise a limitation on the baseline theory, which would effectively drive the baseline lower for certain societies. One can fashion various philosophical justifications for the societal variability of the baseline: for example, one can defend this variability on the basis that it would be a massive autonomy violation to bankrupt a society so that no one has any resources, or perhaps if the entire society has a lot less resources. Of course, setting the baseline too high may deeply infringe on the autonomy of the autonomy-advantaged.

Avoiding such questions is one reason I propound a theory of distributive autonomy rather than baseline autonomy. As we shall see, notions of baselines inform distributive autonomy, but the principle also incorporates weighted balancing in the requirement of an undue constriction.

A society can only go so far in diminishing the autonomy of some to bring all to a certain baseline. If the society goes too far, the measures will likely be draconian. Moreover, in the medium to long run, they will reduce the amount of first-order rights for all because the autonomy-givers will likely leave the society for greener pastures, thus impairing even what mediocre ability exists to establish some minimal baseline.

Much more important than pragmatic constraints, however, is the context of first-order rights. The baseline cannot be set too high without exacting unfair impositions on the first-order rights of those above the baseline. Now for certain rights, this problem will not prove difficult. Protecting all against self-incrimination does involve some exaction on the autonomy of victims of crime to be free from the autonomy infringements (sometimes severe infringements) imposed by criminal behavior. Moreover, the autonomy infringements imposed by this baseline may fall disproportionately on the autonomy-disadvantaged as statistically they live in communities that are more subject to crime. (They also live in communities that are more subject to police abuses.) In spite of the autonomy exactions on victims of crime, we maintain a fairly high (albeit thinning) baseline of minimal protection against self-incrimination.

Courts have historically set the baselines on protecting the rights of the accused fairly high despite the danger that the potential imposition on some above the baseline may be profound.[20] For example, let's take the case of the victim of criminal behavior who becomes paralyzed for life. Any observer would agree that this person has suffered a severe constriction of her autonomy. Suppose further that the criminal behavior of some would have been successfully deterred had the prohibition against self-incrimination not existed. That is, the criminal would have made a calculus that without such protection, committing the crime was too risky and consequently, she would have avoided it. Yet we maintain the baseline very high because we count this privilege as very important to an overall state of autonomous being.

For many years, courts in the United States have maintained pretty high (albeit thinning) baselines with respect to other criminal procedure rights. For example, we could predict with some confidence that if rights to search one's home or other property are relaxed, or if prison conditions are made even more harsh, the propensity to commit crime including violent crime will decline. The violence frequently involved in crime, by its very nature, severely constricts autonomy. Yet we tolerate strong rights of the accused even in this context. Distributive autonomy will certainly countenance these in part because the autonomy infringements of victims are uncertain but probabilistic, whereas the autonomy infringements of compelled self-incrimination are not. The same can be said of other rights of criminal defendants.

In free speech, the baseline has also traditionally been set quite high: for example, during the 1960s the Warren Court in particular enforced a baseline of autonomy to conduct a considerable amount of what might typically be thought of as civil disobedience in the interests of protecting rights of protest and free speech.[21] Of course, civil disobedience can often descend into violence. Although the Supreme Court will not tolerate actual violence, it has frequently protected many situations in which there is a high risk of violence, and set very high standards even when violence has occurred.[22] The Court has also afforded a similarly high level of protection to a speaker's right to say whatever she wants to say even though this may result in some pretty harsh consequences to the autonomy of others. For example, in a recent case, the Court extended strong constitutional protection to video games, even those that involved racism, race-based violence, and rape.[23]

Strangely, when it comes to the distribution of resources for political campaigns, however, the Court has almost completely ignored any baseline of autonomy rights beyond assuming that everyone can articulate her own opinion about the candidate. The notion that some can project their own ideas about a candidate to hundreds of thousands or even millions of people whereas others can project them, for all practical purposes, only in personal conversations, doesn't seem to trouble the Court. The Court wishes to avoid what it perceives as a deep autonomy infringement by endorsing congressionally-imposed limits on how much one can spend on speech to support or oppose a particular candidate. Even if autonomy afforded a right to spend unlimited amounts of money on campaign speech, there is the deeper autonomy infringement of allowing the few to dramatically skew legislative and other legal autonomy benefits and restrictions in their favor by affording them immensely disproportionate voices.

This dramatically differential voice would appear to be more characteristic of aristocracy or rule by the few than of a democracy. It is improbable that aristocracy fosters individual liberty.

Addressing distributional concerns with regard to campaign finance would appear to be at once more foundational and more tricky. The greater fundamentality stems from the centrality of political campaigns in a democracy. After all, in a democracy, campaigns lead to elections. Elections choose legislatures that make laws that circumscribe the autonomy of many, in some cases quite severely. Validating those autonomy restraints would appear to require them to have resulted from a fair process. A deeply skewed electoral process would call into question the entire legal system that effectuates the many subtractions from and additions to individual autonomy that are part and parcel of the lawmaking process.

Moreover, because the electoral process legitimates the autonomy decisions made by the legislative process, the electoral process must be fair in the sense that everyone has an equal voice in electing those representatives who will make those decisions. Political theorist Alexander Meiklejohn used the metaphor of a town hall meeting in which everyone had an equal voice and an equal vote. This was Meiklejohn's ideal to validate the democratic process.[24] Although the town hall meeting is an ideal to be aspired to, actual equality of voice is probably unachievable. But we have strayed so far from that actual equality as to undercut the very legitimacy of our governing process, which centrally affects the overall distribution of autonomy in our country. Legitimacy does not simply introduce additional reasons that citizens should obey the law. Legitimacy relates to people's ability to affirm their sense of justice and to support a just constitution. It shows a constitution is worthy of support, and therefore legitimacy is important to stability.[25]

As we shall see, the Supreme Court has striven mightily to achieve equality in voting. This sharply contrasts with its approach to equalizing the voices of the electorate. The Court has explicitly and repeatedly rejected this objective as violating libertarian interests. But again, the defense of our entire system of restraining the autonomy of some while enhancing that of others is substantially predicated on and justified by democracy. Democracy is constructed on distributive autonomy. "Democracy" comes from the Greek and means power or rule of the people. For those who contend that this is really a republic, "republic" comes from the Latin and means a concern or entity of the people or public.[26] Our social contract relinquishes considerable autonomy to legislatures only if elected by the voices and votes of all the people. Unleashing the staggering differences in American wealth and income on the political process shreds that social contract. Without significantly restricting the amounts that people can spend on the electoral process, there will be no baseline autonomy for the overwhelming majority of the electorate. Instead, the voices of a few will be allowed to drown out the voices of everyone else. Their legal preferences will subdue the autonomy of the rest of us.

Realistically, there is no way to equalize the voices in the electoral process. However, the only way to avoid drowning out the voices of the many is by capping the amount that can be spent on influencing political campaigns. Otherwise, this process of the few marginalizing the voices of the many necessarily and inescapably results in no baseline of minimal autonomy for the vast majority of American citizens in what is perhaps their most important activity as citizens. Basic autonomy theory dictates, and the American Constitution mandates, that each citizen has a fair, meaningful say in electing those representatives who will make those momentous decisions that routinely will positively or negatively affect a citizen's autonomy.

F. The Disconnect of Modern Liberty and Autonomy Theory from Founding Fathers Mill and Kant

Now that I have sketched a first approximation of what distributive autonomy for first-order rights might look like, let me backfill and contextualize this notion in philosophical tradition. Far from being radical or heretical, concern for the distribution of autonomy deeply resonates with big ideas in libertarian theory but also in philosophical thinking more generally. Modern, radically individualistic libertarians have strayed far from the roots of the libertarian theory articulated by John Stuart Mill.

Mill was a complex fellow: besides being one of the founders of modern libertarianism, Mill was also one of the founders of utilitarian theory. So one cannot simplistically analogize Mill to a modern libertarian. One could argue that Mill embraced utilitarianism for non-first-order rights and was a committed libertarian in protecting first-order rights. However, this may comprise too much of a modern gloss on Mill's thought as he was also a committed utilitarian. His concept of liberty itself exhibits some influence of a utilitarian style of thinking. Mill's libertarian commitments are qualified by deep utilitarian notions of achieving the greatest good or happiness for the greatest number.[27] His celebrated essay *On Liberty* is concerned not just with the liberty of particular individuals, but with the liberty of all. Importantly, his concept of what counts as an infringement on one's liberty is much narrower than Robert Nozick's and consequently he would afford legislatures a much broader range of action than would Nozick.

Moreover, Mill's utilitarianism drives him to emphasize the fundamental interconnectedness of human beings. Owing to Mill's utilitarian commitments, he thought that the legislature could do a lot to advance the greatest good for the greatest number. He had a much more robust view of government than Nozick. Mill did not think of persons as ensconced in virtually impervious and extensive side constraints that tremendously restrict what legislatures can do.

Whereas Mill may be the founder of libertarianism, the founder of autonomy theory must be Immanuel Kant.[28] Kant clearly believed in free will but this free will was heavily circumscribed by his very rich and deep concept of duty toward others. One could not be actually free unless one took these duties quite seriously and acted not simply according to whim or desire, but instead with the controlling rudder of a duty-infused morality. Far from being Kantian, Nozick and other modern libertarians are quite distant from their professed Kantian roots. I will have much more to say about both Kant and Mill in Chapter 8.

As another initial impressionistic perspective, the notion of distributive autonomy certainly harkens back to the ideal of distributive justice in Aristotle. However, the notion of distributive justice really relates to just deserts in terms of merit, including virtue; for Aristotle, in a democracy, being a free person counts as merit. This implies that in a democracy there is some baseline distribution of resources for all citizens. Thus, distributive justice is fundamentally concerned with the actual distribution of resources in a fair way that is proportionate to one's merit; it is a theory of just deserts.[29] In contrast, distributive autonomy is concerned with first-order rights and resources, including what is a fair political or constitutional system through which the distribution of second-order economic resources and other first- and lower-order legislative and constitutional rights and resources is decided. Unfairness in erecting the institutions that apportion these goods is more basic than unfairness in any particular actual distribution with which Aristotle is primarily concerned. In contrast to individual decisions to distribute resources, the structure of the distributional system involves all decisions to allocate resources because it involves the distributional decision-making *process*. Once the allotment process itself is corrupted, unjust distributions, in the sense of violating Aristotelian ideas of distributive justice, are highly probable. Chapters 10 and 11 show that unfair distributions have actually transpired.

Unfairness in the constitutional order is foundational in effectuating the distribution of resources. Again, I am using resources in a general way not only to refer to specific material items but instead to things that are good in the sense of being beneficial to human flourishing. Resources could certainly include individual merchandise or commodities but the concept would extend far beyond to metaphysical resources that are beneficial such as self-respect, love, or the ability to determine one's own fate. Unfairness in the constitutional/legislative/judicial processes that determine the distribution of goods continually fabricate increasingly unjust distributions, causing burgeoning problems. These distributions are unjust as being produced by a corrupted political system in the sense of violating the social contract. *Buckley* and the campaign finance cases also violate Aristotelian distributive justice in rewarding wealth and political manipulation rather than merit.

The notion of distributive justice is more closely connected with my principle for distribution of lower-order economic kinds of rights called the principle of aggregate autonomy.[30] I will briefly discuss aggregate autonomy later in the text, primarily to contrast the first-order principle of distributive autonomy with the principle of aggregate autonomy.

As a fairly simplistic but useful starting point, aggregate autonomy is primarily concerned with the distribution of economic resources. These are lower-order rights. In contrast, the principle of distributive autonomy is concerned with first-order rights such as free speech, voting, and due process in court.

In a deep sense, distributive autonomy relates to Aristotle's fundamental conception of the state. Aristotle believed that participation in governance is noble.[31] As the initial quote to Part I demonstrates, Aristotelian notions certainly do connect with distributive autonomy. Moreover, Aristotle thought that political participation was fundamental to the political and moral development of the citizen.[32] At the beginning of *The Politics*, he bluntly says: "Hence it is evident that the state is a creation of nature, and that man is by nature a political animal."[33] Although he expressed mixed feelings about democracy,[34] he thought that democracy was inherently participatory. Participatory deliberation was central to governance and to the formation of character.

The ideal of participatory deliberation forging group governance and individual character animates distributive autonomy. In the context of this text, we engage the fundamental problem of unequal participation in the electoral process, which diminishes the citizenship of the vast majority of the American electorate. But the tale was not always that way. As we shall see in Chapter 3, the Supreme Court violated distributive autonomy (and for that matter, distributive justice) by becoming deeply involved in the distribution of resources and protection of economic rights in a way that grossly disproportionately benefited the already greatly autonomy-advantaged. The Court did this using highly individualistic libertarian economic theories.

The Court abandoned that strategy for a number of years under pressure from a constitutional revolution led by President Franklin Roosevelt. Although Roosevelt lost the battle with the Supreme Court, he won the war: the Court abandoned its radical protection of economic interests. For forty years after that, what I shall call the *Carolene Products* constitutional settlement between the elected bodies of government and the judiciary prevailed and defined the American political system. Essentially, the *Carolene Products* settlement allocated decisions about the distribution of most resources, except constitutionally-specified first-order rights, to the elected branches but ensured that the process of selecting those branches was fair in the sense of meeting baseline, bounded, and distributive autonomy.

Then, in the mid-1970s, the Court once again strongly embraced highly individualistic libertarian theories across a broad swath of its jurisprudence, including its free-speech decisions as Chapter 1 suggests. Notably, the Court guaranteed the right of an individual to influence elections with virtually whatever resources he had available. This approach heavily advantaged property interests whom, as we shall see, were, predictably, highly successful in remolding public policy to their own benefit, particularly in their common interest of further increasing their wealth. As I shall describe in Chapter 11, this approach not only adversely has affected the American poor and middle class but works against the interests of all Americans by enervating the very important economic demand curve of consumption, and incenting increased debt.

But this anticipates the story too much. Let us turn for now to examine first the U.S. Supreme Court's embrace of strong libertarian economic rights and how that embrace lead to disastrous consequences. Chapter 4 chronicles the Court's abandonment of protection of property rights with the strong exceptions of the takings clause and the due process requirement that courts must be involved in property deprivations. This armistice, or peace treaty, settled the constitutional crisis—almost a political war—between the Supreme Court and President Roosevelt. One strong lesson that emerges from the constitutional history in Chapter 3 is that strong embraces of naked self-interest fueled by robust individualistic libertarian theories bereft of duties hurt everyone, including property interests.

Notes

1. *Cf.* J.R. R. TOLKIEN, THE SILMARILLION (George Allen & Unwin, 1977) (mythological divine concepts of free will).

2. *See generally* John Attanasio, *The Principle of Aggregate Autonomy and the Calabresian Approach to Products Liability*, 74 VA. L. REV. 677 (1988).

3. *See* U.S. CONST. amend. V.

4. ROBERT NOZICK, ANARCHY, STATE, AND UTOPIA 12–25 (Basic Books, 1974).

5. In advocating the minimalist state, Nozick allows some redistributive taxation to pay for protection for disadvantaged persons. *Id.* at 26–27.

6. ROBERT NOZICK, PHILOSOPHICAL EXPLANATIONS 355–58 (Harvard University Press, 1981).

7. Peter Westen, *The Empty Idea of Equality*, 95 HARV. L. REV. 537 (1982).

8. In *Political Liberalism*, Rawls takes the position that some minimal level of resources may be necessary to satisfy the principle of equal liberty. Martha C. Nussbaum, *Introduction*, in RAWLS'S POLITICAL LIBERALISM 1, 18–19 (Thom Brooks & Martha C. Nussbaum eds., Columbia University Press, 2015).

9. Of course, in suggesting that a dead person has no autonomy, I leave to one side any eschatological arguments about an afterlife.

10. NOZICK, ANARCHY, *supra* note 4, at 74–78.

11. I am excepting out instances when one uses the bathroom for a long period of time purposefully to exclude others.

12. *See* H.L.A. HART, THE CONCEPT OF LAW (Oxford University Press, 2d ed., 1994). Positivism was positioned in part as a counterpoise to extremely ideological or "idealized" conceptions of law such as fascism and communism. *See generally* Donato, James, *Dworkin and Subjectivity in Legal Interpretation*, 40 STAN. L. REV. 1517, 1529 (1988).

13. An important exception is the European Union, which proscribes monopolistic behavior as part of its fundamental treaty protections.

14. NOZICK, EXPLANATIONS, *supra* note 6, at 355-58, 511-12; *See also* NOZICK, ANARCHY, *supra* note 4, at 58–59, 331.

15. *Compare* PLATO, THE REPUBLIC (R.E. Allen trans., Yale University Press, 2006) *with* ARISTOTLE, NICOMACHEAN ETHICS I.2 at 1094a18-b12 (David Ross trans., Oxford University Press, 1998). I don't mean to draw the distinction between Plato and Aristotle too sharply. Aristotle was Plato's student. Aristotle countenanced slavery and was ambivalent about democracy, preferring a mixed government of oligarchy and democracy.

16. NOZICK, EXPLANATIONS, *supra* note 6, at 291. For further discussion, see Chapter 8(A).

17. *See, e.g.,* MODEL PENAL CODE § 2.02(2)(c), (3) & (9) (1985). The definitions of criminal law and the law of civil wrongs, or torts, are similar. *See generally* Kenneth W. Simons, *A Restatement (Third) of Intentional Torts?*, 48 ARIZ. L. REV. 1061 (2006).

18. Onora O'Neill, *Changing Constructions*, in RAWLS'S LIBERALISM, *supra* note 8, at 57–61, 63. Rawls confines the ability to participate in the discourse to citizens of a particular country rather than global or multinational discourse. Martha C. Nussbaum, *Introduction, supra* note 8, at 48.

19. I will not speculate as to why law tends to be a national rather than supranational phenomenon, but it could be owing to age-old concepts of national sovereignty whose discussion is well beyond the scope of this text.

20. There is a very real argument that courts have been watering down some of the baselines in the criminal protection area, for example, by not always keeping abreast of new capabilities supplied by new technologies. Such issues range far beyond the scope of this volume.

21. *See, e.g.,* Cox v. Louisiana, 379 U.S. 559 (1965).

22. In *Hess v. Indiana*, 414 U.S. 105, 106–08 (1973), the Court overturned the conviction of a student for disorderly conduct during an antiwar demonstration. "The events leading to Hess' conviction began with an antiwar demonstration on the campus of Indiana University. In the course of the demonstration, approximately 100 to 150 of the demonstrators moved onto a public street and blocked the passage of vehicles. When the demonstrators did not respond to verbal directions from the sheriff to clear the street, the sheriff and his deputies began walking up the street, and the demonstrators in their path moved to the curbs on either side, joining a large

number of spectators who had gathered. Hess was standing off the street as the sheriff passed him. The sheriff heard Hess utter the word 'fuck' in what he later described as a loud voice and immediately arrested him on the disorderly conduct charge. It was later stipulated that what appellant had said was 'We'll take the fucking street later,' or 'We'll take the fucking street again.' Two witnesses who were in the immediate vicinity testified, apparently without contradiction, that they heard Hess' words and witnessed his arrest. They indicated that Hess did not appear to be exhorting the crowd to go back into the street, that he was facing the crowd and not the street when he uttered the statement, that his statement did not appear to be addressed to any particular person or group, and that his tone, although loud, was no louder than that of the other people in the area."

The Court said: "[At] best, [appellant's] statement could be taken as counsel for present moderation; at worst, it amounted to nothing more than advocacy of illegal action at some indefinite future time."

23. Brown v. Entm't Merchants Ass'n, 564 U.S.786 (2011).

24. ALEXANDER MEIKLEJOHN, POLITICAL FREEDOM: THE CONSTITUTIONAL POWERS OF THE PEOPLE 25 (Harper & Brothers, 1960).

25. JOHN RAWLS, POLITICAL LIBERALISM 322–33 (Columbia University Press, 1993).

26. OXFORD ENGLISH DICTIONARY, https:en.oxforddictionaries.com/ (last visited Oct. 19, 2017).

27. *See infra* Chapter 8(B).

28. *See, e.g.,* IMMANUEL KANT, GROUNDWORK OF THE METAPHYSICS OF MORALS (Mary Gregor & Jens Timmermann eds., Cambridge University Press, 2012); IMMANUEL KANT, THE METAPHYSICS OF MORALS (Mary Gregor ed., Cambridge University Press, 1996); IMMANUEL KANT, CRITIQUE OF PURE REASON (Paul Guyer & Allen Wood eds., Cambridge University Press, 1998); IMMANUEL KANT, CRITIQUE OF PRACTICAL REASON (Mary Gregor ed., Cambridge University Press, rev. ed., 2015) and IMMANUEL KANT, CRITIQUE OF THE POWER OF JUDGMENT (Paul Guyer, ed., Cambridge University Press, 2000).

29. ARISTOTLE, NICOMACHEAN ETHICS, BOOK V (W.D. ROSS trans., Batoche Books, 1999).

30. Attanasio, *Aggregate Autonomy, supra* note 2.

31. In *The Politics*, Aristotle says:

> Our conclusion, then, is that political society exists for the sake of noble actions, and not of mere companionship. Hence they who contribute most to such a society have a greater share in it than those who have the same or a greater freedom or nobility of birth but are inferior to them in political virtue; or than those who exceed them in wealth but are surpassed by them in virtue.

ARISTOTLE, THE POLITICS, Book III, Part IX (Benjamin Jowett trans.) (last visited Oct. 19, 2017) http://classics.mit.edu/Aristotle/politics.3.three.html.

32. GERAINT PARRY, GEORGE MOYSER & NEIL DAY, POLITICAL PARTICIPATION AND DEMOCRACY IN BRITAIN 286 (Cambridge University Press, 1992).

33. ARISTOTLE, THE POLITICS, *supra* note 31, at Book I, Part II. http://classics.mit.edu/Aristotle/politics.1.one.html.

34. Miriam Galston, *Taking Aristotle Seriously: Republican-Oriented Legal Theory and the Moral Foundation of Deliberative Democracy*, 82 CAL. L. REV. 329, 397–98 (1994).

II The Decline of Libertarian Protection of Property Rights

The *extreme* of liberty (which is its abstract perfection, but its real fault) obtains nowhere, nor ought to obtain anywhere. Because extremes, as we all know, in every point which relates either to our duties or satisfactions in life, are destructive both to virtue and enjoyment. Liberty too must be limited in order to be possessed. The degree of restraint it is impossible in any case to settle precisely. But it ought to be the constant aim of every wise public council, to find out by cautious experiments, and rational, cool endeavours, with how little, not how much, of this restraint, the community can subsist. For liberty is a good to be improved, and not an evil to be lessened. It is not only a private blessing of the first order, but the vital spring and energy of the state itself, which has just so much life and vigour as there is liberty in it.

Edmund Burke, A Letter to the Sheriffs of Bristol, On the Affairs of America 1777[1]

Note

1. Edmund Burke, Speeches on the American War and Letter to the Sheriffs of Bristol, on the Affairs of America 206 (Greeg Press, 1972).

3   The Direct Judicial Protection of Property Rights

PROTECTION FOR PROPERTY rights resonated with the Framers of the Constitution. They connected possession of property with political rights by disenfranchising those who lacked property. They also viewed private property rights as vital to the creation of a realm of civil society removed from, and independent of, government.[1] Being insulated from the power of government was central to the Framers' conception of liberty. The Framers were concerned with the possession rather than the distribution of property. This was because they assumed that land was so plentiful that anyone could acquire it to achieve wealth.[2]

Thus, the Framers connected the possession of property with the exercise of meaningful autonomy—political and otherwise. Because land was so abundant, however, the Framers could view protecting property rights as strongly advancing individual liberty. During the 1890s and the first third of the twentieth century,[3] the Supreme Court magnified protection for property rights using substantive due process, federalism, and other constitutional doctrines.[4] This amplification occurred simultaneously with the shift from a primarily agrarian society to an industrial one. The shift meant that people no longer could own land as a way of exercising a baseline of autonomy. Instead, they lived in tenements owned by others and worked in factories, also belonging to others. As part of the normal workings of the democratic process, the majority sought to regulate the owners' use of property so as to guarantee rights of health and safety, and economic rights involving wages and other compensation.

Politics and Capital. John Attanasio.
© John Attanasio 2018. Published 2018 by Oxford University Press.

Treating economic rights as first-order autonomy rights, the Court used a doctrine commonly referred to as "substantive due process" to insulate liberty of contract from government interference.[5] Protecting freedom of contract is in some ways a logical extension of protecting property from outright governmental expropriation, a practice prohibited by the Fifth Amendment ban on government takings of property: if a society guarantees the right to retain property, then a next logical extrapolition is protecting one's right to acquire it.[6] However, in newly industrialized turn-of-the-century America, labor was no longer scarce but plentiful, and property was no longer plentiful but scarce. As the Court had thought that protecting property was necessary to protecting political autonomy, the Court expanded its conception of property rights to include liberty, not just from physically taking one's property, but also liberty from economic regulation of one's property.

Among the most extreme and neglected examples of the sacred treatment of property rights is the Court's striking down the income tax. In *Pollock v. Farmers Loan & Trust Co.*,[7] the Court invalidated the tax not as a violation of liberty of contract but as a violation of the capitation requirement of Article I, Section 9. Rendering the case both more poignant and pertinent, the tax invalidated in *Pollock* specifically focused on property that was disconnected from labor. The specific tax invalidated was levied on income from dividends, rents, interest, and capital gains rather than wages paid for labor. *Pollock* was reversed by the promulgation of the Sixteenth Amendment.[8]

The key instruments that the Court used to strike down economic regulations were substantive due process and federalism. The Court read into the due process clause a right of liberty of contract. The clause itself says that one cannot be deprived "of life, liberty, or property, *without due process of law*."[9] This implies strongly that one can be deprived of life, liberty, or property with due process of law. Besides breathing substantive content into the clause, the Court read a new right of liberty of contract into it. In its application of the doctrine of substantive due process, the Court conceptualized liberty of contract as one of a number of ways that it limited governmental power to preserve liberty.[10]

In *Allegeyer v. Louisiana*, the connection between liberty and property is also evident. The Court summarized the liberty guaranteed by substantive due process as follows:

The "liberty" mentioned in [the Fourteenth Amendment] means not only the right of the citizen to be free from the mere physical restraint of his person, as by incarceration, but the term is deemed to embrace the right of the citizen to be free in the enjoyment of all his faculties; to be free to use them in all lawful ways, to live and work where he will, to earn his livelihood by any lawful calling, to pursue any livelihood or avocation, and for that purpose to enter into all contracts which may be proper, necessary, and essential to his carrying out to a successful conclusion the purposes above mentioned.[11]

The key case epitomizing the Court's approach was *Lochner v. New York*.[12] *Lochner* invalidated a maximum hours law forbidding bakery workers from working more than sixty hours per week. The Court held that the law violated the liberty of contract of both employees and employers. Writing for the majority, Justice Peckham rejected the state's assertion that the law advanced worker health: "Under such circumstances, the freedom of master and employee to contract with each other in relation to their employment, and in defining the same, cannot be prohibited or interfered with without violating the Federal Constitution."[13]

Lochner was one of many cases that used substantive due process to protect liberty of contract.[14] During this era, the Court also used the contracts clause of Article 2, Section 10[15] and the equal protection clause[16] to protect property rights. Along the same lines, the Court's invalidation of the federal income tax also protected the existing distribution of societal wealth.[17]

Around this same time, many of the Court's federalism decisions invalidated congressional regulations of business interests.[18] The Supreme Court viewed substantive due process and federalism as integrally related in protecting liberty of contract. In turn, the Court explicitly recognized that protecting freedom of contract constitutionally safeguarded a fairly pure form of laissez-faire capitalism.[19] The substantive due process decisions directly protected laissez-faire capitalism. Federalism decisions protected this economic system indirectly but just as effectively. Although federalism decisions invalidating congressional laws technically left open the possibility of states promulgating economic regulations in the these areas, the existing economic milieu often rendered this option impractical: states wishing to regulate feared that businesses would simply move to friendlier states that lacked such restrictions.[20]

This argument does not rely on any foul motives on business's part. Many businesses would move to other states whether they wanted to or not. Businesses located in states that had costly regulatory requirements would have systematic competitive disadvantages compared with businesses located in states that lacked such requirements. Of course, in making such decisions, businesses would consider a range of factors including the cost of moving out-of-state. Nevertheless, economic theory would predict that many economic regulations would cause, at the margin, some businesses to move out of a state enacting certain regulations. Particularly states at the margin would have great incentives not to regulate as keeping or attracting businesses might ease budgetary shortfalls or increase prosperity—at least in the short run. Consequently, the national government was the only viable regulator possible. However, commerce clause decisions frequently precluded the national government from regulating at all.[21] Hence, no one regulated and economic liberty was preserved.

Many Progressives of the time including Theodore Roosevelt, Charles Beard, and Learned Hand viewed such decisions as capitulating to business interests.[22] One author has argued that the Court did not regard its decisions as protecting business interests. Instead, the Court was advancing a regime of neutral legal rules by striking down legislation that favored a particular class or group of people.[23] The majority in the campaign finance case, *McCutcheon v. FEC*, makes a similar argument about the campaign finance restrictions discriminating against a particular class of people, property interests.[24]

Characterizing the *Lochner* Court as purposefully fostering business interests is not necessary to the argument. Purposeful or not, promoting class-neutral regulations would favor the economic status quo, viz. property interests.[25] The decisions could be characterized by protecting everyone's liberty equally by promoting the "neutral" rule of liberty of contract. However, this approach is hardly neutral; it safeguards the liberty of those who have resources. At best, the approach ignores the liberty of those who lack the resources to have any meaningful liberty. At worst, it protects the ability of those with resources to undercut any prospect of securing distributive autonomy for those who lack meaningful liberty. As I shall elaborate in succeeding chapters, decisions requiring that legislation ignore the existing resource positions of citizens can severely impair autonomy.

The Court itself viewed its commerce clause and substantive due process jurisprudence analogously, as both protected individual liberty by limiting the power of government.[26] The substantive due process and income tax cases directly protected property rights. In addition to the federalism decisions, other cases indirectly protected the liberty of contract of property interests using separation of powers. For example, the delegation doctrine restricted the amount of regulatory power that the legislative branch of government could delegate to administrative agencies, which are in the executive branch.[27] Congress itself simply could not feasibly engage in daily regulatory oversight on any widespread or sustained basis. Consequently, these decisions had much the same effect as the Court's federalism decisions, which primarily used the commerce clause but restricted other Article I, Section 8 congressional powers as well. Analogously, by restricting Congress's delegation power, the Court effectively restricted not merely the methods that Congress could use to regulate or tax but also whether, as a practical matter, Congress could regulate at all.[28]

Another area in which the Court also protected property rights was by fashioning a federal common law. In the sense that I am using it here, common law simply means judge-made law. In old England, judges made law, for example regulating property and contracts. Predictably, the common law fashioned by national courts strongly favored national businesses particularly against state and local regulations. In broadly limiting governmental authority, the cases involving federalism, delegation, and federal common law protected laissez-faire individual choice.[29] Laissez-faire is a French word which according to the Oxford English Dictionary, literally means " 'allow to do' "—or to use the vernacular, "anything goes."

During the 1930s, Supreme Court decisions invoking federalism and other doctrines invalidated key portions of President Franklin Delano Roosevelt's New Deal.[30] Against the backdrop of the Great Depression, these decisions precipitated a constitutional crisis. In an attempt to circumvent the five-justice majority who had struck down important swaths of his "New Deal," President Roosevelt proposed a "court packing" plan that would have allowed him to appoint a new justice for every one over the age of seventy (amounting to six additional new justices to the nine-member Court).[31] "During a critical

4 The *Carolene Products* Paradigm of Participatory Democracy

A. The *Carolene Products* Constitutional Settlement

Although slightly earlier cases had begun to reverse judicially-crafted protections that the Supreme Court had afforded to economic rights through such doctrines as federalism[1] and substantive due process,[2] *Carolene Products* sketched the blueprint for a way forward.[3] The case amounted to a kind of peace treaty proposal between the political branches— particularly the President—and the Court.[4] It sketched a modus vivendi between the Court and the elected branches—particularly for how to navigate the tension between a constitutional, countermajoritarian rule of law and majoritarian democracy.

A common way of thinking about the change wrought by *Carolene Products* focuses on the difference between property rights and personal rights. Justice Potter Stewart has often been quoted as declaring:

[T]he dichotomy between personal liberties and property rights is a false one. Property does not have rights. People have rights. The right to enjoy property without unlawful deprivation, no less than the right to speak or the right to travel, is, in truth, a "personal" right.[5]

The Court on which Justice Stewart sat had roundly rejected the doctrine of liberty of contract, which its predecessors had conceptualized as a personal right. With the exception of the Fifth Amendment's requirement of compensation for outright government

Politics and Capital. John Attanasio.

takings of property mentioned by Justice Stewart, and the due process clause, the Court has treated property rights as lower-order rights and personal rights as first-order rights. The distinction has some resemblance to the difference between what Chapter 2 describes as distributive autonomy, which affects first-order rights and aggregate autonomy, which affects lower-order economic rights. But not all the first-order rights discussed in Chapter 2 are constitutional rights.

To alleviate the ambiguity with the terms "property rights," and "personal rights," we can overlook their common or ordinary meanings and instead adopt the meanings assigned to them by the modern Supreme Court. In a general sense, then, personal rights receiving strong constitutional protection can be summarized as follows: the safeguards protecting the rights of those accused of a crime;[6] the vast array of First Amendment protection comprehended by freedom of expression and religion; the Fifth Amendment prohibition against government takings of property; the right not to have one's life, liberty, or property taken away without due process of law; the proscriptions in equal protection jurisprudence against discrimination based on race, gender, and several other impermissible categories including the right to vote and to appellate review; and the guarantee of a sphere of individual liberty largely confined to procreation, sexual matters, marriage, and the family.

Still, the line between personal and property rights remains murky. For example, the prohibition against takings of property[7] is treated as a first-order right.[8] The more accurate distinction may be between personal rights and economic rights, but even that has severe limits as the Constitution does not treat healthcare, education, or sustenance as a first-order right.

As a starting point, we can say that the modern Court's protection for property is at least the following: the requirement of just compensation for government takings of property, procedural safeguards before one can be deprived of property,[9] the weak protections of government's contractual obligations with private entities,[10] and procedural protection for certain statutory entitlements such as welfare.[11]

With the important exception of strong protection for compensation for government takings of property, this list does not suggest robust protection. The metamorphosis proposed by *Carolene Products* marked the decline of direct judicial protection for property rights, or more precisely, economic rights. Instead, the Court tried to guarantee fairness in the distribution of economic and other resources by ensuring broad-based, fair participation in the democratic processes.

Although *Carolene Products* surely stands as one of the most discussed cases in modern American constitutional law,[12] commentators generally focus on its renowned footnote 4, which was for decades the lodestar of the modern Court. It safeguards such individual rights as freedom of speech, freedom of religion, the rights of the accused, and equal protection against discrimination based on race, gender, voting, etc.[13] Until the Court extended substantive due process protection to such areas as procreation, family, and sexual privacy, the footnote presaged virtually all of the constitutional individual rights work of the modern Court. Scholars commonly overlook the holdings of *Carolene Products* that rejected claims involving liberty of contract, federalism, and economic equal protection. The author of the opinion, Justice Harlan Fiske Stone, certainly cared about these main themes of the case. Favoring diminished protection for liberty of contract, Justice Stone had frequently joined Justices Holmes and Brandeis in dissenting against the Court's decisions striking down social welfare legislation.

Around the time of the *Carolene Products* decision, the Court also relinquished heightened scrutiny over the contracts clause of Article I, Section 10;[14] restrictions on Congress's delegation power;[15] and over various Article I, Section 8 restrictions on congressional authority, which overwhelmingly involved federalism issues.[16] The constitutional doctrines listed above were the key ones that the Supreme Court had previously invoked to fashion a liberty-of-contract regime that had afforded freedom from economic regulation. Around this time, the Court also largely released its claimed authority to fashion a federal common law, often used to protect economic liberty.[17] The main prohibitions that survive are the takings clause and the requirement that one cannot be deprived of property without due process of law.

Strong philosophical undercurrents nurtured by robust scholarship drove this metamorphosis. In the *Carolene Products* settlement, protecting economic liberty was reconceptualized as a complex matter that necessitated the careful balancing of competing interests in a highly complex, modern economic milieu. The elected branches seemed better structured and staffed for this task. The judiciary was functionally ill-suited to fashion public policy, particularly economic policy.[18] The earlier *Lochner* analysis could be understood as a matrix. The *Lochner* majority saw itself as protecting both the liberty of employees and employers to contract as they saw fit.[19] One view maintains that around the turn of the twentieth century, the justices viewed liberty as "the opportunity to acquire property."[20]

Protecting this opportunity to acquire property also served utilitarian objectives.[21] Employers and others argued that freedom of contract best maximized the greatest good for the greatest number.[22] The underlying premise was that safeguarding freedom of contract would increase societal wealth, which would in turn increase total societal happiness.[23] Consequently, even if the Court accepted that the maximum hours legislation at issue in *Lochner* was enacted by the legislature, an institution better able than courts to represent the greatest good for the greatest number, three of the four squares of the following matrix—and notably both individual rights/liberty squares—recommended striking down the law. Figure 4.1 illustrates the *Lochner* Court's approach:

EMPLOYER LIBERTY (Invalidate)	EMPLOYEE LIBERTY (Invalidate)
EMPLOYER/ SOCIETAL UTILITY (Invalidate)	EMPLOYEE UTILITY (Uphold?)

FIGURE 4.1: *Lochner* Liberty/Utility Matrix.

The above matrix was shattered when the Court granted the possibility that the employers' and employees' liberty interests may actually stand in opposition to each other. To some degree, the efforts of Progressives and the perceptions of the Court may have been held back by the view that a labor shortage—which had existed in the nineteenth century—and other factors afforded American workers a strong bargaining position.[24] In light of decisions such as *Lochner*, Progressives began to compile statistics demonstrating the differences in worker bargaining power.[25] The reality of grossly unequal bargaining power made it highly unlikely that freedom of contract would advance the liberty of employees.

Prominent voices such as Harvard Law School dean Roscoe Pound began to question this premise: "Freedom of contract in *Lochner*, Pound argued, represented a conception of 'equal rights' between employees and employers that could only be called a 'fallacy' to 'everyone acquainted at first hand with actual industrial conditions.'"[26] Moreover, the Great Depression had demolished the assumption that strict laissez-fare capitalism always advanced the utilitarian interests of society. The key realizations were that property rights could actually threaten liberty, and that government regulation of the marketplace could sometimes advance individual liberty better than government noninterference.[27] Regardless of what the right answers to public policy questions might be, the *Carolene Products* settlement determined that the political process should resolve these issues.

The following matrix in Figure 4.2 aptly illustrates the indeterminate nature of courts dealing with *Lochneresque* issues, which, for the most part, involve fashioning economic and social policy:

LIBERTY EMPLOYER (Invalidate)	LIBERTY EMPLOYEE (Uphold)
UTILITY EMPLOYER (Invalidate)	UTILITY EMPLOYEE (Uphold)

FIGURE 4.2: *Carolene Products* Liberty/Utility Matrix.

In the above framework, courts would find it difficult to prefer one party's liberty interests in freedom of contract over another's. Moreover, legislatures are better-equipped than courts to ascertain the greatest good for the greatest number. Resting such utilitarian determinations in non-majoritarian courts would have been undemocratic, or even somewhat oligarchical, and also less effective as courts lack the expertise, or staff, to deal with economic issues.

To some extent, the matrix offers a foundation for treating economic rights as lower-level rights. To begin with, the matrix illustrates the indeterminate nature of economic rights because inherently they have a utilitarian dimension in terms of the distribution of resources. The conflict of liberty rights also illustrates the indeterminacy of the liberty rights question and consequently the difficulty of judicial resolution. But more fundamentally, the matrix illustrates the relativistic nature of one's economic position. Beyond extremes such as outright takings of property or depriving someone of a baseline level of economic resources, it is difficult to argue that regulating one's use of economic resources is a fundamental imposition on one's autonomy. This is particularly true as all economic activities have distributional and efficiency consequences. A separate, deeper infringement would be lack of meaningful participation in the legislative process that led to the regulation. In illustrating the conflict of economic liberties—in this instance, employers and employees—the matrix emphasizes the necessity of taking everyone's economic interests into consideration in trying to fashion a system that maximizes the economic liberty and well-being of every individual. In its constituent representation structure, the legislature is functionally designed to balance these competing utility interests.

The matrix also supplies the beginnings of a claim that economic rights are lower-order rights. If we move a bit beyond the matrix itself, it is difficult to claim that someone who has been deprived of his freedom of conscience or protection against self-incrimination or the privacy of his home has not had his dignity violated in some much more fundamental way than someone who cannot make as much profit because she is forced to pay her employees minimum wage. Intuitively, it simply does not seem as deep an infringement on the employer's humanity to be economically regulated. If anything, there seems to be a more profound incursion on the autonomy of the workers who frequently were toiling for what the workers themselves refer to as "slave wages."

Consequently, as epitomized in the *Carolene Products* footnote, the modern Court has left balancing the competing utility interests to the democratic institutions.[28] On the other hand, the Court retains power or jurisdiction to decide first-order rights. The first paragraph of the footnote focuses on the Bill of Rights:

> There may be narrower scope for operation of the presumption of constitutionality when legislation appears on its face to be within a specific prohibition of the Constitution, such as those of the first ten amendments, which are deemed equally specific when held to be embraced within the Fourteenth.[29]

The second and third paragraphs expand participation in the democratic process that would decide property rights and other important questions of public policy:

> It is unnecessary to consider now whether legislation which restricts those political processes which can ordinarily be expected to bring about repeal of undesirable legislation is to be subjected to more exacting judicial scrutiny under the general prohibitions of the Fourteenth Amendment than are most other types of legislation. On restrictions upon the right to vote, *see . . . ;* on restraints upon the dissemination

of information, *see* . . . ; on interferences with political organizations, *see* . . . ; as to prohibition of peaceable assembly, *see* . . .

Nor need we enquire whether similar considerations enter into the review of statutes directed at particular religious, or national, or racial minorities; whether prejudice against discrete and insular minorities may be a special condition, which tends seriously to curtail the operation of those political processes ordinarily to be relied upon to protect minorities, and which may call for a correspondingly more searching judicial inquiry.[30]

The idea in the second and third paragraphs was that everyone has a fair say in the formulation of public policy, including the distribution of societal resources.[31] The second paragraph talks explicitly about protecting the political process, particularly the rights to vote, speak, and associate with others that comprise the core of that process. The third paragraph focuses on protecting discrete and insular minorities. Definitionally, these are groups whom the democratic process has historically excluded or disfavored, such as African Americans.

It is inherent in the nature of law to draw lines, which reduce or enhance the autonomy of certain individuals. Surely, a necessary part of any justification for allowing law commonly to effect autonomy incursions must be that the process of fashioning the law is fair. This, as we shall discuss, is one of the reasons for treating rights such as the right to vote, speak, and associate as first-order rights.

B. Voice and Vote as Pillars of Participatory Democracy

Paragraphs two and three of the footnote stand in some tension with each other.[32] To protect minorities, the Court has often compromised the democratic process concerns of the second paragraph. For example, to remedy violations of minority rights, courts often have usurped or altered democratic decision-making in such areas as voting and school desegregation. These tensions stem from the subtlety and complexity of the footnote itself.[33]

At one level, the footnote provides a strong defense for judicial review.[34] The tasks outlined in the footnote are ones that the judiciary is functionally and structurally better suited to perform than the democratically-elected branches. Louis Lusky, Justice Stone's clerk when the footnote was drafted, said the second and third paragraphs of the footnote articulated "governmental dynamics, delineating the scope of legitimate judicial review in terms of the Court's appropriate place in the scheme of government."[35]

The judiciary was better-suited to perform the tasks it articulated than the democratically-elected legislature, as those holding political power would have difficulty impartially policing the political process in which they themselves engaged. Instead, a neutral referee should oversee the democratic contests.[36] Similarly, defending discrete and insular minorities is a task that the majoritarian process has historically failed to accomplish. Consequently, the need arises for some sort of countermajoritarian body that is shielded from the political process. Again, the countermajoritarian Court seems a natural choice.[37]

The footnote also allocates to the judiciary areas that comprise deeper autonomy infringements. Speech, association, and religious concerns go to the core of what it means to be human. So do the rights of the accused. There are few more fundamental deprivations of autonomy than imprisonment—let alone execution. But many of the rights of the accused also have an inherent fundamentality to them in terms of respecting human dignity. Obvious examples are the protection against self-incrimination or the privacy of one's home. Being discriminated against because of one's race or gender also debases one's humanity in fundamental ways although the Constitution and the Court consider these equality rather than autonomy infringements.

Courts are better at judging fundamental rights, including autonomy infringements, because they are not beholden to the will of any political majority who might even be helping to effectuate those infringements. Protecting against such infringements all comprise at least part of a baseline of first-order rights necessary for human dignity and flourishing. Courts are good at adjudicating whether government has unjustifiably abridged that baseline.

Courts are also necessary to oversee the democratic games. These games have real consequences for individual autonomy. The nature of legislation involves line drawing, and line drawing, more often than not enhances the autonomy of some and detracts from the autonomy of others. Fashioning an electoral process that is fair and overseeing it with a fair and neutral referee seems to be a necessary justification for the autonomy infringements that democratic governments commonly impose.

However, in positioning the Supreme Court as ultimate referee monitoring the democratic games,[38] the footnote thrusts upon the Court the daunting challenge of fashioning a conception of democracy. The footnote itself etches the contours of a broad theory of participatory democracy. Louis Lusky, Justice Stone's clerk, explained that its second and third paragraphs "plainly assume the existence of two national objectives—government by the people, and government for the whole people—and focus attention on the Court's special ability to effectuate them."[39]

Part of the tremendous sway of the footnote derives from its focus on democracy's foundational building blocks of speaking and voting.[40] These elements have been amplified in the scholarship of two of the foremost exponents of the footnote, John Ely and Jesse Choper. Both clerked for Chief Justice Earl Warren whose Court was primarily responsible for fleshing out the participatory democracy paradigm whose blueprint appears in footnote 4. Choper has noted that there exists:

[a] large number of varied and often vague theories of "democracy" and to the absence of any clear consensus on its definition and that of such other highly abstract concepts as a "democratic society" and a "democratic political system."

But certain critical elements are beyond reasonable doubt. Whether one looks to such classical theorists as Aristotle, Locke, and Rousseau, to such mainstays of American political thinking as Madison, Jefferson, and Lincoln, or to this nation's constitutional development from its origin to the present time, majority rule has been considered the keystone of a democratic political system in both theory and practice. Effective majoritarianism in turn depends on the preservation of two fundamental rights of the individual, the right to vote and the right freely to express and exchange ideas.[41]

Similarly, John Ely places central importance on protecting the foundational democratic powers of speaking and voting:

Malfunction occurs when the *process* is undeserving of trust, when (1) the ins are choking off the channels of political change to ensure that they will stay in and the outs will stay out, or (2) though no one is actually denied a voice or vote, representatives beholden to an effective majority are systematically disadvantaging some minority out of simple hostility or a prejudiced refusal to recognize commonalities of interest, and thereby denying that minority the protection afforded other groups by a representative system.[42]

The first problem concerns freedom of speech and the right to vote, whereas the second concerns systematic discrimination against particular minorities.[43] According to Lusky, the Court more quickly accepted paragraph two which involves speaking and voting as it had much deeper historical roots.[44]

I do not mean to lessen the importance of the protecting minorities' paragraph that Justice Stone regarded as critically important. He penned the footnote partly in response to the scourge of religious and racial intolerance prior to World War II.[45] Nonetheless, as a discrete and insular minority is a group whom the political process repeatedly abandoned and frequently victimized,[46] the Court protects discrete and insular minorities only after the routine majoritarian processes specified in paragraph two have systematically failed to do so. This priority in ordering appears intentionally to engage the axiom that speaking and voting are logically prior building blocks in establishing representative democracy.

Ely views the footnote as protecting voice and vote in a broad-based, participatory way. He characterizes it as enshrining a "participation-oriented, representation-reinforcing approach to judicial review."[47] Paragraph two demands that "equal participation in the processes of government"[48] exists and that the "channels of participation and communication [be] kept open."[49] In the best traditions of Madisonian pluralist democracy,[50] the paragraph seeks to protect access to the political process.[51] Safeguarding freedom of speech and the right to vote are necessary to achieve the Declaration of Independence's Lockean aspiration of popular consent.[52]

Through assiduous application of the one-person, one-vote principle,[53] the Court has meticulously striven to equalize the power of each citizen's vote.[54] For example, the Court has invalidated an apportionment scheme that had a 0.6 percent deviation in population among congressional districts.[55] The Court has also removed monetary and other impediments to voting.[56] Libertarian free speech jurisprudence sharply contrasts with this inclusive participatory vision of *Carolene Products* to distribute to all citizens the fundamental liberty to choose the leaders who make the laws that govern them. Instead, libertarian free speech jurisprudence is a political theory cousin to the freedom-of-contract vision of *Lochner v. New York*.[57] As such, modern free-speech jurisprudence has tremendously shrunk and distorted meaningful participation in American democracy.[58]

C. Property Rights versus Property Interests

Generally, the modern Court has adhered to that part of the *Carolene Products* constitutional settlement that withdrew strong and direct judicial protection from lower-order economic rights.[59] The Court continues to play an important role in the allocation of economic resources through the takings clause, which safeguards against outright government taking property without just compensation.[60] However, the takings clause only acts as a brake on the distribution of property: it only protects against immediate expropriation of specific pieces of property without just compensation to its owner. If government provides just compensation, it can take private property for virtually any purpose that it desires.[61] If it is patient, the political majority has tremendous authority to dramatically recast the allocation of property and wealth using various taxation and regulatory regimes.

Over the past thirty years, the Court has somewhat increased the Fifth Amendment protection for property.[62] It has been hesitant to use the takings clause to afford strong protection against governmental economic or other regulations.[63] Of course, to the extent that they distort the normal workings of the market, many government regulations diminish the value of property used in a given activity. Exacting just compensation for every regulation that diminishes the value of a property used in a manufacturing or service business would severely chill economic regulation and bring the Court back into the *Lochner* era.[64]

The modern Court also has been quite reluctant to use the contracts clause to fortify economic rights. Although the Court made some moves during the 1970s to revive protection for economic rights under this clause,[65] it subsequently has shied away from this position, particularly when government is not a party to the contract.[66]

The modern Court even expanded its conception of property rights to comprehend some largely procedural protection for the poor and for government employees, without fashioning strong guarantees. For example, the Court has used equal protection to prohibit government from using poverty as a criterion to effectively deprive people of a fundamental right. However, the Court has limited this line of cases to a very few fundamental rights: voting, travel, and judicial access.[67] The Court has declined to extend equal protection to afford substantive constitutional protection for necessities based on indigence.[68] Two other lines of cases impose procedural safeguards before government can deprive someone of private property[69] or government benefits.[70]

Some of the cases referenced above that involve poverty stand at the intersection of personal and property rights, and some commentators classify them as involving personal rights. Protecting against extreme deprivations from those who are indigent is consistent with a theory of distributive autonomy. Some baseline of resources would appear to be consistent, even necessary, to satisfy the most elemental notions of distributive autonomy. After all, someone who lacks some elemental baseline of resources can hardly act autonomously. Indeed, it is arguable that he cannot act in any meaningful sense at all.

Under conditions of massive deprivation, providing substantive rights to minimal necessities such as food may be required to satisfy distributive autonomy. The economic nature of this inquiry may have rendered courts reticent to deal with such questions. Not only does the U.S. Constitution lack clauses that deal with these areas, but structurally the budgetary power is with Congress. Of course, saying that the Supreme Court has not afforded a constitutional right to minimal necessities does not determine whether some right to basic necessities comprises a fundamental dimension of distributive autonomy. In the United States and other wealthy nations, legislatures have at times been somewhat forthcoming in providing some minimal rights to necessities.

Despite weakened protection for *property rights*,[71] the Court has bolstered its free speech jurisprudence to dramatically increase constitutional protection for *property interests*. Paradigmatically, the campaign finance cases hinge on wealth, access to the marketplace of ideas and political influence itself.[72] Even under the best of circumstances, a democracy with a market economy must tolerate considerable disparities in the abilities of citizens to express themselves. Since the mid-1970s, however, free speech jurisprudence has not only tolerated, but systematically facilitated, and even enhanced, enormous differentials in participation.[73]

D. The Weak Libertarian Paradigm of Free Speech Jurisprudence and Participatory Democracy

The *Carolene Products* vision is appealing because it engages deep notions of distributive autonomy: "Give everyone a fair say in who gets what, and let the majority decide." The majority's so-called say only extends to lower order rights; *Carolene Products* says that the Constitution greatly limits the majority's ability to decide the distribution of many first-order autonomy rights. Speech is a core facet of having an equal, or at least a fair, say. The great Justice Benjamin Cardozo famously declared, "[O]f freedom of thought, and speech. . . . one may say that it is the matrix, the indispensable condition, of nearly every other form of freedom."[74] As such, it is a paramount and constitutive autonomy right, as speech dramatically influences the allocation of countless other autonomy enlargements and diminutions.

Vigorous protection for freedom of speech did not emerge until the 1960s, led by the absolute protection position of Justices Hugo Black and William Douglas.[75] Although a majority of the Court never adopted their position that free speech is an absolute,[76] the tremendous influence of their position laid the foundations for at least the weak libertarian paradigm of free speech jurisprudence. The weak libertarian paradigm prohibits content-based speech regulations, or government censorship. *New York Times v. Sullivan*[77] and *Brandenburg v. Ohio*[78] establish the core claim of the weak libertarian paradigm of free speech jurisprudence. In essence, it requires: "Government generally cannot stop me from saying *whatever* I want to say."

The *New York Times* decision articulated the breadth of protection for speech, establishing that virtually no categories of expression are completely bereft of First Amendment safeguards. Emphasizing participation, speech would rarely be excluded based on its content:[79]

> Like insurrection, contempt, advocacy of unlawful acts, breach of the peace, obscenity, solicitation of legal business, and the various other formulae for the repression of expression that have been challenged in this Court, libel can claim no talismanic immunity from constitutional limitations. It must be measured by standards that satisfy the First Amendment.[80]

For virtually all of the time that the Court has protected free speech, the Court had followed a two-tiered theory of speech protection articulated in *Chaplinsky v. New Hampshire* in which certain categories of speech received constitutional protection and certain categories did not.[81] *New York Times* rejected the two-tiered approach and extended a strong presumption of constitutional guarantees to all speech,[82] placing on government the burden of establishing reasons that particular expression should not be protected.[83] Emphasizing broad-based participation, *New York Times* guaranteed that no one's expression would be excluded based simply on its content.

If *New York Times* signaled the breadth of the protection afforded by the weak libertarian paradigm of free speech, *Brandenburg v. Ohio* exemplified the degree or depth of that protection. *Brandenburg* extended strong constitutional shields even to speech threatening violence or advocating government overthrow. To be regulated, the speech had to meet a number of stringent criteria:

> [F]ree speech and free press do not permit a State to forbid or proscribe advocacy of the use of force or of law violation except where such advocacy is directed to inciting or producing imminent lawless action and is likely to incite or produce such action.[84]

The standard required a specific purpose to incite action that is both imminent and lawless. Moreover, the words had to appear likely to succeed in inciting such action.[85] The case exemplifies the stringent protection generally afforded freedom of speech. John Rawls characterized *Brandenburg* as protecting a right to revolution that helps to legitimate democratic governance.[86]

In being centrally concerned with content discrimination, the weak libertarian paradigm deeply resonates with distributive autonomy: it protects the speech of anyone who wishes to participate in the marketplace of ideas equally—irrespective of the content of that person's speech. Obviously, the weak libertarian paradigm of free speech does not always permit a speaker to say anything she wants to say. The *New York Times* and *Brandenburg* decisions themselves allow government to suppress certain defamation and certain incitement.[87]

The vast majority of free speech decisions and scholarship are aimed at and contribute to the weak libertarian paradigm. Elaborating this paradigm with precision, and exploring the extent to which the Court has remained faithful to it, would range far beyond the central concern of this work. For now, suffice it to say that the Burger, Rehnquist, and Roberts Courts have largely adhered to, indeed bolstered, libertarian protection against content discrimination.[88]

One important exception to the Court's continuing attention to protecting all types of speech is the protest cases and the decline of protection for protest speech in general. As Chapter 1 suggests, the Court has dramatically narrowed access to the public forum, that is, places where people can speak for free[89] and also rejected a general right of access to the media, even if the person seeking access offers to pay for it. Although neither of these measures directly affects content, they both disproportionately impact the speech of people who have viewpoints that are not representative of the politically dominant.

A right of access to the media is important to ensuring diversity of viewpoints and subject matter, particularly now. Media ownership has become heavily concentrated: five major conglomerates own the overwhelming majority of news and other media.[90] Moreover, *Forbes* reported in June 2016 that fifteen billionaires owned much of the news media, and further alleged that some have exerted control in their financial interests.[91] Control of the Internet is also becoming more heavily concentrated.[92] In addition, advertisers frequently shy away from controversial programming. The Court has denied a right of even paid access to the media. *CBS v. Democratic National Committee (DNC)* upheld a decision by CBS to reject a controversial paid ad by the DNC criticizing the Vietnam War during a presidential election campaign.[93] Moreover, advertisers need to make money. Let's face it; few adverts target poor people; consequently, network news content is unlikely to aim at their interests.

The Court has afforded strong protection to commercial advertising. Edwin Baker has detailed the ways in which advertising narrows broad-based participation, systemically skewing media content in favor of wealth. First, advertisers disfavor critiques of their products. Second, they favor lighter material. Third, advertisers generally avoid controversial issues. Fourth, advertising "subsidizes media that adopt the perspectives and fulfill the information needs of the more affluent." Baker details many more and less direct and successful attempts by advertisers to influence the media.[94]

This book discusses the skewing of the marketplace of ideas to afford a very small group at the top of the income and wealth spectrum overwhelming influence over the vital area of campaign finance. Enforcing virtually unlimited access to those at the top will almost certainly entail drowning out the voices of everyone else, including those at the bottom. Circumscribing a right of access to the media dramatically constricts access to the voting public, and extending constitutional protection to commercial advertising compounds the capture of the marketplace of ideas.[95] Not only is this point extremely important to free speech theory, but it is also important to distributive autonomy theory. It illustrates the idea that the distribution of speech rights shapes the cumulative content of all the speech in the society. Libertarian denials of this point are counterfactual. Far from building on the weak libertarian paradigm, the strong libertarian paradigm of free speech jurisprudence threatens to gobble up the central content-based and viewpoint-based protections of the weak libertarian ancestor. As I will further illustrate in Chapter 9, the campaign finance cases have enabled certain ideas, viewpoints, and entire subjects to be excluded or marginalized in the critical area of political discourse.

Notes

1. *See* National Labor Relations Board v. Jones & Laughlin Steel Corp., 301 U.S. 1 (1937).

2. *See* West Coast Hotel v. Parrish, 300 U.S. 379 (1937) (substantive due process). The Court also allowed Congress broad discretion to delegate authority to administrative agencies. *See, e.g.*, Yakus v. United States, 321 U.S. 414 (1944).

3. *See* John Attanasio, *Everyman's Constitutional Law: A Theory of the Power of Judicial Review*, 72 GEO. L.J. 1665, 1677–81 (1984) (describing how *Carolene Products* addresses some of the problems catalyzed by the constitutional crisis of the late 1930s).

4. One may argue that the settlement envisioned in the footnote was never totally realized. Those who take this position would probably agree that a considerable portion of its vision was achieved—at least for a time.

5. Lynch v. Household Fin. Corp., 405 U.S. 538, 552 (1972).

6. *See, e.g.*, Duncan v. Louisiana, 391 U.S. 145, 148 (1968).

7. U.S. CONST. amend. IV.

8. *See generally* Keystone Bituminous Coal Ass'n v. De Benedictis, 480 U.S. 470 (1987).

9. Sniadach v. Family Fin. Corp., 395 U.S. 337 (1969).

10. Exxon v. Eagerton, 462 U.S. 176 (1983).

11. Goldberg v. Kelly, 397 U.S. 254 (1970). For additional discussion of the distinction between personal rights and property rights, see John Attanasio, *Personal Rights and Economic Liberties: American Judicial Policy*, in GERMANY AND ITS BASIC LAW, 14 SERIES DRÄGER FOUNDATION 222–24 (Paul Kirchoff & Donald Kommers eds., Nomos Verlagsgesellschaft 1993); *see also* C. Edwin Baker, *Property and Its Relation to Constitutionally Protected Liberty*,

134 U. Pa. L. Rev. 741 (1986). For discussion of the modern property rights regime, see *infra* text accompanying notes 58–72.

12. *See, e.g.*, Bruce Ackerman, We The People: Foundations 119 (Harvard University Press, 1991); John Hart Ely, Democracy and Distrust: A Theory of Judicial Review 75–77, 151–53 (Harvard University Press, 1980); Louis Lusky, By What Right? (The Michie Company, 1975); Attanasio, *Judicial Review, supra* note 3, at 1678–81; Robert Cover, *The Origins of Judicial Activism in the Protection of Minorities*, 91 Yale L.J. 1287 (1982); Lewis F. Powell, Jr., Carolene Products *Revisited*, 82 Colum. L. Rev. 1087 (1982).

13. Bruce Ackerman has described the footnote as "synthesiz[ing] the Founding into the New Deal revolution." Ackerman, Foundations, *supra* note 12, at 123.

14. Home Bldg. & Loan Ass'n v. Blaisdell, 290 U.S. 398 (1934). The contracts clause forbids states from impairing the obligation of contracts. Although this is a plausible route to stronger protection for some economic rights of existing contracts, the *Lochner* era Court did not invoke it very much, perhaps because it only protected existing contracts from ex post regulation. Instead, the doctrine of liberty of contract was much more vigorous protecting potential contracts ex ante against economic regulation. For a time, the Court increased scrutiny under the contracts clause. *See* United States v. New Jersey Trust, 431 U.S. 1 (1977); Allied Structural Steel Co. v. Spannaus, 438 U.S. 234 (1978). The Court has withdrawn from this position, however. *See* Energy Reserves Group, Inc. v. Kansas City Power & Light Co., 459 U.S. 400 (1983); Exxon Corp. v. Eagerton, 462 U.S. 176 (1983).

15. *See, e.g.*, Yakus v. United States, 321 U.S. 414 (1944); *see also* Gary J. Greco, *Standards or Safeguards: A Survey of the Delegation Doctrine in the States*, 8 Admin. L.J. Am. U. 567, 573–77 (1994).

16. *See, e.g.*, Steward Mach. Co. v. Davis, 301 U.S. 548 (1937) (spending power); Sonzinsky v. United States, 300 U.S. 506 (1937) (taxing power).

17. *See* Erie v. Tompkins, 304 U.S. 64, 145–46 (1938); Cass R. Sunstein, The Partial Constitution 54–55 (Harvard University Press, 1993); Morton J. Horwitz, *The Constitution of Change: Legal Fundamentality Without Fundamentalism*, 107 Harv. L. Rev. 32, 77–79 (1993). To both of these challenges the Court applied a relaxed rationality standard in which it almost completely deferred to Congress's judgment.

18. Attanasio, *Judicial Review, supra* note 3, at 1680.

19. Lochner v. United States, 198 U.S. 45, 56 (1905).

20. *See* Walton H. Hamilton, *Property. According to Locke*, 41 Yale L.J. 864, 877 (1932).

21. I am using utilitarianism simply as hedonistic act utilitarianism in its classic way articulated by its founder Jeremy Bentham. *See* Jeremy Bentham, An Introduction to the Principles of Morals and Legislation 11–16 (J.H. Burns & H.L.A. Hart eds., Oxford University Press, 1996). For purposes of this work, I need not discuss other variants of utilitarianism.

22. *Lochner*, 198 U.S. at 57.

23. *See* Herbert A. Hovenkamp, Enterprise and American Law, 1836–1937, 180–82 (Harvard University Press, 1991); 8 Encyclopedia Of Philosophy 209 (Paul Edwards, ed., Macmillian, 1967); J.J.C. Smart & Bernard Williams, Utilitarianism for and Against 12–27, 79–81 (Cambridge University Press, 1973).

24. Barry Cushman, *Doctrinal Synergies and Liberal Dilemmas: The Case of the Yellow-Dog Contract*, 1992 Sup. Ct. Rev. 235, 250–55.

25. Herbert Hovenkamp, *Labor Conspiracies in American Law, 1880–1930*, 66 Tex. L. Rev. 919, 928 (1988).

26. *See* Horwitz, *supra* note 17, at 54.

27. OWEN M. FISS, TROUBLED BEGINNINGS OF THE MODERN STATE 1888–1910, at 392, THE OLIVER WENDELL HOLMES DEVISE HISTORY OF THE SUPREME COURT (Vol. 8) (Macmillan, 1993).

28. *See* Frederick Schauer, *Principles, Institutions and the First Amendment*, 112 HARV. L. REV. 84, 112 (1998) (explaining that courts make decisions based on principle not policy).

29. United States v. Carolene Products, 304 U.S. 144, 152, n.4 (1938).

30. *Id.* at 152 n.4 (citations omitted). The first paragraph primarily concerns selective incorporation of the protections of the Bill of Rights against the states. *Id.* Justice Stone, who drafted the opinion, added the paragraph in response to an inquiry by Chief Justice Hughes, and this paragraph should be considered the chief justice's contribution. LUSKY, RIGHT, *supra* note 12, at 110; Louis Lusky, *Footnote Redux: A* Carolene Products *Reminiscence*, 82 COLUM. L. REV. 1093, 1096–100 (1982). The first paragraph initially received expression in the "preferred position" doctrine, which maintained that the judiciary should afford certain provisions of the Bill of Rights greater constitutional protection. After the Court rejected that preferred position doctrine, the paragraph led to the doctrine of selective incorporation. LUSKY, RIGHT, *supra* note 12, at 124–30.

31. *See* Powell, *supra* note 12.

32. Louis Lusky, who helped to draft the footnote as Justice Stone's clerk, maintained that the selective incorporation method of the first paragraph is independent of the rest of the footnote. Added at the request of Chief Justice Hughes, the first paragraph is textual and contrasts with the functional approach of paragraphs two and three. LUSKY, RIGHT, *supra* note 12, at 111–12; Lusky, *Footnote Redux, supra* note 30, at 1099–100 (1982). *See* Cover, *Origins, supra* note 12, at 1291–92; Bruce A. Ackerman, *Beyond* Carolene Products, 98 HARV. L. REV. 713, 743–44 (1985). Bruce Ackerman has characterized the last two paragraphs as stemming from a positivist, "pluralist bargaining" position, and the first as based on "higher-law" or "tradition." Ackerman, *supra.*

33. Cover, *Origins, supra* note 12, at 1304–10.

34. Attanasio, *Judicial Review, supra* note 3, at 1678–84. LUSKY, RIGHT, *supra* note 12, at 109, 123, 125.

35. Lusky, *supra* note 30, at 1096.

36. *See* Powell, *supra* note 12, at 1088–89.

37. *See* Attanasio, *Judicial Review, supra* note 3, at 1680.

38. *See* Powell, *supra* note 12, at 1088–89.

39. LUSKY, RIGHT, *supra* note 12, at 109. Richard Pildes has remarked: "This is the Age of Democracy. In the last generation, more new democracies, all constitutional ones, have been forged than in any comparable period." Richard H. Pildes, *Foreword: The Constitutionalization of Democratic Politics—The Supreme Court, 2003 Term*, 118 HARV. L. REV. 28, 28 (2004). *See also* Richard H. Pildes, *Democracy, Anti-democracy, and the Canon*, 17 CONST. COMMENT. 295 (2000).

40. *Cf.* Bradley A. Smith, *Money Talks: Speech, Corruption, Equality, and Campaign Finance*, 86 GEO. L. J. 45, 95–98 (1997) (arguing that the Constitution applies egalitarian values to voting, but not to speech).

41. JESSE H. CHOPER, JUDICIAL REVIEW AND THE NATIONAL POLITICAL PROCESS 4 (University of Chicago Press, 1979) (footnote omitted). Choper details the myriad ways in which the majoritarian process fails to work; he argues that these lapses are not as severe as one might

suppose. On the whole, he praises the internal workings of Congress and the presidency as reflecting the will of the American people. *Id.* at 12–47.

Steven Shiffrin has criticized characterizing the democratic process as majoritarian. STEVEN H. SHIFFRIN, THE FIRST AMENDMENT, DEMOCRACY AND ROMANCE 46–85 (1990). "Only someone with a mature capacity for strained metaphor or serious self-delusion could endorse the idea that governmental decisions are made *of* the people or *by* the people." SHIFFRIN, *supra* at 85. Shiffrin founds free speech jurisprudence on the concept of dissent. SHIFFRIN, *supra* at 86–109, 167. The narrowing of participatory channels impairs dissent just as surely as it skews the majoritarian process.

Drawing on the Civic Republican tradition, Cass Sunstein has said that "democracy is concerned with much more than numbers and intensities of preferences." Cass R. Sunstein, *Political Equality and Unintended Consequences*, 94 COLUM. L. REV. 1390, 1394 (1994). Instead, he posits goals avoiding corruption, maintaining political equality, and advancing political deliberation. Sunstein, *supra*, at 1391–94. Political equality entails people being equal in the political arena rather than being advantaged based on wealth. Sunstein, *supra*, at 1392.

42. ELY, DEMOCRACY *supra* note 12, at 103.

43. Many of Ely's critics have disputed his process characterization of protecting discrete and insular minorities; few have criticized his process characterization of the judiciary's role in preserving the political process of "voice and vote." *See, e.g.*, Symposium, *Democracy and Distrust: Ten Years Later*, 77 VA. L. REV. 631 (1991); Symposium, *Judicial Review Versus Democracy*, 42 OHIO ST. L.J. 1 (1981). *See generally* Michael J. Klarman, *The Puzzling Resistance to Political Process Theory*, 77 VA. L. REV. 747, 748, 773 (1991) (arguing that critics of Ely's process theory have been more insistent and more successful in criticizing his ideas about paragraph three).

44. LOUIS LUSKY, OUR NINE TRIBUNES: THE SUPREME COURT IN MODERN AMERICA 130–31 (Praeger, 1993). Lusky traces paragraph two back to Chief Justice Marshall's opinion in *McCulloch v. Maryland*, 4 U.S. (19 Wheat) 316 (1819). In a long footnote in *South Carolina Hwy. Dep't v. Barnwell Bros., Inc.* 303 U.S. 177 (1938), decided earlier in 1938, Justice Stone demonstrated how the Court had implemented Chief Justice Marshall's vision between 1819 and 1938 in its dormant commerce clause rulings. *Id.*

45. ALPHEUS THOMAS MASON, HARLAN FISKE STONE: PILLAR OF THE LAW 515 (Viking Press, 1956).

46. *See* LUSKY, TRIBUNES, *supra* note 44, at 130–31.

47. *See* ELY, DEMOCRACY, *supra* note 12, at 87. *See also* SUNSTEIN, PARTIAL CONSTITUTION, *supra* note 17, at 143–44 (agreeing with many of Ely's positions); James E. Fleming, *Constructing the Substantive Constitution*, 72 TEX. L. REV. 211, 216–17 (1993) (noting parallels in Ely's and Sunstein's positions).

48. ELY, DEMOCRACY, *supra* note 12, at 77.

49. *Id.* at 76.

50. *Id.* at 80. Lusky has disputed Ely's construction of the footnote as "limiting judicial review to procedural and structural interventions." LUSKY, TRIBUNES, *supra* note 44, at 123.

51. ELY, DEMOCRACY, *supra* note 12, at 100.

52. *Id.* at 89–90.

53. *See, e.g.*, Reynolds v. Sims, 377 U.S. 533 (1964).

54. *See generally*, John Rawls, *The Basic Liberties and Their Priority* 77–78 (Tanner Lecturers April 10, 1981) http://tannerlectures.utah.edu/_documents/a-to-z/r/rawls82.pdf; CASS

R. SUNSTEIN, DEMOCRACY AND THE PROBLEM OF FREE SPEECH 20 (Free Press, 1993);
LAURENCE TRIBE, CONSTITUTIONAL CHOICES 192 (Harvard University Press, 1985).

55. *See* Karcher v. Daggett, 462 U.S. 725 (1983) (failure to meet Congressional equal representation standard of Article 1 Section 2); *see also* JOHN ATTANASIO & JOEL GOLDSTEIN, UNDERSTANDING CONSTITUTIONAL LAW 299–300 (4th ed., LexisNexis, 2012).

56. *See, e.g.,* Harper v. Va. Bd. of Elections, 383 U.S. 663 (1966) (invalidating a $1.50 poll tax in state elections).

57. 198 U.S. 45 (1905). For an interesting argument maintaining that intellectual roots of *Lochner* might be traced to the free labor movement or to the southern secessionist movement in the antebellum era, see ROBERT A. BURT, THE CONSTITUTION IN CONFLICT 248–51 (Harvard University Press, 1992).

58. I agree with John Rawls that speech rights merit far greater protection than economic rights. *See* John Attanasio, *The Principle of Aggregate Autonomy and the Calabresian Approach to Products Liability*, 74 VA. L. REV. 677, 728–29 (1988).

59. *See* SUNSTEIN, PARTIAL CONSTITUTION, *supra* note 17, at 45–46, 51. Sunstein argues that property rights are creatures of law and also cites Jeremy Bentham for that proposition. He appears to view property rights largely in positivist, Benthamite terms.

60. *See, e.g.,* BRUCE ACKERMAN, PRIVATE PROPERTY AND THE CONSTITUTION (1977); RICHARD A. EPSTEIN, TAKINGS: PRIVATE PROPERTY AND THE POWER OF EMINENT DOMAIN (Harvard University Press, 1985); Symposium, *The Jurisprudence of Takings*, 88 COLUM. L. REV. 1581 (1988).

61. *See* Hawaii Hous. Auth. v. Midkiff, 467 U.S. 229 (1984); Kelo v. New London, 545 U.S. 469 (2005). This provision does not safeguard ownership or possession of a particular piece of property; it simply exacts just compensation for governmental takings of property.

62. *See, e.g.,* First English Evangelical Lutheran Church of Glendale v. Cty. of Los Angeles, 482 U.S. 304 (1987) (temporary taking); Nollan v. Ca. Coastal Comm'n, 483 U.S. 825 (1987) (higher scrutiny of land-use regulations).

63. The reluctance of the Court to use the takings clause to enter the realm of economic regulation may be quite different when the government takes the property outright. *Compare* Horne v. Dep't of Agriculture, 135 S. Ct. 2419 (2015) (pricing schema) *with* Ruckelshaus v. Monsanto, 467 U.S. 986 (1984) (pesticide regulations) *and* Duquesne Light Co. v. Barasch, 488 U.S. 299 (1989) (utility rate regulations).

64. *See* EPSTEIN, *supra* note 60, at 277–82 (Epstein argues that the takings clause requires that each government regulation satisfy Pareto optimality by increasing the size of the economic pie). *Id.* at 199–200. The Court has ratcheted up the level of Fifth Amendment protection for property to some extent. *See, e.g.,* Dolan v. City of Tigard, 512 U.S. 374 (1994) (applying "rough proportionality" test in zoning case to invalidate zoning commission's conditioning a building permit on the dedication of some property for public cases). However, it has thus far not used the takings clause to afford strong protection for freedom of contract. *See, e.g.,* United States v. Sperry Corp., 493 U.S. 52 (1989) (tribunal fee); Duquesne Light Co. v. Barasch, 488 U.S. 299 (1989) (utility rate regulations).

65. U.S. CONST. art. I, §10, cl. 1. *See* United States Trust Co. v. New Jersey, 431 U.S. 1 (1977); Allied Structural Steel Co. v. Spannaus, 438 U.S. 234 (1978).

66. Energy Reserves Group v. Kansas Power & Light Co., 459 U.S. 400 (1983); Exxon Corp. v. Eagerton, 462 U.S. 176 (1983).

67. *See* Harper v. Va. Bd. of Elections, 383 U.S. 663 (1966) (vote); Shapiro v. Thompson, 394 U.S. 618 (1969) (travel); Ake v. Oklahoma, 470 U.S. 68 (1985) (judicial access), and Douglas v. California, 372 U.S. 353 (1963) (appellate review).

68. *See,* generally, San Antonio Independent Sch. Dist. v. Rodriguez, 411 U.S. 1, 31–44 (1973).

69. *See, e.g.,* Sniadach v. Family Fin. Corp., 395 U.S. 337 (1969) (garnishment of wages).

70. Goldberg v. Kelly, 397 U.S. 254 (1970) (deprivation of a government benefit, welfare). Mathews v. Eldridge, 424 U.S. 319 (1976) (social security disability benefits). *See also* Nelson v. Colorado, 137 S. Ct. 1249, 1255–56 (2017) (unconstitutional deprivation of private property for someone acquitted of crime).

71. Railway Express Agency, Inc. v. New York, 336 U.S. 106 (1949). William Eskridge and Phillip Frickey have argued that the Court "is prone to expand protection of property rights, albeit cautiously and incrementally." William N. Eskridge, Jr. & Philip P. Frickey, *Foreword: Law as Equilibrium*, 108 HARV. L. REV. 26, 44 (1994).

72. *See, e.g.,* Rawls, *Basic Liberties, supra* note 54. Owen M. Fiss, *Free Speech and Social Structure,* 71 IOWA L. REV. 1405, 1411–13 (1986); Norman Dorsen & Joel Gora, *Free Speech, Property, and the Burger Court: Old Values, New Balances,* 1982 SUP. CT. REV. 195, 240; FISS, TROUBLED BEGINNINGS, *supra* note 27.

73. Nicholas Confessore, Sarah Cohen & Karen Yourish, *Small Pool of Rich Donors Dominate Election Giving,* N.Y. TIMES, Aug. 2, 2015, at A1; *Million-Dollar Donors in the 2016 Presidential Race,* N.Y. TIMES, Aug. 2, 2015, at A1.

74. Palko v. Connecticut, 302 U.S. 319, 326–27 (1937).

75. *See, e.g.,* Hugo Black, *The Bill of Rights,* 35 N.Y.U. L. REV. 865 (1960).

76. William J. Brennan, Jr., *The Supreme Court and the Meiklejohn Interpretation of the First Amendment,* 79 HARV. L. REV. 1 (1965).

77. 376 U.S. 254 (1964).

78. 395 U.S. 444 (1969).

79. I say "virtually" as *New York Times* did not extend protection to all types of speech. The case itself continued to place purely commercial advertising beyond the constitutional protection. 376 U.S. at 265–67. Since then, commercial speech has received constitutional protection. *See* Va. State Bd. of Pharm. v. Va. Citizens Consumers Council, 425 U.S. 748 (1976). But certain kinds of commercial speech lack constitutional protection as do certain types of, for example, defamation. *Cf.* Wojciech Sadurski, *Does the Subject Matter? Viewpoint Neutrality and Freedom of Speech*, 15 CARDOZO ARTS & ENTM'T. L.J. 315 (1997) (arguing that the Court still makes distinctions in constitutional protection based on the subject matter of speech).

80. *New York Times,* 376 U.S. at 269 (citations omitted). Harry Kalven talked about the revolutionary change in free speech jurisprudence that *New York Times* signaled. Harry Kalven, Jr., *The* New York Times *Case: A Note on "The Central Meaning of the First Amendment,"* 1964 SUP. CT. REV. 191.

81. 315 U.S. 568 (1942).

82. Kalven, *supra* note 80, at 216–18. *See also* Kenneth L. Karst, *Equality as a Central Principle in the First Amendment,* 43 U. CHI. L. REV. 20, 30–33 & nn.52–70 (1975). Cass Sunstein has argued that the Court has not really abandoned a two-tier theory of speech. Although it does protect speech generally, in contrast to *Chaplinsky,* some types of speech receive more constitutional protection than others. SUNSTEIN, DEMOCRACY, *supra* note 54.

83. Kalven also emphasized that *New York Times* declared unconstitutional the criminal offense of seditious libel. Kalven, *supra* note 80, at 204–10. The importance of rejecting seditious libel was emphasized in Wechsler's brief in *New York Times*. *See* Vincent Blasi, *The Checking Value in First Amendment Theory*, 1977 AM. B. FOUND. RES. J. 521, 574, n.187. John Rawls sees this aspect of *New York Times* as naturally leading to strong protection for even subversive speech in *Brandenburg v. Ohio. See* JOHN RAWLS, POLITICAL LIBERALISM 343, 345 (Columbia University Press, 1993).

84. 395 U.S. 444, 447 (1969).

85. *Id.* at 447–49.

86. RAWLS, POLITICAL LIBERALISM, *supra* note 83, at 344–48.

87. New York Times v. Sullivan, 376 U.S. 254, 279–80 (1964); *Brandenburg*, 395 U.S. at 447. *See also* THE BURGER COURT: THE COUNTER-REVOLUTION THAT WASN'T (Vincent Blasi ed., Yale University Press, 1983).

88. *See, e.g.*, R.A.V. v. City of St. Paul, 505 U.S. 377 (1992) (protecting hate speech); Texas v. Johnson, 491 U.S. 397 (1989) (protecting flag burning); ATTANASIO & GOLDSTEIN, UNDERSTANDING, *supra* note 55, at 611–12 (recounting the Burger Court's treatment of hate speech in the *Skokie* case).

89. *See e.g.*, Perry Educ. Ass'n v. Perry Educators' Ass'n, 460 U.S. 37 (1983); Hudgens v. NLRB, 424 U.S. 507 (1976).

90. Independent Lens, PBS, *Who Owns the Media*, November, 2006. http://www.pbs.org/independentlens/democracyondeadline/mediaownership.html; BEN H. BAGDIKIAN, THE NEW MEDIA MONOPOLY: A COMPLETELY REVISED AND UPDATED EDITION WITH SEVEN NEW CHAPTERS (Beacon Press, 2004).

91. Kate Vinton, *These 15 Billionaires Own America's News Media Companies*, FORBES, June 1, 2016, http://www.forbes.com/sites/katevinton/2016/06/01/these-15-billionaires-own-americas-news-media-companies/#26ece53c30b4.

92. Independent Lens, *supra* note 90.

93. 412 U.S. 94 (1973). There is an exception for candidates for federal office.

94. C. Edwin Baker, *Advertising and a Democratic Press*, 140 U. PA. L. REV. 2097, 2167 (1992). *See also* SUNSTEIN, PARTIAL CONSTITUTION, *supra* note 17, at 217; SUNSTEIN, SPEECH, *supra* note 54, at 62–66; Jonathan Weinberg, *Broadcasting and Speech*, 81 CAL. L. REV. 1101, 1153 (1993); Owen M. Fiss, *Why the State?*, 100 HARV. L. REV. 781, 788 (1987).

95. *See generally* Attanasio, *Economic Liberties*, *supra* note 11.

III The Rise of Constitutional Libertarian Protection for Property Interests: Campaign Finance

" 'money talks.' "
Justice Byron White,
Buckley v. Valeo, dissent

5 The *Buckley* Constitution and the Strong Libertarian Paradigm of American Politics

A. Seeds: The Absolutist Speech Protection of Justices Black and Douglas

Although I do not endorse every case decided under it, the weak libertarian paradigm of free speech jurisprudence has played a very valuable role in advancing distributive autonomy and broad-based participatory democracy. Unhappily, however, its individual liberty dimension carried with it the philosophical seeds of the strong libertarian paradigm, which has so ravaged the *Carolene Products* settlement. The latent seeds in the libertarian genetics of the weak paradigm legally and philosophically risked mutation into the stronger variant.

Recall Louis Lusky, Justice Stone's clerk, said that the footnote's aims were "government by the people, and government for the whole people."[1] Just as the weak libertarian paradigm respects the distribution of autonomy by bestowing on everyone a robust baseline presence in the marketplace of ideas, the strong one profoundly violates the distribution of autonomy by affording some people overwhelmingly greater influence over the marketplace of ideas. Although this differential access extends well beyond the campaign finance area, the differentials are disproportionately important here as campaign finance involves the area of democratic elections and governance, which are uniquely constitutive of an individual's overall autonomy.

As Chapter 1 suggested, during the 1960s, the Court under Chief Justice Earl Warren moved dynamically toward erecting a highly participatory form of democracy. Of course,

Politics and Capital. John Attanasio.
© John Attanasio 2018. Published 2018 by Oxford University Press.

this idea was hardly new; in some sense, it has been the inspirational model that has animated American governance since the time of the Framing. As the great constitutionalist John Ely has said in *Democracy and Distrust*, at some level the history of the American polity has been defined by moving toward more and more robust and inclusive democracy.[2] Ely argued that, over time, America has grown more and more democratic. As evidence of this, he noted that, excluding the Prohibition Amendments, six of the last ten constitutional amendments directly involved broadening popular control over government.[3] Ely thought that the judicial project should advance this historic national quest through a "participation-oriented, representation-reinforcing approach to judicial review."[4]

The Warren Court exemplified this movement toward participatory democracy—perhaps most vividly through its voting rights decisions of "one person, one vote" and through its free speech jurisprudence. Nevertheless, the *New York Times* and *Brandenburg* decisions moved strongly toward, without ever adopting, the position of Justices Hugo Black and William Douglas that free speech is an absolute.[5] In many cases, their position effectively gave voice to unpopular views—to civil rights protestors, Vietnam War protestors, Communist Party members, and others who typically had been excluded from the marketplace of ideas. So the jurisprudence of the Warren Court advanced both liberty and equality. Their decisions furthered the distribution of autonomy for all. One way of thinking about their constitutional conception was that they would protect the ideas and viewpoints of all persons on an equal basis. This constitutional vision bolstered distributive autonomy.

But their ideas also were imbued with deep libertarian content in protecting each person's claim to say whatever he or she wanted to say. It is this strand of their thinking that came to dominate contemporary free speech jurisprudence. For example, a key thrust of the Warren Court was to expand protection to free access to the marketplace of ideas for everyone. Perhaps, the main area of the law in which the Warren Court protected this free access is called the public forum. Essentially, the public forum cases protected everyone's ability to access public parks, streets, sidewalks, and certain other governmental property, to convey their ideas.[6] Importantly, the Court also protected considerable access to the media of radio and television.[7] This notion of free access to the marketplace of ideas nurtures distributive autonomy. Guaranteeing everyone's ability to have their say in particular protects the rights of political protestors, members of minority political parties, and others whom Ely calls political "out" groups.[8] Political out groups are those who lack the ability to influence the political process. This lack of influence can exist to varying degrees. Some groups have been political out groups over centuries of history, such as African Americans. Others have been political outs since the beginnings of time, such as the poor.[9]

The Warren Court paid careful attention to the distribution of autonomy in the core area of free speech. Its jurisprudence championed the rights of political out groups.[10] Ely utilizes the idea of protecting political out groups as aptly describing that Court's jurisprudence, not only as a normative ideal. The Court's jurisprudence exhibited an ideal that John Rawls would dub "equal liberty." As Chapter 1 notes, Rawls published his magisterial *A Theory of Justice* just two years after Warren retired.[11]

For example, the Warren Court's pioneering work in guaranteeing an equal right to vote for all exhibited strong distributive autonomy sensibilities. So did its decisions in the area of free speech. In particular, the public forum cases evidence deep commitments to distributive autonomy.[12] So did that Court's approving discussion in *Red Lion v. FCC*[13] of the Federal Communications Commission's Fairness Doctrine that requires broadcast media to permit access to and present diverse viewpoints.

However, the positions of Justices Black and Douglas affording absolute protection for speech had stronger libertarian roots. Paradoxically, in absolutely protecting discrimination against speech based on its content, Justices Black and Douglas afforded each individual the absolute claim "to say whatever I want to say." The individualistic thrust of their absolutist position led facilely, but certainly not inexorably, from the weak libertarian paradigm of free speech jurisprudence to its stronger distant cousin.

Technically, the absolutist position of Justices Black and Douglas never triumphed on the Court.[14] Nevertheless, the Court has come fairly close to affording a person absolute protection to say whatever he wants to say.[15] Perhaps, the premier example is *National Socialist Party of America v. Village of Skokie*.[16] In that case, the Court effectively upheld the right of the National Socialist Party (Nazi) to demonstrate in a community heavily populated by Jewish Holocaust survivors. In dissenting from denial of certiorari when the case came up a second time,[17] Justice Blackmun opined:

> . . . the present case affords the Court an opportunity to consider whether, in the context of the facts that this record appears to present, there is no limit whatsoever to the exercise of free speech. There indeed may be no such limit, but when citizens assert, not casually but with deep conviction, that the proposed demonstration is scheduled at a place and in a manner that is taunting and overwhelmingly offensive to the citizens of that place, that assertion, uncomfortable though it may be for judges, deserves to be examined.[18]

Applied uncritically, the absolutist position of Justices Black and Douglas led simplistically—but not necessarily—from the weak libertarian paradigm elaborated in those cases to the strong libertarian paradigm that dominates today. The weak libertarian paradigm merely claims, "I can say whatever I want to say." In contrast, the strong libertarian paradigm shouts, "I can say whatever I want to say *with whatever resources I have to say it*." The differential access to the marketplace of ideas permitted by this latter claim has greatly constricted the participatory democracy essence of both the *Carolene Products* settlement and paradoxically, of the weak libertarian paradigm. Moreover, the strong libertarian paradigm has dramatically distorted the distribution of autonomy in the core autonomy areas of free speech and elections.

Ironically, the strong libertarian paradigm uses wealth to constrict the autonomy of many in ways that have interesting political theory parallels with *Lochner*. Both approaches limit participation in the democratic process. *Lochner* removed certain questions from democratic decision-making altogether. By affording *property interests* Brobdingnagian political influence, the strong libertarian paradigm of free speech jurisprudence connects influence to wealth at least as much as to number of votes or preference intensities.

As both are grounded in the absolutist libertarian positions of Justices Black and Douglas, the weak libertarian paradigm readily mutated into its stronger manifestation. In a farsighted 1967 article, Jerome Barron argued that the *New York Times v. Sullivan*[19] decision itself helped to initiate this process. The absolutist approach of Justices Black and Douglas further advantaged the position of already powerful speakers in society, including the media, by immunizing them from much governmental regulation.[20]

In addition, the libertarian political theory underlying the absolutist position certainly did not require, but did take an important step toward, connecting money with speech. In a footnote that criticized affording individuals a limited free right of reply to media attacks, Justice Douglas fused—or actually conflated—spending money to speak, with speaking:

> The monetary and other burdens imposed on the press by the right of a criti-cized person to reply, like the traditional damage remedy for libel, lead, of course, to self-censorship respecting matters of importance to the public that the First Amendment denies the Government the power to impose.[21]

Once one accepts a broad right to say whatever one chooses in a strict libertarian sense, a logically possible but certainly not necessary next step is that government cannot inter-fere with one's using whatever resources one has to say it.[22]

Mark Graber traces the roots of the contemporary "civil libertarian" paradigm to noted speech theorist Zechariah Chafee in the 1920s. According to Graber, "conserv-ative libertarians" protected both speech and property. The Progressives—whose ideas became dominant during the New Deal—rejected constitutional protection for prop-erty. Chafee's crucial intellectual move was to apply libertarian thinking (albeit in some progressive garb) to speech.[23] The resultant prohibition on government interference with the marketplace of ideas led facilely to noninterference with using one's wealth to speak.[24] Ignoring the tremendous disparities in the financial capacity to speak would be contrary to any notion of distributive autonomy, which premises any authentic autonomy partly on some minimal baseline of resources. Particularly in the area of elections, when the speech of some can effectively drown out that of all others, free speech theory has led to very few people exercising disproportionate control over public policy.

Some contend that conservative libertarians who defended the property rights regime of *Lochner* did not actually afford much protection to free speech. Under this view, Chafee introduced libertarian thinking (again, in some progressive garb) to free speech theory.[25] As described in the discussion of *Lochner* in Chapter 3, this position reflects the contemporaneous jurisprudence of the Supreme Court, which strongly protected economic rights but not free speech rights. The Court's approach also found support in the literature of the time. As the position afforded muscular libertarian protection to property rights and exalted them over first-order rights such as free speech, it was antithetical to notions of distributive autonomy.

In sharp contrast, G. Edward White has maintained that Chafee sought to distance himself, albeit not altogether successfully, from contemporary libertarians.[26] Instead, White argues that Thomas Emerson reinjected strong libertarian ideas into free speech theory in the 1960s. Emerson's writings emphasized the highly individualistic libertarian idea of individual self-actualization or self-fulfillment.[27] As Chapter 9 elaborates, these self-fulfillment notions of autonomy contrast sharply with distributive autonomy. Distributive autonomy respects the liberty of each individual more than highly individualistic libertarian accounts, which refuse to consider the liberty of all.

Whether their route traveled through the theories of Emerson or Chafee, libertarian spores philosophically similar to those from the *Lochner* era survived in post-New Deal thinking. What makes White's story particularly intriguing is his theory that the highly influential Emerson reintroduced powerful libertarian ideas into free speech jurisprudence only a few short years before the Court began to erect the strong libertarian paradigm—preeminently in *Buckley v. Valeo*.[28] As recounted in Chapter 9, Emerson may have exerted more influence on the modern Court's free speech approach than any other free speech theorist.

B. The Strong Libertarian Paradigm of Free Speech and the Decline of Democracy in America

1. Equating Campaign Speaking and Campaign Spending: The Supreme Court's Momentous Pivot

The law of campaign finance is extremely complex to the point of being like the tax code. One reason is the sheer length of the cases. For example, *Buckley v. Valeo* alone is 294 pages, *McConnell v. Federal Election Commission* is 131 pages, and *Citizens United v. Federal Elections Commission* is 175 pages. The length and complexity of the campaign finance cases is extraordinary among categories of Supreme Court cases. It is not the point of this book to rehearse the complex law of campaign finance, but instead to probe the seismic shift in constitutional jurisprudence and the philosophical foundations upon which this shift rests. Consequently, I will provide a concise account focusing on the more recent cases. For readers who are interested in a fuller understanding of the law, the footnotes recount these decisions in greater detail.

Some grasp of the case law is important to understanding the problems described in this text and what potential solutions might exist. Strong First Amendment protection to spend money on political campaigns transfers the disparities of the economic marketplace to the marketplace of ideas. But committed individualistic libertarians believe that economic rights are also first-order rights. Consequently, they would broadly reject regulation in *both* the economic marketplace and the marketplace of ideas.

Constitutionally, not just in the United States, but in other constitutional democracies, speech regulations are not equated with regulations involving property rights. With the exception of the takings clause, economic regulations affecting the distribution of wealth do not even engage constitutional rights, first-order or otherwise. The analysis illustrated by the *liberty/utility* matrices has become mainstream so that there is virtually no constitutional scrutiny of legislation affecting the distribution of wealth.

A sustained philosophical discussion of what economic rights might comprise first-order or lower-order rights ranges beyond the scope of this text. Suffice it to say that I agree with Rawls's distinction that economic regulations, with the exception of the takings clause, do not violate first-order rights. The principle I have fashioned affecting lower-order rights is the principle of aggregate autonomy. It sanctions small wealth incursions to avoid severe autonomy incursions for as many individuals as possible in the society. Generally the U.S. Constitution offers no protection for either wealth infringements through taxation, or against more severe autonomy incursions in areas such as healthcare or sustenance. The *Carolene Products* settlement leaves such areas to the elected branches.

Assuming that economic rights are not first-order rights, the campaign finance cases attempt to re-elevate economic rights to nearly a first-order status by ensconcing them in free speech shields. The critical move that *Buckley* and its progeny make is equating the expenditure of funds for speech, with speech. It is not intuitive that these are equivalents.

First of all, as I shall discuss, spending money to speak is not the same as speaking. Consequently, the former can be regulated much more than actually speaking. As we shall see, the Court itself accepts this distinction to some extent in allowing the government to regulate campaign contributions to a much greater extent than campaign expenditures. The standard of scrutiny for campaign contributions has always been much lower than what is traditional for pure speech.

Even if one refuses to accept any distinction between spending money to speak and speaking, the principle of distributive autonomy allows much greater regulation of campaign finance than of the content of speech. Recall that the principle prohibits unduly constricting the first-order rights of others. Accordingly, in the instant context, the principle requires that affording certain free speech rights to some people does not unduly infringe on the free speech rights of others. Content-based restrictions on speech unduly constrict first-order rights; they do not respect the distributive autonomy of the speaker to express all, or nearly all, ideas, or the distributive autonomy of the listener to be exposed to all ideas and to make autonomous decisions about which ones to accept or to reject.

In sharp contrast, allowing individuals to spend as much money as they please on political campaigns floods the vast inequities in the economic marketplace into the marketplace of ideas allowing, indeed enabling, some speakers to unduly constrict, indeed "submerge," the ideas of other speakers. These autonomy-advantaged speakers can also contravene the distributive autonomy of listeners to select which ideas they choose to be exposed to and which ideas have merit. Plainly, these are violations of first-order speech rights.

In the electoral context, a second distributive autonomy infringement occurs that might be even more serious than the first. Elections involve self-government. They are crucial to justifying the myriad autonomy infringements that laws routinely make—many times even involving first-order rights such as imprisonment or execution. We could certainly debate, and societies hotly debate, whether certain of these infringements such as the death penalty are justified at all. But to be justified, autonomy infringements—particularly of first-order rights in a democracy—must be legitimatized in part by an actual democratic process of voices and votes that will decide what those infringements shall be.

The context of selecting political leaders is special in that the campaign connection to fashioning law is much closer than with virtually any other type of speech. This connection allows any distributive autonomy infringements made at the stage of the political campaign to multiply during the ensuing lawmaking process: laws draw lines that afford or deny countless rights, duties, and even capacities that can advance or restrict liberty.

Thus, even if one accepts (using considerable powers of imagination) a precise equation between spending money on speech and speaking, regulating traditionally understood oral and written communication violates the principle of distributive autonomy in a way that regulating campaign contributions and expenditures does not. This is because traditionally understood oral and written communications per se generally cannot unduly constrict the liberty of another, whereas campaign expenditures and contributions frequently can. I am assuming in this analysis that persuasion by rational argument when everyone has a fair opportunity to speak does not unduly constrict the autonomy of another. If anything, being persuaded by rational argument would generally appear to enhance one's autonomy in expanding the opportunities for rational, or even advantageous, choice.

Of course, we might also be persuaded by emotion, or deception and other forms of manipulation. Yet free speech theory protects emotional speech. As Justice Oliver Wendell Holmes Jr. famously put it, "Every idea is an incitement. . . . Eloquence may set fire to reason."[29] But what about deceptive speech? The Supreme Court has also said: "there is no such thing as a false idea."[30] But it does permit lawsuits for defamation when the libelous opinion implies underlying facts that are false.[31] It also unanimously allows outright prohibition of fraud in fundraising even for such a worthy charitable cause as advancing the welfare of Vietnam War veterans.[32]

But what counts as an undue constriction under distributive autonomy theory? We might think of an undue constriction partly as an unreasonable constriction. Adding the ingredient of reasonableness introduces an imprecise but objective rudder into the analysis. If one claims an absolute liberty to influence public policy using campaign expenditures, why cannot one simply bribe a public official to do one's will? Something intuitive has from time immemorial considered bribery wrong and impermissible.

In his book entitled *Bribes*, Judge John Noonan discusses the various ways in which a campaign contribution can influence a public official:

1. A gives to X, a candidate, out of dislike or distrust of Y, X's opponent.
2. A gives to X out of admiration for his character and a belief that the country will be better with him in office.
3. A gives to X because of X's general sympathy to a particular industry, section of the country, or economic class.
4. A gives to X because X has a principled stand on a specific issue.
5. A gives to X because he needs "an insurance policy" guaranteeing he can present his position to X—that is, although A has such status that legislators listen to him, he wants to be sure that he will always have access to X.
6. A gives to X because he has no other way of getting access to him.
7. A gives to X because he expects X to vote for a specific bill.[33]

Noonan wrote eight years after the Court extended strong First Amendment protection to spend money on political campaigns. He expressed particular concern about large contributions, as candidates will likely notice them. In this connection, he voiced deep concerns about PACs.[34]

Inherently, bribes involve the crucial issue of money influencing the lawmaking process. This itself is an autonomy incursion in enabling the briber to use money to subjugate the will of the public official to the will of the briber rather than follow her own thinking as to what is the will of the majority of her constituency or at least what policy is in the best interests of her constituency. The briber doubly violates autonomy because the monetary payment then affords the briber a disproportionate say, perhaps even a trump, in fashioning legislation. The bribe thus constricts the autonomy of the representatives' legal constituency to influence their elected representative. Moreover, the bribe's adverse impact on autonomy multiplies with the public official's time in office as laws inherently expand the autonomy of some and contract the autonomy of others. For Noonan there exists a continuum between a patently illegal bribe and a less direct, but still problematical, influencing of legislative decisions through campaign contributions.[35]

The primogenitor case affording free speech protection to campaign financing is *Buckley v. Valeo*.[36] *Buckley* upheld congressional limitations on contributions to political campaigns, but struck down limitations on a candidate's personal and total campaign expenditures.[37] Contributions were only a symbolic expression of support for a candidate, and contribution limitations advanced Congress's primary purpose of eliminating political corruption or its appearance. Accordingly, limitations on contributions imposed little direct restraint on the contributor's political expression.

The Court stated that there is no indication that the contribution limitations imposed by the Act would have any dramatic adverse effect on the funding of campaigns and political associations. The overall effect of the Act's contribution ceilings is merely to require candidates and political committees to raise funds from a greater number of persons and to compel people who would otherwise contribute amounts greater than the statutory limits to expend such funds on direct political expression, rather than to reduce the total amount of money potentially available to promote political expression.[38]

Importantly, the Court also invalidated limits on independent expenditures made by others, including PACs, to elect a particular candidate.[39] These regulations did not deter political corruption as they concerned expenditures made independent of the candidate and his campaign.[40]

The per curiam[41] opinion equated spending money to advance an idea with speaking. Because spending caps limited the quantity and diversity of political speech,[42] they infringed on the core First Amendment rights of political expression and association.

The Court's concern for the diversity of speech should not be mistaken as exhibiting concern for distributive autonomy. Ensuring diversity of speech seeks to avoid diminishing protection of speech based on its content. Avoiding content-based distinctions advanced the weak libertarian paradigm articulated in *New York Times v. Sullivan* of protecting all categories of speech.[43] *New York Times* prohibits government from interfering with what a speaker wants to say.[44] Going well beyond *New York Times*, *Buckley* protects the speaker's ability to use whatever economic resources he pleases in order to speak. *Buckley* and its progeny protect immense, virtually limitless differentials in the quantity of the speech different speakers can express.

Far from enhancing speech diversity, the Court's position diminished it. The Court's decision allowed far greater speech from property interests than from non-property interests. Let's assume that one-third of the donations are from the wealthiest 0.01 percent of society. As the statistics in Chapter 11 demonstrate, this is a realistic assumption. It might be true that there may be more speech in absolute terms. It is almost certainly true that the percentage of the total campaign speech that exhibits diverse ideas will decline, particularly in areas in which the wealthiest 0.01 percent share common economic or other interests. Why do I say this? There is not a confluence of interests among those donors from the 0.01 percent. They are a politically diverse group of people. However, on the many issues that affect their self-interest, such as regulation of business, taxation, and government spending, there will be a great congruence of interests, affording a small group a grossly disproportionate effect on the election and public policy. This is a very realistic proposition considering the dramatic rise in income and wealth of that group since *Buckley,* as demonstrated in Chapter 10. Particularly considering that people have limited time to study campaigns, the percentage or proportion of diverse ideas in the campaign will likely decline.

Buckley rejected the government's interest in equalizing the financial resources of candidates.[45] Thus, governmental concern for distributive autonomy was basically per se unconstitutional. In a passage trumpeting the rise of the strong libertarian paradigm, the Court declared that governmental restrictions on the speech of some "to enhance the relative voice of others is wholly foreign to the First Amendment."[46] This famous line echoed in countless subsequent campaign finance opinions plainly rejects any notion of distributive autonomy. Instead, it posits a false libertarianism, which protects the autonomy of a few at the expense of trampling the autonomy of many more citizens to have any meaningful influence over the crucial area of elections.

In his partial concurrence and partial dissent, Justice White stated that *Buckley* stands for the proposition "'money talks.'"[47] Nothing in the record before the Court indicated that the limitations at issue on overall campaign expenditures, candidate personal expenditures, or outside contributions would cripple campaigns.

In his partial concurrence and dissent, Justice Marshall argued that the decision would diminish confidence in the political system because it would be perceived that the wealthy have a distinct advantage in elections. He would have upheld both the contribution limitations and the provision limiting how much a candidate could contribute to his own campaign.[48]

Buckley did uphold expenditure limitations on a presidential candidate from a major party who has accepted public funding under subtitle H of the Act.[49] The Court upheld subtitle H because it furthered the electoral process by providing more money for that process. In addition, the candidates had to voluntarily accept the expenditure ceilings in exchange for federal funds.[50] The voluntary nature of this limitation rendered it consistent with the strong libertarian paradigm.

The public financing provision also stated that a candidate from a new or minor party could spend no more money than a major party candidate, and would only get federal funding (according to a special formula for minor party candidates) if her party received more than 5 percent of the vote in the *preceding* election.[51] In his partial concurrence and dissent, Justice Rehnquist argued that this provision essentially "enshrined the Democratic and Republican parties in a permanently preferred position."[52] This criticism highlights yet another example of the strong libertarian approach advantaging entrenched power over broad participation, and hence adversely affecting distributive autonomy.

The *Buckley* Court also upheld provisions requiring candidates to disclose contributions and campaign expenditures. The disclosure provisions would alert voters to the monetary influences on the candidate, and deter corruption by exposing large contributions and expenditures.[53] Minority parties could get an exemption from the disclosure provisions if they showed a probability that compelled disclosure would subject contributors to "threats, harassment, or reprisals from either Government officials or private parties."[54]

Disclosure is consistent with the principle of distributive autonomy. It allows at least some scrutiny of campaign spending, which advances people's autonomy to assess how different candidates are being influenced. One problem with disclosure is that it's like drinking from a fire hydrant. The amount spent on campaigns has topped $7 billion.[55] There are also hidden dark pools of money, discussed later in the text, further impairing the ability to assess how much candidates are being influenced.

2. Bolstering the Strong Libertarian Paradigm: Corporate Spending

Several decisions following *Buckley* invalidated limitations on expenditures by Political Action Committees (PACs). For example, the Court has invalidated bans on PACs expending more than $1,000 to advance the election of a presidential candidate who had accepted public financing.[56] Speech by PACs was fully protected political speech notwithstanding the inability of PAC contributors to control how the PACs used their funds.[57]

The Court has also invalidated a municipal ordinance that established a contribution limit for groups formed to support or oppose a measure placed on the ballot for popular vote.[58] The Court distinguished contribution limits supporting or opposing measures on the ballot from the limits upheld in *Buckley* that involved large contributions to individual candidates.[59] Somewhat moderating the effects of wealth on the majoritarian process, the Court did for a time uphold an annual $5,000 limitation on contributions made by individuals or corporations to PACs.[60] This has now been effectively reversed.[61]

Another cluster of early cases protect certain political expenditures made by corporations. *First National Bank of Boston v. Bellotti* held that government cannot prohibit corporations from spending money to express their views on referenda—even if the referenda are not directly related to their property, business, or assets.[62]

The Court reiterated that the First Amendment did not permit government to equalize the relative voices of speakers in the society, a line that these cases constantly repeat.[63] The Court rejected the state's argument that the statute protected the interests of individual shareholders who might disagree with the corporation's expressed views.[64] Justice White's dissent argued that incorporation is a privilege in which the state bestows on a corporation the power to amass wealth. He remarked: "The State need not permit its own creation to consume it."[65]

In *Federal Election Commission v. National Right to Work Committee (NRWC)*, the Court refused to afford corporations a right to solicit campaign contributions from nonmembers.[66] Corporations and unions could establish segregated funds to which those directly involved with the entity could contribute.[67] This case upheld the government's determination that the persons from whom the not-for-profit corporation was soliciting were not members.[68]

Writing for a unanimous Court, Chief Justice Rehnquist acknowledged Congress's broad power to regulate elections. Congress's interests superseded the associational rights that the corporation asserted in this case. Congress's first stated interest was "to ensure that substantial aggregations of wealth amassed by the special advantages which go with the corporate form of organization should not be converted into political 'war chests' which could be used to incur political debts from legislators."[69] Second, Congress had an interest in protecting shareholders and union members from having funds they have given these institutions used to support candidates whom these individuals opposed. Restricting corporations or unions from making direct contributions to candidates advanced the interest in preventing corruption, broadly conceived. The Court accepted "Congress' judgment that it is the potential for such influence that demands regulation. Nor will we second-guess a legislative determination as to the need for prophylactic measures where corruption is the evil feared."[70]

Federal Election Commission v. Massachusetts Citizens for Life, Inc. (MCFL),[71] struck down limitations on expenditures by a nonprofit corporation to influence the election of particular candidates. MCFL was a nonprofit corporation formed to disseminate ideas rather than earn profits. Since MCFL's goal was not to amass capital, the nonprofit corporation did not present the same threat of corruption as a typical for-profit corporation. Moreover, it had no shareholders who might disagree with its ideas.[72] In another early case, the Court invalidated limitations on independent expenditures made by a political party to elect a particular candidate.[73]

C. *Austin* and *McConnell*: A Brief Turn toward the Participatory Democracy Paradigm

Following fifteen years (1976–1991) of fairly robust constitutional protection, the Court's campaign finance jurisprudence took a fairly sharp turn to briefly embrace the participatory democracy approach that advanced distributive autonomy.[74] In *Austin v. Michigan Chamber of Commerce*,[75] the Court upheld a ban on corporations using general treasury funds for contributions or independent expenditures to support or oppose candidates for state office.[76] The statute focused on "the corrosive and distorting effects of immense aggregations of wealth that are accumulated with the help of the corporate form and that have little or no correlation to the public's support for the corporation's political ideas."[77]

The statute did not ban all political expenditures by a corporation but instead only required that the money be spent through segregated funds.[78] In this way, the corporation's political expenditures could accurately reflect the views of those contributing to the separate fund while allowing those not contributing to remain associated with the corporation for economic and other nonpolitical reasons.[79] *Austin* in its reasoning and its result represented a sharp turn away from the ascendant strong libertarian approach to give greater consideration to the distribution of autonomy.

Justice Kennedy's dissent contended that this was the first time that the Court allowed restrictions on political expenditures.[80] His views prevailed twenty years later when the Court overturned *Austin* in *Citizens United v. Federal Election Commission*,[81] detailed in Chapter 6.[82]

Since *Buckley*, the Court has consistently allowed fairly tough restrictions on contributions to individual candidates.[83] It has, however, invalidated exceptionally low contribution limits.[84] The Court's upholding tough contribution limits shifted the political and constitutional battlefield to soft money, defined as money contributed to political parties rather than to specific candidates. In 1984, soft money accounted for only 5 percent of the two main political parties' spending; but by 2000, that number had ballooned to 42 percent. Moreover, of the total amount of soft money raised, 60 percent came from just 800 donors.[85]

Initially, congressional attempts to regulate soft money encountered what appeared to be a fairly receptive Supreme Court. In *FEC v. Colorado Republican Federal Campaign Committee*,[86] the Court upheld restrictions on a political party's coordinated expenditures with a candidate, as equivalent to a direct contribution to the candidate. Colorado had capped such coordinated expenditures at $2,000 per election cycle. [87]

In *McConnell v. Federal Election Commission*, the Court seemed to even more intensely embrace a participatory democracy paradigm in what some commentators thought was a landmark decision.[88] The *McConnell* opinion, over 131 pages long, largely rejected a facial challenge to the wide-ranging Bipartisan Campaign Reform Act of 2002 (BCRA).[89] The Act limited the use of "soft money" by political parties and for issue ads. However, facial challenges of a statute are difficult to come by, particularly soon after a law has been passed. Consequently, no one knew at this early juncture how much of the decision was attributable to the Court's refusal to strike down the entire Act, or substantial parts of it, based on a very limited record, and how much indicated actual approval of regulating soft money.[90]

BCRA § 323 restricted soft money contributions. "Hard money" included money contributed to a particular candidate's campaign.[91] This definition extended to money given to political parties for the purpose of influencing the election of a particular candidate.

In contrast, "soft money" is largely comprised of funds that individuals, corporations, unions, or other organizations contribute to political parties so long as the funds were not to be used specifically to influence the election or defeat of a particular candidate. The parties could deploy these contributions to influence elections, including even naming particular candidates in advertising.[92]

So even though an individual or organization had contributed the maximum amount to a particular federal candidate, each could still contribute additional amounts of soft money directly to political parties to finance their activities in a wide variety of other areas, which directly influenced that candidate's election, such as get-out-the-vote drives or issue ads naming the candidate.[93] Consequently, the amount of soft-money contributions skyrocketed. Against this backdrop, Congress acted in a broadly bipartisan way to stem soft money contributions.

The BCRA subjected hard money raised and spent on candidates to the same source and amount limits as if it had been contributed directly to the campaign.[94] The Court upheld this regulation, subjecting it to only a moderate level of scrutiny.[95] The relaxed standard of scrutiny was designed to allow Congress latitude to anticipate and avert attempts to circumvent regulations.[96]

BCRA § 323 also limited individuals, corporations, and unions from making large contributions of soft money in federal elections. The majority thought that limiting the dollar amounts or forcing unions and corporations to contribute them through PACs did not alter the political message bound up with the solicitation. Instead, the restriction promoted wider "dissemination of information by forcing parties, candidates, and officeholders to solicit from a wider array of potential donors."[97] As in *Austin*, the Court overtly espoused an approach that was much more consonant with the distribution of autonomy.

Limits on soft-money contributions advanced the important governmental interests in preventing actual corruption that may be related to large contributions, and the lost public confidence spurred by the appearance of corruption. The possibility of corruption or its appearance existed when large contributions were made to a national party.

The Court maintained that the amount of soft money a candidate raises for the party often affects the degree to which the party assists her campaign. Donors often request parties to use hard-money and soft-money contributions for specific candidates. National party committees and candidate committees often organize joint fundraising committees. National parties could manipulate the legislative calendar, could create access to candidates or officeholders in exchange for large donations, or influence decision-making based on donor wishes. Even if such abuses are infrequent, "the potential for such undue influence is manifest."[98] Such concerns over corruption clearly are sufficiently important governmental interests.[99] The various opinions in *McConnell* used the word "corruption" eighty-eight times, defining the concept expansively, relying in part on an extensive record below.[100]

BCRA § 323(f) limited the source and the amount of soft-money contributions that state and local candidates or officeholders could raise or spend to support "a clearly identified candidate for federal office."[101] It forbade federal candidates and officeholders from soliciting, receiving, directing, transferring, or spending soft money in federal elections.[102] In accordance with *Buckley*, the Court upheld these restrictions as contribution limitations "subject to less rigorous scrutiny."[103]

The Court upheld restrictions on "'electioneering communication,'" including any "'broadcast, cable or satellite communication'" that "'refers to a clearly identified candidate for Federal office.'"[104] The Court rejected plaintiffs' argument that *Buckley* protected such communications as "issue advocacy."[105]

The Court also rejected a facial challenge to the part of the statute that required disclosure of the names of people contributing $1,000 or more to a person, or a group that spent more than $10,000 per year on electioneering communications. *Buckley* had rejected facial challenges against such requirements, absent "'reasonable probability'" of harm.[106]

The Court also rejected a facial challenge against treating all payments for "'electioneering communications'" coordinated with a candidate or party as contributions to and payments by that candidate or party. Such coordinated disbursements could be regulated in the same way as other coordinated disbursements.[107] The Court also upheld including electioneering communications in the prohibition against corporations and unions using funds to expressly advocate for or against a federal candidate.[108] Corporations or unions could still fund such electioneering communications using segregated funds or PACs. Issue ads broadcast shortly before federal elections were the "functional equivalent of express advocacy."[109]

The Court also rejected vagueness and overbreadth challenges against BCRA § 214 as § 214 required no agreement for a coordinated expenditure.[110] Unspoken agreements could exist that would benefit the candidate in the same way as a cash donation.[111]

Justice Scalia's dissent in *McConnell* noted that incumbents received much larger hard-money contributions than challengers.[112] Precedent required "'exacting scrutiny'" of the statute in this case.

The right to free speech "would be largely ineffective if it did not include the right to engage in financial transactions that are the incidents of its exercise."[113] Freedom of speech included the right to pool money to disseminate ideas. Given the premise of democracy, there was no such thing as too much speech. It was also the nature of democracy that supporters enjoy greater access to elected officials. Justice Scalia noted that the $3.9 billion spent on the 2000 election was about half as much as Americans spent on movie tickets and a fifth of the expenditure on cosmetics and perfume.[114]

Justice Thomas dissented in part and concurred in the judgment in part.[115] Broad bribery prohibitions would have better deterred corruption and the appearance of corruption.[116] The restrictions at issue were not simply contribution limits, but rather "limitations on independent expenditures."[117] Past cases recognize that corporations face difficulties when forced to communicate through PACs.[118]

Dissenting, Justice Kennedy maintained, "Democracy is premised on responsiveness."[119] The "generic favoritism" rationale adopted by the majority sharply contrasted with *Buckley's* focus on corruption or its appearance.[120]

The joint opinion for the majority written by Justices Stevens and O'Connor concluded that government could protect the political system against the ill effects of aggregated wealth. Obviously, *McConnell* amounted to a warm embrace of a distributive autonomy approach that allows broad-ranging regulations, particularly of soft money. However, as recounted in Chapter 6, the facial nature of this challenge turned out to be pivotal. Moreover, the opinion's coauthor, Justice O'Connor, retired.[121]

Notes

1. Louis Lusky, By What Right? 109 (The Michie Company, 1975).

2. For an elaboration of the origins of majority rule in the American polity, see John Hart Ely, Democracy and Distrust: A Theory of Judicial Review 5–7 (Harvard University Press, 1980).

3. *Id.* at 7.

4. *Id.* at 87.

5. Hugo L. Black, *The Bill of Rights*, 35 N.Y.U. L. REV. 865 (1960).

6. *See* JOHN ATTANASIO & JOEL GOLDSTEIN, UNDERSTANDING CONSTITUTIONAL LAW 311–12 ch. XIV (4th ed., LexisNexis, 2012).

7. Red Lion Broad. Co. v. FCC, 395 U.S. 367 (1969).

8. *See* ELY, DEMOCRACY, *supra* note 2, at 120.

9. Racial minorities and women have over time been afforded far greater protection in constitutional law than the poor. Although poverty can be escaped, race and gender are immutable. Although all of this is true to a certain extent, the poor have tended to be long-standing political outs. Moreover, poor people lack much access to the marketplace of ideas. Although the condition of poverty is not immutable, it is very difficult to shed.

10. *See* ELY, DEMOCRACY, *supra* note 2, at 120.

11. *See supra* text accompanying note 15, Chapter 1.

12. *Red Lion*, 395 U.S. 367. During the Reagan administration, the FCC abrogated the fairness doctrine.

13. 395 U.S. 367 (1969).

14. *See* William J. Brennan, Jr. *The Supreme Court and the Meiklejohn Interpretation of the First Amendment*, 79 HARV. L. REV. 1 (1965).

15. *See* NORMAN REDLICH, JOHN ATTANASIO & JOEL GOLDSTEIN, CONSTITUTIONAL LAW 950–52 (LexisNexis, 5th ed., 2008).

16. 432 U.S. 43 (1977).

17. *See* Smith v. Collin, 439 U.S. 916, 919 (1978).

18. *Id.* at 919 (1978).

19. *See supra* text accompanying notes 77–87, Chapter 4.

20. *See* Jerome A. Barron, *Access to the Press—A New First Amendment Right*, 80 HARV. L. REV. 1641, 1651–52 (1967). Barron argued that *New York Times* placed the media beyond governmental regulation without exacting any commitments that would foster the robust exchange of ideas sought by the case. *Id.* at 1656–60.

21. Columbia Broad. Sys., Inc. v. Democratic Nat'l Comm., 412 U.S. 94, 168 n.18 (1973) (Douglas, J., concurring in the judgment) (denying a right of reply to defamatory falsehoods because of its expense to the press). Drawing libertarian parallels between financial and any other burdens on speech, Justice Douglas continued:

> The burdens certainly are as onerous as the indirect restrictions on First Amendment rights which we have struck down: (1) the requirement that a bookseller examine the contents of his shop; (2) the requirement that a magazine publisher investigate his advertisers; (3) the requirement that names and addresses of sponsors be printed on handbills; (4) the requirement that organizations supply membership lists; and (5) the requirement that individuals disclose organizational membership. In each instance we held the restriction unconstitutional on the ground that it discouraged or chilled constitutionally protected rights of speech, press, or association.

Id. (citations omitted).

22. The free speech tradition assumed that the liberty to speak automatically fostered the broad-based exchange of ideas that democracy required. Owen Fiss argues that the libertarian approach to free speech may reduce rather than enhance diversity of ideas and views by only

giving access to those who have resources. Owen M. Fiss, *Free Speech and Social Structure*, 71 IOWA L. REV. 1405, 1408–11 (1986).

23. MARK A. GRABER, TRANSFORMING FREE SPEECH: THE AMBIGUOUS LEGACY OF CIVIL LIBERTARIANISM 1–14 (University of California Press, 1991). *See also id.* at 156.

24. *Id.* at 206–15.

25. Charles L. Barzun, *Politics or Principle? Zechariah Chafee and the Social Interest in Free Speech*, 2007 B.Y.U. L. REV. 259.

26. G. Edward White, *The First Amendment Comes of Age: The Emergence of Free Speech in Twentieth-Century America*, 95 MICH. L. REV. 299, 316–17, 325–26 (1996).

27. *Id.* at 354–57. *See also* Chapter 9(B).

28. 424 U.S. 1 (1976).

29. Gitlow v. New York, 268 U.S. 652, 673 (1925).

30. Gertz v. Welch, 418 U.S. 323, 339 (1974).

31. Milkovich v. Lorain Journal Co., 497 U.S. 1 (1990).

32. Illinois v. Telemarketing Assocs., Inc. 538 U.S. 600 (2003).

33. JOHN J. NOONAN, BRIBES 623 (Macmillan, 1984).

34. *Id.* at 647–51.

35. Id. at 621–51 (Noonan entitles his Chapter 19, "The Donations of Democracy.").

36. 424 U.S. 1 (1976). Cass Sunstein has analogized *Buckley* to *Lochner*: "Just as the due process clause once forbade government 'interference' with the outcomes of the economic marketplace, so too the First Amendment now bans government 'interference' with the political marketplace . . . ." Cass R. Sunstein, *Political Equality and Unintended Consequences*, 94 COLUM. L. REV. 1390, 1398 (1994).

37. *Buckley*, 424 U.S. at 3.

38. *Id.* at 21–22. *See also id.* at 25–26.

39. *Id.* at 45.

40. *Id.*

41. A per curiam opinion is an opinion that is written by some or all of the justices in the majority in which no one claims authorship. Per curiam opinions are unusual, particularly in landmark cases such as *Buckley*. The typical majority opinion of the Supreme Court has one named author. Drafts are circulated, and other justices participate through suggesting revisions.

42. *Buckley*, 424 U.S. at 54–57.

43. *See supra* notes 77–87 and accompanying text, Chapter 4.

44. 376 U.S. 254, 268 (1964).

45. *Buckley*, 424 U.S. at 54–57.

46. *Id.* at 48–49. Cass Sunstein has argued that in a *Lochneresque* fashion the Court simply accepted the existing distribution of wealth as neutral. CASS R. SUNSTEIN, THE PARTIAL CONSTITUTION 84–85 (Harvard University Press, 1993).

47. *Buckley*, 424 U.S. at 262.

48. *Id.* at 288–90.

49. *Id.* at 86–88, 98–99.

50. *Id.* at 95, 101.

51. *Id.* at 89, 91–99. Major party candidates also received some funding for their primary campaigns. *Id.* at 89–90, 99–100.

52. *Id.* at 293.

53. *Id.* at 66–68.

54. *Id.* at 74. Brown v. Socialist Workers '74 Campaign Committee, 459 U.S. 87 (1982) required an exemption from disclosure of contributions for a minor party suffering harassment.

55. In her effort to reconcile libertarian and egalitarian values, Kathleen Sullivan would hold limits on campaign contributions unconstitutional, and would strengthen disclosure rules. *See* Kathleen M. Sullivan, *Two Concepts of Free Speech*, 124 HARV. L. REV. 143 (2010).

56. Federal Election Comm'n v. Nat'l Conservative Political Action Comm. ("NCPAC"), 470 U.S. 480, 501 (1985).

57. *Id.* at 494.

58. Citizens Against Rent Control v. Berkeley, 454 U.S. 290, 299 (1981).

59. *Id.* at 297.

60. Ca. Med. Ass'n v. FEC, 453 U.S. 182 (1981). A plurality of four justices analogized the amounts that can be contributed to PACs to limitations, upheld in *Buckley*, on the amounts that can be contributed to candidates. Concurring in the judgment, Justice Blackmun would uphold the limits on contributions to PACs as advancing the compelling state interest of preventing corruption in political campaigns.

61. *See infra* text accompanying notes 56–60, Chapter 6.

62. 435 U.S. 765, 784 (1978). The corporations sought to publicize their views on a proposed referendum for a graduated personal income tax. There was no showing that the corporations' political speech had "been overwhelming, or even significant in influencing referenda in Massachusetts, or that there has been any threat to the confidence of the citizenry in government." *Id.* at 789–90. Importantly, the Court indicated that these arguments would have merited consideration had there been such showings. *Id.* at 795.

63. *Id.* at 790–91.

64. The Court found the statute underinclusive because it did not cover other corporate activities, such as lobbying, which might also offend minority shareholders. The statute was also underinclusive in not mentioning groups such as labor unions, trusts, and other associations that might also have minorities with differing views. The statute was overinclusive in that it prohibited corporate speech even if all the members of the corporation agreed with the speech. *Id.* at 792–93.

65. *Id.* at 809. For additional discussion of *Bellotti*, see MICHAEL J. GRAETZ & LINDA GREENHOUSE, THE BURGER COURT AND THE RISE OF THE JUDICIAL RIGHT 256–68 (Simon & Schuster, 2016).

66. 459 U.S. 197 (1982). *NRWC* established a segregated campaign fund because federal law prohibited corporations or unions from directly contributing to political campaigns. Federal Election Campaign Act of 1971 § 441(a) & (b).

67. For corporations, employees and directors could contribute to the segregated fund. For nonprofit corporations such as the National Right to Work Committee (NRWC) that don't have stockholders, members could contribute to a segregated fund.

68. The Court upheld the FEC's denial of the NRWC's segregated fund soliciting these 267,000 persons who had contributed to the NRWC itself and had received membership cards, because, among other reasons, the Committee's own documents stated that it had no members. The Court noted:

> Although membership cards are ultimately sent to those who either contribute or respond in some other way to respondent's mailings, the solicitation letters themselves make no reference to members. Members play no part in the operation or administration

of the corporation; they elect no corporate officials, and indeed there are apparently no membership meetings. There is no indication that NRWC's asserted members exercise any control over the expenditure of their contributions. Moreover, as previously noted, NRWC's own articles of incorporation and other publicly filed documents explicitly disclaimed the existence of members.

Id. at 206.

69. *Id.* at 207.

70. *Id.* at 210.

71. 479 U.S. 238, 265 (1986). The Court found that MCFL had a constitutional right to publish a newsletter disseminating the voting records of candidates.

72. *Id.* at 264.

73. Colo. Republican Fed. Campaign Comm. v. Fed. Election Comm., 518 U.S. 604 (1996).

74. See Richard L. Hasen, Buckley *Is Dead, Long Live* Buckley: *The New Campaign Finance Incoherence of* McConnell v. Federal Election Commission, 153 U. PA. L. REV. 31, 57 (2004) (arguing that *McConnell* "appears to be a transitional case, with even stronger signals pointing to the participatory self-government rationale"). Stephen Loffredo said that *Austin* is a rare decision in which "the Court squarely acknowledged—for the first time in constitutional discourse— that inequalities of private economic power tend to reproduce themselves in the political sphere and displace legitimate democratic governance." Stephen Loffredo, *Poverty, Democracy and Constitutional Law*, 141 U. PA. L. REV. 1277, 1285 (1993).

75. 494 U.S. 652 (1990).

76. The statute did permit corporations and unions to make political expenditures from segregated political funds, to which employees could choose to contribute. *Id.* at 660.

77. *Id.* Multinational structures and different packaging of securities further attenuate any actual ability of the corporation to represent individuals. *See* Charles D. Watts, Jr., *Corporate Legal Theory Under the First Amendment:* Bellotti *and* Austin, 46 U. MIAMI L. REV. 317, 375–76 (1991).

78. Justice Marshall found the statute narrowly tailored to prevent corruption because it did not ban all political expenditures by a corporation but instead only required that the money be spent through segregated funds.

79. 494 U.S. at 663. The Court rejected the argument that the statute was underinclusive because it did not cover entities such as labor unions. Whatever capital such unincorporated associations may amass was done without the special state help of the corporate form. *Id.* at 661.

The Chamber of Commerce asserted that the law was unconstitutional as applied to nonprofit corporations. In rejecting this contention, the Court distinguished *FEC v. Mass. Citizens for Life*, text accompanying *supra* notes 71–73, Chapter 5, on several grounds. Most important, three-quarters of the members of the Chamber of Commerce were for-profit corporations. *Id.* at 663–64.

80. *Id.* at 698–700 (Kennedy, J., dissenting). Justice Kennedy maintained that the decision also permitted some nonprofit corporations to speak but not others. He argued that the statute's distinctions were based on the content of the speech (political campaigns) and the identity of the speaker.

81. 558 U.S. 310 (2010).

82. *See infra* text accompanying notes 19–55, Chapter 6.

83. In *Nixon v. Shrink Mo. Gov't PAC*, 528 U.S. 377 (2000), the Court upheld fairly small campaign contribution limitations, provided for state candidates, as long as the candidate could still run an effective campaign.

84. In *Randall v. Sorrell*, 548 U.S. 230 (2006), Vermont limited contributions for governor and lieutenant governor to $400, contributions for state senator to $300, and contributions for state representative to $200. When *Buckley* was decided, $200 would have totaled approximately $57 per election, rather than the $1,000 per election limit upheld in *Buckley*. The Vermont statute also limited individual contributions to a political party to $2,000 every two years. *Id.* at 250.

Dissenting, Justice Stevens would overrule those parts of *Buckley* that invalidated expenditure limits. As Justice White's dissent in *Buckley* recognized, "'it is quite wrong to equate money and speech.'" *Id.* at 276. Justice Stevens analogized expenditure limits to time, place, and manner restrictions rather than to content-based restrictions. *Id.* at 277.

85. McConnell v. Federal Election Commission, 540 U.S. 93, 124 (2003).

86. 533 U.S. 431 (2001).

87. Colorado feared that donors could circumvent contribution limitations by giving up to the $20,000 annual limit to political parties, which the parties could then pass along to candidates. The Colorado Act had capped coordinated expenditures at $2,000 per election cycle. The evidence "shows that even under present law substantial donations turn the parties into matchmakers whose special meetings and receptions give the donors the chance to get their points across to the candidates." *Id.* at 461. The Party, however, argued that more effective safeguards, such as the earmarking rule, were already in place to prevent circumvention. The earmarking rule treated contributions that were directed to a particular candidate as direct contributions. The Court countered that the earmarking provision "would reach only the most clumsy attempts to pass contributions through to candidates." *Id.* at 462. The Court rejected the alternative proffered by plaintiffs that circumvention could be avoided by capping contributions to parties at less than $20,000 as opposed to limiting coordinated spending. The majority said that "Congress is entitled to its choice." *Id.* at 465.

Justice Thomas dissented, joined by Justices Scalia and Kennedy, and by Chief Justice Rehnquist as to part II. Coordinated expenditures were not the same as contributions, and political parties were not the same as political committees. A political candidate's activities and a party's public image were intertwined. Moreover, the restriction did not serve the important interest of curbing corruption, as the "'aim of a political party is to influence its candidate's stance.'" *Id.* at 476. Finally, government could avoid circumvention problems with more narrowly tailored alternatives, such as enforcing the earmarking provision or simply lowering the $20,000 cap on annual contributions to political parties. *Id.* at 481.

88. 540 U.S. 93 (2003).

89. The Bipartisan Campaign Reform Act (BCRA) amended the Federal Election Campaign Act of 1971 (FECA).

90. The Supreme Court hears two types of challenges to laws. One is a facial challenge which seeks to strike down the law entirely. These are difficult to obtain. The other is an "as applied challenge," which only strikes down the application of the law to the particular facts before the Court.

91. "FECA defines the term 'contribution,' however, to include only the gift or advance of anything of value 'made by any person for the purpose of influencing any election for *Federal* office.'" *McConnell*, 540 U.S. at 122.

92. Using soft money, political parties could influence the election of federal, state, or local candidates.

93. In a somewhat controversial construction expanding the scope of the Act, the Federal Election Commission (FEC) allowed soft-money contributions to political parties for the

purpose of funding "mixed-purpose activities—including get-out-the-vote drives and generic party advertising—in part with soft money." *Id.* at 123. In another controversial construction, the FEC allowed political parties to spend soft money on the "costs of 'legislative advocacy media advertisements,' even if the ads mentioned the name of a federal candidate, so long as they did not expressly advocate the candidate's election or defeat." *Id.*

94. BCRA § 323(a).

95. In *Buckley v. Valeo*, 424 U.S. 1 (1976), and *Nixon v. Shrink Missouri Government PAC*, 528 U.S. 377 (2000), the Court recognized, as in earlier cases, that limits imposed on hard money contributed directly as campaign contributions to a specific candidate affected freedom of association more than freedom of speech, because contributions were used " 'to affiliate a person with a candidate' and 'enabl[e] like-minded persons to pool their resources.' " *McConnell*, 540 U.S. at 135 (quoting *Buckley*, 424 U.S. at 22). Even if contribution limits significantly interfere with freedom of association and (as the Court has noted) those limits more substantially interfere with freedom of association than freedom of speech, they needed only to be "closely drawn" to serve a "sufficiently important interest." *Id.* (quoting *Shrink*, 528 U.S. 387–88). This was the same lower standard of review that *Buckley* had applied to campaign contributions. This standard afforded "proper deference to Congress' ability to weigh competing constitutional interests in an area in which it enjoys particular expertise." *Id.* at 137.

96. The plaintiffs also claimed the statute was substantially overbroad because § 323(a) comprehended minor parties, which received very few large soft-money contributions. *Buckley* rejected similar arguments. In order to ensure the integrity of the electoral process, it was reasonable that all parties and candidates abide by the same rules regardless of the size of their political party. Moreover, § 323(a) applied only when an organization had official status. A "minor party can bring an as-applied challenge if § 323(a) prevents it from 'amassing the resources necessary for effective advocacy.' " *Id.* at 159.

The plaintiffs attempted to argue that section 323(a) was substantially overbroad because it included all money raised by the national parties even when the money was ultimately used for state or local elections. Federal officeholders and candidates primarily populated and ran the national committees of the two major political parties. Regardless of the ultimate use of the money, the close connections between the federal officeholders and the national parties were "likely to create actual or apparent indebtedness on the part of federal officeholders." *Id.* at 155.

97. *Id.* at 140.

98. *Id.* at 153. *See also* McCutcheon v. FEC, 134 S. Ct. 1434, 1470, 1483–85 (2015) (Breyer, J., dissenting) (soft-money donations garner access and influence).

99. Plaintiffs asserted that FECA § 323(a) "impermissibly interferes with the ability of the national committees to associate with state and local committees," *McConnell*, 540 U.S. at 159, but the Court found nothing on the face of the provision that prevented collaboration in raising and spending soft money.

100. BCRA § 323(d) "prohibits national, state, and local party committees from making or directing 'any donatio[n]' to qualifying" tax-exempt organizations or from soliciting tax-exempt organizations that are engaged in political activities. Once again, the Court upheld this ban as a reasonable "anticircumvention measure." *McConnell*, 540 U.S. at 178. Moreover, national party officials could collaborate in their official capacities with their state and local counterparts in raising and spending hard money and could do the same with soft money in their unofficial capacities.

BCRA § 323(b) prevented state and local committees from using soft-money donations or becoming conduits for such donations. However, the Levin Amendment in BCRA§ 323(b)(2) allowed state and local parties to use annual "Levin" donations of up to $10,000 per person to fund "voter registration activity, voter identification drives, [Get Out the Vote] drives, and generic campaign activities" that promoted a party rather than a specific candidate. *McConnell*, 540 U.S. at 163.

In upholding BCRA § 323(b), the Court afforded Congress substantial deference to prevent funds donated to state and local parties from being used to circumvent the national limits on soft money. Section 323(b) was "narrowly focused on regulating contributions that pose the greatest risk" of corruption and was "a closely-drawn means of countering both corruption and the appearance of corruption." *McConnell*, 540 U.S. at 167.

Similarly, BCRA§ 323(b)'s prohibition on transferring "Levin" funds among state parties was necessary to prevent circumvention of the $10,000 limit. This ban prevented donors from making "multiple $10,000 donations to various committees that could then transfer the donations to the committee of choice." *McConnell*, 540 U.S. at 171. Rejecting a facial challenge that BCRA§ 323(b) overly restricts the amount of funds available, the Court said that the standard was not whether it reduced the amounts available in previous elections but whether it drove the party's "'voice below the level of notice.'" *McConnell,* 540 U.S. at 173 (quoting *Shrink Missouri*, 528 U.S. at 397). Section 323(b) was "closely drawn to match the important governmental interest of preventing corruption and the appearance of corruption." *Id.* The Court left open the possibility of as-applied challenges.

101. *Id.* at 184. Section 323(f) did not limit the total amount a state or local candidate or officeholder could spend on such "'public communications.'" Instead, it limited the source and the amount of contributions that could be used to directly influence federal elections. BCRA § 323(f) also limited the ability of federal candidates and officeholders from soliciting, receiving, directing, transferring, or spending soft money in state or local elections.

102. FECA § 323(e).

103. *McConnell*, 540 U.S. at 182.

104. *Id.* at 189–90 (BCRA Title II).

105. *Id.* at 192. Plaintiff argued that an ad was "issue advocacy" if it avoided using such "'magic words'" as "'vote for'" or "'defeat.'" *Id.* at 191.

106. *Id.* at 199–200 (BCRA § 201). Similarly, the Court allowed disclosure of executory contracts for electioneering communications. Such disclosures would not have to reveal in advance the content of future advertisements, but would afford pre-election disclosure of who supported a candidate.

107. *Id.* at 202–03 (BCRA § 202).

108. *Id.* at 203–05 (BCRA § 203).

109. *Id.* at 206. BCRA § 204 extended to nonprofit organizations the prohibition against using general treasury funds to pay for electioneering communications, but the Court previously had determined that such a restriction did not apply to *MCFL* organizations such as those in *Federal Election Comm'n v. Mass. Citizens for Life*, 479 U.S. 238 (1986). However, this provision's lack of an explicit exemption for *MCFL* nonprofit corporations did not invalidate it, as Congress was aware of the *MCFL* exemption and the government conceded it applied.

The restrictions upheld on electioneering communications only applied to the broadcast media but not to print media or the Internet. Reform could occur one step at a time. *McConnell*,

540 U.S. at 206–08 (BCRA § 203). The Court also rejected the challenge that the restriction on electioneering communications discriminated in favor of media companies, as media companies are different.

110. *Id.* at 220–23. The Court did invalidate BCRA § 315(d)(4). This provision required that if a party wanted to spend more than $5,000 for its candidate, it had to forgo ads that used the "magic words" of "elect" or "defeat." *Id.* at 213–19. Having political parties avoid these words failed to qualify as a meaningful governmental interest as candidates could easily evade the "magic words" requirement.

111. In another portion of the Court's opinion, Chief Justice Rehnquist invalidated BCRA § 318's prohibition on donations by minors to candidates or political parties as an anti-circumvention measure. There were more tailored ways to prevent this problem, such as establishing a total allotted family donation or prohibiting contributions by very young children. As minors were protected by the First Amendment, the provision "sweeps too broadly." *McConnell*, 540 U.S. at 232.

Another part of the Court's opinion written by Justice Breyer rejected a facial challenge to BCRA § 504, which required broadcasters to keep records of all "'election message request(s)'" made by the public about a candidate or a federal election. The FCC already required that a record be kept of all "'candidate request(s)'" (requests made by or on the behalf of a candidate), showing the "'classes of time,'" "'rates charged,'" and "'when the spots actually aired.'" *McConnell* left open the possibility of as-applied challenges. *Id.* at 235.

This data would make the public aware of how much money candidates had been spending to publicize their messages, and would facilitate compliance with the disclosure and source requirements. Broadcasters were also required to keep a record of all "'issue request(s)'" made by the public about legislation or any "'political matter of national importance.'" *Id.* at 240. This requirement allowed for a determination of whether the "broadcasters are too heavily favoring entertainment" or were offering opportunities to discuss different views on public issues. *Id.*

In partial dissent, Chief Justice Rehnquist maintained that this requirement could reveal sensitive campaign strategy. *Id.* at 361–62. The majority rejected this position stating that it was unclear whether the First Amendment protected the confidentiality of campaign strategy in the first place in light of the "interest in free and open discussion of campaign issues." Assuming that there was such First Amendment protection, the majority did not think this provision unconstitutional on its face. *Id.* at 242–43.

112. *Id.* at 264. Justice Scalia dissented on Titles I and IV, and dissented in part on Title II.

113. *McConnell*, 540 U.S. at 264. Justice Scalia did think that, of course, "the government may apply general commercial regulations to those who use money for speech if it applies them evenhandedly." *Id.* at 272.

114. *Id.* at 261–62.

115. Justice Thomas concurred in the judgment on Title II, and dissented on Titles I, V, and § 311.

116. *McConnell*, 540 U.S. at 264.

117. *Id.* at 272.

118. Justice Thomas also criticized the forced disclosure requirements of BCRA § 201, stating that they violated the right to anonymous speech that has existed since the founding generation. *Id.* at 275.

119. *Id.* at 297 (Kennedy, J., concurring in the judgment in part and dissenting in part). Chief Justice Rehnquist joined Justice Kennedy's opinion and Justices Scalia and Thomas joined parts.

Justice Kennedy thought that the majority incorrectly assumed that the regulations were contribution rather than expenditure limits and therefore entitled to less scrutiny. Actually, the regulations were "neither contribution nor expenditure limits, or are perhaps both at once." *Id.* The restrictions created "significant burdens on speech itself" and even greater burdens on association. *Id.* at 313. *Austin v. Mich. Chamber of Commerce* was the only other time the Court had allowed the censorship of political speech "based on the speaker's corporate identity." *Id.* at 326.

BCRA § 203's forcing corporations and unions to communicate through segregated funds (PACs) was unconstitutional "compulsory ventriloquism." *Id.* at 333.

120. *Id.* at 296.

121. *Id.* at 114. For further discussion of *McConnell, see* Hasen, *supra* note 74.

6 A Stronger Libertarian Paradigm and The Death of the New Deal Constitution

A. Protecting Campaign Spending by Corporations and Unions

Cases such as *Austin* and *McConnell* seemed to be moderating the strong libertarian implications of *Buckley*. Suddenly, the Court reversed course again. In a series of cases beginning in 2007, the Court moved beyond the outer perimeters of *Buckley* to establish an even more robust libertarian paradigm of free speech jurisprudence. The first such decision was *Federal Election Commission v. Wisconsin Right to Life, Inc. (WRTL),*[1] which invalidated a ban on issue advocacy.

As part of a lobbying campaign, WRTL aired three commercials prior to the 2004 federal primary election that referred to Washington senators by name. The commercials encouraged citizens to contact these senators to request that they oppose a federal judicial nominee filibuster.

The Act had made it a federal crime for any labor union or incorporated entity to "pay for any 'electioneering communication'" from general treasury funds within thirty days before a primary or general election that named a specific candidate for federal elected office.[2]

In *McConnell v. Federal Election Commission,*[3] the Court had rejected a facial challenge to the Bipartisan Campaign Reform Act § 203. However, the *WRTL* Court found that the interests justifying regulation of campaign speech did not justify restrictions on issue advocacy.[4] Writing the main opinion,[5] the chief justice declared that under *McConnell* only regulation of express campaign speech "survives strict scrutiny."[6] An ad comprises

Politics and Capital. John Attanasio.
© John Attanasio 2018. Published 2018 by Oxford University Press.

express campaign speech if its only reasonable interpretation is as "an appeal to vote for or against a specific candidate."[7] The ads in *WRTL* focused on issue promotion and advocated contacting public officials to take a position on the particular legislative issue.[8] The Court rejected the government's position that an expansive definition of " "functional equivalent' " was necessary to prevent issue advocacy from circumventing "the rule against express advocacy."[9]

The government's " 'desire for a bright-line rule' " did not establish a compelling state interest.[10] However, Chief Justice Roberts did acknowledge that the state had a compelling interest in addressing " 'the corrosive and distorting effects of immense aggregations of wealth that are accumulated with the help of the corporate form.' "[11] *Austin* held that this interest justified regulating corporate campaign speech, not "issue advocacy."[12] Although the chief justice tried to distinguish *McConnell*, four other justices suggested that it would not survive.[13]

Justice Souter dissented, joined by three other justices. "Devoting concentrations of money in self-interested hands to the support of political campaigning . . . threatens the capacity of this democracy to represent its constituents and the confidence of its citizens in their capacity to govern themselves."[14]

McConnell was decided in 2006. The *Wisconsin Right to Life* decision reversed course in 2007 turning sharply back toward the strong libertarian paradigm. In 2008, *Davis v. Federal Election Commission*[15] (discussed after *Citizens United*[16]) reinforced this movement back toward the strong libertarian paradigm. In January 2010 came the dramatic move toward the strong libertarian paradigm in *Citizens United v. Federal Election Commission*.[17] *Citizens United* extended protection to independent electioneering expenditures made by corporations. This move cuts sharply against distributive autonomy by tremendously increasing disparate access to the marketplace of ideas: *Citizens United* allows those who control corporations to leverage their autonomy by leveraging their assets with the immense treasuries of corporations.[18]

Writing for the majority, Justice Kennedy applied strict scrutiny[19] to invalidate a law that made it a felony for any corporation—even nonprofit advocacy corporations—to broadcast " 'electioneering communication' " or "speech expressly advocating the election or defeat of a candidate" shortly before elections.[20] The statute's exception permitting corporate political action committees (PACs) did "not alleviate the First Amendment problems" with the law. PACs are burdensome alternatives and "fewer than 2,000 of the millions of corporations in this country have" them.[21]

Austin had upheld such a ban, finding a compelling governmental interest in preventing " 'the corrosive and distorting effects of immense aggregations of wealth that are accumulated with the help of the corporate form and that have little or no correlation to the public's support for the corporation's political ideas.' "[22]

Citizens United explicitly overruled *Austin*. Justice Kennedy—who had vigorously dissented in *Austin*—declared that *Austin* and its progeny collided with pre-*Austin* precedent that prohibited restricting speech based on corporate identity.[23] The *Buckley* majority explicitly rejected any governmental interest in equalizing the ability to influence elections. *Austin* had distinguished corporations from wealthy individuals on the ground that state law afforded the corporate structure special financial advantages. Whatever those may be, "'the State cannot exact as the price of those special advantages the forfeiture of First Amendment rights.'"[24] Also, it was irrelevant for First Amendment purposes that corporate funds were amassed without regard to public support for the corporation's political ideas.[25] The majority stated that it was returning to the principle of *Buckley* and *Bellotti* that a speaker's corporate identity did not allow government to suppress political speech.[26]

Greater influence over government officials did not necessarily entail corruption. "'Favoritism and influence are not . . . avoidable in representative politics.'"[27] Moreover, the government's other asserted interest in protecting dissenting shareholders from funding political speech, with which they disagreed, would even ban political speech by media corporations.[28]

Importantly, the Court also invalidated a ban on independent corporate campaign expenditures, overruling part of *McConnell*.[29] The Court did uphold the disclaimer and disclosure requirements.[30]

Chief Justice Roberts concurred.[31] He thought that *Austin* was inconsistent with *Buckley's* "explicit repudiation" of a governmental interest in equalizing the ability to influence elections.[32] Justice Scalia's concurrence argued that an original understanding of the Constitution disfavored the regulation even if the Founders disliked corporations.[33]

Writing for three other justices in dissent,[34] Judge Stevens extensively recounted the findings made by the District Court Judge Kollar-Kotelly in *McConnell*, who first reviewed the BCRA.[35] Quoting from that opinion:

> The factual findings of the Court illustrate that corporations and labor unions routinely notify Members of Congress as soon as they air electioneering communications relevant to the Members' elections. The record also indicates that Members express appreciation to organizations for the airing of these election-related advertisements. Indeed, Members of Congress are particularly grateful when negative issue advertisements are run by these organizations, leaving the candidates free to run positive advertisements and be seen as 'above the fray.' . . . .
>
> "The Findings also demonstrate that Members of Congress seek to have corporations and unions run these advertisements on their behalf. The Findings show that Members suggest that corporations or individuals make donations to interest groups with the understanding that the money contributed to these groups will assist the Member in a campaign. After the election, these organizations often seek credit for their support. . . .[36]

The findings further concluded that 80 percent of Americans think that public officials give corporations and other organizations "'special consideration'" for electioneering communications.[37]

Reflecting on the District Court opinion in *McConnell*, Justice Stevens remarked:

> Many of the relationships of dependency found by Judge Kollar-Kotelly seemed to have a *quid pro quo* basis, but other arrangements were more subtle. Her analysis shows the great difficulty in delimiting the precise scope of the *quid pro quo* category, as well as the adverse consequences that *all* such arrangements may have.[38]

There was no such record in *Citizens United* because "the Government had no reason to develop a record at trial for a facial challenge the plaintiff had abandoned."[39]

Citizens United, a wealthy nonprofit corporation with millions of dollars in assets, could have spent unrestricted sums to broadcast the film *Hillary* at any time other than thirty days before the primary election. This ruling "threatens to undermine the integrity of elected institutions across the Nation."[40] The Court here negated Congress's efforts to combat corruption when previous legislation had failed, and overruled a "virtual mountain of research"[41] without any evidence except how the law affected Citizens United.[42]

The dissent stated that the Court's central argument for ignoring stare decisis "is that it does not like *Austin*."[43] More than half of the states, along with leading groups in business, organized labor, and nonprofit organizations sought to preserve *Austin*, including the United States Chamber of Commerce and the AFL-CIO. The "only relevant thing that has changed since *Austin* and *McConnell* is the composition of this Court."[44]

Existing law still permitted corporations to put dollars into their own PACs.[45] This had proven quite effective as corporate and union PACs in the prior election cycle had raised nearly $1 billion.

Corporations also had tremendous liberty to spend unlimited sums to communicate with their executives and shareholders to "fund additional PAC activity through trade associations, to distribute voting guides and voting records, to underwrite voter registration and voter turnout activities, to host fundraising events for candidates within certain limits, and to publicly endorse candidates through a press release and press conference."[46]

It had long been recognized that corporations have the "distinctive potential" to corrupt the electoral process.[47] In the context of campaign spending, corruption is just another way of saying that one can coercively bend others to one's own will. In 1907, the Tillman Act banned corporate contributions to federal candidates.[48] The Founding generation approached corporate power cautiously, viewed corporate rights narrowly, and "conceptualized speech in individualistic terms."[49] Those who pay for an electioneering communication should actually support its content.[50]

To establish the link between campaign finance and corruption, Justice Stevens's dissent again relied on the District Court in *McConnell*, which had also made extensive findings connecting campaign finance with ingratiation and access:

> Witnesses explained how political parties and candidates used corporate independent expenditures to circumvent FECA's "hard-money" limitations. One

former Senator candidly admitted to the District Court that ' "[c]andidates whose campaigns benefit from [phony 'issue ads'] greatly appreciate the help of these groups. In fact, Members will also be favorably disposed to those who finance these groups when they later seek access to discuss pending legislation." (quoting declaration of Sen. Dale Bumpers). One prominent lobbyist went so far as to state, in uncontroverted testimony, that ' "unregulated expenditures—whether soft money donations to the parties or issue ad campaigns—can sometimes generate *far more* influence than direct campaign contributions." ' In sum, Judge Kollar-Kotelly found, "[t]he record powerfully demonstrates that electioneering communications paid for with the general treasury funds of labor unions and corporations endears those entities to elected officials in a way that could be perceived by the public as corrupting."[51]

The dissent observed that corruption could take many forms, as the congressional record for the BCRA also evidenced.[52] "The majority appears to think it decisive that the BCRA record does not contain 'direct examples of votes being exchanged for . . . expenditures.' It would have been quite remarkable if Congress had created a record detailing such behavior by its own Members."[53]

Clearly, *Citizens United* is entirely inconsistent with any notion of distributive autonomy. If anything, it is wholly removed from any notion of individual autonomy, except insofar as it allows those who control corporations to magnify their autonomy through the corporate form, eclipsing the autonomy of those who are neither officers nor directors of corporations. Corporations cannot vote in elections; why should they be allowed to influence elections far more than ordinary citizens through free speech?

Citizens United was decided on January 21, 2010. Its impact was immediate and far-reaching. Two months later, in *Speechnow.org v. FEC* the Federal Appeals Court for Washington, D.C., sitting *en banc*,[54] struck down governmental limitations on the amounts that an individual could contribute to an independent PAC. The invalidated law had capped at $5,000 per election individual contributions to PACs if the PACs used these to support or oppose political candidates. The D.C. Circuit Court of Appeals rejected the government's argument that unlimited contributions could lead to corruption, as it could give these contributors favored access to beholden elected officials. Relying on *Citizens United*, the D.C. Circuit Court, stated: "In light of the Court's holding as a matter of law that independent expenditures do not corrupt or create the appearance of *quid pro quo* corruption, contributions to groups that make only independent expenditures also cannot corrupt or create the appearance of corruption."[55] Consequently, "the First Amendment cannot be encroached upon for naught."[56] As a result of this decision, PACs could collect unlimited contributions, which they could use to purchase ads supporting or opposing candidates.

Speechnow.org marked the emergence of the "Super PAC." Soon after the case was decided, the FEC extended to corporations and unions the right to give unlimited contributions to PACs. The FEC also decided that even those PACs that made direct contributions to candidates could become Super PACs as long as they kept separate accounts for independent giving and candidate contributions.[57] Eliminating these regulations had the effect of shifting funds away from candidates' campaigns and political parties, and toward independent organizations.[58]

B. Invalidating Reciprocal Public Funding

The strong libertarian paradigm continued to wax in *Davis v. Federal Election Commission*. There, the Court invalidated two provisions known as the " 'Millionaire's Amendment.' "[59] BCRA considered a candidate self-financed if she personally spent more than $350,000 on her own campaign. When a self-financing candidate ran against a non-self-financing candidate, the non-self-financing candidate could accept a maximum of three times the normal limit of individual contributions and unlimited coordinated party expenditures until his total contributions were equal to the personal expenditures of his self-financed opponent.[60]

Justice Alito observed that the Court had never upheld disparate campaign contribution limits for candidates competing in the same election. The majority thought that the BCRA effectively penalized self-financing candidates for exercising their First Amendment right to personally finance their own campaign speech. Candidates were forced to choose between limiting their personal expenditures, and consequently their speech, and accepting "discriminatory contribution limits." *Buckley* had rejected leveling candidates' financial resources. This sort of equalization would allow Congress to infringe on the voters' right to independently evaluate candidates based on all their strengths. The Court's complete list of candidate strengths was: "wealth," "wealthy supporters," being "celebrities" or "well-known family name."[61]

Dissenting with three other justices, Justice Stevens would reverse *Buckley's* rejection of candidate expenditure limits. Quantity limitations on expression often benefit speakers and their audiences, unlike content restrictions, which violate free speech. He endorsed Justice White's *Buckley* dissent, which analogized quantity limits on speech to time, place, and manner regulations, rather than to direct limitations on speech.[62]

The BCRA did not restrict any speech at all, but allowed the non-self-financing candidate a voice equal to that of his opponent.[63] Without quantity restrictions, candidates could overwhelm voters and cloud important issues. Government had legitimate, long-standing interests in minimizing the effects of a candidate's wealth on an election and the perception that wealth was the sole determinant of winning elections.[64]

Davis aptly illustrates the contrast between cramped, individualistic notions of liberty, and distributive autonomy. Congress tried to distribute autonomy more equitably. Rather than viewing this as an autonomy enhancement of candidates and voters alike, the majority regarded this attempt to address disparate campaign resources, and resulting disparities in autonomy positions as an infringement on the liberty of the self-financed candidate. No matter what position one takes on *Davis*, it poignantly illuminates the tremendous differences between a distributive autonomy approach and a highly individualistic libertarian focus. I call the latter approach individualistic for lack of a better term; indeed, a theory of distributive autonomy is much more respectful of the individual because it considers the autonomy of each individual rather than only of those who have the good fortune to have the resources to have the capacity to exercise their first-order rights.

Further bolstering the strong libertarian paradigm, *Arizona Free Enterprise Club's Freedom Club PAC v. Bennett*[65] invalidated a different matching funds scheme. Arizona granted publicly funded candidates "additional 'equalizing' or matching funds" in both primary and general elections.[66] "During the general election, matching funds were triggered when the amount of money a privately financed candidate receives in contributions, combined with the expenditures of independent groups made in support of the privately financed candidate or in opposition to a publicly financed candidate, exceed the general election allotment of state funds to the publicly financed candidate."[67] Once that occurred, every expenditure made by a privately financed candidate, or by an independent group supporting him, triggered a parallel increase in public funding to all publicly financed opponents. However, the state did not match independent expenditures made to oppose a privately financed candidate. Total matching funds could not exceed three times the funding initially received by the publicly financed candidate.[68]

Chief Justice Roberts found the Arizona law "*more* constitutionally problematic" than the one in *Davis*.[69] Particularly egregious was the fact that uncoordinated spending by an independent group activated state matching funds that government would give directly to a publicly financed candidate. A candidate "at least has the option of taking public financing" unlike independent expenditure groups.[70] For a privately financed candidate running against multiple publicly financed candidates, one dollar spent by him could trigger one dollar to each of his publicly financed opponents. Alternatively, one dollar spent by an independent group to support his candidacy could trigger sending equivalent state dollars to multiple candidates whom the group opposes.[71]

Arizona argued that the law was designed to " 'level the playing field.' "[72] Nonetheless, "even if the ultimate objective of the matching funds provision is to combat corruption— and not 'level the playing field,' "[73] the matching funds scheme unacceptably burdened political speech. *Buckley* emphasized that limits on "overall campaign expenditures could not be justified by a purported government 'interest in equalizing the financial resources of candidates.' "[74] Not all public financing was suspect; the specific system of public funding mattered.[75]

Justice Kagan dissented.[76] For over a century, campaign finance reform has focused on preventing "massive pools of private money from corrupting our political system." In effect, Justice Kagan pointed out what amounts to a broad-based violation of distributive autonomy: "If an officeholder owes his election to wealthy contributors, he may act for their benefit alone, rather than on behalf of all" constituents.[77] Again, officeholders make laws that enhance or constrain personal autonomy.

Justice Kagan noted that nearly one-third of the states have adopted public financing. Even Congress's presidential public financing system, specifically approved in *Buckley*, awarded a lump sum at the start of the election campaign.[78] Arizona's subsidy increased speech.[79] Expenditures by private groups increased by 253 percent since the Arizona law had existed.[80] Petitioners essentially demanded "a right to quash others' speech" by prohibiting "a (universally available) subsidy program."[81]

The facts of *Bennett* present a complex case for distributive autonomy. The law at issue infringed on the liberty of independent groups to make independent expenditures for the election or defeat of a particular candidate. Of course, that begs the question of whether distributive autonomy allows or may require government to impose upper boundaries on outside groups. In Chapter 2, I suggested that it does. Regardless of the answer to this question, the triggering effect of independent expenditures on the amount of public funding that a publicly financed candidate receives may render the law in *Bennett* offensive to distributive autonomy. Moreover, counting such independent expenditures against the self-financed candidate *may* also violate his autonomy if he genuinely cannot coordinate his campaign with those making these independent expenditures. Even if the candidate cannot so coordinate expenditures, those making them may still be rewarded later on. These are difficult, fact-intensive questions. Nevertheless, distributive autonomy allows, probably requires, imposing upper limits on candidate and PAC expenditures. These are common in other countries.

C. Purchasing Entire Election Cycles: Invalidating Limits on Aggregate Contributions

In *McCutcheon v. Federal Election Commission*,[82] the plurality struck down aggregate limitations on how much individuals and certain entities could donate as political contributions over an election cycle.[83] These aggregate limits were in addition to individual contribution limits, which had already been upheld in previous cases. For the 2013–2014 election cycle, BCRA imposed contribution limits on an individual of "up to $2,600 per election to a candidate ($5,200 total for the primary and general elections); $32,400 per year to a national party committee; $10,000 per year to a state or local party committee; and $5,000 per year to a political action committee, or 'PAC.' "[84] These contribution limits included earmarks made through conduits to a particular candidate. In addition to imposing contribution limitations to individual candidates and other entities specified above, the statute also imposed aggregate contribution limits. Over the two-year 2013–2014 election cycle, the statute limited individuals to aggregate contributions of $123,200: $48,600 to federal candidates and $74,600 to other political committees, including PACs.[85] These aggregate limits were in addition to individual contribution limits already upheld in previous cases.

The trial court dismissed the challenge to aggregate contribution limits. It viewed the aggregate and individual contribution limitations as part of one coherent system; the aggregate limits helped prevent circumvention of regular contribution limits.[86] Writing for the plurality, Chief Justice Roberts began by saying:

> There is no right more basic in our democracy than the right to participate in electing our political leaders. Citizens can exercise that right in a variety of ways: They can run for office themselves, vote, urge others to vote for a particular candidate, volunteer to work on a campaign, and contribute to a candidate's campaign.[87]

Although government can prevent corruption or its appearance, precedent contrasts regulable "*'quid pro quo'*" exchanges for money, with "'[i]ngratiation and access,'" which is simply part of the democratic process.[88]

The chief justice's plurality invalidated the aggregate limitations whether they were evaluated under the strict scrutiny standard for expenditure limitations or under the lower "'closely drawn'" standard for contribution limitations.[89] In so doing, it explicitly overruled a holding of *Buckley v. Valeo*.[90] *Buckley* had upheld a $25,000 aggregate contributions limit.

The plurality stated that it was not bound by *Buckley* because the *Buckley* Court had devoted only three sentences to upholding the aggregate contribution limitations at issue. Moreover, the overall statutory schema presented in *McCutcheon* contained important innovations. Since *Buckley*, Congress limited contributions to PACs. Congress also prohibited donors from creating or controlling multiple PACs, which could be used as tools to circumvent contribution limitations.[91] Although earmarking regulations existed when *Buckley* was decided, Congress had since increased the difficulty of earmarking contributions to a particular candidate through conduits.[92]

The *McCutcheon* plurality exemplifies the strong libertarian paradigm of free speech jurisprudence:

> The First Amendment "is designed and intended to remove governmental restraints from the arena of public discussion, putting the decision as to what views shall be voiced largely into the hands of each of us . . . in the belief that no other approach would comport with the premise of individual dignity and choice upon which our political system rests."[93]

The plurality disagreed with *Buckley's* characterization of the $25,000 aggregate contribution limitation as "modest": the aggregate limitation constricted how many candidates, committees, or policy concerns an individual could support.[94]

The only interest upon which the plurality would uphold the law was actual corruption or the appearance of corruption. The plurality honed narrowly to quid pro quo corruption.[95] Obviously, what counts as corruption matters. Lawrence Lessig contends that dependence corruption is more consistent with the understanding of the Framers than is individual quid pro quo corruption:

> Congress was intended to be "dependent on the people alone." It has become dependent upon an additional group, "the funders" of campaigns. Because of who "the funders" are, this additional dependence is a conflicting dependence, and that conflict constitutes the "corruption."[96]

The plurality explicitly rejected this concept of dependence corruption. For example, they refused to characterize as corruption "the possibility that an individual who spends large sums may garner 'influence over or access to' elected officials or political parties.'"[97] For the plurality, Congress had already determined that an individual contribution limitation of $5,200 was the threshold for corruption of a candidate. Consequently, if Congress thought that there was no danger of corruption below that amount, then Congress had to defend its aggregate limits on the grounds of circumvention of that limitation rather than on corruption grounds.[98] In any event, tough restrictions on earmarking donations to a particular candidate rendered circumvention improbable.[99]

The plurality also rejected the District Court's example of a $500,000 gift to a joint committee: the District Court maintained that an individual donor could give to a joint committee comprised of national and state committees, and then all of the committees comprising the joint committee could turn around and give this money to one candidate's committee.[100]

The plurality maintained that the anti-coordination regulations had proven effective: in 2012, despite candidates, political parties, and PACs spending $7 billion on political campaigns, coordinated expenditures were quite low.[101] If the aggregate restriction did not serve the purpose of averting circumvention of contribution limitations, it "impermissibly restrict[ed] participation in the political process."[102]

The plurality did suggest several alternative measures that legislatures might use to avoid large sums being channeled to a small group of candidates.[103] It made clear that it was not pre-approving any of these ideas. Moreover, consistent with previous cases, the plurality did approve the disclosure requirements. Although disclosure of contributions also burdened speech, such disclosure was a less restrictive alternative than limiting aggregate contributions.[104]

In summary, campaign finance jurisprudence should focus "on the need to preserve authority for the Government to combat corruption, without at the same time compromising the political responsiveness at the heart of the democratic process, or allowing the Government to favor some participants in that process over others."[105] As described in Chapter 3, the logic of the last phrase bears some resemblance to that of the *Lochner* line of cases.[106]

Dissenting, Justice Breyer stated that *McCutcheon* overruled that part of *Buckley* permitting limitations on aggregate campaign contributions. The decision created a loophole empowering "a single individual to contribute millions of dollars" to a political party or to a candidate's campaign. With *Citizens United*, this decision "eviscerates our Nation's campaign finance laws, leaving a remnant incapable of dealing with the grave problems of democratic legitimacy that those laws were intended to resolve."[107]

The plurality disconnected large aggregate contributions from corruption or its appearance by defining corruption quite narrowly as quid pro quo corruption, which is "akin to bribery."[108] The plurality's narrow definition, which specifically excluded influence and access, violated precedent. Prior cases treated corruption "'not only as *quid pro quo* agreements, but also as undue influence on an officeholder's judgment.'"[109] The *McConnell* Court had specifically rejected the plurality's approach to defining corruption.[110] *McConnell* relied on an extensive record of over 100,000 pages and over 200 witnesses compiled by the District Court, which carefully depicted "the web of relationships and understandings among parties, candidates, and large donors that underlies privileged access and influence."[111] Yet that voluminous record did not contain one instance of an actual bribe.

Citing Justice Brandeis and others, the dissent emphasized the essential relation of free speech to democracy.[112] Corruption "derails the essential speech-to-government-action tie. Where enough money calls the tune, the general public will not be heard."[113] Again, the tie to distributive autonomy theory is obvious.

The dissent gave several elaborate examples of the vast donations that the removal of the aggregate contribution limitations could produce. The first example showed how the aggregate contribution limit capped at $74,600 the amount that a donor could give to a Joint Party Committee during a two-year election cycle. Removing the aggregate limits allowed the same donor to contribute a total of $1.2 million.[114] In example two, when one adds that same donor contributing to congressional candidates, the $1.2 million increases to $3.6 million every two years.[115] The entire $3.6 million in contributions by a single donor could be channeled to a single candidate. These funds could be targeted to embattled candidates in hotly contested races. Before *McCutcheon*, the aggregate contribution limit had been $123,200.[116]

The dissent's third example demonstrated how PACs would be able to channel $2 million from each of ten wealthy donors to ten candidates in close races.[117] In 2012, the average House race cost the winning candidate $1.6 million, and the average Senate race cost the winning candidate $11.5 million.[118]

The dissent contested the plurality's claim that these examples could simply not happen.[119] Even with aggregate contribution limits, joint fundraising committees, "'Leadership PACs,'" and multicandidate PACs had already been proliferating.[120] The dissent rejected the alternatives offered by the plurality as ineffective substitutes for the aggregate contribution restrictions.[121] Finally, the dissent questioned why the plurality did not send the case back to the three-judge District Court, as it had come to the Supreme Court on a motion to dismiss, yet there were large factual disagreements remaining that the trial court had to resolve.[122]

D. The Stronger Libertarian Archetype: Transforming the Playing Field Again

McCutcheon and *Citizens United* represent a new archetype that has transformed the electoral playing field. Most argue that they have recast the discourse in quantitative ways. As with most real metamorphoses, however, the key change is qualitative. *Citizens United* opens the floodgates for campaign spending by corporations and unions.

The corporate form is a government-created vehicle that provides corporations singular legal advantages to amass wealth. *Citizens United* empowers individuals who control corporations to highly leverage their political influence using the corporate form. Indeed, fiduciary duties running to officers and directors may sometimes nudge these individuals to use corporate wealth aggressively in the political arena to maximize corporate profits or otherwise advance the interests of the corporation. Of course, fiduciary duties may somewhat constrain officers and directors from using corporate funds to advance their personal political agendas, but officers and directors have a broad range of discretion. Moreover, officers and directors are commonly major shareholders. Thus their economic interests will typically be closely aligned with those of the corporation.

Permitting those who run corporations and unions, within certain limitations, to leverage their influence by using the massive funds accumulated by these entities decimates distributive autonomy. Within certain boundaries, it allows people who control these organizations to eclipse the autonomy of others to influence elections.

The *McCutcheon* case permits purchasing, or at least influencing, entire election cycles. As insightful as it is, the *McCutcheon* dissent may not describe what may sometimes be the optimal strategy. Rather than focus contributions on a few hotly contested races, they sometimes might be spread around the country to influence all races, especially all races of incumbents who are overwhelmingly likely to win. Some money should be concentrated to defeat a few bothersome independent incumbents who won't cooperate. Defeating them or at least giving them a good scare will also keep others in line.

McCutcheon is breathtaking. It empowers a few individuals to make contributions to multiple campaigns to influence elections *around the entire country*—essentially to purchase public policy. Astonishingly, *McCutcheon* affords the right to influence not only individual races but entire election cycles.

One can see the immediate and profound impact that these cases have had on political donations. It may not be a coincidence that just one year after *Citizens United* was decided, the amount contributed by a few top donors skyrocketed. For some time now, grossly disproportionate donations had come from the top 1 percent of the top 1 percent. In the 2000, 2004, and 2008 presidential election cycles, their slice of the total donations pie "held solidly around 17 percent." However, their jump to 28.1 percent of total donations in the 2010 election cycle "marks a significant break with the past."[123]

Another big leap occurred in 2014; *McCutcheon* was decided on April 2, 2014. "In 2010, only 17 individuals contributed a total of $500,000 or more, while members of the $1 million-plus club numbered only nine. In 2014, the number of $500,000 and up donors ballooned to a whopping 135, and 63 people gave more than $1 million."[124]

Two other disturbing phenomena also emerged: "The 2014 election was the most expensive midterm election in history, costing a grand total of $3.77 billion. But for the first time since 1990, fewer Americans donated money in this midterm election than the one before."[125] The total number of donors declined by nearly 20 percent—from 541,256 to 434,256. For the 2014 election cycle, spending by outside groups, which are largely funded by a few large donors, jumped from 9 percent of total campaign spending to 14.9 percent. Chapter 11 discusses the 2016 election.

McCutcheon breaks completely new ground. During the 2016 presidential campaign, *Citizens United* received the lion's share of criticism with *McCutcheon* hardly being mentioned. In upholding aggregate limitations, *Buckley* had acknowledged the importance for some upper boundaries on individual autonomy in the interests of not making the playing field too disparate. However, after *McCutcheon*, the already tremendous disparities in individual citizens' abilities to influence political campaigns grew geometrically. After all, how many citizens have the wherewithal to contribute the invalidated aggregate total of over $120,000 to a particular election cycle every two years? How many fewer have the wherewithal to contribute what Justice Breyer predicts will be over $3.5 million every two years? The Federal Reserve Bank says U.S. median family income is "between $40,000 and $49,999."[126] *McCutcheon* could almost be called the "un-distributive autonomy" decision. Its philosophical commitments are almost antithetical to any concept of every citizen being able to enjoy some minimal influence over elections.

Don't believe me. Believe Congress. One newly elected member of Congress recently said that both parties tell newly elected members that they should spend thirty hours a week "dialing for dollars." A model daily schedule given to new Democratic members of Congress at an orientation meeting recommended they spend four hours a day soliciting funds and two hours a day on their work in Congress.[127] Which constituents will Congress persons listen to? How many of their actual constituents will they listen to when passing most laws (autonomy restrictions or enhancements)? How does this impact the distribution of autonomy in the society? As the last section of this chapter demonstrates, this is not speculation. Money doesn't just talk; it is eloquent.

E. Protecting the Rule of Law: Upholding Limits on Judicial Fundraising

In the judicial elections context, the Court finally upheld a substantial restriction on asking for campaign donations. Let's start with some background. The Court first became involved in judicial electioneering in *Republican Party of Minnesota v. White*.[128] That case invalidated, as violating free speech, a Minnesota law that forbade a candidate for judicial office from announcing " 'his or her views on disputed legal or political issues.' "[129]

Justice Scalia rejected Minnesota's asserted interests in judicial impartiality and the appearance of impartiality. A court must be impartial toward the parties, but not necessarily the issues before it. Judges always have biases about legal views. Justice Scalia thought that Justice Ginsburg's dissent "greatly exaggerates the difference between judicial and legislative elections," as state judges make common law and shape state constitutions.[130] The electioneering context does not justify "an *abridgement* of the right to speak" with voters, which lies at the core of both the First Amendment and the electoral process.[131] The Court did not suggest that the First Amendment requires judicial campaigns to be the same as legislative campaigns.

Justice Stevens dissented.[132] Unlike executives and legislators who are supposed to respond to the popular will, judges are supposed to decide issues of law and fact. Moreover, judges announcing their views mislead voters into thinking that judges decide cases based on their "personal views rather than precedent."[133] Justice Ginsburg dissented: "'judges represent the Law,'" not voters.[134] Prohibiting judicial candidates from announcing their position on specific issues protects judicial integrity and impartiality.

Caperton v. A.T. Massey Coal Co.[135] first embroiled the Court in judicial campaign contributions. The Court required the recusal of a state Supreme Court justice under the due process clause. A jury found defendant Massey Coal Co. liable and awarded $50 million to plaintiff Caperton. While Massey Coal's appeal was pending, the company's CEO donated almost $2.5 million to a political organization that opposed an incumbent state Supreme Court justice, and supported his opponent. The CEO also made over $500,000 of independent expenditures to support the opponent's campaign.

Following the opponent's election, the plaintiff unsuccessfully moved to recuse the newly elected justice on three separate occasions. The West Virginia Supreme Court of Appeals, voting 3-2, reversed plaintiff's jury verdict on hearing and then again on rehearing.

In requiring judicial recusal, Justice Kennedy stated that the Constitution rarely requires it, as the "'probability of actual bias'" rarely rose to the level of a due process violation.[136] "Not every campaign contribution by a litigant or attorney creates a probability of bias" requiring recusal.[137] Here, the Court analyzed "the contribution's relative size in comparison to the total amount of money contributed to the campaign, the total amount spent in the election, and the apparent effect such contribution had on the outcome of the election."[138]

Justice Kennedy focused on the CEO's $3 million contribution to the incumbent justice's opponent, candidate Benjamin. This "eclipsed the total amount spent by all other Benjamin supporters and exceeded by 300% the amount spent by Benjamin's campaign committee."[139]

Chief Justice Roberts dissented.[140] Beyond the CEO's direct $1,000 contribution, the victorious opponent and his campaign had no control over the CEO's other expenditures. Another independent group received $2 million from the plaintiffs' bar. Moreover, the CEO had spent heavily during many prior state elections.

Caperton may have led the Court finally to uphold (5-4) a substantial restriction on campaign fund raising beyond disclosure requirements and contribution limitations. In *Williams-Yulee v. Florida Bar*,[141] the Court sustained a Florida ethical rule banning judicial candidates from personally soliciting campaign funds.

Chief Justice Roberts, writing for the majority, emphasized preserving judicial neutrality, independence, and fairness. At least in the judicial electioneering context, the majority relaxed the stringent compelling state interest test of constitutional scrutiny. Consequently, *Williams-Yulee* could be viewed as cabining in the strong libertarian paradigm to prevent its compromising the judiciary and the rule of law. In this way, *Williams-Yulee* may have been swayed by the *Caperton* case.

In thirty-nine states, trial judges or appellate judges were elected. Many of those states prohibited judicial candidates from personally soliciting campaign funds. Elected judges "are not politicians."[142] Government must be able to assure people "that judges will apply the law without fear or favor—and without having personally asked anyone for money."[143] In "exercising strict neutrality and independence," judges "cannot supplicate campaign donors without diminishing public confidence in judicial integrity."[144] This principle dated back at least eight centuries to Magna Carta.

The state had an interest in protecting the "'public confidence in the fairness and integrity of the nation's elected judges.'" As Alexander Hamilton noted in Federalist No. 78, the judiciary lacks the power of "'the sword or the purse.'"[145] Unlike candidates for political office, judges should not be responsive to the interests of those who elected them.[146]

Justice Scalia dissented. "When a candidate asks someone for a campaign contribution, he tends (as the principal opinion acknowledges) also to talk about his qualifications for office and his views on public issues."[147] Also, the ban favored incumbents, well-to-do candidates, and well-connected candidates who could readily secure fundraising committees. "This danger of legislated (or judicially imposed) favoritism is the very reason the First Amendment exists."[148]

Judicial elections are the public's reaction to exerting control over a judiciary that could rule them. "A free society, accustomed to electing its rulers, does not much care whether the rulers operate through statute and executive order, or through judicial distortion of statute, executive order, and constitution." One cannot allow speech abridgments "for the benefit of the Brotherhood of the Robe."[149]

The *Yulee* case can be taken two ways. It could be interpreted as calling a halt to the influence of money—or at least some moderation—when one departs from the realm of democracy and enters the realm of the rule of law. After all, Chief Justice Roberts eloquently articulates the deep problems that unconstrained judicial fundraising could inflict on the rule of law. At some level, the rule of money could substitute for the neutrality and fairness that are so core to the rule of law.

At another level, *Yulee* can be taken as a foil to at least *McCutcheon* and probably *Buckley*. If we focus on *McCutcheon*, its definition of corruption and influence stand at the opposite end of the spectrum to the one embraced by the Court in *Yulee*. After all, *Yulee's* definition of corruption eclipses the narrow quid pro quo formulation of *McCutcheon*. The *Yulee* Court is certainly correct that democracy differs from the rule of law. However, the Constitution endeavors to make elected officials responsive to the interests of their constituents, not to the wallets of a very few who might not even be constituents. Again, as the last section of this chapter shows, this is not speculation. Judges impose very direct circumscriptions on autonomy through the imposition of sentences of imprisonment, or even execution, and in overseeing, sometimes with juries, civil trials, which can impose injunctions or very large monetary damage awards. Whether the autonomy constrictions exacted by judges exceed those imposed by legislatures is at best doubtful. After all, legislation affects everyone; judicial decisions primarily affect the parties before the court. Still, for those parties, the autonomy consequences are immediate and life altering. But legislation usually governs judicial decisions. Although the precedential effects of judicial decisions can be far-reaching these precedential effects usually pale against the far-reaching sway of legislation.

One is tempted to suggest that the Court did not wish influence pedaling or corruption to pollute its own realm, but is untroubled by its affecting the political branches. Of course, the nature of the judicial process is quite different from the legislative one, and the procedures by which courts can be influenced differ dramatically from the ways in which legislatures can be influenced. Nevertheless, distributive autonomy theory does not supply a ready answer or justification to distinguish these lines of cases. Money influencing both legislative and judicial decisions violates distributive autonomy. One could maintain that the individuated nature of the judicial process that carries with it immediate, profound consequences (execution, imprisonment, large monetary awards) makes the judicial process more susceptible of autonomy violations. But legislation frequently spells out the consequences that judiciaries mete out—execution, imprisonment, monetary awards, etc. Perhaps the judicial process is designed to be influenced in much more circumscribed ways than legislation. Although this distinction has merit, it also has limits: the procedural rules of discovery were just dramatically revised because of abuses in burying the other side in litigation bills.[150] Perhaps the dangers that monetary influences portend for the judiciary are easier for judges and justices to see and grasp. Perhaps this insight will make threats to the other branches more readily visible, too.

F. The Death of the New Deal Constitution

The *Carolene Products* Court was the architect of a new model that replaced the *Lochner* libertarian property rights paradigm. It left the distribution of property rights and other resources to the democratic, majoritarian processes. The courts' role was to enforce the Bill of Rights and to ensure that the democratic process that allocated resources was fair. Fairness entailed equal voting rights, equitable speech rights, and protection for identifiable minority groups who were repeat losers in the democratic contests. Although the right to vote empowers one voter to cast a ballot, a speaker can leverage her ideas by influencing countless others.

The weak libertarian paradigm that reached its peak during the 1960s made an extremely valuable contribution to broad-based democratic participation by combating content discrimination disfavoring certain kinds of speech—most problematically, speech that the government, and politically and economically powerful groups, did not like. In contrast, the strong libertarian paradigm fashioned during the 1970s narrows participation by empowering *each* person to use her own economic resources to influence elections and public officials. As I have suggested, its autonomy infringements travel far beyond campaign finance, but its largest autonomy infringements lie in this area. Consequently, this text focuses on this facet of the strong libertarian paradigm.

A different libertarian paradigm based on freedom of contract infected constitutional jurisprudence during the *Lochner* era. Ironically, the strong libertarian paradigm of free speech may safeguard property more vigorously than the *Lochner* era protection of liberty of contract. Although the free speech libertarian paradigm only indirectly protects property interests, it shields them more broadly than its liberty-of-contract predecessor. During the *Lochner* era, the Court did not strike down every regulation that affected liberty of contract.[151] Nor did the Court invalidate every congressional foray into economic regulation as violating the commerce clause.[152] In contrast, the strong libertarian paradigm broadly advantages property interests with respect to all public policy issues. The impact of this tremendously disproportionate access to the electoral process can be negated only if one assumes that spending money to help candidates win does not influence them, or that extremely wealthy donors habitually behave much more altruistically than the rest of the population, commonly ignoring or acting against their own political/economic interests. A tremendous amount of data recounted in Chapters 10 and 11 suggests otherwise.

But the demise of the *Carolene Products* constitutional paradigm represents much more than the death of *Carolene Products*. It also represents the passing of a theory of democracy that was broad-based, participatory, and robust. It represents the collapse of a relatively equitable political process to decide the distributing of resources, which resulted in a relatively equitable distribution of resources. A tremendous amount of data in Chapters 10 and 11 attests to its success in this regard.

The demise of the *Carolene Products* paradigm led to the dismantling and death of the New Deal. By the New Deal political arrangement, I am referring to the social welfare state embodying a broad participatory democratic ideal, broad-based rule of law with fair access to courts, judicial restraints on the behavior of police, and a relatively equitable distribution of resources that exhibited vast disparities of wealth but also had a large, robust middle class and a sturdier safety net for the poor. All this was married with a very vibrant economy boasting considerably higher growth. The changes wrought by *Buckley* and its progeny are so far-reaching because what is described above is the death of the *Carolene Products* Constitution, which was really the New Deal Constitution. That was the Constitution upon which the New Deal welfare state was built. That Constitution is aptly described in John Ely's celebrated work, *Democracy and Distrust*. When that Constitution collapsed, so did the New Deal approach to governance and some of its core ideas such as redistribution, fair wages, full employment, rights-driven enforcement of the criminal law, and a substantial safety net protecting the poor and disadvantaged.

The strong libertarian paradigm has led to dramatic inequities in the distribution of resources and the distribution of power. Disparities in wealth and policy influence wrought by the strong libertarian paradigm of free speech jurisprudence will continue to grow quickly and unpredictably. In our electronic age, information is the most valuable asset. Unfortunately, free speech jurisprudence and scholarship have not examined or thought systematically about the implications of ideas being perhaps the key economic asset or driver.[153] Viewing information as the key economic asset of our time connects the strong libertarian paradigm even more closely to *Lochner*.

The Court has not systemically deconstructed the *Carolene Products* constitutional settlement. Indeed, some of the key architects of the *Buckley* Constitution have openly expressed disdain for *Lochner*.[154] However it happened, one thing we know for sure: *Carolene Products*—the blueprint for the New Deal paradigm of constitutional democracy—is dead.

G. The Constitutional Content of Distributive Autonomy

The entire *Buckley* line of cases rests on an interpretation of liberty in the Constitution based on modern, highly individualistic (in the sense of being self-focused) libertarian theory. To the extent that distributive autonomy displaces that theory, it undermines the very foundations of *Buckley* and its progeny.

But that still begs the question of where can you find distributive autonomy in the Constitution? Recall that the Constitution talks about freedom or liberty, but does not define what it means by, for example, freedom of speech.

Although the Constitution does not speak of distributive autonomy, it does not elaborate what it means by liberty at all beyond the fairly generic and open-textured language of the amendments, particularly the Bill of Rights. Surely, it cannot accept the notion of liberty for some. Our very Pledge of Allegiance talks about "liberty and justice for all." One might consider this argument trite as the Pledge has no constitutional status.

But what about the Fourteenth Amendment to the Constitution? That enjoys constitutional content. One might usefully compare the current state of extremely libertarian case law on campaign financing with the egalitarian values enshrined in the Thirteenth, Fourteenth, and Fifteenth Amendments promulgated shortly after the Civil War. The importance of these Amendments renders their collective promulgation nothing less than a Second Framing of the Constitution. Yet the egalitarian values enshrined in those

Amendments are nowhere to be found in the Court's campaign finance jurisprudence. I suppose one could argue that campaign finance jurisprudence is entirely based on the First Amendment, which lacks egalitarian values and talks about "freedom of speech." Even if such a narrow reading of the Constitution were possible and part of it should be divorced from other overarching values within it, one would still have to contend with a vexing problem that the First Amendment is incorporated against the states through the Fourteenth Amendment. Thus, it is difficult for extreme libertarian theories to contend that the values of equality that pervade, indeed dominate, the Thirteenth, Fourteenth, and Fifteenth Amendments can simply be ignored in free speech cases. After all, the First Amendment doesn't apply to the states at all except through the Fourteenth Amendment, which has both a privileges and immunities clause and an equal protection clause, both strong egalitarian provisions. Moreover, the Fourteenth Amendment states that all citizens are "citizens of the United States," apparently placing all of our citizenship rights under the Constitution on an equal footing.[155]

One could argue that the Fourteenth Amendment, including the equal protection clause, does not apply to the federal government. That might remain a controversy among a few academics but the Supreme Court applies the clause to the federal government.[156]

These three Amendments present considerable problems for the committed individualistic libertarian because the Constitution itself has strongly embraced egalitarian values, which the campaign finance cases explicitly reject. For example, the Fourteenth and Fifteenth Amendments broadly reject discrimination in voting. As Chapter 9 demonstrates, the campaign finance cases are in irreconcilable tension with cases protecting an equal vote more generally. Moreover, the equal protection clause would appear to guarantee attention to equality in the distribution of constitutional rights, including speech.

1. Liberty and Equality

In his seminal work on the Fourteenth Amendment, William Nelson states that the core concern of the Fourteenth Amendment was equality of citizenship.[157] Nelson's book demonstrates how three core concerns dominated our early constitutional discourse in the early days of the Republic. These were liberty, equality, and federalism or local government. Moreover, federalism was key to their notions of constituent representation and democracy.[158]

Equality was a multi-variegated and complicated subject in early America, extending to political equality of citizenship and frequently to social and economic equality in deploring concentrations of wealth and monopolistic privilege.[159] Originally, the draft of Section 1 of the Fourteenth Amendment extended "to all citizens ... the same political rights and privileges."[160] Of course, these sentiments would resonate deeply with notions of distributive autonomy, which incorporate at least some minimal exercise of autonomy for all, particularly in the crucial area of governance.

Liberty was viewed as a second crucial aspect of citizenship and connected to self-governance. Nelson explains:

> Libertarian talk assumed three distinctive forms, each of which will be considered in turn: first, claims that people obtained their liberty through the natural law from God; second, analysis of how liberty flowed from the nature of republican government; and third, discussion of the relationship between liberty and practices of local self-government formalized in the federal system.[161]

According to Nelson, the most common articulation of liberty of citizenship in the period between 1830 and 1860, and quoted by the Framers of the Fourteenth Amendment[162] came from the case of *Corfield v. Coryell*,[163] which describes privileges and immunities of citizenship:

> which are, in their nature, fundamental; which belong, of right, to the citizens of all free governments; and which have, at all times, been enjoyed by citizens of the several States which compose this Union, from the time of their becoming free, independent, and sovereign. What these fundamental principles are, it would perhaps be more tedious than difficult to enumerate. They may, however, be all comprehended under the following general heads: Protection by the government; the enjoyment of life and liberty, with the right to acquire and possess property of every kind, and to pursue and obtain happiness and safety; subject nevertheless to such restraints as the government may justly prescribe for the general good of the whole.[164]

The last line suggests that the Framers of the Fourteenth Amendment did not view liberty as unbounded individual choice to the point of whimsy as *Buckley* and its progeny do. Instead, they thought the government could restrain liberty "for the general good of the whole." This is copacetic with John Stuart Mill's conception. Mill published *On Liberty* about ten years before the adoption of the Fourteenth Amendment. This caveat is also very revealing in exhibiting a concern for the common good, which is absent from individualistic or egocentric, libertarian notions but deeply resonates with the notion of distributive autonomy.

Coryell also talks about the electoral franchise as part of its core concept of liberty.[165] This statement implies not only that the franchise, understood against the egalitarian backdrop of the times, was part of the fundamental notion of liberty: it also states bluntly that the franchise is subject to state regulation.

This statement in *Coryell* is also reflective of a widespread movement to extend the vote to all white male citizens. The idea was that each white male should have an equal vote. Unfortunately, except in parts of the northeast where some states extended the vote to certain black men, there was no thinking to extend this right to women, black persons, or others. But this extension was still a large step forward. This extension of the franchise was one of the key strands of egalitarian thinking during the period immediately after the ratification of the Constitution. This thinking was influenced by Thomas Jefferson's celebrated statement in the Declaration of Independence:

> We hold these truths to be self-evident, that all men are created equal, that they are endowed by their Creator with certain unalienable Rights. . . .[166]

Again, these notions are in profound tension with *Buckley* and its progeny and congruent with greater regulation of the electoral process to ensure that all have a meaningful right of participation. They are also in tension with the argument that an originalist understanding of the First Amendment supports *Buckley* and its progeny. The concept of electoral opportunity deeply resonates with distributive autonomy.

2. Federalism, Constituent Representation, and Divided Power

The Framers of the Fourteenth Amendment viewed "federalism as a bulwark of liberty."[167] This is quite relevant in the context of the campaign finance cases. These cases not only violate authentic understandings of liberty and equality—they also violate the Framers' understanding of federalism.

Buckley and its progeny have undermined the American federal system. The Framers of the American Constitution intended a federal system in which members of Congress represented their states or their individual constituencies. This was particularly true of members of the Senate as each state has two senators regardless of its population.[168] To illustrate the importance of this provision, it is the only remaining non-amendable provision of the Constitution. The entire schema of the Senate being apportioned by state and the House being apportioned by population was perhaps the key compromise in the entire constitution-making process. The small states dreaded being effectively subjugated by the population-rich big states. The Framers certainly debated this prospect ad nauseam. The small states only agreed to sign on if there was a chamber in which they had equal votes. Hold that thought for a few pages.

Indeed, the Senate is more powerful than the House. Uniquely, it ratifies treaties (by two-thirds of its members), and approves the appointment of federal judges including the Supreme Court, ambassadors, the cabinet, and other top members of the bureaucracy.

Perhaps, even more sacred than federalism was the concept of genuine representation. The inviolate idea that underlay this was that representatives should represent their constituencies.[169] After all, the United States got started with the cry "No taxation without representation!"—the mantra of the entire Revolution. Hence it must be treated as a foundation of the entire Constitution. But the other aspect of that cry was to fend off tyrannical power like that exhibited by King George. If one key aim of the Constitution was constituent representation, perhaps even more central was dividing power. To avert tyrannical power, the Framers developed an elaborate system of divided power. The key to that system was creating a legislative authority that was dispersed, bicameral, and constituent-based. They also created different branches of government so that no one power could dominate. They further divided power between the federal government and the states. *Buckley*, however, allows a very small group of people to dominate the entire system. And extensive data shows that this group shares common interests, as one would expect, driven by their common economic situations. Contrary to the warnings of Michael Walzer in *Spheres of Justice*, the political power is not separated from the economic. Instead, *Buckley* has united them or really empowered the economic sphere to subjugate the political sphere.

The empirical data demonstrates just how far we have departed from the Fourteenth Amendment's schema that Nelson describes. Political scientists have developed an empirical approach to measuring representation, called alignment. Alignment seeks to measure the congruence between what voters want and what government actually does. Within a constituency, the views of the median voter of that constituency should align with the views of the representative of that constituency. In addition, within a particular jurisdiction—local, state, or national—the views of the median voter should align with the "median legislator's positions," and with the actual policy outcomes in that jurisdiction.[170]

Predictably, *Buckley* and its progeny have prompted a major shift by legislators away from the views of their constitutional constituents and toward the views of their donors. "Over the last generation, the share of campaign funds provided by the wealthiest 0.01% of Americans has surged from about 10% to more than 40%."[171] Concurrently, candidates have become more monetarily dependent on these donors while these donors have grown more extreme in their political views, exhibiting a bimodal distribution of political views that sharply contrasts with the normal distribution of the views of the electorate at large.[172] Since the 1970s and 1980s, the representation gap has grown geometrically in favor of property interests.[173]

So what has become of constituent representation? A broad swath of studies have concluded:

> [P]oliticians and donors have nearly identical ideal point distributions: highly bimodal curves in which they cluster at the ideological extremes and almost no one occupies the moderate center. Voters' views, in contrast, exhibit a normal distribution whose single peak is in the middle of the political spectrum. It is fair to say that donors receive exquisitely attentive representation—and that voters receive virtually no representation at all.[174]

What about federalism? And related but separate, what has become of the only remaining non-amendable constitutional provision protecting equal representation of the small states in the Senate? Even before *McCutcheon*, "a majority of individual contributions now come from out-of-state donors."[175] Donors disproportionately come from a few states. So, for example, in the 2013–2014 election cycle, the average House of Representatives candidate "received on average 61.3 percent of their itemized individual contributions from donors *outside* their districts." The average House winner received 64.3 percent from outside their districts, and 26 percent of winners received over 80 percent of their largest contributions from non-constituents. In the Senate, nineteen of the twenty-eight incumbents running for re-election received over 50 percent of their itemized ($200+) donations from out-of-staters.[176]

The 2014 election was not an outlier. "Since the late 1970s, out-of-district donations have consistently accounted for roughly half the itemized individual donations to House candidates, and since the late 1990s that number has regularly been in the three-fifths to two-thirds range."[177] Of course, the late 1970s is a few years after *Buckley* was decided. Moreover, in the 2013-14 election cycle, 77 percent of $200+ donations came from 5 percent of the zip codes.

> Indeed, ten zip codes (all in New York, Washington, San Francisco, and Chicago) generated more than $233 million in itemized campaign contributions, or roughly the same amount as the total sum provided by the bottom twenty-five states (ranked by the amount of their campaign donations).[178]

During the 2013-14 federal election cycle, PACs and individuals from "Washington, D.C.—which elects no senators and has a single nonvoting representative in the House of Representatives—" donated as much money to federal candidates, PACs, parties and outside spending groups "as the residents of twenty-nine states."[179]

In 2016, of the top twenty donors to outside spending groups such as PACs, six came from New York, three from California, four from Illinois, one from Arkansas, Nevada, Nebraska, Arizona, Wisconsin, Georgia, and Connecticut.[180] Historians will have a difficult time scraping together any Framer intent behind the idea that members of Congress, elected to represent Maine or a particular congressional district in Maine should be indebted to donors from New York, California, and Illinois. These donations magnify the voices and interests of the wealthiest states. Nobel Laureate economist Paul Krugman recently commented: "inequality of both wealth and income increased to levels not seen since the Great Gatsby days."[181] Without mentioning law, he described the property rights reawakening sketched in these chapters from *Lochner* to *Carolene Products*, back to *Buckley, Citizens United*, and *McCutcheon*:

> For the first time since 1917, then, we live in a world in which property rights and free markets are viewed as fundamental principles, not grudging expedients; where the unpleasant aspects of a market system—inequality, unemployment, injustice—are accepted as facts of life.[182]

Notes

1. 551 U.S. 449 (2007) (BCRA § 203).

2. *Id.* at 457. Moreover, the ads did not mention an election, candidacy, political party, or challenger; and they [did] not take a "position on a candidates' character, qualifications, or fitness for office." *Id.* at 470.

3. 540 U.S. 93 (2003).

4. The *WRTL* Court considered issue advocacy "not the 'functional equivalent'" of campaign speech or express advocacy of a particular candidate. 551 U.S. at 478.

5. Only Justice Alito joined parts III and IV of the chief justice's opinion in *WRTL*. However, these parts of the opinion effectively stated the law on these issues as those concurring in the judgment generally agreed with the majority's conclusions.

6. *WRTL*, 551 U.S. at 465. Regulating WRTL's ads was not narrowly tailored to achieve a compelling state interest.

7. *Id.* at 470.

8. *Id.* BCRA § 203 prevented WRTL from broadcasting these commercials less than thirty days before the primary election.

9. *Id.* at 479.

10. *Id.* This is in part IV of the chief justice's opinion. However, it effectively stated the law on these points. *See supra* note 2, Chapter 4.

11. *Id.* at 479.

12. *Id.* at 480. Austin v. Mich. Chamber of Commerce, 494 U.S. 652 (1990). *Austin* is discussed *supra* in text accompanying notes 75-82, Chapter 5. Chief Justice Roberts distinguished the Court's holding from *McConnell* and assured that its precedent was undisturbed. "*McConnell* held that express advocacy of a candidate or his opponent by a corporation shortly before an election may be prohibited, along with the functional equivalent of such express advocacy." *WRTL*, 551 U.S. at 482. However, when the issue was "what speech qualifies as the functional equivalent of express advocacy subject to such a ban" the Court would "give the benefit of the doubt to speech, not censorship." *WRTL*, 551 U.S. at 482.

13. Concurring in the judgment, Justice Scalia would reconsider *McConnell* as it forced the Court to differentiate "issue-speech from election-speech with no clear criterion." *WRTL*, 551 U.S. at 484. Justice Scalia was joined by Justices Kennedy and Thomas. For Justice Scalia, no test for distinguishing between express and issue advocacy "can both (1) comport with the requirement of clarity that unchilled freedom of political speech demands, and (2) be compatible with the facial validity of § 203 (as pronounced in *McConnell*)." *Id.* at 483–84. Justice Alito's concurrence predicted that if the *McConnell* Court's test "impermissibly chills political speech," then the Court might reconsider *McConnell*. *Id.* at 482–83.

14. *Id.* at 507 (Souter, J., dissenting). Justice Souter also criticized the interpretive approach of the plurality:

> The no other reasonable interpretation test flatly contradicted *McConnell*. This decision permitted companies and unions to easily circumvent the ban on their making campaign contributions "simply by running 'issue ads' without express advocacy, or by funneling the money through an independent corporation like WRTL."

Id. at 536.

15. 554 U.S. 724 (2008).

16. Although *Davis* was decided before *Citizens United*, this text's discussion of *Davis* occurs after that of *Citizens United* because the *Davis* case treats an issue very similar to that in *Arizona Free Enterprise Club's Freedom Club PAC v. Bennett*, decided after *Citizens United*. 564 U.S. 721 (2011). Hence I will discuss *Davis* and *Arizona Free Enterprise* together.

17. 558 U.S. 310 (2010). The organization Citizens United released a film in 2008 that criticized Senator Hillary Clinton, entitled *Hillary: The Movie*. Citizen's United received most of its funds from individuals, but in addition accepted a small portion from for-profit corporations. It sought to make its film available through video-on-demand within thirty days of the 2008 primary election, which would have violated the restrictions on corporate expenditures.

18. The Court allowed a facial challenge because the distinction between facial and as-applied challenges was "not so well defined." *Id.* at 331. Only addressing an as-applied challenge would prolong the chilling effect of BCRA § 441b on corporate expenditures. Corporations fearing the possibility of civil and criminal penalties would either refrain from speaking or requesting an advisory opinion from the FEC. This was an "unprecedented governmental intervention into the realm of speech." *Id.* at 336.

19. *Id.* at 340.

20. *Id.* at 319. The law prohibited broadcasting an "'electioneering communication'" within thirty days of a primary election or sixty days of a general election. *Id.* at 321. It did uphold disclaimer and disclosure requirements on corporate political speech.

21. *Id.* at 337–38 (§ 441b). "PACs are burdensome alternatives; they are expensive to administer and subject to extensive regulations." *Id.* at 337. Every PAC had to file an organizational statement and detailed monthly reports with the FEC. Also, each PAC had to have a treasurer who received donations, kept detailed records of the donations and the identity of donors, and preserved receipts for three years.

22. *Id.* at 348. *First National Bank of Boston v. Bellotti* had extended free speech protection to corporations. *See supra* text accompanying notes 62-65, Chapter 5. *Bellotti* struck down a ban on independent corporate expenditures for referenda. However, *Bellotti* did not address state bans on independent expenditures to support or oppose candidates.

23. *Austin's* reasoning would allow the government to prohibit a corporation from printing books expressing political views. Citizens United v. FEC, 558 U.S. 310, 337, 349 (2010).

24. *Citizens United*, 558 U.S. at 351.

25. *Id.* Although some media corporations had "'immense aggregations of wealth,'" they were all exempt from § 441b, even if media was only part of the corporation's business. *Id.*

26. *Id.* at 365. The Court determined whether to adhere to stare decisis based on the precedent's workability, antiquity, "'the reliance interests at stake, and of course whether the decision was well reasoned.'" *Id.* at 363. As neither party defended *Austin's* rationale, the pull of stare decisis diminished. Apparently, BCRA § 441b would prohibit a corporate blog post. The First Amendment does not allow "categorical distinctions based on the corporate identity of the speaker and the content of the political speech." *Id.* at 364. In addition to *Austin*, the Court overruled that part of *McConnell* prohibiting independent electioneering expenditures by corporations.

27. *Id.* at 359.

28. *Id.* at 361. In addition, the statute was underinclusive in protecting dissenting shareholders because it only prohibited speech within thirty or sixty days of an election. The statute also was overinclusive by covering all corporations, including nonprofit and single-shareholder corporations.

29. *Id.* at 366.

30. BCRA § 311 required independent electioneering communications to include a statement disclaiming candidate authorization and also the name and address or website address of the person or group funding the communication. Under BCRA § 201, organizations must also file FEC statements disclosing the person making the expenditure, the amount, the election to which it is directed, and the names of certain contributors. *Citizens United*, 558 U.S. at 366. *Buckley* subjects disclosure and disclaimer "requirements to 'exacting scrutiny,' which require[s] a 'substantial relation' between the disclosure requirement and a 'sufficiently important' governmental interest."

The disclosure and disclaimer requirements were substantially related to a sufficiently important government interest in informing the electorate "about the sources of election-related spending." *Id.* at 367. The *McConnell* Court used this interest to reject facial challenges to BCRA §§ 201 and 311. Disclosure helped to identify groups running advertisements using "' dubious and misleading names.'" As-applied challenges to disclosure requirements would succeed if a group showed a "'reasonable probability'" that disclosure of its contributors' names "'will subject them to threats, harassment, or reprisals from either Government officials or private parties.'" *Id.*

31. *Id.* at 372. The chief justice's concurrence was joined by Justice Alito. Regardless of whether the Court labeled *Citizens United's* challenge "'facial' or 'as-applied,'" the consequences were the same. *Id.* at 376. Chief Justice Roberts termed stare decisis, or precedent, a "'principle of policy.'" *Id.* at 378.

32. *Austin* was "uniquely destabilizing" by threatening to subvert decisions beyond corporate speech. The Court should be more willing to depart from a precedent that did more damage than good to the orderly development of the law. *Id.* at 380.

Chief Justice Roberts also noted that according to the Court, the government's arguments did little to defend *Austin's* "concerns about the corrosive and distorting effects of wealth on our political process." *Id.* at 381.

33. Justice Scalia concurred, joined by Justice Alito and in part by Justice Thomas. Even if the Founders disliked Founding-era corporations and it was proper to exclude them from First Amendment coverage, most modern corporations were very different and might not have been excluded. In any event, most of the Founders' resentment focused on corporations with state-granted monopolies. *Id.* at 387–88.

Justice Thomas concurred in part and dissented in part. He would invalidate the disclosure, disclaimer, and reporting requirements, to protect anonymous speech. *Id.* at 480. (Thomas, J., concurring in part and dissenting in part).

34. Justice Stevens dissented in part, joined by Justices Ginsburg, Breyer, and Sotomayor.

35. *Citizens United*, 558 U.S. at 448. "*See McConnell*, 251 F. Supp.2d, at 555–60, 622–25; *see also id.* at 804–805, 813, n.143 (Leon, J.) (indicating agreement)."

36. *Id.* at 448–49 (*quoting* 251 F. Supp. 2d at 623–24 (citations and footnote omitted)).

37. *Id.* at 449.

38. *Id.*

39. *Id.* at 457. Plaintiff had abandoned its facial challenge in its motion for summary judgment. Therefore the court below developed no record on the legislation, and Justice Stevens used the record on the BCRA that had been developed by the trial court in *McConnell*.

40. *Id.* at 396.

41. *Id.* at 400.

> In fact, we do not even have a good evidentiary record of how § 203 has been affecting Citizens United, which never submitted to the District Court the details of *Hillary's* funding or its own finances. We likewise have no evidence of how § 203 and comparable state laws were expected to affect corporations and unions in the future. It is true, as the majority points out, that the *McConnell* Court evaluated the facial validity of § 203 in light of an extensive record. *See id.*, at 331–32. But that record is not before us in this case. And in any event, the majority's argument for striking down § 203 depends on its contention that the statute has proved too 'chilling' in practice—and in particular on the contention that the controlling opinion in *WRTL*, 551 U.S. 449 (2007), failed to bring sufficient clarity and 'breathing space' to this area of law. *See* [*Citizens United*, 558 U.S.], at 329, 333–336. We have no record with which to assess that claim. The Court complains at length about the burdens of complying with § 203, but we have no meaningful evidence to show how regulated corporations and unions have experienced its restrictions.

Id. at 400, n.5.

42. Justice Stevens disagreed with treating this case as a facial challenge. The Court had "repeatedly emphasized in recent years that '[f]acial challenges are disfavored.'" *Id.* at 398. The Court could have decided the case narrowly by expanding "the *MCFL* exemption to cover § 501(c)(4) nonprofits that accept only a *de minimis* amount of money from for-profit corporations." *Id.* at 406. There were other narrower grounds to decide this case. As one alternative, "the Court could have ruled, on statutory grounds, that a feature-length film distributed through video-on-demand does not qualify as an 'electioneering communication'" under § 441b. *Id.*

43. *Id.* at 409.The majority's arguments against stare decisis say almost nothing about the Court's standard considerations of the precedent's antiquity, workability, and the reliance interests at stake. The *Austin* decision was twenty years old. The Court offers no argument that *Austin* and *McConnell* were unworkable. Many statutes that *Citizens United* called into question had existed for at least fifty years. *Id.* at 412.

44. *Id.* This ruling "strikes at the vitals of *stare decisis.*" *Id.* at 414. Overlooking precedent, the "majority opinion is essentially an amalgamation of resuscitated dissents." *Id.* For Justice Stevens, *First National Bank of Boston v. Bellotti* did not apply as it dealt with dramatically different facts than *Austin.*

Id. at 414. All six members of the *Austin* majority were on the Court for *Bellotti*, and none even hinted at a tension between the decisions. *Id.* at 445. *See also* Richard L. Hasen, Citizens United *and the Illusion of Coherence*, 109 MICH. L. REV. 581 (2011). (arguing that the campaign financing cases are incoherent).

45. Unlike the majority's position, channeling the donations of people associated with corporations through PACs protected the autonomy of shareholders from coerced speech. PACs offered some protection by ensuring that those who pay for an electioneering communication actually support its content. *Citizens United*, 558 U.S. at 475.

46. Specifically, the statute prohibited broadcast, cable, or satellite communication by a labor union or a corporation. *Id.* at 417–18. It did not apply to nonprofit, MCFL corporations or to media corporations. These were non-media, non-*MCFL* corporations. For unions and these companies, the law only prohibited a broadcast, cable, or satellite communication that could

reach 50,000 persons in the relevant electorate, made within thirty days of a primary or sixty days of a general federal election, paid for with general treasury funds, and that could only be interpreted as a solicitation to vote for or against a specific candidate. *Id.* at 418.

47. *Id.* at 423.

48. In the Tillman Act, Congress expressly distinguished between corporate and individual spending on elections.

49. *Citizens United,* 558 U.S. at 430. The dissent suggested that equating corporate rights to speak with those of the press reads the press clause out of the Constitution. *Id.* at 431. Issues "about Congress' authority to regulate electioneering by the press" were not before the Court. *Id.* at 474.

50. *Id.* at 475. The District Court judge in *McConnell* concluded that the government's interest in preventing the appearance of corruption, as that concept was defined in *Buckley,* was itself sufficient to uphold BCRA §203. *See, e.g., Citizens United,* 558 U.S. at 479. *See also id.* at 456.

51. *Id.* at 456.

52. Corruption dangers existed "that are far more destructive to a democratic society than the odd bribe." *Id.* at 449. The majority's understanding of corruption forbade regulation of all but the most extreme abuses. *Id.* at 449. *See McConnell,* 251 F. Supp. 2d. at 555–60, 622–25. The BCRA legislative and judicial "'record powerfully demonstrates that electioneering communications paid for with the general treasury funds of labor unions and corporations endears those entities to elected officials in a way that could be perceived by the public as corrupting.'" *Id.* at 456. The *McConnell* Court found corporate spending restrictions "faithful to the compelling governmental interests in '"preserving the integrity of the electoral process, preventing corruption,"'" sustaining confidence in government, and securing the individual citizen's active, alert responsibility that is necessary for good democratic governance. *Id.* at 440.

Members of the Court suggested in *McConnell* that the BCRA "may be little more than 'an incumbency protection plan'"; however, there is no evidence in the record of "'invidious discrimination against challengers.'" *Id.* at 460–62.

53. *Id.* at 455.

54. 599 F.3d 674 (2010).

55. *Id.* at 694.

56. *Id.* at 695.

57. RICHARD L. HASEN, PLUTOCRATS UNITED: CAMPAIGN MONEY, THE SUPREME COURT, AND THE DISTORTION OF AMERICAN ELECTIONS 39 (Yale University Press, 2016).

58. *See* Michael S. Kang, *The End of Campaign Finance Law,* 98 VA. L. REV. 1 (2012).

59. 554 U.S. 724, 729 (2008).

60. Moreover, the self-financed candidate faced more demanding disclosure requirements. The self-financing candidate had to file: within fifteen days of entering a race, a "'declaration of intent'" to spend more than $350,000, an "'initial notification'" within twenty-four hours of crossing the $350,000 mark, and an "'additional notification'" within twenty-four hours of each additional expenditure from personal funds of $10,000 or more.

The non-self-financing candidate faced less demanding disclosure requirements. These candidates were required to report only when: after certain notifications by a self-financing opponent, they believed that the opponent had spent $350,000 in personal funds, their additional contributions received under the Act became equal to that opponent's personal expenditures, or they had to return "'excess funds.'" *Id.* at 730–31.

61. *Id.* at 740–42. The Court found no " 'compelling state interest' " in eliminating real or perceived corruption: If the current contribution limits did not serve permissible interests of preventing corruption or the perception that congressional seats may be bought, those limits should be uniformly raised or eliminated altogether.

Davis also invalidated the asymmetrical candidate disclosure requirements contained in the law. Justice Alito subjected these to " 'exacting scrutiny,' " requiring a court to find a substantially " 'relevant correlation' " between the claimed governmental interest and the disclosed information. *Id.* at 744. As the seriousness of the burden on First Amendment rights increases, so also must the strength of the government's interest. The BCRA requirements failed this standard, as the government could not justify the severity of the burden these asymmetrical contribution limits and disclosure requirements imposed on First Amendment rights.

62. *Id.* at 749–50.

63. *Id.* at 753–54.

64. Moreover, the self-financing candidate's opponent received no unfair advantage as he could only take advantage of the increased limits until he was financially equal to his opponent. Preventing real and perceived corruption are not the only governmental interests weighty enough to justify campaign finance regulations.

Justice Ginsburg wrote a separate dissent, joined in part by Justice Breyer. She agreed with Justice Stevens that the challenged provisions did not violate *Buckley's* holding, but thought that the issues presented in this case did not require reconsideration of *Buckley*. *Id.* at 758.

65. 564 U.S. 721 (2011).

66. *Id.* at 729. Arizona's scheme "substantially burdens protected political speech without serving a compelling state interest." *Id.* at 728.

67. *Id.* at 729.

68. *Id.* at 729–30.

69. *Id.* at 737.

70. *Id.* at 739.

71. As the law "imposes a substantial burden on the speech," it must be " 'justified by a compelling state interest.' " *Id.* at 748.

72. *Id.* "Any increase in speech resulting from the Arizona law is of one kind and one kind only—that of publicly financed candidates." *Id.* at 741. This increase came at the expense of "privately financed candidates and independent expenditure groups" as the law decreased their speech. *Id.* at 741. The Court has "rejected government efforts to increase the speech of some at the expense of others." *Id.*

73. *Id.* at 751.

74. *Id.* at 750.

75. *Id.* at 754.

76. Justice Kagan was joined by Justices Ginsburg, Breyer, and Sotomayor.

77. *Bennett*, 564 U.S. at 757 (Kagan, J., dissenting).

78. *Id.* at 758–59. *Buckley* rejected the challenge to federal funding for presidential candidates from minor-party candidates ineligible for it, as public funding supported rather than hindered, speech. *Id.* at 767. It is nearly impossible to predict campaign expenditures ex ante; "that creates a chronic problem for lump-sum public financing programs." The Arizona "program's designers found the Goldilocks solution, which produces the 'just right' grant to ensure that a participant in the system has the funds needed to run a competitive race." *Id.* at 760–61.

79. *Id.* at 767.

80. *Id.* at 768, n.5.

81. *Id.* at 766. The publicly financed candidate can only receive three times the amount of the initial public funding disbursement received from the government, gets 94 cents for every dollar the self-funding candidate spends, and cannot receive private contributions, "no matter how much more his privately funded opponent spends." *Id.* at 762. Arizona's subsidy "produces *more* political speech." *Id.* at 763. That "additional speech constitutes a 'burden' is odd and unsettling." *Id.* at 768. The Court has "never, not once, understood a viewpoint-neutral subsidy given to one speaker to constitute a First Amendment burden on another. (And that is so even when the subsidy is not open to all, as it is here.)" *Id.* at 769.

82. 134 S. Ct. 1434 (2014).

83. *Id.* at 1442-43.

84. Federal Election Campaign Act of 1971, as amended by the Bipartisan Campaign Reform Act of 2002, 2 U.S C. § 441a(a)(1); 78 Fed. Reg. 8532 (2013), *quoted at McCutcheon,* 134 S. Ct. at 1442.

85. BCRA § 441a(a)(3); *McCutcheon,* 134 S. Ct. at 1442–43.

86. The trial court expressed its alarm with the following hypothetical:

> A single donor might contribute the maximum amount under the base limits to nearly 50 separate committees, each of which might then transfer the money to the same single committee. That committee, in turn, might use all the transferred money for coordinated expenditures on behalf of a particular candidate, allowing the single donor to circumvent the base limit on the amount he may contribute to that candidate. [Citations omitted].

McCutcheon, 134 S. Ct. at 1443.

87. *Id.* at 1441.

88. *Id.* For an account of corruption focusing on government outputs and clientelist behavior, *see* Samuel Issacharoff, *On Political Corruption,* 124 HARV. L. REV. 118, 127–29 (2010). "Clientelist pressures erode public institutions with incentives to increase the size, complexity, and nontransparency of governmental decisionmaking, with the corresponding impetus simply to increase the relative size of the public sector, often beyond the limits of what the national economy can tolerate." *Id.* at 129.

89. *McCutcheon,* 134 S. Ct. at 1437. Later that term the Court said that the *McCutcheon* plurality assumed without deciding that it was applying intermediate scrutiny because applying any other standard "would have required overruling a precedent." McCullen v. Coakley, 134 S. Ct. 2518 (2014). Presumably the Court was referring to treating contribution limits under intermediate scrutiny. If so this might suggest higher effective scrutiny for all contribution limits going forward.

90. 424 U.S. 1 (1976).

91. *McCutcheon,* 134 S. Ct. at 1446–47. Before the regulation, the same donor could have created and funded multiple PACs, and each could have contributed to the same candidate.

92. *Id.* at 1446-47. "For example, the regulations construe earmarking to include any designation, 'whether direct or indirect, express or implied, oral or written.' 11 CFR §110.6(b)(1). The regulations specify that an individual who has contributed to a particular candidate may not also

contribute to a single-candidate committee for that candidate. §110.1(h)(1). Nor may an individual who has contributed to a candidate also contribute to a political committee that has supported or anticipates supporting the same candidate, if the individual knows that 'a substantial portion [of his contribution] will be contributed to, or expended on behalf of,' that candidate. §110.1(h)(2)" *Id.* at 1447.

93. *Id.* at 1448 [citation omitted].

94. "The Government may no more restrict how many candidates or causes a donor may support than it may tell a newspaper how many candidates it may endorse." *Id.* at 1448.

95. *Id.* at 1450–52.

96. Lawrence Lessig, *What an Originalist Would Understand "Corruption" to Mean*, 102 Cal. L. Rev. 1, 7 (2014).

97. *McCutcheon,* 134 S. Ct. at 1451 [citation omitted].

98. *Id.* at 1452.

99. *Id.* at 1447.

100. However, the donor could not telegraph, or even imply, her desire to earmark the gift to a particular candidate. Moreover, the $500,000 example is crafted around contributions to a presidential candidate, not just any candidate. In any event, that state committees would channel donations given them to committees in other states was highly improbable. *Id.* at 1455.

101. In 2012, the four Democratic and Republican senatorial and congressional committees were: the National Republican Senatorial Committee (NRSC), the National Republican Congressional Committee (NRCC), the Democratic Senatorial Campaign Committee (DSCC), and the Democratic Congressional Campaign Committee (DCCC). Combined, these four committees "spent less than $1 million each on direct candidate contributions and less than $10 million each on coordinated expenditures." Similarly, of the $1.1 billion spent in 2012 by candidates for the House of Representatives, less than 0.3 percent was given to other candidates. The Democratic and Republican state party senatorial and congressional committees spent $500 million in 2012, of which 0.003 percent ($17,750) was given to candidates from other states. There was no reason to believe that these patterns of behavior would change absent the aggregate limitations. *Id.* at 1457.

102. *Id.* at 1457. The contribution limitations for each election cycle further constrict circumvention possibilities for donations to a particular candidate. For example, even if a donor gave $2,600 to each of 100 congressmen who were in safe races in hopes that they would all reroute $2,000 to one particular candidate in a contested race, only one private donor to the various individual congressional campaigns could do this. This is because for that particular election cycle, the 100 congressmen would have reached their contribution limits to the single congressman in the contested race. *Id.* at 1457–58 & n.10.

103. In addition to more robust enforcement, one measure involved limiting targeted transfers between party committees and candidate committees. "There are currently no such limits on transfers among party committees and from candidates to party committees. *See* 2 U. S. C. §441a(a) (4); 11 CFR §113.2(c)." *McCutcheon,* 134 S. Ct. at 1458. A "possible option for restricting transfers would be to require contributions above the current aggregate limits to be deposited into segregated, nontransferable accounts and spent only by their recipients." *Id.* Another possibility would be to require any donations made to joint committees to be spent by the joint committee. *Id.* at 1458–59. Another was further restrictions on earmarking. For example, a PAC might be required to contribute to a minimum number of candidates to ensure that funds contributed to that PAC

were not earmarked to a specific candidate. *Id.* at 1459. Alternatively, donors who had already given the maximum contribution to particular candidates could be prohibited from giving additional contributions to PACs that have indicated they will support the same candidates. *Id.*

104. Disclosure was also a more effective alternative in an Internet world than it had been when *Buckley* was decided. At that time, the disclosures would sit in the FEC office. *Id.* at 1459–60. Organizations such as Open-Secrets.org and FollowTheMoney.org rendered disclosure far more effective. Aggregate contribution limits encouraged contributions to 501(c) organizations, which tallied $300 million of independent expenditures in the 2012 election cycle. Unlimited contributions can be made to such organizations and they escape disclosure. *Id.* at 1460.

The plurality also rejected the suggestion that contributions of a large check to an individual legislator presented an opportunity for corruption even when the check was divided among other candidates, the political party, and PACs who supported that party. This definition of corruption went far beyond the Court's requirement of quid pro quo corruption. The plurality further opined: "We have no occasion to consider a law that would specifically ban candidates from soliciting donations—within the base limits—that would go to many other candidates, and would add up to a large sum." *Id.* at 1461.

105. *Id.* at 1461. Concurring in the judgment, Justice Thomas reprised his view that contribution limitations should be struck down. The plurality's rationale for invalidating aggregate contribution limitations could not be squared with *Buckley's* basic rationale for allowing any contribution limitations at all. *Id.* at 1463. The plurality effectively continued to chip away at that part of *Buckley's* holding that sustained contribution limitations. *Id.* at 1464.

106. *See* note 23 & accompanying text, Chapter 3.

107. *McCutcheon*, 134 S. Ct. at 1465 (Breyer, J., dissenting). Justice Breyer's dissent was joined by Justices Ginsburg, Sotomayor, and Kagan [citations omitted].

108. *Id.* at 1466.

109. *Id.* at 1469 (*quoting* FEC v. Beaumont, 539 U.S. 146, 155–56 (2003)).

110. *Id.* at 1470 (quoting *McConnell*, 540 U.S. at 153).

111. *Id.* at 1469 (citing *McConnell*, 540 U.S. at 146–52, 154–57, 167–71, 182–84).

112. *Id.* at 1467 (citing *Whitney v. California*, 274 U.S. 357, 377 (1927) (Brandeis, J., concurring).

113. *Id.* at 1467. The plurality quotes the following language from *Citizens United* as supporting its definition of corruption:

> "[w]hen *Buckley* identified a sufficiently important governmental interest in preventing corruption or the appearance of corruption, that interest was limited to *quid pro quo* corruption." 558 U. S., at 359. Further, the Court said that *quid pro quo* corruption does not include "influence over or access to elected officials," because '"generic favoritism or influence theory . . . is at odds with standard First Amendment analyses.'" *Id.* (quoting *McConnell* . . . (Kennedy, J., concurring in judgment in part and dissenting in part)).

Id. at 1471. But not a single opinion in *Citizens United* had interpreted this language as overruling the *McConnell* decision. Yet the plurality rejected the definition of corruption upon which *McConnell's* holding rested. *Id.* at 1471–72.

114. *Id.* at 1472. A donor could give $64,800 to each of the three national committees of each party, and $20,000 to each of the fifty state political party committees in the same time frame. *Id.*

115. The $3.6 million could be distributed: $64,800 to national party committees, $20,000 to state committees, and $5,200 to individual candidates. The donor could give $5,200 to each of 435 congressional candidates and 33 senatorial candidates. Each candidate could give $4,000 for the primary and the election for a total of $1,872,000, and each party committee could give $10,000 for a total of $530,000. Alternatively, the joint committee could give $2.37 million to a single candidate. In addition, for a general election, coordinated expenditures valued between $46,600 and $2.68 million could be directed at the candidate. The amount depended on the size of the candidate's state and whether the election was for the House or the Senate. *McCutcheon*, 134 S. Ct. at 1473–75.

116. *Id.* at 1472–75.

117. Justice Breyer elaborated his example:

> Groups of party supporters—individuals, corporations, or trade unions—create 200 PACs. Each PAC claims it will use the funds it raises to support several candidates from the party, though it will favor those who are most endangered. (Each PAC qualifies for "multicandidate" status because it has received contributions from more than 50 persons and has made contributions to five federal candidates at some point previously. §441a(a)(4); 11 CFR §100.5(e)(3)). Over a 2-year election cycle, Rich Donor One gives $10,000 to each PAC ($5,000 per year)—yielding $2 million total. Rich Donor 2 does the same. So, too, do the other eight Rich Donors. This brings their total donations to $20 million, disbursed among the 200 PACs. Each PAC will have collected $100,000, and each can use its money to write ten checks of $10,000—to each of the ten most Embattled Candidates in the party (over two years). Every Embattled Candidate, receiving a $10,000 check from 200 PACs, will have collected $2 million.

Id. at 1474–75.

118. *Id.* at 1475.

119. First, although contribution limits to political committees have been added since *Buckley*, there was still no limit on the number of political committees that could be created that supported a party or a group of party candidates.

Second, although the nonproliferation rule attributes all contributions to political committees given by the same corporation, labor union, or person to the contribution limit of that organization, there were still 2,700 nonconnected political committees operating during the 2012 election. Removal of aggregate contribution limits will only cause that number to grow. 134 S. Ct. at 1475–76. "Just because a group of multicandidate PACs all support the same party and all decide to donate funds to a group of endangered candidates in that party does not mean they will qualify as 'affiliated' under the relevant definition." *Id.* at 1476.

Third, the earmarking restrictions in political committees when *Buckley* was decided are virtually the same as the provisions in place today.

Fourth, although the contribution limitations apply to multiple single candidate political committees, they do not apply to one political committee supporting a particular candidate and another supporting multiple candidates including that one. The briefs before the Court suggested that this was a realistic option. *Id.* at 1475–77.

Fifth, the FEC could attribute to the contributors' grand total both contributions to an individual candidate and contributions to a "'political committee that has supported or anticipates supporting the same candidate if the individual knows that "a substantial portion [of his contribution] will be contributed to, or expended on behalf of," that candidate.'" (plurality quoting 11 CFR §110.1(h)(2)). *Id.* at 1477. Since 2000, the FEC has been able to meet this heavy burden in only one case. *Id.*

120. Demonstrating the lack of efficacy of this FEC regulation, political parties and candidates had over 500 joint fundraising committees in the last election, and candidates established over 450 "'Leadership PACs.'" At the same time party supporters had established over 3,000 multicandidate PACs. 134 S. Ct. at 1478. These groups were not prosecuted under the $123,200 aggregate contribution limit. They will certainly not be prosecuted under limits of several million dollars.

121. The dissent noted that the plurality did not endorse the constitutionality of any of these proposals and the plurality admitted they could be subject to challenge. *Id.* at 1479–80.

122. *Id.* at 1479. The plurality itself noted the substantial factual disputes between the dissent and the plurality. The dissent emphasized: "We disagree, for example, on the possibilities for circumvention of the base limits in the absence of aggregate limits. We disagree about how effectively the plurality's 'alternatives' could prevent evasion." *Id.* at 1480.

The plurality also left open a tremendous number of fact questions, including the existence of a compelling state interest, the fit between that interest and statute, and the extent to which the plurality should defer to the judgment of Congress. "Determining whether anticorruption objectives justify a particular set of contribution limits requires answering empirically based questions, and applying significant discretion and judgment. To what extent will unrestricted giving lead to corruption or its appearance? What forms will any such corruption take? To what extent will a lack of regulation undermine public confidence in the democratic system? To what extent can regulation restore it?" *Id.* A remand would have been consistent with the Court's past practice. *Id.* at 1479–80.

For two interesting but sharply contrasting perspectives on *McCutcheon,* compare Burt Neuborne, *"Welcome to Oligarchs United",* http://www.scotusblog.com/2014/04/symposium-welcome-to-oligarchs-united/ (last visited Apr. 3, 2014) *with* Richard A. Epstein, *'Oligarchs United'? Not So Fast,* http://www.hoover.org/research/oligarchs-united-not-so-fast (last visited Apr. 7, 2014).

123. Lee Drutman, *The Political 1% of the 1% in 2012,* June 24, 2013, http://sunlightfoundation.com/blog/2013/06/24/1pct_of_the_1pct/.

124. Peter Olsen-Phillips, Russ Choma, Sarah Bryner & Doug Weber, *The Political One Percent of the One Percent: Megadonors Fuel Rising Cost of Elections in 2014,* OPENSECRETS.ORG, Apr. 30, 2015, https://www.opensecrets.org/news/2015/04/the-political-one-percent-of-the-one-percent-in-2014-mega-donors-fuel-rising-cost-of-elections/.

125. Russ Choma, *Final Tally: 2014's Midterm Was Most Expensive, With Fewer Donors,* OPENSECRETS.ORG, Feb. 18, 2015, https://www.opensecrets.org/news/2015/02/final-tally-2014s- midterm-was-most-expensive-with-fewer-donors/.

126. FEDERAL RESERVE BANK, REPORT ON THE ECONOMIC WELL-BEING OF U.S. HOUSEHOLDS IN 2015, at 15 (May 2016). The Fed conducted its survey in October and November 2015.

127. http://www.cbsnews.com/news/60-minutes-are-members-of-congress-becoming-telemarketers/.

128. 536 U.S. 765 (2002).

129. *Id.* at 768. The candidate could discuss "'character,' 'education,' 'work habits,'" and administrative approaches. *Id.* at 774.

130. *Id.* at 784.

131. *Id.* at 781.

132. Justice Stevens's dissent was joined by Justices Souter, Ginsburg, and Breyer.

133. *White,* 536 U.S. at 799, n.2.

134. *Id.* at 803.

135. 556 U.S. 868 (2009).

136. *Id.* at 872. Notably, when a judge had a financial interest in the outcome of a case or when a judge participated in an earlier proceeding, judicial disqualification was required. Although actual bias also required recusal, the Court could not easily review the West Virginia justice's finding lack of actual bias. Instead, Justice Kennedy applied an objective standard, asking "whether, 'under a realistic appraisal of psychological tendencies and human weakness,' the interest 'poses such a risk of actual bias or prejudgment that the practice must be forbidden.'" *Id.* at 883–84.

137. *Id.* at 884.

138. *Id.*

139. *Id.* The Court stated that the CEO's "significant and disproportionate influence—coupled with the temporal relationship between the election and the pending case—'"offer a possible temptation to the average . . . judge to . . . lead him not to hold the balance nice, clear and true.'"" *Id.* at 886 (citations omitted). The Court reiterated that these facts are extreme, making a flood of recusal motions unlikely.

140. Chief Justice Robert's dissent was joined by Justices Scalia, Thomas, and Alito. Historically, the due process clause required a judge's disqualification only "when the judge has a financial interest in the outcome of the case, and when the judge is presiding over certain types of criminal contempt proceedings." *Id.* at 891. Bias or the appearance of bias never merited disqualification, at common law or under the Constitution.

141. 135 S. Ct. 1656 (2015).

142. *Id.* at 1662.

143. *Id.* In Florida, the governor selected appellate judges from a group proposed by a nominating committee; they then had to run for retention in office every six years. *Id.* at 1662. Florida disciplined judicial candidate Yulee for signing a letter to prospective donors asking for contributions.

144. *Id.* at 1666.

145. *Id.* (citations omitted)

146. The optics are not appealing when "most donors are lawyers and litigants who may appear before the judge they are supporting." 135 S. Ct. at 1667. Potential litigants may even feel forced to retain a lawyer who did contribute if their lawyer did not. Although campaign committees could still solicit funds, the stakes were higher when the judicial candidate does so personally.

Florida only restricted a "narrow slice of speech." It "leaves judicial candidates free to discuss any issue with any person at any time. Candidates can write letters, give speeches, and put up billboards. They can contact potential supporters in person, on the phone, or online. They can promote their campaigns on radio, television, or other media. They cannot say, 'Please give me money.' They can, however, direct their campaign committees to do so." *Id.* at 1670.

Justice Ginsburg concurred. "'Favoritism,' *i.e.,* partiality, if inevitable in the political arena, is disqualifying in the judiciary's domain." *Id.* at 1674. Judges should be indifferent to constituent concerns and to popularity. "In recent years, moreover, issue-oriented organizations and political action committees have spent millions of dollars opposing the reelection of judges whose decisions do not tow a party line or are alleged to be out of step with public opinion." *Id.*

147. *Id.* at 1676.

148. *Id.* The ban extended to soliciting contributions from "someone who (because of recusal rules) cannot possibly appear before the candidate as lawyer or litigant. Yulee thus may not call up an old friend, a cousin, or even her parents to ask for a donation to her campaign." *Id.* at 1679.

Although the ban "prevents Yulee from asking a lawyer for a few dollars to help her buy campaign pamphlets, it does not prevent her asking the same lawyer for a personal loan, access to his law firm's luxury suite at the local football stadium, or even a donation to help her fight the Florida Bar's charges." *Id.* at 1680.

149. *Id.* at 1682.

150. *See, e.g.,* Elizabeth D. Laporte & Jonathan M. Redgrave, *A Practical Guide to Achieving Proportionality Under New Federal Rule of Civil Procedure 26*, 2015 FED. CTS. L. REV. 19.

151. *See, e.g.,* Muller v. Oregon, 208 U.S. 412 (1908) (upholding a law prescribing a ten-hour work day for women working in factory or laundry); Bunting v. Oregon, 243 U.S. 426 (1917) (upholding a law prescribing a ten-hour day for factory workers).

152. *See, e.g.,* Champion v. Ames, 188 U.S. 321 (1903) (prohibiting lottery tickets in interstate commerce); Houston East & West Tex. Ry. v. United States (Shreveport Rate Case), 234 U.S. 342 (1914) (regulating intrastate railway rates).

153. This asset is protected not only by free speech jurisprudence but also by a variety of copyright, trademark, and patent laws.

154. *See* Morton J. Horwitz, *The Constitution of Change: Legal Fundamentality Without Fundamentalism*, 107 HARV. L. REV. 32, 72 (1993) (citing statements critical of *Lochner* made by Justice Scalia); Jamal Greene, *The Anticanon*, 125 HARV. L. REV 379, 392 n.66 (2011) (citing statements critical of *Lochner* made by Chief Justice Roberts). Although Chief Justice Rehnquist also made statements critical of *Lochner*, he was certainly not an architect of the *Buckley* Constitution, as some people suppose.

155. Initially the Bill of Rights only applied to the federal government. It was incorporated against the states through the Fourteenth Amendment in a process called selective incorporation. *See* John Attanasio, *Everyman's Constitutional Law: A Theory of the Power of Judicial Review*, 72 GEO. L.J. 1665, 1682–87 (1984).

156. Bolling v. Sharpe, 347 U.S. 497 (1954) (applying *Brown v. Board of Education* to the federal government).

157. WILLIAM E. NELSON, THE FOURTEENTH AMENDMENT: FROM POLITICAL PRINCIPLE TO JUDICIAL DOCTRINE 11, 119 (Harvard University Press, 1988).

158. *Id.* at 13.

159. *Id.* at 14–17.

160. *Id.* at 51–52. This version was dropped because of the fear of the rights that it would afford black persons.

161. *Id.* at 21.

162. *Id.* at 24–25.

163. 6 F. Cas. 546 (E.D. Pa. 1823).

164. *Id.* at 551–52.

165. *Id.* at 552.

166. For this idea, I am indebted to William Nelson. See GORDON S. WOOD, EMPIRE OF LIBERTY: A HISTORY OF THE EARLY REPUBLIC, 1789–1815, at 300-05, 542 (Oxford University Press 2009).

167. NELSON, *supra* note 157, at 27.

168. Indeed, until the promulgation of the Seventeenth Amendment, the Constitution specified that senators be elected by state legislatures, not popularly. Justice Scalia thought the Seventeenth Amendment's altering this was the most important change ever made to the Constitution. He favored repealing it because of its anti-federalism implications. David Schleicher, *The Seventeenth Amendment and Federalism in an Age of National Political Parties*, 65 HASTINGS L.J. 1043, 1044–45 (2014). On the Seventeenth Amendment, *see generally* Todd J. Zywicki, *Beyond the Shell and Husk of History: The History of the Seventeenth Amendment and Its Implications for Current Reform Proposals*, 45 CLEV. ST. L. REV. 165 (1997).

169. Daryl J. Levinson, *The Supreme Court 2015 Term: Foreword: Looking for Power in Public Law*, 130 HARV. L. REV. 33 (2016).

170. Nicholas O. Stephanopoulos, *Aligning Campaign Finance Law*, 101 VA. L. REV. 1425, 1428 (2015). At the jurisdictional level, congruity between the legislature's positions and the median voter's positions is called "preference alignment," and the congruence between the median voters positions and actual policy outcomes is called "outcome alignment." *Id.*

171. *Id.* at 1433.

172. *Id.* at 1474.

173. *Id.* at 1433, 1471.

174. Stephanopoulos, *Campaign Finance*, *supra* note 170, at 1431. *See also id.* at 1468. In part of his work, Stephanopoulos claims that single issue PACs and labor union PACs are more likely to make contributions ideologically in line with a bimodal distribution, therefore causing misalignment. In contrast, he claims that corporate PACs and large multi-issue PACs are more moderate, and comprise moderating forces that decrease misalignment between legislators and average voters. Although he suggests that this might entail different treatment for different kinds of PACs, Stephanopoulos recognizes that such differential treatment would discriminate among speakers based on the content and the viewpoint of their speech. Government also cannot restrict speech based on its controversial content or favor moderate viewpoints. Stephanopoulos asserts that corporations establish and contribute to PACs to achieve access and influence post-election and to elect candidates with similar views. Contributions by political parties also favor moderate viewpoints as being politically centrist wins elections. *Id.* at 1479–82. Of course, characterizing corporations' views as moderate is consistent with achieving access and influence which increases profitability using political advantage.

175. Richard H. Pildes, *Romanticizing Democracy, Political Fragmentation, and the Decline of American Government*, 124 YALE L.J. 804, 827 (2014).

176. Richard Briffault, *Of Constituents and Contributors*, 2015 U. CHI. LEGAL F. 29, 34–37.

177. *Id.* at 35.

178. *Id.* at 50.

179. *See Id.* & n.105, *citing* Open Secrets, Contributions by State, 2014 Overview, archived at http://perma.cc/8L89-RY73.

180. https://www.opensecrets.org/outsidespending/summ.php?cycle=2016&disp=D&type=V&superonly=N.

181. PAUL KRUGMAN, THE RETURN OF DEPRESSION ECONOMICS AND THE CRISIS OF 2008, 28 (W.W. Norton & Co., 2009).

182. *Id.* at 28.

IV Distributive Autonomy: Philosophical Origins, Constitutional Applicabilty, and Campaign Finance

The liberty of the individual must be thus far limited;
he must not make a nuisance of himself to other people.
John Stuart Mill, *On Liberty*, Chapter 3

Your freedom and mine cannot be separated.
NELSON MANDELA *message read by*
his daughter at a rally in Soweto
February 10, 1985

7 Philosophical Ruminations

THE TENSION BETWEEN LIBERTY AND EQUALITY

A. Doctrinal Wrong Turns: Equating Spending Money with Speaking

Small changes in constitutional jurisprudence can effect large changes in the government policymaking process and in government policy. Constitutional changes are like launching satellites into space. Even a small modification in the trajectory at the launch site can result in the projectile's being millions of miles off course deep in space.

Ideas matter. Constitutional jurisprudence often reflects overreaching intellectual trends in our society. For example, Justice Holmes criticized *Lochner* as codifying the dominant social Darwinist, laissez-faire thinking of the time.[1] As I have already contended, the *Buckley* Constitution in many ways reflects the sway of modern individualistic libertarian thinking. Until fairly recently, many free speech theorists advanced a narrow libertarianism with scant attention to the philosophical underpinnings or inegalitarian consequences of this approach.

Occasionally, some commentators have glimpsed the contours of a more egalitarian approach to free speech jurisprudence. For example, renowned First Amendment theorist Alexander Meiklejohn sought to capture an inclusive approach to freedom of speech in his timeless metaphor of the town meeting:

> The town meeting, as it seeks for freedom of public discussion of public problems ... is not Hyde Park. It is a parliament or congress. It is a group of free and

Politics and Capital. John Attanasio.
© John Attanasio 2018. Published 2018 by Oxford University Press.

equal men, cooperating in a common enterprise, and using for that enterprise responsible and regulated discussion. It is not a dialectical free-for-all. It is self-government.[2]

Other theorists have sought to legitimate free speech in part on the basis that it embraces everyone in society.[3]

My aim is not that we jettison the libertarian paradigm but only that we take the liberty of all seriously by developing a free speech jurisprudence informed by distributive autonomy. A good starting point for this jurisprudence is a return to something like the weak libertarian paradigm, refashioned to pay more attention to advancing broader access to the marketplace of ideas irrespective of wealth.[4]

Tinkering with the libertarian speech paradigm can be dangerous, because striving to achieve too much equality in the distribution of autonomy can paradoxically have authoritarian consequences.[5] But, as I will demonstrate, autonomy also suffers from ignoring the vast disparities in its distribution. As one example of the danger of status quo bias,[6] Stephen Carter once warned, "unless we act to stop our slide, we will continue downward toward the New First Amendment, with its guaranties of freedom of speech for those who can afford it, and freedom to listen for those who cannot."[7] As Chapter 9 recounts, even the freedom to listen has been seriously impaired.

These breaches of distributive autonomy eventually will make almost everyone suffer. There will be almost no winners here. The constitutional, philosophical, political science, and economic analyses in this work all arrive at the same destination, the same simple idea: society is one fabric in which its members succeed or fail, prosper or crash, together. Chapters 10 and 11 advance a lot of compelling statistics that indicate how closely society is bound together in its economic destiny, and more generally in its successes and failures. The principles of distributive and aggregate autonomy at some level are merely lodestars to engage this seemingly inescapable truth. Let me offer some initial reflections as to how we might afford greater attention to distributive autonomy in our conception of free speech. The *Buckley* line of cases could be rethought. For starters, the cases probably should not strictly equate spending money with speaking. This wrong turn conflates property rights with speech rights.

As the Federal Court of Appeals for Washington, D.C. suggested in *Buckley v. Valeo*,[8] spending money to speak could be protected by the middle-tier standard of *United States v. O'Brien*,[9] an analytical tack that the Supreme Court decision in *Buckley* specifically rejected.[10] *O'Brien* imposes a lesser level of scrutiny on government regulation if the activity regulated involves speech mixed with action, and if the regulation focuses on the conduct rather than the speech. For example, the Court in *O'Brien* upheld a government regulation broadly banning the destruction of draft cards. The fact that the person in that case burned his draft card to protest the draft did not render his behavior protected speech. The government could broadly protect the draft card from mutilation whether that mutilation was intended to express an idea or not.

The Court of Appeals in *Buckley* specifically relied on *O'Brien*:

[W]e think it clear that a government regulation is sufficiently justified if it is within the constitutional power of Government; if it furthers an important or substantial governmental interest; if the governmental interest is unrelated to the suppression of free expression; and if the incidental restriction on alleged First Amendment freedoms is no greater than is essential to the furtherance of that interest.[11]

Rejecting the applicability of *O'Brien*, the Supreme Court in *Buckley* maintained that the expenditure limitations regulated speech, rather than speech plus conduct. Moreover, the campaign finance restrictions suppressed speech; consequently, they were not unrelated to the regulation of speech. Importantly, the Supreme Court did concede that: "*Some forms of communication made possible by the giving and spending of money involve speech alone, some involve conduct primarily, and some involve a combination of the two.*"[12] I have italicized this sentence to emphasize its importance. This consequential passage in *Buckley* is rarely referenced. It has been lost in the many pages of that book-length, complex decision.

Even if the *O'Brien* standard had applied, *Buckley* said that the statute would still have failed the *O'Brien* requirement of being unrelated to suppressing communication, as the government had intended to restrict communication. The Court also rejected the characterization of the contribution and expenditure limitations as time, place, and manner restrictions because they directly restricted the quantity of political communication.[13]

Content neutral regulations on speech that regulate the time, place, or manner of speaking do not violate the weak libertarian paradigm. Speech regulations focused on suppressing a particular subject matter or viewpoint do violate the weak libertarian paradigm which focuses on content neutrality. Once the Court equated spending money on speech with speaking, any restrictions on spending money to speak became restrictions on speech. Consequently this logical jump of equating spending money to speak with speaking was crucial to the analysis in *Buckley*.

But this jump leads naturally from the weak libertarian paradigm which merely protects against *qualitative* restrictions on speech based on their content to its strong cousin that protects against *quantitative* restrictions on speech. Recall that the weak paradigm allows me to say whatever I want to say whereas the strong one proclaims that I can say whatever I want to say with whatever resources I have to say it. One can see the seeds of the problem in the weak libertarian paradigm. If I can truly say whatever I want to say, that might protect against both qualitative restrictions based on the content of my speech and quantitative restrictions based on how much I can speak. The *Buckley* Court specifically prohibited restricting the quantity of political speech.

The problem with this position that quantitative restrictions on speech are per se unconstitutional is not merely that it is counterintuitive but also that it is ahistorical as it is against well-established Supreme Court precedent. When people are competing for air time in the marketplace of ideas, as will naturally and inevitably occur, the weak libertarian paradigm—which was after all predicated on the Constitution's vision of participatory democracy—tried to structure an accommodative marketplace of ideas that endeavored to afford everyone some opportunity to speak. That is, after all, what time, place, and manner restrictions are all about. To accomplish this, quantitative restrictions on speech are logically inevitable.

If two groups want to parade down the same stretch of Fifth Avenue in New York City, they can't both do it at the same time. Moreover, one group couldn't parade constantly to the exclusion of the other. Time, place, and manner restrictions require accommodating both—actually fairly equally. In *Ward v. Rock against Racism*,[14] the Court upheld a New York City regulation on the volume of a concert in Central Park as a content neutral manner regulation. And this regulation was permitted not to accommodate other speech but to keep noise down for surrounding residents. So there wasn't a countervailing constitutional interest of accommodating other speech. We have already seen the case of *Red Lion v. FCC* which tried to achieve a similar objective in the broadcast media: it approved government's limiting the speech that broadcasters wanted to undertake in order to accommodate diverse viewpoints. The Court's enforcing antitrust legislation against the print media tried to accomplish similar objectives as did the sound truck case. We shall see these cases in chapter 9. In short, free-speech jurisprudence was geared to be accommodative of all *speakers* partly because that was the only way to accommodate all *views*. Achieving this accommodation inevitably involves limiting the quantity of speech of those who have the resources to monopolize the marketplace of ideas.

Moreover, giving some groups unlimited access to the marketplace of ideas will necessarily violate the weak libertarian paradigm because it will skew the marketplace of ideas based on content. All that I have to assume here is that the point of view of people who have greater resources is partly shaped by those resources and more importantly, that those marginalized or excluded from the marketplace of electoral ideas—the key marketplace in the democracy—have different points of view shaped by their economic interests. To deny this is essentially to deny most of modern economics which is based on the theory that people act significantly in their self-interest. If all this is true, then the weak libertarian paradigm and the strong one are not really cousins at all but fundamentally at odds with one another. All this begins with the doctrinal wrong turn of equating spending money to speak with speaking.

Since *Buckley*, the Court has reflexively equated spending money to express ideas with speaking or writing. Intuitively, one does not analogize spending money with speaking; the former is generally viewed as a form of conduct rather than as an expression of ideas. At most, as *Buckley* itself suggests, spending money to speak involves elements of speech and conduct. If this is the case, the *O'Brien* standard would apply.

Application of the *O'Brien* standard might involve distinguishing between asking for money, which along a continuum more closely engages speech rights, and giving or spending money for speech, which may more closely implicate property rights and more resembles action than speech. This might be particularly true when one is simply paying money for someone else's speech. I am not suggesting that no connection exists between spending money to speak and speaking. Obviously, much expression requires spending money.

But really the expenditure is not so much for the speech as for its *dissemination*. Usually, money does not impact the quality of the expression but only how broadly it circulates. The spread of an idea is a quotient of the quality or attractiveness of the idea (which are not the same thing, but we will put that to one side for now) and the dissemination capacity of the person who propagates the idea. It is widely assumed that these two variables are mutually sustaining. The quality of an idea and its widespread circulation are not completely unrelated but that relationship is limited at best. The ability to spread one's ideas is a blend of at least one's ability to generate quality ideas, one's ability to communicate them, one's wealth capacity to disseminate these ideas, and one's profession. Certain professions have greater access to the marketplace of ideas. Think of journalists, politicians, professors, professional athletes, movie stars, etc.

Which one of these variables matters most is controversial. Indeed, there is a prominent school of psychological thinking that maintains that the repetition of an idea is an extremely important element in persuasion.[15] If this is true, one can immediately grasp the power and unfairness of *Buckley* and its progeny. Extending equal constitutional protection to the content of the idea and to the quantitative means to expose it to a broad-based audience rearranged the entire election landscape. Indeed, if repetition counts so much, *Buckley* allows the strong libertarian paradigm of free speech to swallow the weak libertarian one. Although the strong libertarian paradigm does not allow suppressing ideas based on their content, it does safeguard the rights of one speaker to drown out the speech of all others, even if the speaker does this based on the content of the idea or even based on the viewpoint of the speaker. If I don't like your idea, I don't have to persuade others not to accept it. I can suppress it more successfully by simply repeating my point of view so many times that yours gets physically or psychologically drowned out. If this is true, the strong libertarian paradigm can gobble up its weaker ancestor, and the autonomy to speak in general, distributive or otherwise.

Limiting the quantity of speech in a content-neutral way is not the same as limiting speech because of its qualitative or content characteristics. The latter should be given much more intense constitutional scrutiny than the former. *O'Brien* would not allow government to cut funding as a pretext for censorship. Government may restrict expenditures involving candidates not to suppress speech but to ensure that communications by a particular candidate are not marginalized or drowned out. More importantly, protecting access for all voters and candidates in the metaphorical town meeting advances authentic participatory democracy.[16] These are content-neutral substantial state interests which easily meet the *O'Brien* standard. Indeed, they are compelling state interests more than adequate to hurdle even the highest level of constitutional scrutiny. So are such interests as federalism, constituent representation, equal say in elections, divided power, and avoiding corruption discussed toward the end of the previous chapter.

Thus, adopting an *O'Brien* approach to campaign finance jurisprudence may be helpful but it is not necessary to the argument. Even supposing, counterintuitively, that campaign finance should be treated as pure speech, the current legal regime constitutionally enables deep autonomy infringements against the vast majority of Americans. I will return to whether the *O'Brien* standard applies to campaign expenditures after I have more fully developed the principle of distributive autonomy.

B. Philosophical Expressions of the Tension between Liberty and Equality

Some theorists have overtly proffered a more inclusive approach to free speech jurisprudence using egalitarian values. It is worth exploring these at this juncture in part because they expose the theoretical problems with the Court's analysis that any restrictions on the quantity of speech violate the Constitution. The speech autonomy of many people—in the electoral context, the overwhelming majority of the population—will be decimated under this approach. As the analysis in chapter 6 suggests, the Framers of the Constitution and the ethos that pervaded the country in the immediate aftermath of the Constitution exalted the idea of an equal say and equal vote. While the idea was then only extended to a limited part of the population, it was gradually expanded to include more and more people until fairly recently when there have emerged many stark allegations about undermining the right to vote. For the Framers, the electoral process was key to representative democracy, which was at the core of their new Constitution.

Egalitarian perspectives on broad-based speech rights have been advanced by Jürgen Habermas, Bruce Ackerman, and Ronald Dworkin. Taking these three is not meant to be exhaustive of competing approaches. For example, I treat both John Rawls's and Michael Walzer's approaches to campaign finance and elections in chapters 8 and 9 respectively. I touch on Habermas, Ackerman, and Dworkin here simply to illustrate how sharply the *Buckley* campaign financing regime contrasts with three very different inclusive approaches, and also to begin to expose a range of moral problems with highly self-focused libertarian approaches to speech in the electoral process.

Jürgen Harbermas encapsulates free speech protection in the following three rules defining his "ideal speech situation":

(1) *Rule of Participation.*—Each person capable of engaging in communication and action is allowed to participate;

(2) *Rule of Equality of Communicative Opportunity.*—Each participant is given equal opportunity to communicate with respect to the following:
   a. Each is allowed to call into question any proposal;
   b. Each is allowed to introduce any proposal into the discourse;
   c. Each is allowed to express attitudes, sincere beliefs, wishes and needs;

(3) *Rule against Compulsion.*—No participant may be hindered by compulsion— whether arising from inside the discourse or outside of it—from making use of the rights secured under (1) and (2).[17]

Elaborating, the rule of participation requires that all persons and groups must be included in reaching a particular agreement. The rule of equal communicative opportunity requires that each individual or group enjoy the same quantity and quality of speech.[18] Habermas posits this theory as an aspirational ideal. I am not espousing Habermas's theory as an attractive, viable, or even practical conception of free speech jurisprudence. I use it simply to offer a foil. Even this small taste of Habermas's theory signals how far removed it is from the strong libertarian paradigm. In an ironic way, the radicalness of Habermas's theory exposes the radical and rigid nature of *Buckley*, both in its rejection of any quantitative restrictions on speech and of its embrace of the strong libertarian paradigm. These moves lie at the opposite end of the spectrum from Habermas's preoccupation with equal communicative opportunity.

Bruce Ackerman advances an egalitarian justification for the liberal state, which is premised on deliberative democracy. He begins by placing every individual in an equal position and then putting her in a dialogic conversation. Three principles govern the conversation. The first is the principle of *Rationality*. It requires:

Whenever anybody questions the legitimacy of another's power, the power holder must respond not by suppressing the questioner but by giving a reason that explains why he is more entitled to the resource than the questioner is.[19]

The second is the principle of *Consistency*. It requires: "The reason advanced by a power wielder on one occasion must not be inconsistent with the reasons he advances to justify his other claims to power."[20]

Ackerman's third principle requires *Neutrality*:

No reason is a good reason if it requires the power holder to assert: (a) that his conception of the good is better than that asserted by any of his fellow citizens, *or* (b) that, regardless of his conception of the good, he is intrinsically superior to one or more of his fellow citizens.[21]

Ackerman begins by postulating the equal worth of every individual. Equal worth requires that any departure from equality of resources be predicated on what Ackerman calls a "neutral justification."[22]

From this dialogue, citizens will fashion the kind of liberal state that they have in mind. Ackerman's theory is extremely democratic and egalitarian; he discusses democracy at length.[23] Not only does everyone begin equally, but also everyone participates equally. His principles are egalitarian for those who can participate in his dialogic process. His is a conversational theory of the state. Within the boundaries of the above principles or premises, conversation serves as a constructive process by which to build the state, and more important, the lives of people within the state. Indeed, conversation is more important than voting: "It is not the act of voting but the act of dialogue that legitimates the use of power in a liberal state. When an outcome is not justified through Neutral dialogue, a liberal voting procedure *cannot* remain indifferent about its adoption."[24] But the process itself for Ackerman is affirming in a way that is deeply egalitarian.[25] Conversation is also empowering as it enhances the autonomy of the individual participant in the conversation; Ackerman's rules strive to protect that autonomy.

His dialogic process is so egalitarian in providing equal opportunity to influence the marketplace of ideas that each speaker can determine the size and identity of his audience and the media by which he wishes to reach that audience.[26] To put the question almost tautologically, how could one erect a state in which only a few participate equally in the dialogue and others participate in the dialogue on a grossly unequal basis? The reason that Ackerman is so particular in maintaining the egalitarian nature of the dialogic process is because it goes to the legitimacy of the liberal state; of the distribution of resources, broadly understood; and of the life opportunities that result.

Voting rights and speech rights during elections are constitutive by nature and are fulcrums in Ackerman's dialogic process. Consequently, Ackerman's position would argue very strongly for a more egalitarian approach to free speech rights in the campaign financing cases. Indeed, in a book written about twenty-five years after *Social Justice in the Liberal State*, Ackerman proposes a robust campaign finance regulatory structure defined by anonymous contributions, expenditure restrictions, and stout public financing.[27]

In *Social Justice in the Liberal State*, Ackerman discusses free speech rights in the same chapter that he treats freedom from monopolization: "This freedom from censorship is but an aspect of an even broader right to free competition." He places freedom from censorship and from monopolization as the two crucial freedoms as the dialogic process proceeds. That process requires the leader of the liberal dialogue to block every "effort at self-aggrandizement" by the participants in the dialogue.[28]

Ronald Dworkin was a relentless critic of *Buckley*. He noted that all European countries limit campaign spending.[29] Dworkin repeatedly advocated rigorous campaign spending limits. These limits derived from his following two "essential conditions of fair political engagement, and hence of self-government, for all":[30]

First, each citizen must have a reasonably equal opportunity not only to hear the views of others as these are published or broadcast, but to command attention for his own views, either as a candidate for office or as a member of a politically active group committed to some program or conviction. No citizen is entitled to demand that others find his opinions persuasive or even worthy of attention. But each citizen is entitled to compete for that attention, and to have a chance at persuasion, on fair terms, a chance that is now denied almost everyone without great wealth or access to it. Second, the tone of public discourse must be appropriate to the deliberations of a partnership or joint venture rather than the selfish negotiations of commercial rivals or military enemies. This means that when citizens disagree they must present their arguments to one another with civility, attempting rationally to support policies they take to be in the common interest, not in manipulative, slanted, or mendacious pitches designed to win as much of the spoils of politics as possible by any means.[31]

Dworkin derives these conditions from the civic republican ideal. That ideal posits a deliberative rational discourse of the kind he describes in the above quote. This contrasts with rational interest group politics as a means of decision-making.

Resonating with a host of free speech theorists, Dworkin engages the historical mother lode for protecting free speech, viz. advancing democracy. For him, "self-government means more than equal suffrage and frequent elections. It entails a partnership of equals, reasoning together about the common good."[32] He discusses at some length the very large expenditures on political campaigns and their continual increases coincident with case law that increasingly enables this behavior. He admits that we can never fully achieve his ideal of a dialogic partnership among equals—no nation could. "But when politics are drenched in money, as our politics now are, then we risk not simply imperfection but hypocrisy."[33]

In *Justice for Hedgehogs*, Dworkin elaborates his ideas in important ways, but he appears to remain committed to the view that liberty hinges on the distribution of resources:

You cannot determine what liberty requires without also deciding what distribution of property and opportunity shows equal concern for all. The popular view that taxation invades liberty is false on this account provided that what government takes from you can be justified on moral grounds so that it does not take from you what you are entitled to retain. A theory of liberty is in that way embedded in a much more general political morality and draws from the other parts of that theory. The alleged conflict between liberty and equality disappears.[34]

The two key principles of equal concern and personal responsibility animate Dworkin's entire political structure.

First, [government] must show equal concern for the fate of every person over whom it claims dominion. Second, it must respect fully the responsibility and right of each person to decide for himself how to make something valuable of his life.[35]

The second principle supports the "rights of free speech and expression, conscience, political activity and religion."[36] That is how valuable and constitutive Dworkin views free speech. Elucidating his first principle of equal concern and respect, he analogizes to members of society treating each other as though they were members of a constitutional convention.[37] This is reminiscent of Alexander Meiklejohn's town meeting.

The critiques and perspectives on *Buckley* outlined above are all premised on egalitarian thinking. But *Buckley* is a libertarian decision; it explicitly rejects the egalitarian value. As chapters 1 and 2 suggest, the theory of distributive autonomy is confined to autonomy values. The principle's concern with the distribution of autonomy has quite a respectable pedigree starting with the founders of libertarian and autonomy theory, John Stuart Mill and Immanuel Kant.

Notes

1. *See* Lochner v. New York, 198 U.S. 45 (1905); *see also* Russell W. Galloway, Justice For All? The Rich and Poor in Supreme Court History, 1790-1990, 75-100 (Carolina Academic Press, 1991). Moreover, Herbert Hovenkamp has argued that the law of race relations in the late nineteenth and early twentieth centuries was partly driven by racist social scientific theories. Herbert Hovenkamp, *Social Science and Segregation Before Brown*, 1985 Duke L.J. 624.

2. Alexander Meiklejohn, Political Freedom: The Constitutional Powers of the People 25 (Harper & Brothers, 1960). The Civic Republican tradition also supports a broad-based participatory ideal. For example, Frank Michelman conceptualizes democracy as a dialogic process that is participatory and inclusive. Frank I. Michelman, *Conceptions of Democracy in American Constitutional Argument: Voting Rights*, 41 U. Fla. L. Rev. 443 (1989); Frank Michelman, *Law's Republic*, 97 Yale L.J. 1493 (1988). Leaning more heavily on the ideals of liberalism, Edwin Baker arrives at a similar dialogic, inclusive position. C. Edwin Baker, *Republican Liberalism: Liberal Rights and Republican Politics*, 41 Fla. L. Rev. 491 (1989). Both authors rely heavily on the ideal of one person, one vote as grounding their participatory ideal. For a discussion of the importance of political participation in the thought of Civic Republicans, see Miriam Galston, *Taking Aristotle Seriously: Republican-Oriented Legal Theory and the Moral Foundation of Deliberative Democracy*, 82 Cal. L. Rev. 329, 340-49 (1994).

3. *See generally* Cass R. Sunstein, Democracy and the Problem of Free Speech (Free Press, 1993); Mark A. Graber, Transforming Free Speech: The Ambiguous Legacy of Civil Libertarianism 226–34 (University of California Press, 1991) (arguing that a diverse group of lawyers, philosophers, and political scientists favor a broad-based, participatory ideal for free speech); Stanley Ingber, *The Marketplace of Ideas: A Legitimizing Myth*, 1984 Duke L.J. 8–12 (surveying various theorists who legitimate free speech protection in part on the basis that it extends to everyone in the society).

4. Nor would I discard the asymmetry that exists between the amount of regulation allowed over the economy and over speech. *See* Kathleen M. Sullivan, *Free Speech and UnFree Markets*, 42 U.C.L.A. L. Rev. 949 (1995).

5. John Attanasio, *The Constitutionality of Regulating Human Genetic Engineering: Where Procreative Liberty and Equal Opportunity Collide*, 53 U. Chi. L. Rev. 1274, 1310–14 (1986).

6. *See* John Attanasio, *Lawyer Advertising in England and the United States*, 32 Am. J. Comp. L. 493, 540–41 (1984) (cautioning against status quo bias in comparing "the dangers of changing and the dangers of not changing").

7. Stephen L. Carter, *Technology, Democracy and the Manipulation of Consent*, 93 YALE L. J. 581, 607 (1984) (book review).

8. 519 F.2d 821, 840 (1975).

9. 391 U.S. 367 (1968).

10. Buckley v. Valeo, 424 U.S. 1, 16–19 (1976).

11. *Buckley*, 519 F.2d at 840–41 (citing United States v. O'Brien, 391 U.S. 367, 376–77 (1968)).

12. *Buckley*, 424 U.S. at 16.

13. *Id.* at 15–19.

14. 491 U.S. 781 (1989).

15. Richard E. Petty & Duane T. Wegener, *The Elaboration Likelihood Model: Current Status and Controversies* 4, 61–63, in SHELLY CHAIKEN & YAACOV TROPE, DUAL-PROCESS THEORIES IN SOCIAL PSYCHOLOGY (Guilford Press, 1999); R.B. Zajonc, *Mere Exposure: A Gateway to the Subliminal*, 10 CURRENT DIRECTIONS PSYCHOLOGICAL SCI. 224–28 (Dec. 2001); ENCYCLOPAEDIA BRITANNICA https://www.britannica.com/topic/persuasion-psychology.

16. Edwin Baker argues that the institutional context in which speech occurs defines its regulatory regime. *See* C. Edwin Baker, *Campaign Expenditures and Free Speech*, 33 HARV. C.R.-C.L. L. REV. 1, (1998). "For example, legislative debates, committee hearings, judicial proceedings and agency proceedings are contexts where political speech occurs within legally structured or institutionally bound parts of government." *Id.* at 2. Elections also comprise an institutionally bound part of governance, and speech should be constrained to advance their fairness. *Id.* at 3.

In an illuminating article, Burt Neuborne adopts a more circumscribed version of this approach, specifically taking aim at the electoral process and comparing it to other contexts where the Court allows institutionally bounded speech. Burt Neuborne, *The Supreme Court and Free Speech: Love and a Question*, 42 ST. LOUIS U. L.J. 789, 801 (1998).

17. JÜRGEN HABERMAS, MORALBEWUSSTSEIN UND KOMMUNIKATIVES HANDELN 99 (1983), *quoted in* Lawrence Byard Solum, *Freedom of Communicative Action: A Theory of the First Amendment Freedom of Speech*, 83 Nw. U. L. REV. 54, 96 (1989).

18. *Id.* at 96–97. Solum describes Habermas's equal communicative opportunity thusly:

> Participants must have the same opportunities to initiate and perpetuate communication. They must have the same chance to employ each of the various classes of speech acts. Thus, each participant must have equal opportunity to assert or deny propositions about states of affairs (constative speech acts), to refer to the common social world so as to establish legitimate interpersonal relationships (regulative speech acts), to make public his private experiences (expressive speech acts), and to order the organizations of speech, through questioning, answering, and so forth (communicative speech acts). The discussion must provide adequate opportunity to subject every assertion, indeed every relevant speech act, to adequate scrutiny.

Id. at 97.

19. BRUCE A. ACKERMAN, SOCIAL JUSTICE IN THE LIBERAL STATE 4 (Yale University Press, 1980).

20. *Id.* at 7.

21. *Id.* at 11.

22. An important caveat in Ackerman's thought is that one must be able to actually engage in dialogue in some rudimentary way in order to have rights. For further discussion of the merits of this caveat, *see* Attanasio, *Liberty and Equal Opportunity Collide, supra* note 5, at 1333–34.

23. *See* Chapter 9 entitled "Liberal Democracy" in ACKERMAN, SOCIAL JUSTICE, *supra* note 19.

24. *Id.* at 297.

25. *Id.* at 342.

26. *Id.* at 174.

27. *See infra* note 44 and accompanying text, Chapter 9.

28. ACKERMAN, SOCIAL JUSTICE, *supra* note 19, at 178.

29. Ronald M. Dworkin, *The Curse of American Politics*, 43 N.Y. REV. BOOKS 19, 23 (Oct. 17, 1996).

30. *Id.* at 19.

31. *Id.*

32. RONALD DWORKIN, SOVEREIGN VIRTUE 385 (Harvard University Press, 2000). *See also* Ronald Dworkin, *The Decision That Threatens Democracy*, 57 N.Y. REV. BOOKS (May 13, 2010) http://www.nybooks.com/articles/2010/05/13/decision-threatens-democracy/ (critique of *Citizens United* and the campaign financing decisions generally).

33. DWORKIN, SOVEREIGN VIRTUE, *supra* note 32, at 385.

34. RONALD DWORKIN, JUSTICE FOR HEDGEHOGS 4 (Harvard University Press, 2011).

35. *Id.* at 17.

36. *Id.* at 349.

37. *Id.* at 79.

8 The Principle of Distributive Autonomy

A. Modern Libertarianism: The Influential Theory of Robert Nozick

Modern libertarians regard themselves as ideological opposites to egalitarians. As Chapter 2 suggests, the principle of distributive autonomy, which I shall presently proffer, is at strong odds with popular modern conceptions of libertarianism, but perhaps not so much with the original conception of John Stuart Mill. As it represents perhaps the preeminent example of modern individualistic libertarianism, I shall use Robert Nozick's widely acclaimed, and richly elaborated, conception of liberty as a starting point to demonstrate how my own theory of distributive autonomy differs.

In *Philosophical Explanations*, Nozick connects autonomy to the essence of being human. He analogizes the idea of autonomy to the powerful notion of free will.[1] I do not wish to overstate the value of autonomy. In my view, although autonomy may be a necessary feature of human dignity and flourishing, it is not sufficient.[2] For example, Augustine insists that the exercise of free will must be guided by the rudders of virtue and love.[3]

Perhaps to justify bestowing so much protection on autonomy, Nozick first defends why it is so valuable. He conceives of autonomy as a social condition that is instrumentally necessary for true free will to exist. At the same time, autonomy is also intrinsically valuable because when expressed as an individual state of being rather than a social condition, it becomes cognate to the concept of free will itself. Autonomy, or free will, has

Politics and Capital. John Attanasio.
© John Attanasio 2018. Published 2018 by Oxford University Press.

intrinsic value because it endows individuals with dignity. Without autonomy, human beings become trivialized playthings of external forces.[4]

In Nozick's view, only personal acts of free will can originate value. His concept of value is closely connected with pursuing knowledge and transcendent truth. The components of value are diversity and unity. A shorthand definition is "organic unity": "The more diverse the material that gets unified (to a certain degree), the greater the value."[5] Nonautonomous acts must slavishly accept or blindly replicate value that already exists.[6] Illuminating Nozick's notion of autonomy is his evocative metaphor of a "self-chooser."[7] Although Nozick acknowledges competing causes of behavior, his self-chooser plans behavior by weighing reasons.[8]

At bottom, the rational self-chooser represents an ideal to aspire to rather than a description of reality. For example, one's ability to choose is at least currently constrained by extant physical boundaries such as the speed of light. Even more basic, we are born irrespective of our will. Indeed, one who truly was a self-chooser might not choose to be like the rest of us at all. Thus, Nozick only talks about guaranteeing autonomy within the confines imposed by the milieu in which we live.[9]

The range of autonomy Nozick permits is quite broad with the limitation that one individual may not infringe on the autonomy of another.[10] Significantly, Nozick has a fairly expansive idea of what states or individuals can do to harm others that would violate their autonomy. To protect his notion of individual free will, then, Nozick conceptualizes people as being protected by relatively impervious side constraints, which cannot be infringed either by governmental or private actors.[11] He sees each individual as being clothed in what amounts to an armor of rights: "Individuals have rights, and there are things no person or group of persons may do to them (without violating their rights). So strong and far-reaching are these rights that they raise the question of what, if anything, the state . . . may do."[12]

As against the state, these side constraints completely prohibit countless regulations such as taxation of earnings, which Nozick views as akin to forced labor or slavery.[13] Consistent with his night watchman's theory of the state,[14] his robust notion of stringent "side constraints"—almost like a spherical shield ensconcing individuals—ranges far beyond physical harm.[15] But, as we shall see, Nozick has an important escape hatch—a robust theory of contract—one that even prevails over generations so that contracts entered into centuries ago protect the status quo today, even their deeply inegalitarian or morally repugnant aspects. This robust theory of contract derives from his robust theory of free will: one has the free will to enter into contracts, even a repugnant one such as slavery.

So Nozick's conception of liberty has deep inegalitarian qualities. Some of this is also justified by a deeply inegalitarian notion of human nature. When a person employs her free will to originate value, she both creates greater value for society and renders herself more valuable.[16] Nozick's schema ranks organisms by their relative degree of "organic unity"—that is, how many diverse elements they can discover and comprehend. He postulates a hierarchy, in declining order, from people to animals to plants to rocks. Individual persons themselves have different levels of value within the hierarchy. Moreover, in this scheme, the value of superintelligent, extraterrestrial beings would exceed the value of humans.[17]

In the logic of Nozick's conception, the superior positions of superior beings are merited. People who are harmoniously ordered will inspire everyone.[18] They also may discover transcendent truths that expand the horizons of humanity.[19] "There is reason to believe that the developed person will come to treasure all beings, wanting to aid them along a similar path of development to the extent this is possible."[20] Lesser individuals should not feel lower self-esteem because of the superiority of others, as they should not measure their self-worth by comparing themselves with more developed people.

Interfering with self-actualization and the resultant pursuit of transcendent truth is virtually never justified. This pursuit is perhaps the most personal and important endeavor in which individuals can engage. Nozick claims that limiting individual liberty with countervailing egalitarian claims[21] degrades persons by treating them as means rather than ends—in violation of the famous Categorical Imperative of Immanuel Kant.[22]

Nozick breezes past the inegalitarian implications of his virtually absolute protection of the inviolability of persons and their property.[23] His absolutist libertarian theory vindicates economic inequality. It also justifies inequality of moral worth that, in turn, justifies differential treatment. Although a superior person cannot demand superior rights, one must change one's behavior toward a superior person in order to be responsive to his identity.

> It may be that at a certain level of someone's development, others ought to treat him in certain ways, yet at a higher level of his development others no longer ought to do so, for their previous behavior no longer would be responsive to his (now) most valuable characteristics.[24]

Indeed, Nozick's theory can even be used to justify slavery, especially if such slavery would advance the search for the perfection of the few. Honestly recognizing the moral and logical vectors of his theory, Nozick admits that slavery would be permissible if it resulted from freely made transactions.[25] He tries to evade this problem by claiming that developed persons will not enslave others because they will treasure all people and all things.[26]

We are only equal to start with in the original position. Nozick justifies his inegalitarian theories by resting a lot of weight on his concept of freely entered into transactions. Nozick's concept of transactions is rather thin. At the beginning of *Anarchy, State and Utopia*, he defends the current distribution of property based on transactions entered into millennia ago. Ironically, he takes those transactions as a given without ever examining the autonomy or other characteristics of any of the countless numbers of transactions entered into across history.[27] The move of using transactions—freely entered into over millennia—to justify contemporary autonomy infringements simply does not appear to take autonomy seriously. Instead, it feels more like a post-hoc rationalization used to justify my infringing on your autonomy.

Nozick also places a lot of weight on the admittedly appealing notions of free will and transcendent being. In my view, although free will is an important value, it must be constrained by the countervailing claims of others to their own freedom and dignity. Although Nozick does argue that failure to conform one's behavior to goodness diminishes one's value,[28] he does not relate autonomy to pursuing goodness. Unlike the Kantian paradigm, which requires truly free acts to conform to the moral law,[29] Nozick focuses laser-like on protecting individual choice. He does predict that higher order beings will value others more, but this is conjecture informed by other aspects of his theory, which have frequently been proven counterfactual by historical realities. As an illuminating counterfactual, imagine for a moment the various geniuses across the expanse of history who were appalling villains.

Having lived in and dealt with Communist systems of government-enforced equality, I am drawn to some of Nozick's liberty sympathies. In a vain and oftentimes cynical quest to achieve equality, these systems inflicted horrific violations of autonomy on their citizens—more accurately called subjects. I say "cynical" because oftentimes the quest to achieve equality paralleled the Orwellian nightmare depicted in the notorious *Animal Farm*.[30]

Stringent theories of equality seek to level all inequalities, sometimes in naïvely idealistic ways, such as those of Karl Marx, and other times as a subterfuge to acquire brute power, such as Josef Stalin. Even when idealistically motivated, these utopian adventures have commonly resulted in tragedy. The pursuit of these strong theories of equality has also proven quite barbarous and has repeatedly resulted in greater inequality. Witness the Soviet Union or the French Revolution. Brutality might be expected in any leveling process involving human beings who are individuals and very different from one another in ability, character, work ethic, etc.

The leveling process habitually associated with strong equality theories makes me much more sympathetic to weak conceptions of equality focusing on some floor of baseline dignified existence for everyone including those who lack sufficient wherewithal with which to fashion some minimally decent life. But as Chapter 2 suggests, this is where equality and autonomy have common interests or overlaps. These types of concerns inform my principle of aggregate autonomy, which monitors lower-order rights. Similar worries animate the new principle of distributive autonomy.

B. The Contrasting Libertarian Ideas of Nozick and Mill

The libertarian theories of Nozick venture far beyond the libertarian roots developed by John Stuart Mill in his pathbreaking essay, *On Liberty*. A thrust of Mill's essay is a spirited defense of free speech. Central to this defense, Mill exalted diversity of ideas as necessary for rational debate. Rationally debating diverse ideas lead to the "'judgment of a completely informed mind.'"[31] This approach contrasted with relying on the vagaries of public opinion.

Consequently, Mill strongly defends—arguably fathers—what I have called the weak libertarian paradigm of free speech jurisprudence. However, his reasoning does not appear to protect the strong libertarian paradigm. As suggested throughout this work, particularly in Chapters 5, 6, and 9, the strong libertarian paradigm diminishes diversity of ideas.

Reinforcing a key concern about contrasting opinions, Mill says:

> The liberty of the individual must be thus far limited; he must not make himself a nuisance to other people. But if he refrains from molesting others in what concerns them, and merely acts according to his own inclination and judgment in things which concern himself, the same reasons which show that opinion should be free, prove also that he should be allowed, without molestation, to carry his opinions into practice at his own cost. That mankind are not infallible; that their truths, for the most part, are only half-truths; that unity of opinion, unless resulting from the fullest and freest comparison of opposite opinions, is not desirable, and diversity not an evil, but a good, until mankind are much more capable than at present of recognizing all sides of the truth, are principles applicable to men's modes of action, not less than to their opinions. As it is useful that while mankind are imperfect there should be different opinions. . . .[32]

The Millian conception of liberty does not envision unfettered individual choice. The essential Millian idea circumscribes individual freedom of action insofar as it harms others.[33] All therefore hangs on how one defines harm. In the foundational *On Liberty*, Mill equivocated as to what comprised harm:

> [T]wo maxims . . . together form the entire doctrine of this Essay. . . .
> The maxims are, first, that the individual is not accountable to society for his actions, in so far as these concern the interests of no person but himself. . . . Secondly, that for such actions as are prejudicial to the interests of others, the individual is accountable, and may be subjected either to social or to legal punishments, if society is of opinion that the one or the other is requisite for its protection.[34]

This last sentence would appear to give considerable authority to the legislature to define harm if it involves "actions which are prejudicial to the interests of others." This definition of harm itself would appear to be a much more far-reaching concept of harm than anything articulated by Nozick. This definition seems to comprehend one's actions that would violate—directly or indirectly—another's baseline autonomy.

Moreover, Mill places heavy weight on the authority of the legislature:

> The aim, therefore, of patriots, was to set limits to the power which the ruler should be suffered to exercise over the community; and this limitation was what they

meant by liberty. It was attempted in two ways. First, by obtaining recognition of certain immunities, called political liberties or rights, which it was to be regarded as a breach of duty in the ruler to infringe, and which, if he did infringe, specific resistance, or general rebellion, was held to be justifiable. A second, and generally a later expedient, was the establishment of constitutional checks; by which the consent of the community, or of a body of some sort, supposed to represent its interests, was made a necessary condition to some of the more important acts of the governing power.[35]

Hence Mill's concept of liberty appears to permit much greater regulation by legislation, or popular consent, than anything permitted by Nozick. It is difficult to invoke Mill to justify anything like the strong libertarian paradigm of free speech jurisprudence. Beyond a fairly narrow concept of political rights focused on something that loosely resembles the weak libertarian paradigm of free speech jurisprudence, Mill appears to have a vigorous concept of popular consent for elaborating what comprises harm. One can retreat to the simple equation that spending money on speech equals speech, but one suspects making this a core political right would have tested Mill's imagination. A committed utilitarian—one who believes in the greatest good for the greatest number—would certainly not approve a right to purchase legislation, let alone the legislature.

Mill was a complex figure who at once propounded theories of libertarianism and utilitarianism.[36] As Onora O'Neill points out, Mill's theory of liberty constrains choice with reason and character; to maximize the happiness of all and one's value to others, Mill requires that persons make choices not simply to suit their individualistic fancies, but that persons inform their choices with reason, individuality, and character. Choice by itself has no moral content for Mill.[37]

Of course, to suggest that Nozick's definition of liberty differs from that of one of the founders of libertarian thought does not mean Nozick is wrong, only that there are other coherent ways to think about liberty. Just because he was first is no reason to prefer Mill's account over Nozick's. But contrasting Mill's conception does at minimum free libertarianism of the monolithic conception in which it is currently confined.

C. Kantian Autonomy Theory and Libertarianism

If Mill can be counted as arguably the preeminent founder of libertarianism, then the primogeniture of this entire realm of philosophy must be Immanuel Kant. After all, Kant first elaborated autonomy theory, and his entire philosophical conception revolves around autonomy. Modern libertarianism has strayed quite far from its Kantian groundwork.

Perhaps the foremost modern scholar of Kantian theory is Onora O'Neill; interestingly, she must also be counted as a prominent critic of modern libertarian theory. O'Neill's powerful critiques demonstrate the virtually total disconnect between Kant's conception of autonomy and modern conceptions of libertarianism articulated by Nozick and others. For example, Kant's theory of autonomy is inextricably tied to morality.[38]

O'Neill characterizes Kant as representing "*principled autonomy*," contrasting him with contemporary theorists who focus on "*individual autonomy*."[39] Kant's starting points of reason and morality are central to his theory of practical reason. That theory comprehends two basic ideas. First, practical reasoning must be law-like in form. Second, the principles it articulates must be universalizable. O'Neill maintains that Rawls and Habermas closely connect their concept of public reasoning to democracy, "in particular of participatory or deliberative democracy, but they do not attempt any wider vindication of reason."[40] Kant's theory of reasoning is fundamentally practical in being applicable to behavior in everyday life. Second, the norms adduced "must be followable by others: they must be norms that can be used by a *plurality* of agents."[41] Moreover, the reasoning itself is autonomous so that neither reason nor the individual exercising it is bound by any other assumptions or values.

Kant fashions a general ethical system.[42] His practical reasoning formulates principles whose applicability aims for universality in the strict sense of the word. He specifically states:

> But it is requisite to reason's lawgiving that it should need to presuppose only *itself*, because a rule is objectively and universally valid only when it holds without the contingent, subjective conditions that distinguish one rational being from another.[43]

The quest for universality extends the reach of Kant's practical reason far beyond democratic regimes. Practical reason also seeks principles that are lawful. "Lawlessness undermines reasoning. It undercuts the very possibility of offering others reasons for believing or for acting."[44]

Practical reason also requires principles that are universal in scope: only principles that can be grasped by reason alone, acting without preconceived assumptions, are principles of practical reason. These same two conditions of lawfulness in form and universality in scope are requirements of autonomous acts. Kant analogizes his concept of autonomy to the notion of self-legislation, that is, the ability to govern one's own actions. This governance must be based on practical reasoning. Otherwise, the self is governed by external forces rather than by practical reasoning acting autonomously.[45] In order to exercise its powers, reason requires freedom. Agreements on principles, thoughts, or actions secured by coercion are not agreements at all.[46] Thus, autonomy is the necessary partner of practical reason.

As O'Neill points out, however, the idea of "'self'" in "'self-legislation' is *reflexive rather than individualistic*; it applies to certain justifications of principles rather than to certain agents or 'legislators.'" It is also impersonal in the sense that the principles chosen must be universally applicable rather than individualistic.[47] At the end of the day,

Kantian autonomy, which he views as cognate to self-legislation, really amounts to law-giving by pure practical reason rather than by an individual.

These steps build Kant's famous Categorical Imperative. Kant considers autonomy, universality, and the Categorical Imperative as cognate ideas, indeed as alternative forms of one another.[48] The Categorical Imperative is an attempt at universalizability. For O'Neill, the strictest form of Kant's Categorical Imperative is: "'[A]ct only on that principle through which you can at the same time will that it be a universal law.'"[49]

This formulation of the Categorical Imperative illustrates the stringency of the universalizability condition. Any principle that makes people victims will not achieve universal acceptance as naturally it will be rejected by at least those whom it treats as victims. So universalizability protects against infringements on broad-based agency.[50] For example, it will be difficult to gain universal acceptance of laws that permit false promising,[51] violence, deception,[52] or monopolizing resources.[53] Ergo, it is difficult to imagine how to articulate the principles enunciated in the *Buckley* line of cases in universalizable terms.

Devolving from Kant's Categorical Imperative is his Universal Principle of Justice, which applies the Categorical Imperative in the public domain. The principle contains three elements of what Kant refers to as republican justice. Those are freedom, dependence on legislation, and equality within the law. Freedom is required to obtain consent and engage in dissent. Second, there must be subordination to law; if anyone is outside law, freedom is broadly undercut. Third, there must be legal equality of citizens; otherwise freedom would be impaired as would the possibility of authentic consent or dissent.[54] Kant thinks that nature imposes scarcity in the world having given just enough so that people may coexist together.[55] Because we are not sufficiently altruistic, there must be some principles that allow people to coexist on the planet.[56]

Equality in Kant's Universal Principles of Justice focuses on legal equality. In discussing legal equality, Kant specifically alludes to "legislation." The idea of legislation is central to Kant's thinking; he uses the word repeatedly in the *Critique of Practical Reason*. Individuals must be subordinate to laws rather than some individuals being subordinate to others, which curtails freedom. Subordination to others rather than to law would also destroy consent and dissent.[57] Everyone is subordinate to laws, which guarantees legal equality. *Societies that fail to secure such equality under law represent feudal or caste societies.*[58] Keep in mind that the foregoing is a core claim of the consensus founder of autonomy theory. It is difficult to square Nozick's ideas—or modern campaign finance jurisprudence—with these claims.

The Universal Principle of Justice also "demands both the same freedom of choice and the same basic restrictions for all agents."[59] Consequently, they impose very deep constraints forbidding all actions—including laws—that maximize one's individual autonomy at the expense of the autonomy of others. As introduced in Chapter 2, this idea of the reciprocity of any coherent theory of autonomy figures prominently in the principle of distributive autonomy. Reciprocity is also the key to the liberty/order paradox.

D. The Liberty/Order Paradox: The Weakness of Strong Libertarian Theories

Law by its nature imposes certain restraints on individual liberty. Perhaps more than some authors,[60] I differentiate the concepts of liberty and autonomy. Distinguishing between liberty and autonomy is not traditional, possibly even heretical. From this point forward, I use the term "liberty" to describe a condition in which society can impose no immediate restrictions on individual choice to pursue preferred aims. Although this is an extreme version of liberty, it can be defended on the grounds that, in an ideal world, this is what committed libertarians would want. Even in the world as it exists, committed modern libertarians try to get as close as possible to this state of being.

Although I can imagine coherent but implausible defenses for this extreme definition of liberty, I do not share them. Instead, I use this version of liberty simply for illustrative purposes. I further depart from traditional libertarian theory by defining liberty as an instrumental value that, together with order, seeks to foster the intrinsic value of autonomy.[61]

I define autonomy more traditionally as that intrinsically valuable condition that involves the right to fashion one's own life plan within the constraints of one's own personal abilities and circumstances. Notice that this definition lacks the reciprocal quality of distributive autonomy. There is a very cogent position that the notion of some egalitarian distribution of autonomy is inherent in this value. Kant essentially had this view. I use the term "distributive autonomy" in part because notions of the distribution of autonomy are so foreign to modern libertarian theory. It also aptly describes the content of the value that I am describing.

My definition of liberty is unorthodox. Mill's foundational idea allows circumscribing freedom of action insofar as it harms others. In contrast, my definition of liberty creates the opportunity to explore the extent to which totally unfettered individual choice can actually harm others and circumscribe their autonomy. This unbounded concept of liberty advances autonomy in important ways yet constricts it in others. This radical definition of liberty affords the opportunity to explore how liberty sometimes does not advance autonomy, using the lens of the liberty/order tension.

Let us begin. In accepting a need for criminal law, even the most committed libertarian universally permits grave governmental infringements on individual liberty involving fines, imprisonment, and even capital punishment. So, even the most committed libertarian embraces the night watchman vision of government. Nozick's conception of the minimal state embraces the "night-watchman state of classical liberal theory, limited to the functions of protecting all its citizens against violence, theft, and fraud, and to the enforcement of contracts."[62] There are two plausible rationales for the night watchman vision of government. A fairly common justification is averting the deep liberty infringements caused by personal injury or property loss.

A second more complex rationale for the night watchman theory—not necessarily inconsistent with the first—is the paradox that autonomy is actually advanced by some imposition of order. I call this paradox the liberty/order tension. This problem is well-stated in a famous old free speech case styled *Cox v. New Hampshire*.[63] The case explores the simple mechanism of a traffic light, or stoplight. Clearly the stoplight constrains the unfettered liberty of a vehicle or a pedestrian to cross the street. Obviously, if everyone tries to cross a busy intersection at the same time, only the most powerful will cross—measured by size of vehicle or some other way. In that circumstance, we can expect even more serious infringements on autonomy in the way of accidents, which cause loss of limbs, even death. Thus, the liberty/order continuum requires that to maximize—and even to create—the conditions for personal autonomy, liberty must paradoxically be somewhat constrained. Even more paradoxical, frequently the *government* imposes some order (for example, in the way of a simple traffic light) on liberty to dramatically increase autonomy.

The criminal law imposes liberty constraints ex post, that is, for acts already perpetrated. In contrast, the traffic light constricts liberty ex ante on the theory that certain regulatory conditions are necessary to realize meaningful, let alone attractive, levels of autonomy. Put more bluntly, the traffic light infringes on some individuals' immediate freedom of action or liberty to generate much more autonomy for a broad swath, arguably all, of the population.

I equivocate here because one can argue that the autonomy of larger, more powerful cars is diminished rather than enhanced by the traffic light. As they are larger and more powerful, they might be able to pass through the busy intersection more frequently without a traffic light than with one. I admit that the traffic light may disadvantage or diminish the autonomy of the more powerful. However, the opposite could easily be true. After all, even large cars will sometimes be hit in the continual melee that will ensue at an unregulated intersection. Although larger cars will have an easier time getting through the intersection, the probability of injury to those cars and its passengers increases. So does the number of tense close calls. Consequently the traffic light probably will enhance the long-run autonomy of all—even the most powerful.

One can imagine less ambitious rationales justifying the traffic light. Specifically, one can posit that the traffic light is necessary to prevent the deep and long-lasting autonomy infringements caused by personal injury. Arguably, this rationale does not require a traffic light. Instead, it only requires a rule mandating that at intersections, smaller vehicles must give way to larger ones, and pedestrians must give way to vehicles. Such a rule would allow individuals to exercise the power of the liberty afforded them by larger vehicles. (A larger vehicle can be taken as a metaphor for greater resources.)

Of course, far from escaping the liberty/order tension, the larger car rule, with the pedestrian corollary, reinforces its inevitability. To the extent that this or any other alternative rule emerges, a measure of order frequently would have been imposed to paradoxically increase autonomy: more vehicles—and perhaps the occasional pedestrian—would now be able to safely pass through the intersection under the larger car rule than could pass with no rule at all.

Indeed, in some ways, the larger car rule restricts the liberty of the drivers of larger cars less than the traffic light. One could lodge efficiency objections against the proffered alternative rule, arguing that the traffic light is more efficient in that it would let more cars pass through in the aggregate. However, we normally do not count efficiency rationales as justifying autonomy infringements on freedom of movement. Freedom of movement is generally considered a first-order autonomy right whereas efficiency advances lower-order utilitarian rights or interests.[64] Constitutional jurisprudence generally does not count efficiency reasons as a sufficient reason to abridge first-order rights.

If efficiency fails, traffic lights could be defended on more typical autonomy rationales: (1) to avoid the deeper autonomy infringement of personal injury, or (2) to protect the autonomy of as many people as possible to traverse the intersection. Let us call both of these rationales equally plausible autonomy accounts of why we might permit traffic lights. The traffic light is also substantially egalitarian—certainly much more than the larger car rule. The traffic light equitably distributes both autonomy enhancements and infringements. If designed correctly, the traffic light seeks to maximize the traffic flow of all, not of any specific car or set of cars. It treats all cars the same regardless of whether they are large or small, luxurious, or jalopies.

However, the traffic light example in *Cox v. New Hampshire* does not legitimate the result in that case.[65] After all, *Cox* does not involve traffic lights, but restrictions on speech. The threat of personal injury is not nearly as large as it is in the stoplight situation. Moreover, *Cox* recognized the need for time, place, and manner restrictions on the liberty to speak in long-standing free speech zones—public parks, streets, and sidewalks.

Even assuming that the systemic restrictions on freedom of movement imposed by the traffic light really are de minimis, time, place, and manner restrictions on speech are not. They delay or prevent a person from expressing herself wherever, whenever, or however she chooses on public property. This is a significant infringement on the core autonomy interest in free speech. In *Cox* and other cases, the Supreme Court allows these substantial autonomy infringements. Although the Court forbids government from censoring the content of speech, it allows government to regulate when, where, and how the speech can occur.

One can contend that today these time, place, and manner constraints are de minimis in a world where people have far greater access to the marketplace of ideas through the ability to speak on the Internet and various social media. But there are several problems with this Internet mitigation argument. First, the Supreme Court considerably expanded government's ability to impose time, place, and manner restrictions during the 1980s[66]—well before the widespread use of the Internet. Moreover, some posit that the Internet will exacerbate communication disparities as money can buy bytes on social media and other virtual venues to replace, for example, the importance of grassroots workers in elections.[67] Still, even today, when people get angry and really serious about protests, they still "take to the streets."

Some radical libertarians may regard time, place, and manner restrictions as abridgments of liberty. But just as traffic lights increase autonomy of movement, reasonable time, place, and manner restraints increase the autonomy to speak for all or certainly for the overwhelming majority of people.

Thus, the liberty/order paradox demonstrates that theories of unfettered choice do not advance liberty but constrict it. One could speculate that the most powerful will at least in the short run benefit by regimes governed by unfettered choice, but in the longer run even the more powerful will not. Paradoxically, then, some imposition of order actually maximizes not only the amount of liberty that the overall society enjoys, but also the liberty of virtually everyone in the society.

The liberty/order tension demonstrates the necessity for reciprocity. Nozick recognizes the need for some reciprocity in his idea of protective associations. He assumes that the reciprocity entailed in forming a protective association will advantage all and hence people will voluntarily enter into such associations. That is quite a logical leap. Rather than form protective associations, groups in a Hobbesian state of nature might well form "war associations" on the theory that they perceive themselves able to attack and conquer the weak and less powerful. Of course, far from advancing liberty, such war associations would advance the subjugation of the less strong.

Nozick could defend against the war association problem by pointing out that aggressive war associations would violate the liberty of those whom they attacked. Still, those who form such associations might not care. They could also call themselves protective associations when they were in actuality war associations and attack others on what they claim are defensive grounds—a claim that has been reiterated time and again throughout history. They could even claim—sincerely or insincerely—that they were invading to impose some order on the chaos in a particular area so as to increase liberty or that they were invading an authoritarian state in order to increase liberty.

Once we reduce the concept of the state to merely a protective association, the possibilities for rationalization are far-reaching. After all, part of the inherent nature of a protective association is violence and the threat of violence. To be effective, protective associations have to be good at violence. In contrast, the modern state is a profound mixture of violence and beneficence.

For those who dismiss the account of the war association, consider that a protective association is a state formed solely to protect people against immediate incursions of their persons or property. Hence the main instrument of such a state would be violence. A protective association forged around preventing violence could easily mutate into inflicting it. This would be particularly true if its members lacked resources but were good at violence. Think of ancient Sparta.

Once a protective association is formed, it also poses the danger of smaller protective associations forming within the larger one. This danger is particularly pronounced in systems that feature federalism and free enterprise. The worry is not just idle theorizing. In the context of the United States, mini protective associations—the southern states— fought a civil war. As far as free enterprise goes, the Mafia is a well-known protective association based on a metastasized version of free enterprise. Predictably, such organizations will burgeon in countries where wealth is highly unequal. Persons with immense amounts of wealth will feel the necessity to protect it from those who lack wealth, and even from each other. They could even co-op parts of government.

Nozick does not appear to give any satisfying account of how to guard against such mini protective associations. Moreover, his schema will likely result in wealth becoming highly unequal as he protects unequal distribution of wealth forged from the beginnings of time.

The Framers of the American Constitution had a much better—and more successful—account of the state. The Preamble to their/our Constitution reads in pertinent part "to form a more perfect union, establish justice, insure domestic tranquility, provide for the common defense, promote the general welfare, and secure the blessings of liberty to ourselves and our posterity." They certainly ensured domestic tranquility and provided for a common defense but did this in the context of establishing justice. Many had studied the great philosophers and had rich understandings of justice. More importantly, they went far beyond a protective association. They not only provided for the common defense and domestic tranquility but they also wished to promote the general welfare and secure not just liberty but the *blessings* of liberty. Perhaps they did this because they recognized that protective associations can easily degenerate into aggressive war associations. But they seem to have had a richer account of the state in mind. The powers that the Constitution itself bestows on the government reinforces the notion that the Framers had a more productive idea of the state than Nozick.

So like the Framers, once people recognize the advantages of reciprocity, why wouldn't they enter into associations more robust than protective associations? For example, why wouldn't they enter into a kind of insurance arrangement in which each person would commit to protect the other against certain kinds of catastrophic losses: Of expression? Of privacy? Of torture? Of health? Of education? Of employment? Of food? Of shelter?

I have purposely chosen a broad array of arrangements—some of which would, in some conceptions, entail first-order rights and others of which would not. Modern constitutions usually articulate more robust forms of protective associations installing many more rights than the minimalist state. Such more extensive constitutional arrangements are virtually universal.

Nozick's protective association is only one logical possibility. It does admit to the usefulness, if not necessity, of a minimum amount of reciprocity. But that minimum amount will still give tremendous advantages to the strongest, smartest, fairest, luckiest, most successful in the society. I am not suggesting that societies should ignore these traits; nor should they ignore hard work. But the minimalist protective association again seems to advance, indeed *maximize* the positions of the top end of the society, while overlooking the autonomy of many, possibly most, others. When viewed against the backdrop of the protective association, Nozick's stringent side constraints position seems more of a rationalization of the positions of the strong rather than a broad-ranging justification for autonomy.

What about the side constraints of the beggar who can't eat? Does that person really have any authentic side constraints at all? Libertarians and non-libertarians alike would readily agree that the beggar has side constraints against being personally assaulted by others. But what good does that do for the beggar if she is likely to die of starvation within a month anyway? One can say that no one is responsible for the beggar's position, or that to the extent that anyone is, it would be the beggar herself. But at that point the defender of libertarianism must be prepared to make harsh judgments about individual culpability for the beggar's situation. Actually, severely limited information on the situations of millions of people will force the committed libertarian to make harsh (perhaps smug, self-serving) assumptions about how the beggar got to be the beggar.

To his credit, Nozick is not completely unresponsive to the moral nature of the demand for reciprocity. He mandates redistributive taxation to provide for the needy joining the protective association: "Under this plan all people, or some (for example, those in need), are given tax-funded vouchers that can be used only for their purchase of a protection policy from the ultraminimal state."[68] Subsidizing membership in the protective association concedes some concern for reciprocal autonomy. Nozick is even-handed and consistent in this way: he guarantees to the poor the same level of autonomy that he guarantees to everyone else, that is, the minimalist state. But this accommodation protects minimal autonomy to join the protective association. It ignores any reciprocal autonomy, or authentic autonomy, for the vagaries of life throughout the many generations after the protective association is first formed. Thus, Nozick's redistributive taxation to join the protective association seems more like an inadequate rationale for the minimalist state rather than part of a larger architectural blueprint for realizing authentic autonomy.

Distributive autonomy might have been termed the "reciprocal autonomy." However, this alternative conception could be both too rigid and too weak. Reciprocal autonomy could be considered too rigid, if it is thought to impose a duty to reciprocate any action by another that advances one's autonomy. Obviously, this would be an untenable situation and a society that few of us would want to inhabit. At the other end of the spectrum, the notion of reciprocal autonomy could convey the idea of loose reciprocity with comparative inattention to the distribution of autonomy. The idea of reciprocity that even a committed libertarian like Nozick accepts leads naturally into a discussion of egalitarian notions.

E. The Rawlsian Quest to Reconcile Liberty and Equality

For many years, I have been at once troubled and fascinated by the problem of inequality—the problem of why some people have, while others have not. By have not, I do not just mean material goods such as wealth but all resources, including talents, even luck. Although one can posit eschatological explanations for this phenomenon, these are far beyond my range of expertise.

For whatever reason, inequality has been part of the human condition—or crucible. This is a descriptive rather than a normative statement; it is simply describing the world as it is rather than seeking to justify or change this reality. Some political theorists have sought to develop philosophical principles to justify these inequalities whereas others have invoked different philosophical principles to try to justify altering or mitigating these inequalities.

John Rawls made what was perhaps the most celebrated attempt in the twentieth century to reconcile liberty and equality. Like Kant, and less systematically Mill, Rawls explores more robust theories of reciprocity that would appear to take into consideration the autonomy interests of a much larger swath of society. Rawls's approach to reciprocity is deeply egalitarian. In some ways, Rawls's influence derives from the descriptive character of his project as much as the normative one. That is, his ideas resonate with people because they didn't only prescribe part of what an attractive set of moral sensibilities ought to be, but they also describe the kind of society that many of his contemporaries sought to build.

Rawls views liberty reciprocally. Rawls begins his magnum opus, *A Theory of Justice*, in a quasi state of nature: He places people behind his famous, if controversial, "veil of ignorance." Those entering into his social contract are shielded from knowledge of their positions in the world by this veil,[69] and they are asked to choose principles of justice for themselves and others under the circumstances.[70]

In *Political Liberalism*, Rawls employs a deliberative process to derive his principles of justice.[71] His notion of deliberative democracy permits a wide-ranging breadth of discourse as part of public reasoning.[72] In *Political Liberalism*, public reasons offered in a deliberative process play the pivotal role in erecting and legitimating the entire political structure. The idea of legitimacy is very important in *Political Liberalism*. It is bound up with the obligation to obey the law, even laws with which one disagrees.[73] Related to the obligation to obey the law is the notion of preserving societal stability.[74]

Rawls arrives at the following principles of justice. Although the statement of these principles is similar in both books, I will use the more recent version in *Political Liberalism*:

a. Each person has an equal right to a fully adequate scheme of equal basic liberties which is compatible with a similar scheme of liberties for all.
b. Social and economic inequalities are to satisfy two conditions. First, they must be attached to offices and positions open to all under conditions of fair equality of opportunity; and second, they must be to the greatest benefit of the least advantaged members of society.[75]

The first principle, which Rawls calls "the principle of equal liberty," includes freedom of speech.[76] The principles are lexically ordered so that none of the equal opportunity or resource concerns of the second principle justify abridging the first principle.[77]

The principle that Rawls is perhaps best known for is called the difference principle. It is a third-order right stated in part (b) of the second principle. It commands that social and economic inequalities be arranged "to the greatest benefit of the least advantaged."[78] Perhaps, Rawls's most common measure of the least advantaged is lack of wealth. Although he does not precisely define the least advantaged, Rawls suggests that they may be those with one-half of the median income, or those whose average income equals that of certain social classes such as unskilled laborers.[79]

Whether they are behind the veil of ignorance or engage in a deliberative process, Rawls posits that people would choose something like the three principles listed above, including the difference principle, to shield themselves against unknown, but potential, conditions of disadvantage in life.[80]

In prior works,[81] I proffered an alternative to the difference principle called the weak principle of aggregate autonomy. It posits: *act to protect the individual from severe constrictions of life plans whenever such protection requires de minimis wealth-related interference with one's own life plans.* I borrow the Rawlsian strategy of lexically prioritized principles. The weak principle of aggregate autonomy focuses on the allocation of economic resources. It can also apply to avoiding or compensating certain kinds of personal injury. Whether the principle is formulated in its weak version or in more vigorous terms, redressing aggregate autonomy concerns neither justifies nor tolerates invasions of higher order rights, such as political and civil rights. It partly aims to give some basic safety net of economic claims to those who are resource disadvantaged over long periods of life or because of mishaps that damage their lives.

As currently formulated, aggregate autonomy does not require anything like equality of resources. Neither, of course, does the difference principle. The weak principle of aggregate autonomy simply requires some attention to a minimal level of autonomy for as many persons as possible. The only liberty intrusion that the weak principle permits is a de minimis wealth incursion. Wealth infringements constitute slight liberty infringements, particularly if they involve small amounts of money, not taken outright, but reallocated through a systematic, participatory form of taxation or regulatory structure such as an insurance plan.

I will further explore this principle in future work. The principle of aggregate autonomy is somewhat hydraulic: it can be stated in weaker and stronger language fairly easily. That is, it could readily be recast up to guard against less severe incursions on the life plans of others, or it could accept greater wealth incursions on one's own life plans. To justify any ratcheting up, we would have to explore what counts as a severe incursion on liberty. Extreme poverty would seem to count, but, for example, how extreme does the poverty have to be before it rises to a severe incursion?

I also put to one side whether someone facing imminent starvation, or other similar catastrophic deprivations, violates first-order rights, which would engage the principle of distributive autonomy. Earlier, I hinted that this may be the case. To some extent, the answers to these questions are imponderables. But they might prove painfully obvious to someone who is gradually or imminently starving, or cannot receive decent medical care for her child.

Rather than use the veil of ignorance or a deliberative process as a justification, the principle of aggregate autonomy uses the value of autonomy or free will itself. It accepts the idea that autonomy is inherently valuable in undergirding free will and human flourishing. Once that is the case, the theory posits that the autonomy of all is valuable.

Consequently, any moral theory that accepts autonomy as valuable has to consider and respect the autonomy of all, and to provide at least some minimal level of autonomy for as many people in the society as possible. This alternative justification to Rawls's veil of ignorance renders the principle of aggregate autonomy difficult for libertarians to jettison or ignore: rather than trump or compromise autonomy with competing equality claims, the principle advances autonomy.

Modern individualistic libertarians are compelled to grapple with aggregate autonomy precisely because aggregate autonomy plays with autonomy marbles: it essentially uses the cherished nature of autonomy itself to justify some reciprocal notions in seeking to achieve some minimal floor in each individual's ability to exercise autonomy. Specifically, it uses the intrinsic and instrumental value of autonomy to impose obligations to recognize the interconnectedness of the autonomy of everyone. As outlined earlier, autonomy is intrinsically valuable as part of the essence of being human and instrumentally valuable as a precondition to choosing other elements of what the ancient philosophers called the good life. Once one considers autonomy centrally valuable, it is difficult in moral theory to justify acts that markedly deprive others of autonomy.

Once one posits autonomy as a core, but certainly not exclusive, value in moral theory, one necessarily accepts obligations to advance the autonomy of others, or at minimum not to engage in behavior that diminishes the autonomy of others. Otherwise, theories of unfettered liberty quickly reduce to perverse "moral" theories attempting to justify unfettered selfishness. Essentially, absolute liberty allows me to use my free will to bend, constrict, or usurp yours as long as I did not actively directly harm you or your property, for example by punching you in the nose.

F. Campaign Finance: Illuminating the Tension between Liberty and Equality

In this work, we are not talking about lower-order rights but the first-order right of speech. I agree with Rawls that speech rights merit far greater protection than property rights.[82] The theory of aggregate autonomy leans heavily on differentiating between economic rights and higher-order rights, including political rights. It posits that economic rights are less fundamental or central to human autonomy than higher-order rights. Consequently, economic rights are susceptible of greater incursion. As outlined in Chapters 3 and 4, this distinction is well-accepted in American constitutional law. For example, the Supreme Court affords free speech rights the highest level of constitutional protection.[83] In contrast, the *Carolene Products* settlement affords far less constitutional protection for economic rights.[84]

The durability of these aspects of the *Carolene Products* settlement intuitively suggests that the Court may have been on to something. In political theory and in legal systems spanning many parts of the world, there is overwhelming endorsement of less protection for economic rights than political rights. This long-standing and broad-based view is evidence supporting these different levels of protection. It does not, however, supply reasons for this lesser protection.

In *A Theory of Justice*, Rawls offers two basic reasons for placing equal liberty lexically ordered ahead of the principle of equal opportunity and the difference principle. The first is a kind of autonomy to advance participatory democracy:

> The basic structure is then to secure the free internal life of the various communities of interests in which persons and groups seek to achieve, in forms of social union consistent with equal liberty, the ends and excellences to which they are drawn. People want to exercise control over the laws and rules that govern their Association, either by directly taking part themselves in its affairs or indirectly through representatives with whom they are affiliated by ties of culture and social situation.[85]

The second reason to rank the principle of equal liberty hierarchically first involves promoting equal citizenship and avoiding envy:

> In a well-ordered society then self-respect is secured by the public affirmation of the status of equal citizenship for all; the distribution of all material means is left to take care of itself in accordance with pure procedural justice regulated by just background institutions which narrow the range of inequalities so that excusable envy does not arise.[86]

Political participation occupies a special place in Rawls's panoply of first-order rights. Jeremy Waldron has stated that, for Rawls, political participation is not just one among many basic liberties. Instead, it is the " ' "right of rights". ' " In this sense, the "right to participate . . . is the direct descendant, in political practice, of the principle of popular sovereignty underlying the whole contractarian approach in political philosophy."[87]

Once one differentiates first-order rights and accepts that first-order rights lexically trump lower-order rights, the problem of allocating those rights becomes far more sensitive. Assuming first-order rights are more valuable, any attempt to equalize first-order rights inherently entails a more fundamental invasion of individual autonomy, and such attempts necessarily constrict the most fundamental and personal human behaviors. The principle of aggregate autonomy is cabined in to lower-order rights.[88] It does not permit differences in economic circumstances to justify invading higher-order rights, such as freedom of speech, freedom of religion, or the right against self-incrimination, the privacy of one's home, disallowing imprisonment without due process, equal opportunity in voting, education, and employment—to give a few examples. Of course, listing these rights only begs further questions of what the contents of each of these higher-order rights should be. As the main discussion of this book involves freedom of speech, I will limit the discussion to what is the appropriate level of protection for free speech rights.

Rawls criticizes the campaign finance cases[89] as violating his principle of equal liberty.[90] Even though he focuses much of his discussion of the principle of equal liberty on free speech rights, Rawls does not elaborate what equal liberty entails.

As articulated in *Political Liberalism*, Rawls's principle of equal liberty declares: "Each person has an equal right to a fully adequate scheme of equal basic liberties which is compatible with a similar scheme of liberties for all."[91] This iteration of his first principle of justice is somewhat different from the one Rawls articulated twenty years earlier in his celebrated *A Theory of Justice*. Rawls's formulation of his first principle in *A Theory of Justice* required: "Each person is to have an equal right to the most extensive total system of equal basic liberties compatible with a similar system of liberty for all."[92]

Rawls says that this statement was not intended to convey the notion that he was maximizing first-order liberties. Rawls's reluctance to maximize liberties stems in part from uncertainty as to what would be maximized, the capacity for a sense of justice or the capacity for a conception of the good. The principle of equal liberty is meant to guarantee both.[93] Although Rawls's theory of equal liberty is intended to govern first-order rights, he does not detail how to equalize first-order rights. In *Theory*, he says that personal liberty may be restricted only in two cases: "(a) a less extensive liberty must strengthen the total system of liberty shared by all; [or] (b) a less than equal liberty must be acceptable to those with the lesser liberty."[94]

Rawls's reticence about elaborating his principle of equal liberty in greater detail may have stemmed from the leveling effect that strong egalitarian theories can—perhaps invariably—have. Nevertheless, Rawls's principle of equal liberty supplies formidable support for a free speech jurisprudence that takes autonomy seriously. Equal liberty is central to the formation or building of " 'moral powers.' "[95] A person must be able to participate fully in the formulation of public affairs and also in the pursuit and formation of that person's conception of the good. One important aspect of this is the ability to participate in the conversation about both of these matters, which implicates the values of free speech and of association.[96]

G. Distributive Autonomy: A Fusion of Liberty and Equality

Let's start with an aggregate autonomy approach to campaign finance disparities, I have defended elsewhere the need for at least a weak principle of aggregate autonomy.[97] By its nature, aggregate autonomy is a distributional theory concerned with the allocation of autonomy.

Although many economists fashion theories that increase the size of the so-called pie or total societal wealth, selecting any economic system has immense distributive consequences. Most democratic polities have some system of progressive, redistributive taxation. This sort of redistribution may be so widespread because free enterprise arrangements have frequently resulted in large disparities in the distribution of wealth and income. It is counterfactual to think that free enterprise systems are alone in producing large disparities in the distribution of wealth and income. Other economic regimes, as different as communism and mercantilism, have produced great disparities as well.

Besides restraining economic disparities, another reason may have greater explanatory force for the widespread use of progressive taxation. Redistributive taxation is quite common and entails taking some money from the wealthier members of society. Taxing an individual who has significant economic resources is not, generally speaking, a substantial infringement on his liberty, or autonomy.

Applying aggregate autonomy to campaign finance, one could subsidize some speech to remedy the profound incursion on first-order rights that the *Buckley* line of cases effectuates. These subsidies could be financed by the relatively small wealth incursions of redistributive taxation. However, in many instances, huge campaign funding disparities will survive even robust public subsidies. The magnitude of the wealth disparities involved inevitably necessitates limiting the amount of money that some can spend to speak in order to limit their abilities to drown out the voices of others. As such limitations implicate first-order rights, they engage distributive autonomy.

Generally, autonomy is not at all a zero-sum game; one person's autonomy does not need to decrease for another's to increase. As the discussion of the liberty/order tension demonstrates, rules can be fashioned that will broadly enhance autonomy. A good example discussed earlier is time, place, and manner restrictions on speech on public property; another is the traffic light.[98] However, in the context of campaign finance, autonomy takes on aspects of a zero-sum game. In the United States, campaigns are competitive, winner-take-all situations. The amount of time that any voter can devote to political campaigns is limited, particularly as multiple campaigns go on simultaneously in our complex federal, separation of powers, bicameral systems. Moreover, political campaigns compete for attention with countless other activities such as work, family and friends, and leisure. If the time that people pay attention to campaigns is limited, bombarding as much messaging time as possible, through massive campaign expenditures, becomes an even greater advantage.

Although it is counterintuitive and counterfactual, let us relax somewhat this position that campaign speech has substantial aspects of a zero-sum game so that voters are willing to spend virtually all of their nonworking hours consuming campaign speech. Even under these counterfactual conditions, a few voices with unlimited resources can overwhelm that limited amount of time so as to drown out, or at least mute, all others. If one person can use $100,000,000 to speak and the remaining 100 people in society can use $100 to speak, the voice of the one can nearly silence the voices of everyone else. Again, a prominent precept in psychology maintains that the repetition of an idea is an important element in persuasion.[99] If this is true, the funding to engage in repetition greatly advantages certain candidates over others. The only way around this problem is to limit how much money the person with $100,000,000 can devote to speech. Whatever one thinks about either the ethics or efficacy of that strategy, it does entail a deeper autonomy infringement than simply taking some money through taxation to help subsidize the candidacy of persons with less funding. Again limiting campaign speech engages distributive autonomy concerns; aggregate autonomy supplies no basis to justify such limits.

Let's review some of the concerns animating the principle of aggregate autonomy:[100] first, aggregate autonomy is interested in the allocation of autonomy, requiring that as many people as possible have at least some minimal level of autonomy. Second, it posits that authentic autonomy hinges partly on the possession of resources and therefore, underwrites some redistribution of property rights to provide some minimum level of autonomy to as many people as possible. Third, all of its redistribution activities are hermetically sealed off from first-order rights.

Working out how some distributional sensibilities could be introduced into first-order rights is tricky. Invading the liberty of some in the fragile realm of first-order rights is sensitive, even for the laudable purpose of trying to increase the number of persons who have some baseline of autonomy. Moreover, redressing allocations of lower-order economic rights involves less of an autonomy incursion particularly when that incursion exclusively exacts small, or even more significant, amounts of wealth. First-order rights are more personal; consequently, limiting them is more invasive.

Again, we might avoid this dilemma altogether if we could repair the maldistribution of first-order rights by invading lower-order rights. For example, the principle of aggregate autonomy could be used to afford some communications resources to those without voice. In the Rawlsian schema, this move could be viewed as redistributing lower-order economic resources, viz. weak property rights, to enhance first-order speech rights. Although this proposal entails some relatively small redistribution of lower-order property rights to attain some baseline influence over the core autonomy area of political campaigns for those who lack ingress, it would still prove controversial.

In the campaign financing context, both the *Arizona* and *Davis* cases invalidated government programs to channel money to candidates who lacked resources.[101] Granted, those cases objected to the subsidies being triggered by private financing for the electoral opponent. Even without this triggering, who knows the extent to which the current Court would consider state subsidization of speech in the competitive electoral setting unconstitutional.

In the 2016 elections, Senate winners raised nearly eight times more than losers, as Chapter 11 chronicles. Consequently, effective subsidization would necessitate giving much more money to some candidates than to others. Remember that in the campaign context, the Court has repeatedly emphasized that it will not countenance efforts to equalize the ability to speak. Unfortunately, this rationale is completely at odds with any notion of distributive autonomy, or aggregate autonomy, or with proper respect for the autonomy of all. Subsidizing campaign funding for candidates who lack it and possibly for citizens who lack the ability to make contributions would appear to respect some baseline or minimum amount of autonomy for those individuals. However, the amount of money being spent on political campaigns makes a subsidy strategy at most only part of any possible solution. After all, over $7 billion was spent on the 2016 federal elections alone.

Upper limits on expenditures by campaigns or outside organizations such as PACs will have to be pursued carefully. Depending on the relationship between spending money and speaking, upper boundaries could involve substantial infringements on autonomy. As I have already suggested and as Chapter 9 will elaborate, campaign expenditures do not involve pure speech. To the extent that the relationship between campaign expenditures and speech is attenuated, so is the protection of campaign expenditures as a first-order right. This analytical tack is facilitated if one hinges speech protection on advancing democracy rather than on some other value such as self-actualization. The committed individualistic libertarian would reject this move.

Even if campaign expenditures comprise speech, distributive autonomy rationales justify fashioning upper boundaries on speech expenditures. A distributive autonomy approach respects the autonomy of all. It also honestly engages the reality that constitutional and other decisions inevitably alter the distribution of autonomy.

There is no holiday or escape from distributive consequences just because one is operating in the area of first-order rights. Most decisions involving first-order rights have distributive consequences—as Chapter 2 discusses, even a right against self-incrimination. They certainly do when it comes to campaign financing because, like it or not, hide it or not, campaign financing, by definition, involves money. Money decisions inevitably have distributive consequences. Consequently, any theory of distributive autonomy will apply with particular force to the area of campaign finance.

Just because campaign financing more directly involves money does not mean that distributive autonomy decisions may be pursued by simply balancing the various interests involved. First-order rights inherently trump lower-order rights.[102] Only a strong interest—a bigger trump—can counterbalance or overcome infringements of first-order rights.

In constitutional cases, the strongest such interests involve what I call countervailing constitutional interests. A good example of this is the case of *Bakke v. Regents of the University of California*.[103] That is the watershed affirmative-action case. There an unsuccessful applicant to medical school claimed that affirmative action violated his equal protection rights by discriminating among applicants based on race. The Supreme Court rejected a number of rationales offered to justify affirmative action. The rationale that Justice Powell, writing for "a majority of one," accepted was the university's interest in a diverse student body with diverse backgrounds and ideas. This educational interest sounded in the First Amendment (free speech) and consequently comprised a countervailing constitutional interest to the equal protection claim.

By analogy, distributive autonomy illustrates that campaign finance implicates competing autonomy interests, the autonomy interests of those who wish to spend an unlimited amount of money to finance campaign speech and the autonomy interests of the vast majority of the society not to have their ideas completely overwhelmed to the point of being drowned out by the unfettered but invasive autonomy of the few. Equally important are the autonomy and decision-making interests of all voters to be exposed to the broad expanse of campaign ideas, not just to the ideas of those who have the funds to project them.

Distributive autonomy reasoning exposes the inevitability of autonomy trade-offs in campaign finance decisions. Chapters 10 and 11 make a strong statistical showing of the extent to which the campaign finance cases have invaded the speaking, listening, or voting autonomy of voters whose choices are being manipulated by money rather than ideas; of constituents whose representatives are beholden to property interests outside their districts; of citizens of less wealthy states whose voices and votes are being overlooked; of candidates who must conform their wills to donors; and of citizens' basic liberty as power is consolidated, not divided. Shortly after *Buckley*, the eminent Judge John Noonan analogized the campaign finance system to bribery. Since he wrote, the system has become much more choked on money. But the biggest autonomy infringements come post-election when public officials pass laws that infringe the autonomy of many nondonors to enhance the autonomy of a very few, very large donors. Again, Chapters 10 and 11 chronicle strong empirical evidence demonstrating this behavior.

Distributive autonomy must, however, be pursued circumspectly: one cannot come close to equalizing the autonomy of all. As the communist experience poignantly demonstrates, extreme trade-offs of liberty for equality can have stark authoritarian consequences.[104] One should be able to avoid potential authoritarian consequences of upper boundaries by predicating them on real and inevitable autonomy trade-offs and premising them on autonomy rationales. Autonomy rationales would be sensitive to authoritarian incursions on the autonomy of those whose campaign speech or expenditures is being limited. However, in the United States today, the authoritarian incursions on autonomy cut the other way by subjecting larger and larger majorities of the citizenry to a form of governance that increasingly resembles oligarchy. So any infringement on autonomy imposed by spending caps is mitigated as those caps limit campaign spending designed to dominate politics and overwhelm the autonomy of the vast majority of the society. The word *designed* suggests some kind of intentionality, which was discussed in Chapter 2.[105]

As with aggregate autonomy, distributive autonomy uses the importance or value of autonomy itself to justify some attention to its distribution. After all, if autonomy is so valuable, it is valuable for everyone—not just for the few who for whatever reason have sufficient resources to exercise it.

It is not evident how to differentiate the value of your autonomy from the value of mine. Autonomy is both intrinsically and instrumentally valuable. It is intrinsically valuable in terms of free will, and human dignity. Unlike in Rawlsian theory then, liberty and equality are not in constant tension, thus prompting continual dilemmas of preferring one or the other. Instead, autonomy is the end and advancing autonomy is the means of achieving that end.

In my account, autonomy is also instrumentally valuable in enabling one to lead a meaningful life, for example, a life in the service of others. I am not suggesting that a life in the service of others is the only meaningful life or that a narcissistic life cannot have meaning. I chose the example of a life in the service of others merely because it is the easier life to defend. With the exception of saints, most lives are at best mixtures of selfish and altruistic behaviors. What matters is the emphasis. For now, I am only suggesting that autonomy is instrumentally valuable in enabling any life that has meaning from the subjective perspective of that individual. The only constraint that distributive autonomy imposes is that one cannot unduly constrict the opportunities of others to pursue their visions of meaningful lives. Providing an account of what might comprise a meaningful life or at least what limits there might be on individual choice to comprise a meaningful life, or indeed whether such limits even exist, are complex questions for another day. Because I consider autonomy just one aspect of the good life, it is also instrumentally valuable in enabling other aspects of whatever might be considered a good life. So guaranteeing some minimal level of autonomy for all members of society is intrinsically and instrumentally valuable.

If autonomy is such an important goal, then it is difficult for a moral theory to ignore, or indeed marginalize, the autonomy of some to advance the autonomy of others. At a minimum, it is very difficult to justify political or legal rules that allow the first-order, core autonomy rights of some to be sacrificed to the autonomy of others. This is doubly true of campaign finance as elections erect the government. By disproportionately influencing the legal lines that government draws, the autonomy-advantaged can constrict the autonomy of others while further enhancing their own. Surely no authentic autonomy theory can tolerate, let alone underwrite, this.

As Martha Nussbaum has noted, Rawls prohibits as unethical trying to have one's comprehensive view codified into law.[106] Chapters 10 and 11 detail how property interests have made phenomenal progress in this direction. Many first-order autonomy decisions have distributional consequences not only on wealth but also on other first-order interests including imprisonment and execution. Addressing these differentials is more important for first-order rights precisely because these rights go to the essence of being human. Especially because first-order rights are involved, one has to pay attention to how its distribution enhances or constricts the autonomy of others. The stark autonomy differentials that highly individualistic libertarian theory protects and indeed facilitates empowers the autonomy-advantaged to further diminish the autonomy of the already autonomy-disadvantaged. Attempts to achieve rigid equality in the distribution of autonomy would bring other adverse consequences. Distributive autonomy endeavors to avoid both of these unhappy extremes.

The principle of distributive autonomy might be stated as follows: *In the realm of constitutive rights and other first-order rights, an individual may choose to maximize her own autonomy so long as her behavior does not unduly constrict—intentionally or unintentionally—the autonomy of other individuals whose elemental humanity also entitles their autonomy to proper respect.* Government cannot truly equalize autonomy in any sense. However, when inevitably choosing among rules that affect people's autonomy such as free speech, it cannot adopt a rule that would allow the unfettered liberty of some to unduly constrict—in the case of certain individuals to virtually trample—the long-run or short-run autonomy or liberty of others.

By constitutive rights, I mean rights in foundational areas that constitute the legal system and the larger society. Preeminently, those are the rights to speak, vote, and associate with others to form political and other organizations and more casual arrangements. These are perhaps the most constitutive rights that exist in the Constitution.[107] Incidentally, the other rights in the First Amendment involving freedom of religion, can also be regarded as constitutive in placing barriers against constructing the state on specific religious beliefs and in protecting an individual right of conscience.

I do not single out these speaking, associating, and voting rights because they are somehow greater than other first-order rights such as the right not to be imprisoned unjustly or not to be tortured. Even among first-order rights, there is something distinctive about speaking and voting because in exercising these rights, citizens construct the government that determines other rights, including many nonconstitutional first-order and lower-order autonomy rights. Even constitutions are interpreted by courts that are elected or appointed by government. Singling out constitutive rights may be taken as more of a rationale for the particular importance of applying distributive autonomy to the campaign finance area and not as a claim that constitutive rights should be treated differently than other first-order rights.

At this point, I am not prepared to examine all of the implications of the principle of distributive autonomy. The principle might also be refined to account for objections when it is applied to other contexts. Moreover, I am not asserting that the principle comprises the only first-order rights principle, or what might happen in collisions between competing first-order rights principles, or values.

There are several notable features of the principle. First, although distributive autonomy is an ethical principle, the principle contains no injunction to maximize one's autonomy. In contrast Nozick's theories march if not toward a moral injunction—at least a hard push—to maximize one's personal autonomy so as to discover transcendent truth. Although I certainly do not preclude an individual's choice to pursue transcendent truth or even a choice to maximize one's personal autonomy, the principle of distributive autonomy does not require such maximizing. Hence, the word *may*. Although Nozick certainly does not advocate denigrating the autonomy of another person, the real life application of his theory inexorably leads in that direction. His thick theory of contractual rights, thickened over generations, leads to tremendous autonomy differentials both in first- and lower-order rights. So do the taste-shaping effects of his broad-based injunction of pursuing transcendent truth.

Urging and justifying personal quests for transcendent truth could incite another problem. People's perceptions of whether they are pursuing transcendent truth can vary widely and wildly. Some people now regarded as nefarious villains certainly may have thought that their quest was for transcendent truth. Moreover, regardless of intentions, the quest for transcendent truth does not always turn out well. As an early biblical portrayal, those who were building the Tower of Babel thought they were going to achieve transcendent truth pursuing the divine. So did those who partook of the fruit of the tree of knowledge. In both stories, God differed. I am not denigrating the quest to pursue transcendent truth. There are also many noble examples of such quests. But under Nozickian autonomy theory, the question of whether one is pursuing transcendent truth is answered by the pursuer. Affording unfettered autonomy to pursue all the different visions of transcendent truth will inevitably cause many collisions among those visions.

The principle of distributive autonomy dramatically reduces such collisions because the principle limits one's ability to choose whatever path, transcendent truth or otherwise, one fancies. The principle does not express a moral injunction to maximize one's autonomy. Moreover, the principle does limit one's autonomy by the requirement of not unduly constricting the autonomy of others.

In applying the principle, a lot hangs on the words *unduly constrict*. Inevitably in life, many of our exercises of autonomy will constrict or interfere with the autonomy of others. For example, if I am going through an intersection, I am constraining the autonomy of someone else to travel through the intersection in a direction perpendicular to mine. Depending on how I proceed through the intersection, however, I will probably not unduly constrict the autonomy of others.

There are dangers in defining these words *unduly constrict* too broadly, as the thrust of the principle involves autonomy. If a wide variety of behaviors qualify as undue constrictions, then the liberty of many could be straightjacketed. There is some inherent deterrent or safety valve against suffocating interpretations of undue constrictions in the principle's inherent reciprocity. This principle applies to all members of society. Consequently, everyone has a strong stake in the words "unduly constrict" not being defined too broadly. However, this is only a starting point for circumscription; we have all witnessed times when autonomy, equality, theological, or other theories have been taken too far.

Undue constrictions are partly defined by the requirement of "proper respect." The words *proper respect* are constrained and defined by that minimum amount of treatment necessary to respect the elemental or basic humanity of others. The word *elemental* is meant to convey the minimum basic autonomy, dignity, or humanity that a person is entitled to in order to value and not abridge her fundamental human nature. The principle could be strengthened by slightly altering it to: "*proper respect for elemental human dignity and flourishing.*" To some extent, dignity is inherent in the concept of elemental humanity but making it more explicit would strengthen the principle. Imposing even thin moral duties to respect human flourishing would strengthen it much more as that would seem to imply some autonomy to develop one's talents. Although the principle lacks either criterion, incorporating either or both would strengthen the requirement of *"proper respect for elemental humanity."*

The principle of distributive autonomy certainly resonates with Kantian ideas. Kant allowed a measure of coercion or law in order to maximize autonomy for all.[108] The principle of distributive autonomy does not seek to maximize autonomy. First, the principle applies only to political and other first-order rights. Even within the realm of first-order rights, distributive autonomy does not seek to maximize autonomy. It does *allow* an individual to maximize his own autonomy with the constraint that he cannot unduly infringe on the autonomy of others.

The principle of distributive autonomy is not nearly as ambitious or far-reaching as the Kantian conception of autonomy. For example, the principle does not elaborate a conception of morality. Although distributive autonomy is largely consistent with Kant's Categorical Imperative in being concerned with the autonomy of others, not just with the autonomy of oneself, its reach is much more confined than the Categorical Imperative, which professes to be a comprehensive moral theory. Neither distributive autonomy nor aggregate autonomy pretends to give a broad-based account of morality. As I have said in a previous work, autonomy, in the narrow sense that I have defined it, is not an account of moral living:

> I want to live in a society where people have forbearance, pull their punches, and do not exercise all of their rights against me, just as I do not exercise all of my rights against them. I also want to live in a society in which people care for each other as human beings, irrespective of what rights they may have or lack. Particularly in a secular society, an important burden of moral philosophy must be to advance conceptions of the good.[109]

Kant is also less concerned with distributive consequences than is distributive autonomy or aggregate autonomy. He only recounts "some duties to limit acute poverty and dependence where they can damage agency."[110] This notion does have parallels with the idea of distributive autonomy for example, with the discussion of whether a starving person actually has anything like autonomy.

Moreover, in his idea of a republican constitution, Kant is not particularly concerned with participatory democracy.[111] This contrasts with the principle of distributive autonomy, which helps to buttress notions of participatory democracy. Although I am not at all limiting the reach of distributive autonomy to democratic polities, democracy is very copacetic with distributive autonomy as democracy inherently distributes the lawmaking power, and laws necessarily constrict or enhance autonomy. I err to say "inherently"; I said it reflexively as something we learned in civics class. We implicitly thought that we had an obligation to obey the laws because we as citizens had a big, if not equal, say in making them. Unfortunately *Buckley* and its progeny have undercut this axiom that has always been taken as a given.

The democratic structure resembled a pyramid in which citizens at its base comprised its ultimate governmental authority. The next layer comprised nongovernmental societal leaders in business, journalism, the professions, etc. who exerted greater control over society. Atop the pyramid was the government. Chapters 10 and 11 demonstrate the extent to which the metaphorical democracy pyramid has been undercut so that a small group has ultimate authority to decide autonomy infringements and enhancements. It may even be something like an inverted pyramid with the group at the bottom or the base—who have ultimate control—being smaller than the group of high-ranking government officials—national, state, and local—who are theoretically at the top. What mitigates the power of the base is that it is so large, that is, it comprehends so many people. When the base is so small and getting smaller—possibly only the 0.01 percent of property interests—power is highly concentrated in the hands of a few as Chapters 10 and 11 demonstrate. Unfortunately, these chapters also hint at the inherent instability of an inverted pyramid arrangement. But then again anyone who looks at an inverted pyramid already knows that.

Notes

1. ROBERT NOZICK, PHILOSOPHICAL EXPLANATIONS 291–93 (Harvard University Press, 1981). I put to one side for the moment the stringent side constraints conception of autonomy that Nozick builds on these theoretical foundations. *See generally* ROBERT NOZICK, ANARCHY, STATE, AND UTOPIA 28–35 (BASIC BOOKS, 1974). For a critique of the side constraints conception of autonomy, *see supra* Chapter 8(A).

2. *See* Donald Kommers, *Review: The Supreme Court and the Constitution: The Continuing Debate on Judicial Review*, 47 REV. POL. 113, 124–25 (1985).

3. *See* AUGUSTINE, THE CITY OF GOD 542 (G. Walsh, D. Zema, G. Monahan & D. Honan trans.) (Image Book Doubleday, 1958).

4. NOZICK, EXPLANATIONS, *supra* note 1, at 291.

5. *Id.* at 416.

6. *Id.* at 310–14.

7. *Id.* at 352–62.

8. *Id.* at 294–362.

9. *Id.* at 312.

10. *Id.* at 501–02.

11. NOZICK, ANARCHY, *supra* note 1, at 169–70.

12. *Id.* at ix.

13. *Id.* at 169–72, 265–94.

14. *Id.* at 26.

15. *Id.* at ix, 26–53.

16. NOZICK, EXPLANATIONS, *supra* note 1, at 519–20.

17. *Id.* at 412–17.

18. *Id.* at 410, 436–40.

19. *Id.* at 618.

20. *Id.* at 512.

21. NOZICK, ANARCHY, *supra* note 1, at 235–38.

22. *Id.* at 30–33.

23. *Id.* at ix, 270.

24. NOZICK, EXPLANATIONS, *supra* note 1, at 504.

25. *Id.* at 356.

26. *Id.* at 511–12.

27. NOZICK, ANARCHY, *supra* note 1, at 18–22.

28. *See* NOZICK, EXPLANATIONS, *supra* note 1, at 409–10.

29. *See id.* at 353–55; *see also* George P. Fletcher, *Why Kant*, 87 COLUM. L. REV. 421, 430 (1987).

30. GEORGE ORWELL, ANIMAL FARM (Harcourt, Brace & Co., 1946).

31. THE BASIC WRITINGS OF JOHN STUART MILL, ON LIBERTY; THE SUBJECTION OF WOMEN & UTILITARIANISM 38 (The Modern Library, 2002).

32. *Id.* at 58.

33. *Id.* at 11. *See also* Jonathan Riley, *"One Very Simple Principle,"* in JOHN STUART MILL'S SOCIAL AND POLITICAL THOUGHT: FREEDOM 170, 179 (G.W. Smith, ed., Routledge, 1998).

34. MILL, LIBERTY, *supra* note 31, at 97–98.

35. *Id.* at 4.

36. *See generally* JOHN STUART MILL, UTILITARIANISM in MILL, LIBERTY, *supra* note 31, at 233.

37. *Id.* at 250.

38. ONORA O'NEILL, CONSTRUCTING AUTHORITIES: REASON, POLITICS AND INTERPRETATION IN KANT'S PHILOSOPHY 109–10 (Cambridge University Press, 2015).

39. *Id.* at 6.[emphasis in the original].

40. *Id.*

41. *Id.* at 2. [emphasis in the original].

42. *Id.* at 76.

43. IMMANUEL KANT, CRITIQUE OF PRACTICAL REASON 18 (Mary Gregor ed., Cambridge University Press, rev. ed. 2015).

44. O'NEILL, CONSTRUCTING AUTHORITIES, *supra* note 38, at 116.

45. *Id.* at 117–18.

46. *Id.* at 25–26.

47. *Id.* at 117–19 [emphasis in original].

48. *Id.* at 119.

49. *Id.* at 148 [emphasis in the original]. IMMANUEL KANT, GROUNDWORK OF THE METAPHYSICS OF MORALS (Mary Gregor & Jens Timmermann trans., Cambridge University Press, 2012). Kant sought to boil down principles to the least number possible. KANT, *supra*, at 34.

50. O'NEILL, CONSTRUCTING AUTHORITIES, *supra* note 38, at 99.

51. *Id.* at 44.

52. *Id.* at 82, n.23.

53. *Id.* at 166.

54. *Id.* at 178–83.

55. *Id.* at 197–200.

56. *Id.* at 182–83.

57. *Id.* at 179.

58. *Id.* at 185. [emphasis added].

59. *Id.* at 201.

60. These distinctions between liberty and autonomy are not traditional. *See generally* I. Berlin, *Two Concepts of Liberty*, in FOUR ESSAYS ON LIBERTY (Oxford University Press, 1969); NOZICK, ANARCHY, *supra* note 1; NOZICK, EXPLANATIONS, *supra* note 1.

61. Although I do not share all of Nozick's account for making autonomy an intrinsic value, *see supra* text accompanying notes 9-15, I do subscribe to parts of it. An independent account of why autonomy may be intrinsically valuable ranges far beyond the scope of this work.

62. NOZICK, ANARCHY, *supra* note 1, at 26.

63. 312 U.S. 569 (1941).

64. *See* JEFFRIE G. MURPHY & JULES L. COLEMAN, THE PHILOSOPHY OF LAW 212–18 (Rowman & Allanheld, 1984).

65. 312 U.S. 569 (1941).

66. *See* JOHN ATTANASIO & JOEL GOLDSTEIN, UNDERSTANDING CONSTITUTIONAL LAW 642–50 (4th ed., LexisNexis, 2012).

67. Joseph Fishkin & Heather K. Gerken, *The Party's Over: McCutcheon, Shadow Parties, and the Future of the Party System*, 2014 SUP. CT. REV. 175, 208.

68. *See* NOZICK, ANARCHY, *supra* note 1, at 27. *See also id.* at 24–27.

69. JOHN RAWLS, A THEORY OF JUSTICE 10–19, 118–23 (Harvard University Press, 1971, rev. ed. 1999).

70. Behind Rawls's veil of ignorance, we don't know our class or social status, or wealth, or natural assets (including our intelligence, strength, age, sex, or race), our conception of the good or life plan, our attitude toward risk, or the society or the generation to which we belong. *Id.* at 118–19, 174–76.

71. Onora O'Neill, *Changing Constructions*, in RAWLS'S POLITICAL LIBERALISM 57 (Thom Brooks & Martha C. Nussbaum eds., Columbia University Press, 2015); JOHN RAWLS, POLITICAL LIBERALISM 57 (Columbia University Press, 1993).

72. Martha C. Nussbaum, *Introduction*, in RAWLS'S LIBERALISM, *supra* note 71, at 32.

73. *See* Paul Weithman, *Legitimacy and the Project of Liberalism,* in RAWLS'S LIBERALISM, *supra* note 71, esp., at 101–02.

74. *See generally* Nussbaum, *Introduction*, *supra* note 72, at 1; O'Neill, *Changing Constructions*, *supra* note 71, at 57; Weithman, *Legitimacy and Liberalism*, *supra* note 73, at 73; and Jeremy Waldron, *Isolating Public Reasons*, at 113 (taking a critical view of public reasons in part because they excluded important aspects of moral debate); Thom Brooks, *The Capabilities Approach and Political Liberalism*, at 139; Frank I. Michelman, *The Priority of Liberty: Rawls and Tiers of Scrutiny*, at 175; all in RAWLS'S LIBERALISM, *supra* note 71.

75. RAWLS, POLITICAL LIBERALISM, *supra* note 71, at 291. As originally stated in *A Theory of Justice*, even in the 1999 revised edition, Rawls formulated the principles slightly differently:

FIRST PRINCIPLE
Each person is to have an equal right to the most extensive total system of equal basic liberties compatible with a similar system of liberty for all.

SECOND PRINCIPLE

Social and economic inequalities are to be arranged so that they are both:

(a) to the greatest benefit of the least advantaged, consistent with the just savings principle, and

(b) attached to offices and positions open to all under conditions of fair equality of opportunity.

RAWLS, THEORY, *supra* note 69, at 266.

76. RAWLS, THEORY, *supra* note 69, at 53, 178. Justice Breyer posits a right of "active liberty" to participate in the democratic process of self-governance, including speech. *See* Stephen Breyer, *Madison Lecture: Our Democratic Constitution*, 77 N.Y.U. L. REV. 245, 257, 258 (2002).

77. RAWLS, THEORY, *supra* note 69, at 264–67.

78. *Id.* at 266.

79. *Id.* at 83–84.

80. *Id.* at 118–23.

81. See generally John Attanasio, *The Principle of Aggregate Autonomy and the Calabresian Approach to Products Liability*, 74 VA. L. REV. 677(1988); John Attanasio, *Aggregate Autonomy, the Difference Principle, and the Calabresian Approach to Products Liability*, in PHILOSOPHICAL FOUNDATIONS OF TORT LAW 299 (David G. Owen ed., CLARENDON PRESS, 1995).

82. *See* Attanasio, *Aggregate Autonomy*, *supra* note 81, at 728–29.

83. *See, e.g.,* Brandenburg v. Ohio, 395 U.S. 444 (1969); New York Times Co. v. Sullivan, 376 U.S. 254 (1964).

84. *See, e.g.,* Railway Express Agency, Inc. v. New York, 336 U.S. 106 (1949); Williamson v. Lee Optical, 348 U.S. 483 (1955). *See also* Chapter 3(C).

85. RAWLS, THEORY, *supra* note 69, at 476.

86. *Id.* at 478.

87. JEREMY WALDRON, LAW AND DISAGREEMENT 156 (Oxford University Press, 1999).

88. *See* Attanasio, *Difference Principle*, *supra* note 81, at 314.

89. RAWLS, POLITICAL LIBERALISM, *supra* note 71, at 356–63. *See also* C. Edwin Baker, *Campaign Expenditures and Free Speech*, 33 HARV. C.R.-C.L. L. REV. 1, nn.2–3 (1998) (describing some prominent critics). *But cf.* Kathleen M. Sullivan, *Political Money and Freedom of Speech*, 30 U.C. DAVIS L. REV. 663 (1997) (defending campaign finance jurisprudence and arguing that Congress should lift limitations on campaign contributions); Kathleen M. Sullivan, *Political Money and Freedom of Speech: A Reply to Frank Askin*, 31 U.C. DAVIS L. REV. 1083 (1998).

90. RAWLS, POLITICAL LIBERALISM, *supra* note 71, at 356–63. *See also* Attanasio, *Difference Principle*, *supra* note 81, at 299. *See also* John Attanasio, *The Constitutionality of Regulating Human Genetic Engineering: Where Procreative Liberty and Equal Opportunity Collide*, 53 U. CHI. L. REV. 1274, 1334–39 (1986).

91. RAWLS, POLITICAL LIBERALISM, *supra* note 71, at 291.

92. RAWLS, THEORY, *supra* note 69, at 220.

93. RAWLS, POLITICAL LIBERALISM, *supra* note 71, at 271, 322–33.

94. RAWLS, THEORY, *supra* note 69, at 220, 266.

95. Michelman, *Priority of Liberty*, *supra* note 74, at 179.

96. *Id.* at 189.

97. *See supra* note 1, Chapter 1.

98. *See supra* text accompanying notes 63-75.

99. See, e.g. GARDNER LINDZEY, DANIEL GILBERT & SUSAN T. FISKE, THE HANDBOOK OF SOCIAL PSYCHOLOGY 65, 317, 326, 335, 341-42, 347, 362, 365-66 (4th ed. McGraw-Hill, Distributed by Oxford University Press, 1998); Richard E. Petty & Duane T. Wegener, *The Elaboration Likelihood Model: Current Status and Controversies* 4, 61–63, *in* SHELLY CHAIKEN & YAACOV TROPE, DUAL-PROCESS THEORIES IN SOCIAL PSYCHOLOGY (Guilford Press, 1999); *Mere Exposure: A Gateway to the Subliminal*, 10 CURRENT DIRECTIONS IN PSYCHOLOGICAL SCI. 224–28 (December 2001); ENCYCLOPEDIA BRITANNICA https://www.britannica.com/topic/persuasion-psychology (last visited October 22, 2017).

100. *See* Attanasio, *Aggregate Autonomy*, *supra* note 81, and Attanasio, *Difference Principle*, *supra* note 81, at 308–09.

101. *See supra* text accompanying notes 65–81, Chapter 6.

102. *See generally* RONALD DWORKIN, TAKING RIGHTS SERIOUSLY (Harvard University Press, 1977).

103. 438 U.S. 265 (1978).

104. *See* Attanasio, *Difference Principle*, *supra* note 81, at 309.

105. *See supra* text accompanying note 17, Chapter 2.

106. Nussbaum, *Introduction*, *supra* note 72, at 23.

107. Another important constitutive right is the right to sit on a jury in criminal and civil cases. *See* U.S. CONST. amends. VI, VII.

108. O'NEILL, CONSTRUCTING AUTHORITIES, *supra* note 38, at 48, 182–85.

109. Attanasio, *Difference Principle*, *supra* note 81, at 318.

110. O'NEILL, CONSTRUCTING AUTHORITIES, *supra* note 38, at 210.

111. *Id.* at 179.

9 Distributive Autonomy, The Constitution, and Campaign Finance

A. A Distributive Autonomy Critique of the Campaign Finance Cases

Because the principle of distributive autonomy is an ethical theory, it operates at the individual level. Thus, besides regulating personal behavior, it requires constitutional and legislative moves by individuals who sought and possess law-making authority and consequent responsibility. This is extremely important. Even if the Supreme Court's constitutional interpretation changes and the *Buckley* line of cases is reversed, there will need to be legislation in order to undo its adverse effects.

Possible legislation that distributive autonomy might require would be to subsidize campaign contributions for citizens or voters who lack adequate resources to make contributions. This would afford those individuals at least some minimal level of influence over elections and public policy. Subsidies would come from the general tax revenues. Subsidizing such speech is the easiest move to make. Redistributive taxation does not violate distributive autonomy because it does not affect first-order rights. The principle of distributive autonomy would require such taxation to avert an undue constriction of the first-order rights of those who lack the resources to contribute. In addition, aggregate autonomy would also require this move as it would comprise a de minimis wealth exaction that would avert a severe constriction on the life plans of those who cannot afford campaign contributions, and consequently have been deprived of influence over elections and resultant public policy.

Politics and Capital. John Attanasio.

Aristotle calls participating in politics noble and part of human nature. He probably could not have imagined our system of campaign donations: Athens had broad-ranging prohibitions against bribery.[1] Conversely, *Buckley* and its progeny actually give rights to drown out the speech of others for the purpose of: (1) making one's own voice heard, or (2) just drowning out the speech of others, for example the opponents of their favored candidates, or (3) for no reason at all. This certainly could not have been what Aristotle and his fellow Athenians had in mind. Moreover, it is hard to argue how constitutionally protecting this behavior advances autonomy.

But then matters grow even worse: the autonomy of those whose voices have been drowned out is then systematically violated by the lawmaking process that has been dramatically skewed against them. So the severely diminished influence of most citizens over elections in a democracy per se violates their natural autonomy as human beings and their socially contracted autonomy in the Constitution. Subsequent legislation enacted by those elected begets further autonomy violations: Of course, legislatures make laws including criminal laws, that can tremendously constrict first-order autonomy, and many laws that impact speech itself such as the prohibition against draft card burning issue in *United States v. O'Brien*. Laws also routinely constrict or advance lower-order autonomy in the area of economics. They may also constrict or advance autonomy rights in such important areas as the environment, information privacy, healthcare, education, etc. These have not been traditionally considered first-order rights in the United States although some are in other countries.

Not all first-order rights are constitutionalized. A few countries do not have constitutions; others have fairly minimalist ones. Some rights strongly protected by the legislature could be considered first-order rights. Healthcare may be starting to look like one in the United States; some states in the U.S. constitutionally protect a right to education. The precise dividing line between first-order and lower-order rights is beyond the scope of this work. There is broad consensus that speaking, voting, and electing one's government count as highest order rights. These are the rights we are discussing here.

Buckley and its progeny inexorably allow relatively few people to effectively constrain the liberty of the vast majority of the population. Generally speaking, constitutional law limits the government's ability to constrict first-order autonomy rights. In an unflattering role reversal, the *Buckley* line of cases violates autonomy by reversing congressional efforts to protect distributive autonomy.

Although the Court's decisions may severely limit government from channeling money to candidates who have received less donations, distributive autonomy would favor such a system. Indeed, the principle may require some action along these lines just to counterbalance the profound violations and distortions of distributive autonomy engendered by the current legal regime. A voucher system in which the government would appropriate funds and allow private citizens to contribute their vouchers to candidates as they saw fit would avoid the Court's aversion to equalizing campaign funds. One potential problem with a voucher system, however, is that it is unlikely to significantly diminish the funding advantages that some candidates already enjoy. Contributions from vouchers are likely to be spread out fairly evenly among candidates. Consequently, no candidate is likely to gain a huge advantage from the voucher system, and the relative disparities in campaign funds from donations, candidates's personal fortunes, and PACs will likely survive. Indeed they may increase because those funds could be targeted to attracting a disproportionate number of vouchers. Moreover, unless a voucher system is extremely well-funded, it will not come close to redressing the disparities in distributive autonomy in the area of elections. In recent presidential year elections, over $7 billion was spent at the federal level alone. If all candidates for at least federal office could receive voucher money, enormous appropriations would be required just to even get noticed.

1. Speech as Reasoned Argument?

In his magnum opus *Spheres of Justice*, distinguished philosopher Michael Walzer supplies strong political theory underpinnings for severely restricting campaign expenditures by both candidates and outside groups. Walzer's "spheres of justice" scrupulously separate money or "property/power" from political power. "The most common form of powerlessness in the United States today derives from the dominance of money in the sphere politics."[2]

Walzer fashions a pluralistic, particularistic approach to justice that is focused on avoiding dominance, or what he calls tyranny. Essentially tyranny refers to various forms of subjugation. Avoiding dominance prompts him to focus on the distribution of social goods. So his is a theory of distributive justice. Walzer's conception of goods is quite broad including not only wealth and property, but also political power, jobs (including professional jobs), religious office, leisure (including vacations), citizenship, marital and familial relationships, education, recognition and honors—even grace. He calls his conception of distributive justice complex equality. The most equitable and effective system for making these distributive decisions is democracy.[3]

The concept of social goods is particularistic and is based on the language, history, and culture of specific societies. Each of the social goods occupies a separate sphere. Spheres are carefully walled off from each other. The distribution of the social goods occupying a specific sphere takes place relatively autonomously within that sphere. By autonomously, Walzer means independent of the distributive patterns in the other spheres that treat different social goods.[4]

Elites can dominate, even monopolize, the distribution of social goods within a particular sphere but they cannot use their influence in one sphere to try to influence the distribution of social goods in another. For example, those who occupy the political sphere cannot use their political power to acquire special educational privileges for their relatives. Moreover, those who dominate the market sphere cannot use their wealth to purchase recognitions and honors. The latter must be distributed fairly through independent juries using transparent and independent standards.

I select these two spheres purposefully as these are perhaps the two that Walzer most fears can be abused by elites to extend their power in one sphere, to dominate another sphere. Walzer describes such aggrandizing behavior as the tyranny of the spheres. Historically, political power has been the most abused sphere in being used to dominate others. This is particularly dangerous because the political sphere is the most powerful. For example, it polices the boundary lines between the spheres. It also decides the goals for society. Its regulations can also invade and override the understandings in other spheres.[5]

When he wrote the book, Walzer was contemporaneously anxious about elites who already dominate the market sphere, extending their sway over other spheres. Money is a unique commodity in terms of being the closest to achieving universal acceptance. So it easily can flow into other spheres. Still, there are many social goods that money can't buy. As money and power occupy separate spheres, Walzer views money invading the political sphere as akin to bribery, and his concept of bribery is far more robust than the narrow quid pro quo view articulated in *McCutheon*. Walzer analogizes money in politics to the ancient vice of money purchasing religious office: for many years, Simony, which is buying religious office, has been forbidden.[6] Because money is the closest commodity to achieving broad-based acceptance, it can easily travel from its own sphere into other spheres in an attempt to distort the distribution of social goods and dominate the spheres generally.

Because the political sphere is the most powerful one, Walzer is especially dismayed that money is currently trying to dominate the sphere of politics. He views this as bribery, which was extensively prohibited even in ancient Athens.

> Freedom of speech, press, religion, assembly: none of these require money payments; none of them are available at auction; they are simply guaranteed to every citizen. It's often said that the exercise of these freedoms costs money, but that's not strictly speaking the case: talk and worship are cheap; so is the meeting of citizens; so is publication in many of its forms.[7]

As he regards the political and market spheres as the most potent and dynamic, Walzer is quite apprehensive that money could come to dominate the entire polity. Money takes on a political character "only when it 'talks' to candidates and officials, only when it is discreetly displayed or openly flaunted in the corridors of power."[8] For Walzer, only reasoned arguments can be brought into the political forum. "And all the other citizens must talk, too, or at least have a chance to talk."[9] He is also worried about the largest estates passing through inheritance, because this would extend the power of wealth into future generations and bring a kind of aristocratic state, breaching the political sphere. Walzer thinks that: "Good fences make just societies."[10]

Amplifying reasoned argument, Walzer moves beyond a right of speech to a right to persuade. The key rights of citizens are voting and arguing: Voting "is the foundation of all distributive activity and the inescapable framework from which choices have to be made."[11] From this necessity of accumulating votes to make a decision comes the necessity of persuasion and influence: "Democracy requires equal rights, not equal power. Rights here are guaranteed opportunities to exercise minimal power (voting rights) or to try to exercise greater power (speech, assembly, and petition rights)." Participation is necessary to justify government's ability to restrict a person's activities.[12] Like Aristotle, Walzer thinks that participation must be broad-based.[13] Walzer also thinks that the opportunity to persuade is crucial to the concept of self-respect.[14] The biggest impediment to this ideal is the presence of money in politics:

> A radically *laissez-faire* economy would be like a totalitarian state, invading every other sphere, dominating every other distributive process. It would transform every social good into a commodity. This is market imperialism. I suppose that is less dangerous than State imperialism because it is easier to control.[15]

The control Waltzer suggests is redistribution. Of course, this is tough to do if the market sphere has essentially purchased a big chunk of the political one.

Spheres of Justice was published in 1982 when the influence of money was only beginning. Chapter 10 of this text demonstrates that disparities in income and wealth in the United States have continued to explode. This has generated an upward spiral further advantaging those with greater means to disproportionately influence policy that will make their means greater still. Thus, the scope of money's invasion of the political sphere continues to grow as do the number and seriousness of distributive autonomy violations.[16]

2. Affording Campaign Finance Mid-level Protection

In a campaign spending market where a few voices can essentially marginalize, if not extinguish, all others, some notions of upper boundaries on expenditures must be discussed. Upper boundaries mitigate but they don't eradicate the invasion by the economic sphere into the political sphere. Any distributive autonomy analysis of upper boundaries would first have to consider the nexus between campaign spending and speech. Walzer argues that equating spending money with speaking profoundly violates the spheres of justice, allowing money to dominate speech and politics. It also transforms speech from reasoned argumentation into something akin to bribery.

The *Buckley* Court specifically rejected treating campaign expenditures as unprotected conduct rather than protected speech. *Buckley* and its progeny also refused to scrutinize campaign expenditure limitations under the middle-level *O'Brien* test, which reduces constitutional scrutiny for laws regulating behaviors that combine speech and action.[17] Instead, *Buckley* and its progeny counterintuitively treat campaign expenditures as pure speech. Even if the *O'Brien* test had pertained, the regulations would still have failed it. As the regulations in *Buckley* sought to redress inequalities in campaign speech, they failed the *O'Brien* test's requirement that the regulations be unrelated to speech.

Other rationales could also meet the content neutrality requirement of *O'Brien*. The Court could accept regulatory rationales not explicitly aimed at limiting campaign speech by candidates or independent groups, even though the regulations may result in such limitations. For example, offering corruption as a rationale might work if the Court adopts a broader, more traditional view of corruption than quid pro quo corruption which really amounts to the crime of bribery. *Buckley* accepted the corruption rationale to allow restricting contributions, and rejected it for limiting expenditures by candidates and outside groups. Rejecting corruption as a rationale to restrain outside groups blinks the reality that many of the groups are frequently not really outside. There is evidence of coordination between specific campaigns and outside groups, and of post-election access and influence.

Federalism rationales articulated earlier also meet the content neutrality requirement, as would preserving the basic constituent representation framework of the Constitution, not to mention the Constitution's most fundamental idea of dividing power. These problems are discussed in Chapter 6: to rehearse them, *McCutcheon* and *Citizens United* allows donors from a few states to dominate entire election cycles, thus undercutting our constitutional federalist and representational structures. After all, a congressperson in Idaho should be representing his constituency, not a donor from California. Divided power, federalism, and representational democracy are three of the most fundamental ideas the Constitution has, as is equal representation in the Senate for small states such as Idaho. If these don't comprise countervailing constitutional interests of the most compelling nature, I'm not sure what does. Countervailing constitutional interests signify values embedded right in the Constitution that the government asserts to justify its alleged abridgment of another constitutional provision.

Drowning out rationales applying to speech of candidates and other speakers of more modest means and of voter/ decision-makers also comprise a group of countervailing constitutional interests of the most compelling sort. These grow even more powerful if bolstered by the anti-distortion rationales described in the next section.

If one takes the facts of *O'Brien* seriously, many speech-neutral rationales should prove acceptable. Again, *O'Brien* endorsed as content-neutral rationales that prohibited burning draft cards even though in that case the cards had been burned to protest the draft during the Vietnam War.

But what does the principle of distributive autonomy tell us about whether *O'Brien* even applies here? Far from exhibiting concern with the distribution of autonomy, *Buckley* explicitly denegrates any attempt to redress inequalities among electoral speakers. *Buckley's* analysis exhibits the strong libertarian paradigm of free speech jurisprudence on steroids. Even *Buckley's* permitting considerable regulation of disclosure and contributions was driven by avoiding corruption, a rationale that is consistent with the strong libertarian paradigm. Beyond contributions, disclosure, and some public financing, *Buckley* and its even more robust offspring do not permit much regulation at all. The Court makes a strong connection between speech rights and property rights, a natural move in modern, highly individualistic libertarian theory.

Whether one professes to adhere to the strong libertarian paradigm or to the weak one would depend on one's philosophical approach. A Nozick libertarian adheres to the *Lochner* position of strong direct protection for property rights. Connecting speech with the liberty to use as much of one's property as one wants in order to speak opens the floodgates to undue constrictions of first-order rights. That move introduces the tremendous inequalities of wealth and income that exist in any free-market system first into the marketplace of ideas, and then transforms government lawmaking into a marketplace, making laws literally up for auction.

Still, what makes the question somewhat difficult—even for one committed to distributive autonomy—is the reality that to express ideas, one frequently has to spend money. But this more protects expenditures on one's own campaign, than contributions to PACs. Even in one's own campaign, the First Amendment may protect a broad but not unlimited ability to get one's message across. But does it really afford a right to drown out the speech of others or to distort the information available to voters? The latter seems at worst anti-speech in the sense of choking off or at least blocking a free marketplace of ideas. At best behaviors choking off speech or effecting wholesale distortion appear much closer to action than speech unless there are other ingredients.

Of course, frequently one does not have to spend money to speak. Writing a letter to the editor, engaging in a protest march, or posting a message on Facebook, Twitter, or a blog does not require much money at all. Where the money comes in is in amplification, distortion, and drowning out.

Someone committed to distributive autonomy might reject any connection between spending money and speaking. But it seems that position is too extreme for two reasons. First, there is a connection between spending money and certain speech activities. So some protection may be warranted for the candidate's own speech. Second, the principle of distributive autonomy allows one to exercise her autonomy so long as that exercise does not unduly constrict that of another. Does a small campaign expenditure by a candidate on her campaign unduly constrict the autonomy of other individuals? The undue constriction requirement must be construed to render the principle of distributive autonomy copacetic with broad-based freedom of action.

Affording some middle level of protection for spending money on one's own campaign would not seem to trespass the undue constriction threshold. After all, the principle sets the undue constriction threshold fairly high, requiring that the constriction be connected to an other actor's basic human dignity. However, the level of constitutional protection for even candidate expenditures would be far less than that afforded pure speech. This position is also congruent with one's intuitions: most people don't equate spending or particularly donating money with speaking.

That begs the further question of what level of protection should spending money to speak be afforded? Perhaps something like the *O'Brien* standard would be appropriate for a candidate expenditure. To be protected under the middle-level *O'Brien* standard, the regulation has to focus on the activity of spending rather than on the speech behavior.[18]

The Court tends to be relatively lax in scrutinizing governmental regulations of expressive conduct under the *O'Brien* standard. The key criterion is that the "governmental interest is unrelated to the suppression of free expression." So if regulating the spending of money is unrelated to the suppression of free speech, the government would then have broad latitude to set fairly low limits on campaign contributions (which already can be done under the *Buckley* line of cases), and substantial but much higher, limits on campaign expenditures by candidates. As suggested earlier, normally contributions to PACs and expenditures by PACs seem to be so far removed from expressing one's ideas that they amount to action, not speech. But what about PACs affiliated with ultra-wealthy donors who take a very active role in shaping the PACs's ideological agenda? This would seem to have some parallels with candidate expenditures. But are either pure speech? What about spending money purely to buy clothes at the store? Is that speech or action? If under normal circumstances, spending money is action, then spending money on speech must be at most speech plus action; as noted earlier, *Buckley* itself partly concedes this point.

An additional problem becomes that large PACs in which donors are very personally involved have the ability to virtually drown out the speech of lots of other people during an election campaign. One may have a constitutional right to spend money to buy a gun, but not a tank. Even if spending money to campaign and get elected were pure speech, spending money to drown out the ideas of others is not. Saying otherwise is a dangerous idea as history has repeatedly proven. Don't believe me; ask the pros. All authoritarians seek to occupy the airwaves to drown out the ideas of others. The key battle in most modern revolutions is over the television station. Of course, property interests will vigorously reject this analogy insisting that they comprehend very diverse points of view. Not on their economic interests, they don't. As the data demonstrates, the diversity quotient plunges on issues relating to lower taxes and less regulation.

A similar line of argumentation would also apply to putting substantial, but perhaps higher ceilings on candidate expenditures. However, candidate expenditure limits should be set higher than the wealthy donors of PACs partly to ensure that the candidate has a meaningful opportunity to convey her views and partly to ensure that the electorate is well informed.

Chapters 10 and 11 statistically demonstrate how dramatically a very small number have drowned out the viewpoints and ideas of virtually everyone else in their economic self-interest. So, one can see right away that any meaningful theory of distributive autonomy would shy away from connections between spending money and speaking. Incorporating the great disparities of American wealth into the marketplace of ideas—particularly into political campaigns, which comprise the core of that marketplace—renders the possibilities for undue constrictions of first-order rights almost limitless. Consequently, the legislature should have broad latitude to cap independent expenditures made by any individual to support or oppose a particular candidate or referendum.

But does diminished scrutiny of spending money to speak only apply to campaign speech, or more broadly to any connection between spending money and speaking? At first blush, distributive autonomy would appear to demand broadly diminished scrutiny, but such questions should be addressed carefully on a case-by-case basis.

A serious argument can be made that the electoral forum is special. In *Kovacs v. Cooper*, the Court permitted government to regulate the volume of sound trucks. The Court viewed this as part of the system of " 'ordered liberty.' " The majority approved the regulation as a time, place, and manner restriction. It was a reasonable, content-neutral regulation of the manner of speaking:

> Opportunity to gain the public's ears by objectionably amplified sound on the streets is no more assured by the right of free speech than is the unlimited opportunity to address gatherings on the streets. The preferred position of freedom of speech in a society that cherishes liberty for all does not require legislators to be insensible to claims by citizens to comfort and convenience. To enforce freedom of speech in disregard of the rights of others would be harsh and arbitrary in itself. That more people may be more easily and cheaply reached by sound trucks, perhaps borrowed without cost from some zealous supporter, is not enough to call forth constitutional protection for what those charged with public welfare reasonably think is a nuisance when easy means of publicity are open. Section 4 of the ordinance bars sound trucks from broadcasting in a loud and raucous manner on the streets. There is no restriction upon the communication of ideas or discussion of issues by the human voice, by newspapers, by pamphlets, by dodgers. We think that the need for reasonable protection in the homes or business houses from the distracting noises of vehicles equipped with such sound amplifying devices justifies the ordinance.[19]

The majority emphasized that in a system of ordered liberty, other interests were to be accommodated such as the peaceful tranquility of one's home and business, particularly when ample opportunities exist to reach the audience. The Court's analysis is just an expression of the liberty/order tension which I derived from another Supreme Court case of this same era. The Court's reasoning at one time was not libertarian but broadly resonated with the more distributive autonomy approach that piloted the Court's First Amendment jurisprudence during the *Carolene Products* participatory democracy paradigm.

Time, place, and manner restrictions such as the one sustained in *Kovacs* typically apply to public forums which are government property.[20] The Supreme Court could easily treat campaigns and elections as public forums created by the government—indeed as constitutionally—mandated public forums established for the purpose of constituting the government itself. The logic of *Kovacs* and other similar cases would treat restrictions on campaign financing as reasonable, content-neutral manner regulations to ensure that the electoral forum is fair and open to all.

The zero-sum game nature of elections, coupled with the massive public policy rewards from electoral investments would render egregious undue constrictions on autonomy considerably more prevalent in the government created electoral forum than in other speech situations. This transforms electoral forums—the heart of democracy—into bazaars where public policy can be bought and sold, rather than voted on. The statistics in chapter 6, 10, and 11 validate this characterization. Autonomy is not a zero sum game. A zero sum game is a game that for someone to win, someone else must lose. Baseball and basketball are good examples. So are elections. Hence, the electoral forum is especially vulnerable to manipulation and the consequences of the manipulation are grave.

Consequently campaign finance can be regulated under the *O'Brien* standard or under the similar standard for reasonable time, place, and manner restrictions. Those standards apply with particular force to speech in the constitutionally-mandated electoral forum.

3. Calabresi: Distortion, Information Economics, and Public Choice Theory

In addition to *O'Brien* or time, place and manner restrictions, the *Buckley* line of cases should also be reversed because the State is protecting a number of compelling state interests involving elections. Some of these interests come from the concurring opinion of Justice Jackson in *Kovacs v. Cooper*. Jackson's opinion, which I have mentioned before, is more famous than the majority's quoted in the previous section: "Freedom of speech for Kovacs does not, in my view, include freedom to use sound amplifiers to drown out the natural speech of others."[21] Justice Jackson's analysis is framed as a countervailing constitutional interest that would satisfy even the highest level of constitutional scrutiny: the speech of some should not be permitted to shut down the speech of others.

The Court adopted his reasoning in a unanimous opinion in *Red Lion Broadcasting Company v. FCC*. That case broadly endorsed the FCC's doctrine of fair access to the broadcast media:

> Just as the Government may limit the use of sound-amplifying equipment potentially so noisy that it drowns out civilized private speech, so may the Government limit the use of broadcast equipment. The right of free speech of a broadcaster, the user of a sound truck, or any other individual does not embrace a right to snuff out the free speech of others.[22]

Although the FCC abrogated the fairness doctrine during the Reagan administration,[23] the Court has repeatedly endorsed *Red Lion* in subsequent cases: *CBS v. FCC*[24] upheld a congressional statute affording candidates for federal office a right to " 'reasonable access' " to paid political advertising on broadcast media once a campaign had commenced.[25] Quoting *Red Lion* but adding the emphasis, the *CBS* case stated:

> Although the broadcasting industry is entitled under the First Amendment to exercise "the widest journalistic freedom consistent with its public (duties)," *Columbia*

Broadcasting System, Inc. v. Democratic National Committee, ... the Court has made clear that:

> "*It is the right of the viewers and listeners, not the right of the broadcasters, which is paramount.* It is the purpose of the First Amendment to preserve an uninhibited marketplace of ideas in which truth will ultimately prevail, rather than to countenance monopolization of that market. . . . It is the right of the public to receive suitable access to social, political, esthetic, moral, and other ideas and experiences which is crucial here." *Red Lion Broadcasting Co. v. FCC* (emphasis added).

The First Amendment interests of candidates and voters, as well as broadcasters, are implicated by § 312 (a)(7). We have recognized that "it is of particular importance that candidates have the . . . opportunity to make their views known so that the electorate may intelligently evaluate the candidates' personal qualities and their positions on vital public issues before choosing among them on election day." *Buckley v. Valeo.* Indeed, "speech concerning public affairs is . . . the essence of self-government," *Garrison v. Louisiana.* The First Amendment "has its fullest and most urgent application precisely to the conduct of campaigns for political office." *Monitor Patriot Co. v. Roy.* Section 312 (a)(7) thus makes a significant contribution to freedom of expression by enhancing the ability of candidates to present, and the public to receive, information necessary for the effective operation of the democratic process.[26]

In the electoral context, *CBS v. FCC* makes three key points: (1) Congress is permitted to avert the monopolization of the marketplace of ideas, particularly in elections, (2) listener rights prevail in elections, and (3) voters must be exposed to a wide variety of information about the candidates because elections are central to autonomous democratic decision-making. These rationales not only have constitutional content, but they also meet the *O'Brien* standard of being disconnected from the regulation of the content of speech. The idea that some campaign speakers would drown out the speech of others violates all three of the *CBS* case's articulated interests.

Although *CBS* made the monopolization point in the context of the broadcast media, the Court has upheld application of the Sherman Antitrust Act to the print media as well. In *Associated Press v. United States,*[27] the Court summarily rejected a First Amendment defense by the Associated Press against application of the Sherman Antitrust Act to the press. It held that the Sherman Act did not give them the right to exclude membership from competing press sources:

> It would be strange indeed, however, if the grave concern for freedom of the press which prompted adoption of the First Amendment should be read as a command that the government was without power to protect that freedom. The First Amendment, far from providing an argument against application of the Sherman Act, here provides powerful reasons to the contrary. That Amendment rests on the

assumption that the widest possible dissemination of information from diverse and antagonistic sources is essential to the welfare of the public, that a free press is a condition of a free society. Surely a command that the government itself shall not impede the free flow of ideas does not afford non-governmental combinations a refuge if they impose restraints upon that constitutionally guaranteed freedom. Freedom to publish means freedom for all and not for some. Freedom to publish is guaranteed by the Constitution, but freedom to combine to keep others from publishing is not. Freedom of the press from governmental interference under the First Amendment does not sanction repression of that freedom by private interests. The First Amendment affords not the slightest support for the contention that a combination to restrain trade in news and views has any constitutional immunity.[28]

If one lacks a First Amendment right to drown out competing press sources, why does one have a right to drown out competing candidates?

Perhaps the most compelling elaboration of the drowning out, or the speech monopolization, rationale in campaign finance cases has been Judge Guido Calabresi's concurring opinion in a U.S. Court of Appeals decision denominated *Ognibene v. Parkes*.[29] That case upheld formidable New York City limits on campaign contributions made by contractors who work for the City. Judge Calabresi's opinion elaborates the drowning out rationale as an anti-distortion rationale. This rationale would appear to certainly pass the *O'Brien* test. It is so fundamental, however, that it may serve as a compelling state interest to sustain a narrowly tailored campaign regulation facing even the highest level of Supreme Court scrutiny.

In Judge Calabresi's view, the campaign speech of property interests drowning out all other campaign speech distorts other speakers' rights to speak and listeners' rights to know. From the perspective of the speech rights of less wealthy "donor-speakers":

> The first benefit of anti-distortion measures is not difficult to see. If an external factor, such as wealth, allows some individuals to communicate their political views too powerfully, then persons who lack wealth may, for all intents and purposes, be excluded from the democratic dialogue. In much the same way that anti-noise ordinances help to prevent megaphone users from drowning out all others in the public square, contribution limits can serve to prevent the wealthiest donors from rendering all other donors irrelevant—from, in effect, silencing them.[30]

From the standpoint of voter-listeners receiving accurate information, and of competing candidates-speakers, drowning out distorts preference intensities:

> To return to the example of the megaphone in the public square, the problem with its loudness is not just that it drowns out the voices of others, but also that it

misrepresents, to an outside observer, the relative intensity of the speaker's views. That is, even if the megaphone user cares little about the issue being discussed, his voice gets heard above all others, while the voices (and intensity of feelings) of those who care passionately about the issue (and shout their beliefs at the top of their lungs) seem small in comparison. The one speaker's relative loudness—along with the other speakers' relative softness—obscures the depth of each speaker's views, thereby degrading the communicative value of everyone's message.[31]

This short but brilliant opinion describes three types of distortion. The first is the distortion of the subject matter and viewpoint in the marketplace of ideas caused by property interests drowning out the voices of less wealthy donors. The second is the distorted preference intensities for particular candidates and campaign proposals observed by voter-listeners, and the third is the distortion of their own preference intensities suffered by candidate-speakers.

The first type of distortion harkens back to Justice Jackson's opinion in *Kovacs*. But Judge Calabresi elucidates the drowning out rationale by focusing on distortion. He says that distortion will occur through the ideas of less wealthy "donor-speakers" being systematically drowned out in the marketplace of ideas by the ideas put forward by property interests. This marginalizes the ideas of the less wealthy. My own small addendum would connect this distortion to three types of content discrimination against less wealthy donor-speakers: there is a systematic underestimating of their preferences that marginalizes: the general subjects they want to discuss, their viewpoints on all electoral issues, and their concrete proposals for change.

Calabresi's second distortion maintains that voter-listeners will observe systemically distorted preference intensities as the preference intensities of less wealthy persons will be systematically underestimated: wealthy persons can amplify even their less intense preferences by spending small sums (relative to their wealth) of money on campaigns. Similar expenditures would crush the budgets of the less wealthy. Because the marginal utility of money is so dramatically different between a poor or a middle class person, as against a wealthy person, the less wealthy will be unable to project even their very intense preferences whereas property interests will be able to express even minor preferences intensely. Bearing out Judge Calabresi's point, the statistics in Chapters 6 and 10 suggest that the distortions are now so dramatic that the super-wealthy—1/100 of 1 percent—have been magnifying their preferences in complete disproportion to even the most intensive preferences held by any other groups in society.

Third, these distortions will also systematically muffle the views, issues, and proposals of less wealthy candidates and candidates who raise less money because their views are less sympathetic to wealthy donors. These are not trivial points; they are the stuff of revolutions and populism—dangers the First Amendment guards against.

In his brief opinion, Calabresi does not explicitly apply his distortion rationale to information economics, but that must be what he had in mind. Information economics relaxes the perfect information assumption of neoclassical microeconomics. Because of the centrality of information in all economic decision-making, this move broadly recasts economic analysis. Joseph Stiglitz, who won the 2001 Nobel Prize for his work on information economics, emphasizes the distortions that asymmetrical information introduces in the marketplace. Similarly, asymmetrical information in electoral speech distorts public policy.

Calabresi's point about preference intensities observed by the voters, and signaled by donors and candidates probably also refers to public choice theory. Again these distortions in preference intensities will skew electoral behavior based on misleading information. Kenneth Arrow won the Nobel Prize in economics for public choice theory. The theory demonstrates how the intensity of preferences figures heavily in democratic decision-making.[32] In its simplest form, public choice theory would predict that voter preferences are a mix of number of votes and intensity of preferences. So public choice theory renders Calabresi's point about preference intensities even more compelling.[33] A small number of voters can express even their less intense preferences much more strenuously, thereby heavily distorting public policy in their favor.

That Judge Calabresi would forge pathbreaking links between the drowning out problem and both information economics and public choice theory is not surprising. Professor Calabresi and Nobel Laureate Ronald Coase were the cofounders of Law and Economics.

From this analysis, Calabresi concludes that courts should allow legislatures a much wider berth of regulatory authority than the current campaign finance case law affords:

> And because wealth inequalities are inevitable, and indeed, many would say are desirable in their creation of incentives, the only way to ensure a truly "unfettered interchange of ideas"—an interchange, that is, where each voice is heard in reasonable proportion to the intensity of the beliefs it expresses—is to give the government some freedom to mitigate the fettering impact of these inequalities.[34]

To expand on Judge Calabresi's points, information economics would suggest that these distortions would alter voter behavior from what it would have been without these distortions. Information economics would also suggest that these information distortions skew the speakers' access to, or at least influence on, the marketplace of ideas. Information economics coupled with public choice theory would predict a systemic skewing of the marketplace of ideas and resultant public policy in favor of property interests, which is exactly what has transpired as the empirical evidence recounted in Chapters 10 and 11 shouts.

In his brief opinion, Calabresi focuses a little more on the speaker's right to speak. I would emphasize the listeners' right to know. Listener interests illuminate the systemic slanting of the marketplace of ideas that the electorate faces in deciding elections.

Applied to listener interests, these distortions generate at least five sorts of countervailing constitutional interests of the highest magnitude. Earlier, I suggested that a countervailing constitutional interest is one that the government can assert to justify its position that is not only powerful, but also has constitutional throw-weight that counterbalances the constitutional violation asserted against the government. First, listener interests have First Amendment content: the voters will mistakenly think that the ideas that they encounter during a political campaign are representative of the electorate as a whole, rather than a small minority who have the wealth and frequently the financial incentives to monopolize the electoral discourse. The more distorted the information is, the greater the violation of distributive autonomy. Distortions can be direct in terms of certain targeted messages or indirect in terms of flooding the electoral marketplace of ideas with certain perspectives. The psychological studies highlighting the persuasive effects of repetition as key to persuasion only strengthen this point. This distorts the public's right to know and will unwittingly or intentionally manipulate their policy preferences.

Second, listener distortions directly impair the right to vote, another countervailing constitutional interest. The essence of voting is choosing. Uninformed choice or misinformed choice is really no choice: If I am offered a choice among three paintings, but am blindfolded, how can I choose? Or even more closely in point, the voters are being shown paintings of politics that are forgeries, depriving them of any meaningful right to vote.

Third, these distortions also undermine our entire representative system delineated in Article I of the Constitution, which has separate structural constitutional content from speech. The distortations systematically alter voters' choices and policy preferences by giving speakers a constitutional right to exert sway over legislative districts that they have never even visited, let alone lived in. As discussed in Chapter 6, this ability to project immense influence all over the country into districts and states one does not inhabit undermines our entire framework of representative democracy. Listeners have to obey legislation without representation—something the Revolutionary War was fought over. Fourth, related to the representational interests, these distortions undermine federalism including the provision that each state has two senators, a key federalism interest and the only unamendable provision of the Constitution. As I have outlined toward the end of Chapter 6, the Senate has certain unique powers to participate in structuring the federal government in the way of approving treaties and key government officials including judges, cabinet officers, and ambassadors.

Fifth, related to the two previous interests, listeners—another term for citizens—will live under a government in which power is concentrated rather than divided, again something hardly copacetic with any conception of autonomy, distributive or otherwise. The ideas of a certain interest group will drown out most others. Although property interests represent a spectrum of political views and ideas, their interests will naturally coalesce around certain issues of particular importance to them because of their wealth. These would include taxation, lack of economic regulation, free trade, keeping inflation low, etc. The economic incentives to distort the electoral marketplace of ideas are enormous. Unsurprisingly, empirical data in Chapters 6, 10, and 11 bears out the theoretical prediction that property interests have common pocketbook interests and some have quite successfully translated them into policy.

If a small minority of citizens are exercising sway over the entire nation, across elections, even state and local ones, this undermines the system of divided power. The statistical data in Chapters 6, 10, and 11 suggests this hypothesis is reality. Dividing power was the core of the Framer's entire constitutional project. The Framers divided power statically by allocating certain powers to certain branches of government—most simplistically the legislature makes laws, whereas the executive branch enforces them. The national government has certain powers, the states have certain powers, and some are shared.

There is also a dynamic division of power in the system of checks and balances: the legislature might make laws, but the president can veto laws, and the legislature can override the veto by two-thirds vote of both houses of Congress. Moreover, the executive branch makes plenty of law in its administrative agencies. Congress can overturn the administrative regulations it does not like by passing new laws—if the President doesn't veto them. And so on and so on. This elaborate division of powers sometimes causes consternation among citizens over government's inability to get things accomplished. However, the Framers intended the division of power as the ultimate protection against their greatest fear—tyranny; that is, rule by one person or a small group of people.

This division of power was the most important idea of the Framers of the Constitution. They fought the Revolutionary War over it. This Constitution was undermined—indeed supplanted by—the *Buckley* Constitution that enables dramatically disproportionate rule by the few donors. Again, the statistics adduced by the political science and economics communities seem strongly to attest that consolidation of power is real not theoretical. At least in terms of the listeners's interests, all of these countervailing constitutional interests should resonate with even modern highly individualistic libertarians. After all, the Framers designed the system of divided power primarily to protect liberty.

Disclosure is simply not nearly enough to counteract these dramatic and systemic distortions. The distortions are thrust on listeners whereas listeners have to seek out most of the disclosures and then assemble the information. There are occasional articles in the press that put some of the information together but the torrent of information unleashed by opening the money floodgates drowns out even these attempts to summarize and analyze the disclosures in a way that is readily accessible by and digestible to voters. The proof is in the pudding: since *Buckley*, public policy has been repeatedly, dramatically, and systemically remolded in favor of the very distortions discussed above. As the numerous studies recounted in Chapters 10 and 11 demonstrate, the temporal correlations between the distortions and dramatic changes in public policy are astonishing.

I also am not generally criticizing all property interests for pursuing their self-interest. Many—actually most—choose to respect distributive autonomy and not play the new, big money campaign finance game. Even they will benefit as free riders from reduced taxes and regulations—at least for a time. But putting aside distributive autonomy ethical considerations, the data in Chapters 10 and 11 suggest that these benefits will be costly and short-lived. This system of political economy is malignant already causing demand weakened by consumer inequality, asset bubbles, diminished growth, skyrocketing debt, and more frequent and bigger economic downturns. Yes 2008 really happened.

On the speaker side, there are countervailing First Amendment interests of not having the viewpoints and the preferred subjects of discussion of less wealthy speaker-candidates or speaker-voters drowned out. In addition, many potential speaker-candidates will simply not run for office because they lack both the funds or campaign platforms that will garner the requisite financial support. Content-based discrimination hinging on subjects to discuss and speaker viewpoints are both flatly unconstitutional. Creating a more level playing field is a speaker right premised on not unduly constricting the autonomy of candidates or other speakers to influence the electorate, and offering all candidates and speakers some measure of proper respect in terms of access to the electorate. However, one whose voice is never heard above the tidal wave of multimedia sight and sound sponsored by property interests has had his autonomy to speak or at least his opportunity to influence an election decimated.

If regulations are permitted to reduce the advantages of property interests, they will still enjoy tremendously disproportionate access to election-speak and consequently much greater relative autonomy. The principle of distributive autonomy entails this. Moreover, if the distortion rationales are correct, it is difficult to articulate a theory of autonomy that affords rights to systematically mislead others. Were that the case, a lot of laws would be unconstitutional, including fraud restrictions, SEC violations, etc. Indeed, the Supreme Court has unanimously rejected a First Amendment right to defraud others.[35] Even if it is unintentional, the First Amendment neither protects nor enables systemic information distortion.

4. The Campaign Finance Cases: Constricting Distributive Autonomy

This claim of drowning out the voices of others only justifies some limitations on speech expenditures; it does not define what those limitations might be. With regard to expenditure limitations more generally, one might err slightly on the high side in setting expenditure limits to avoid purported autonomy infringements (assuming a tight connection between campaign expenditures and speech) on persons seeking to make these expenditures. However, setting the limits too high will result in the speech of the many people who currently lack any meaningful opportunity to influence the election process—who are frequently disproportionately 'political out' groups—remaining totally marginalized.

The current campaign finance legal landscape protects the positions of whom John Ely calls political "ins."[36] Typically, political in groups are defined as incumbents. Chapter 11 certainly demonstrates that incumbents benefit tremendously from the campaign finance regime. But the people who appear to benefit most are a very small group who have the economic resources and the political will to play the game. The overwhelming majority of citizens cannot play and have lost by forfeit. That a clear majority of citizens would count as a "political out" group is a phenomenon that Ely never imagined. In September 2016, the *New York Times* editorialized that both 2016 presidential candidates were catering to their wealthy donors much more than to anyone else.[37] In this milieu, property interest donors comprise the ultimate "political in" groups whom challengers and even office holders appeal to.

Precisely where candidate and independent expenditure limits should be set will require careful analysis. Notably, John Stuart Mill's libertarian theory stressed diversity of opinion. This section does not spell out what standard of review should apply to the cases but instead analyzes them based on whether they violate distributive autonomy. Analyzing the laws at issue in these cases under an *O'Brien* standard would itself change the result in most of them. After all, the foundations for the entire *Buckley* line of cases is that Congress is violating the autonomy of candidates and those wishing to make independent expenditures. If in fact the *Buckley* cases themselves violate the autonomy of candidates and voters who cannot participate in the money game, it is difficult for them to survive any autonomy analysis.

Should courts really strike down laws that prevent undue constrictions of people's fundamental humanity? Imagine the argument one has to make to justify a case striking down a law that has restricted campaign expenditures in the interests of distributive autonomy: a court would have to defend a decision that gives individuals the right to unduly constrict the autonomy of others in the area of first-order rights. That's a mouthful. Most of the cases striking down expenditure limitations are impossible to justify in distributive autonomy terms.

Under any reasonable meaning of "unduly constrict" in the principle of distributive autonomy, *McCutcheon* certainly meets that test. *McCutcheon* is particularly problematical because it is one of the only cases in which the Court has struck down regulations on campaign contributions. More importantly, the aggregate contribution differentials that it allows are staggering. Some simple math illuminates the problem. If the examples of the *McCutcheon* dissent are correct, one individual can channel $3.6 million to a single candidate. Alternatively, one individual could channel vast funds to many candidates. Consequently, a small collection of such individuals can spend enormous sums on whichever candidates they prefer. This *constitutionally-enabled* ability affords these individuals fantastically disproportionate control over the lawmaking process, thereby unduly constricting the autonomy of the overwhelming majority of society who cannot remotely afford—or don't want to make—such expenditures. Moreover, in addition to campaign contributions, these donors can still contribute to outside groups such as PACs.

As discussed earlier, *McCutcheon* also undermines most fundamental structural and individual rights bulwarks of our constitutional system including divided power (including federalism), representative democracy, the right of each state to elect two senators, the right to vote, and ironically free speech itself. Empirical evidence predictably suggests that senators and House members listen to big donors who live out-of-state and outside of their constituencies, more than to their own constituents. Even if there is some autonomy right to constrain the electoral autonomy of the vast majority of citizens and then to further constrict their autonomy in legislation, these appear to be countervailing constitutional interests of the highest magnitude. Divided power, federalism and representative democracy are three bedrock ideas on which the Constitution was founded. So is averting the various kinds of infringements on the free-speech rights of speakers and listeners described in the previous section. The distortion problems described also severely impair—or unduly constrict—the right to vote.

Citizens United multiplies the distributive autonomy and constitutional problems generated by *McCutcheon*. Whether corporations have free speech rights at all is a controversial question in an originalist historical understanding of the Constitution and for many other reasons. First, theories of autonomy are generally captured in individual terms. It is difficult to imagine the rationales of free will, transcendent being, and human dignity that Nozick posits as rationales for protecting autonomy applying to fictional legal entities such as corporations. Nozick posits all of these in individualistic terms. Indeed, the whole point of highly individualistic libertarianism is the individual.

Second, allowing corporations to make unlimited expenditures on campaigns violates distributive autonomy. It allows the immense wealth accumulated in corporations to drown out the voices of people. Third, corporations have strong economic interests in spending vast amounts of money to influence political campaigns and issues because the immediate payoff to the bottom line of changing the law can be immense. Management may even have fiduciary duties to pursue these. Fourth are myriad complicating factors of agency. The few individuals who control corporations can leverage their assets in a way that compounds the already great differential between their abilities to influence elections and the abilities of the overwhelming majority of citizens.

Fifth, as the dissent in *Citizens United* notes, the decision violates the autonomy rights of shareholders who disagree with the corporate contribution. Sixth, it also violates the autonomy rights of all shareholders because they did not purchase shares to advance the politics of the corporation's leaders. Seventh, these severe autonomy infringements could have been mitigated by the corporation's making expenditures through its own PAC, which the legislation permitted. Eighth, *Citizens United* itself listed myriad other ways a corporation could assert its interests in political campaigns, including endorsing candidates, hosting parties for them, etc., that the law already permitted. Ninth, incorporation is a considerable legal privilege granted by the state to make profit. As Justice White remarked in his dissent in *First National Bank v. Belotti*, the state need not allow its own creature to consume it.[38] Thus, *Citizens United* is truly difficult to defend in distributive autonomy theory or any autonomy theory. The ability of corporations and individuals to contribute to dark pools of money will eliminate the deterrent effect of companies losing business by making corporate contributions public.[39]

Similarly, the *Davis* and *Arizona* cases would also seem to violate the principle and the same set of constitutional rights and interests discussed in this chapter. Both cases reversed legislative efforts to protect the autonomy rights of candidates to compete meaningfully in the electoral process and of voters to have a less distorted electoral process. One could argue that the legislature could pursue a different type of public financing as the Court suggested. First, no one knows which type of public financing would be constitutional. Second, and perhaps most important, these programs did not "unduly constrict" the autonomy rights of wealthy candidates who wish to use their own funding. After all, neither program gave the less wealthy candidate greater funding than the privately funded one (although the *Arizona* program did count donations made to independent groups favoring a particular candidate in determining how much financing the publicly financed candidate should receive). Moreover, each of the programs allowed *all* candidates the choice of obtaining public funding.

The great advantage of all public financing programs is to diminish the electoral speech oligopoly of property interests. The current constitutional regime diminishes the distributive autonomy rights of voters because candidates on all sides during the primaries and general elections will continue to focus more and more on property interests to secure all-important donations. One can make a serious claim that the matching funds for independent expenditures provided in *Arizona* do infringe distributive autonomy. After all, in reaction to independent expenditures made by an independent group favoring a particular candidate, the legislature supplied an equal amount of funding directly to the campaign of her opponent (or multiple opponents), which could be used by opponents' campaigns as they saw fit. Arguably, this measure unduly constricted the autonomy of both privately funded candidates and outside groups such as PACs. Something might depend on factual issues such as alleged coordination between campaigns and outside organizations.

Whether *Buckley* was correctly decided is a more interesting and complicated question. If one makes the jump that spending money to speak virtually equals pure speech,[40] a questionable idea, then one can make a plausible case that *Buckley* was correct in striking down limitations on independent expenditures and on a candidate's spending money on her own campaign on the basis that both were too low. One reason repeatedly given for striking down low expenditure limits is that they unfairly disadvantage challengers.[41] The numbers contradict this argument. Senate incumbents won 90 percent of their races in the 2012 election and House incumbents 97 percent.[42] Incumbents in both houses outspent challengers by over 6 to 1.[43]

Detailing a campaign finance regulatory structure ranges far beyond the scope of this work. Bruce Ackerman and Ian Ayres have proposed one of the most comprehensive and thoughtful such structures, which has many innovative features. For example, donors would give to a blind trust to short-circuit the connection between donations and influence. Ackerman and Ayres also give each voter a $50 voucher to spend on federal campaigns.[44]

Precisely what regulations would pass Supreme Court scrutiny is difficult to know. But not many sets of limitations could violate autonomy more than the status quo. Moreover, the electoral autonomy infringements are compounded by electing governments that are hardly representative yet routinely legislate severe autonomy infringements and bounteous autonomy enhancements. To avoid infringing on distributive autonomy, limits on expenditures by candidates and outside groups should be set relatively low.

B. Distributive Autonomy and the Free Speech Theories of Meiklejohn and Emerson

Perhaps the two free speech theorists whose work most influenced the Supreme Court were Thomas Emerson and Alexander Meiklejohn. The Court cited heavily to their work in fashioning muscular protection for speech. This was particularly true of the Warren Court, while it was constructing the weak libertarian paradigm for speech.

Law professor Thomas Emerson premised free speech protection primarily on the highly individualistic notion of self-actualization. Emerson posited that free speech rights are intrinsically valuable as they involve the most fundamental aspects of human personality and development through art, literature, political theory, etc. Emerson, who was a lawyer and not a philosopher, outlined four reasons for protecting free speech.[45] The first and most important is self-actualization. The other three rationales are the pursuit of truth and knowledge, an informed electorate, and social change and stability.[46]

Emerson's concept of self-actualization entails the ability, or right, to develop oneself in whatever direction one sees fit. Certainly this rationale is sufficient to make free speech a first-order right. However, self-actualization has its roots in modern individualistic libertarian theory. For example, it is not self-evident why self-actualization does not lead to elevating economic rights to first-order rights. After all, economic resources dramatically expand one's ability to self-actualize. The highly libertarian nature of Emerson's rationale for protecting free speech leads, naturally but not inexorably, to this result.

The philosophical roots of the strong libertarian paradigm of free speech jurisprudence lie in the basis for protecting free speech supplied by Emerson. If the main basis for speech protection is self-actualization, it readily underwrites not only the ability to say whatever I want to say but also to say it with whatever resources I have at my disposal. If self-actualization would directly protect economic or property rights, then a fortiori it will also protect the libertarian right to use whatever property one pleases to express one's ideas.

In contrast, philosopher Alexander Meiklejohn argued that free speech was instrumentally valuable to the democratic process. Specifically, for the voters to be adequate democratic decision-makers, they have to be informed. Consequently, free speech must be stringently protected. Meiklejohn, like Rawls,[47] focused on advancing the democratic process and empowering an informed electorate. As mentioned above, Emerson also talked about nurturing democracy among his four reasons for protecting freedom of speech, but the key reason was self-actualization.

In *A Theory of Justice*, free speech is one of the key rights falling under Rawls's first-order principle of equal liberty. Rawls imparts two basic reasons for placing equal liberty lexically ahead of his principle of equal opportunity and the difference principle. The first involves participating in fashioning the rules under which one is governed. Second, if everyone has a fair say under a fair governmental process in determining the distribution of societal resources, people won't envy the distribution of resources that others have.[48]

Envy is a very important concept for Rawls. It involves rational resentment over the distribution of resources in society. It can cause considerable instability on the part of those who lack resources when inequalities in resources become too great. Envy can threaten the entire society.[49] As we have glimpsed earlier and will see in much greater detail in Chapters 10 and 11, the potential implications of Rawls's theory of envy for modern American society are worrisome.

At some level, Rawls's first rationale is an instrumental reason for ordering free speech rights above economic rights in exercising control over the legislative processes that so affect individual autonomy. But it's also intrinsically valuable in engaging fundamental aspects of human nature in terms of human beings being both political and social animals. His second reason involving the promotion of self-respect goes more to the intrinsic value of liberty.

Rawls's reasons for giving lexical priority to equal liberty deeply resonate with Meiklejohn's reasons for protecting free speech. Both philosophers' reasons also nurture the core concern of *Carolene Products* of relegating the distribution of societal resources and other public policy decisions to the elected branches, but making sure that the process of electing government is fair. Thus, strong protection for economic rights—other than prohibiting outright takings of private property[50]—infringes on the fundamental project of the democratic, or majoritarian, process that significantly focuses on the distribution of resources.

Meiklejohn's conception of free speech being central to the democratic process affords greater sustenance for the view that free speech rights should receive far greater protection than economic rights. Democracy starts by being agnostic as to the distribution of resources within the society. Arguably, to succeed, constitutional democracy must be agnostic or neutral about this distribution. This is because one of the chief goals of the democratic process is to secure some degree of agreement, if not consensus, among the citizenry about this distributional calculus and the resultant shares of resources. Remember resources includes not just economics but education, healthcare, prison conditions, etc.

Moreover, if the democratic process is fair, it will reflect, or at least approximate, the collective economic self-interests of the citizenry. As far as economics goes, one of the great competitive advantages of a democracy is that it is structured so that the system does not leave people behind. If everyone has an equal say in the laws that will govern, the resultant legal system is more likely to be responsive to the interests of all. Recall that the *Carolene Products* political settlement covered its bets on this score. The second paragraph was devoted to ensuring fairness in speaking and voting, the two fulcrums of democracy. But the third paragraph was a second line of defense protecting discrete and insular minorities—groups who had been systematically excluded from the democratic process and were consequently repeat losers in that process. Of course discrete and insular minorities is a safety valve which has limited application and even then, frequently doesn't work. So the participatory democracy paradigm certainly was not perfect but it was continually striving to grow inclusive. Thus, to the extent that capitalism has tendencies to catalyze inequalities of wealth, which Thomas Piketty believes and Adam Smith does not, a robust democratic system will help, and has helped, to counteract those tendencies.

Not only is an inclusive democratic system fair, as Rawls suggests, but it turns out to be highly economically efficient. As Chapter 11 discusses, a system that tries to provide for all tends to bolster the economic demand curve. Having at least a somewhat equitable distribution of wealth—even a bounded one in which disparities remain large—ensures that consumers will have adequate funds to purchase goods, which sustains the supply of goods and hence the economy. If a democratic system is not representative and skews toward a grossly inequitable distribution of wealth, the demand curve will become anemic over time, and so will the economy.

More speculative, but probably also true, is that workers who have a say in their government—and who are partly as a result of that paid fairly and trained well—are more likely to be efficient and productive, which will inure to the benefit of all. So will the resultant stability of the polity which is also economically efficient.

So free speech is central to participatory democracy, and participatory democracy is central to good government. Both Thomas Emerson's and Alexander Meiklejohn's theories afford very strong constitutional protection for free speech.[51] However, preferring Emerson's more individualistic, speaker-oriented theories or Meiklejohn's listener-oriented, advancing-democracy theories carries dramatically different consequences for this protection. For example, their theories would require different results for constitutional protection of campaign finance. Elevating self-actualization to an almost sacred value would resonate with Nozick's concept of side constraints and would readily lead to strong constitutional protection for being able to say whatever I want using whatever resources I want to say it, and consequently, for the current campaign finance regime. In contrast, if speech is primarily part of an interactive democratic process, as Meiklejohn conceived it, then it deeply resonates with the reciprocal nature of distributive autonomy, and what Kant thought of as the reciprocal, duty-oriented concept of autonomy more generally.

Emerson's focus on self-determination also can lead to distortions in the legislative and regulatory process by justifying, if not exalting, the self-determination of more powerful individuals over the self-determination of the majority of other persons in the society. Emerson hinted strongly that he supported *Buckley*.[52] His highly individualistic libertarian theories would favor the result in *Buckley*.

Consistent with his democratic, distributive approach, Meiklejohn premised protection for speech on listener rights, or the public's right to know, whereas consistent with his individualistic approach, Emerson emphasized speakers' rights. I do not mean to push this distinction too hard as Emerson also relied on the right to know; however, he leaned much more heavily on the right of the speaker to speak.[53] The Court has premised its protections for freedom of speech on both. In myriad cases, the Supreme Court has safeguarded listener rights, but it is fair to say that it has emphasized speaker rights, or both speaker and listener rights in many more cases. Moreover, although the Court has relied on both rationales for protecting free speech, it has for many years relied more on Emerson's than on Meiklejohn's.

Again, the core of the weak libertarian paradigm of free speech is content neutrality. In constructing this paradigm, the Court understandably leaned heavily on speakers' rights in stringently protecting content neutrality across an extremely broad range of issues. There is merit to exalting speakers' rights over listeners' rights if content neutrality is the aim. Emerson's theories of self-actualization, dissent, and the pursuit of knowledge are delineated in extremely individualistic terms. These theories were also a convenient underpinning to enforce the individual's right to "say whatever I want to say." This simple yet far-reaching claim is the core of the content neutrality vision of the weak libertarian paradigm. Far from compromising this content neutrality core, the current Court has vigorously buttressed it.[54]

In this text, I do not want to take a position on the relative merits of the Meiklejohnian or Emersonian approaches across the broad scope of free speech jurisprudence. Engaging in robust debate about the implications of their respective positions for content neutrality also ranges far beyond the scope of this volume.

In the democracy/voting/campaign finance context, both speakers' and listeners' rights should have at least equal sway. And, if put to the test, at least in the election context, listeners' rights should generally prevail.[55] After all, two of the most constitutive and important rights that exist in the Constitution are the right to vote and speak coupled with what Walzer calls the right to persuade. Elections are about voters and voting. Candidates serve the electorate, not the other way around. Consequently, in this of all contexts, the rights of the electorate—listeners–should generally prevail over the rights of candidates or other speakers. But the dichotomy is a false one as *Buckley* and its progeny violate the rights of voter/listeners and less wealthy speakers.

Voters need information about candidates in order to exercise their right to vote in a fully informed way. The right to vote has deep autonomy implications in the way of having a say in governmental decisions that order our lives. The right to speak in the political arena has similar implications. In a way, the democratic process itself can be thought of as an expression of the principle of distributive autonomy in that it seeks to give us say over how our lives will be governed. Although the principle of distributive autonomy does not give all of us equal say, all of us should have a meaningful say.

Candidates become elected officials who make law. Although most laws limit the autonomy of some, many laws involve trade-offs that constrict the autonomy of some while enlarging the autonomy of others. Take the example of maximum hours or overtime laws. Moreover, in a representative democracy, the maxim "equal justice under law" does not only entail equality before the courts. If some have enormous sway over the elected officials who make law while others have virtually none, the entire idea of equal justice under law begins to look hollow. After all, justice involves more than courts; justice is meted out by all of government.

One could posit democracy as an end in itself. This is a difficult argument to maintain unless one has a fetish for the unruly, highly inefficient process (in the short run) of governance that democracy begets. More probably, democracy is a means to the end of achieving greater autonomy in choosing the kind of life one wants to live.[56] After all, government impacts this immensely. I suppose that the highly libertarian theorist could take the position that government should not have power anyway. But this arguably infringes on the autonomy of those who would choose a more ambitious government, particularly if the decision is made through the democratic process.

The principle of distributive autonomy does place side constraints on what type of government one can choose. It would of course violate the principle if one chose a government that permanently subjugated citizens and eliminated choice, including the choice to pick another government. Think of dictatorships or other authoritarian regimes—which sometimes first come to power through elections. What could be a more obvious example of an undue constriction across society and over time?

Not only does the Meiklejohnian approach respect the *Carolene Products* settlement in staying out of the distribution of property rights and in focusing on the fairness of the political process that distributes these and other resources: it also respects autonomy. The very nature of participatory democracy coalesces with, and indeed advances, the idea of distributive autonomy. Although Meiklejohn was not openly concerned with autonomy and Emerson was, paradoxically Meikeljohn's theory advances distributive—authentic—autonomy in the crucially important area of participatory democracy much more than Emerson's. This contrast between Emerson and Meiklejohn further illuminates the differences between modern, highly individualistic libertarian theory and distributive autonomy.

C. Yin and Yang: Libertarian Campaign Financing versus Egalitarian One Person, One Vote

The Court itself illuminates the depth of the autonomy infringement of the campaign finance cases. Their most precise and poignant counterpoint is the Court's jurisprudence stringently commanding one person, one vote.[57] In sharp contrast to its free speech decisions, the Court has been quite avid in its pursuit of weighting votes equally, invalidating even small differences in their relative weights.[58] There could be little reason to do this except to advance democracy, or to protect the autonomy of the individual voter, or to safeguard each voter's influence over the inevitable, and often deep, autonomy infringements and trade-offs effected by law. The aggregate effect of voting in influencing the government and therefore law is immense.[59] Moreover, law largely involves line drawing, which routinely constrains liberty and autonomy.

In sharp contrast, *Buckley* and its progeny use individual liberty reasoning to justify severe disparities in campaign finance. Voting and speaking comprise the fulcrums of democracy. Taken together, they constitute the core of the democratic process protected in the *Carolene Products* decision.[60] The decision's other core functional concern of protecting minorities engages after the democratic process has broken down.

The basic thrust of the Court's voting rights jurisprudence has been guaranteeing the equal weight of each ballot so that everyone equally influences the democratic process of governance. The piloting principle has been one person, one vote; and the watershed case animating this ideal is *Reynolds v. Sims*.[61] *Reynolds* is replete with language guaranteeing the equal weight of each person's vote:

"Obviously included within the right to choose, secured by the Constitution, is the right of qualified voters within a state to cast their ballots and have them counted. . . ." And history has seen a continuing expansion of the scope of the right of suffrage in this country. The right to vote freely for the candidate of one's choice is of the essence of a democratic society, and any restrictions on that right strike at the heart of representative government. And the right of suffrage can be denied by a debasement or dilution of the weight of a citizen's vote just as effectively as by wholly prohibiting the free exercise of the franchise.[62] [Citations omitted].

The *Reynolds* Court continued, quoting from the earlier case of *Gray v. Sanders*:

"How, then, can one person be given twice or ten times the voting power of another person in a statewide election merely because he lives in a rural area or because he lives in the smallest rural county? Once the geographical unit for which a representative is to be chosen is designated, all who participate in the election are to have an equal vote—whatever their race, whatever their sex, whatever their occupation, whatever their income and wherever their home may be in that geographical unit. This is required by the Equal Protection Clause of the Fourteenth Amendment. The concept of 'we the people' under the Constitution visualizes no preferred class of voters, but equality among those who meet the basic qualifications."[63]

Quoting yet another landmark voting rights case, the *Reynolds* Court continued:

"No right is more precious in a free country than that of having a voice in the election of those who make the laws. . . . Other rights, even the most basic, are illusory if the right to vote is undermined. . . ."

. . . *Wesberry* [*v. Sanders*] clearly established that the fundamental principle of representative government in this country is one of equal representation for equal numbers of people, without regard to race, sex, economic status, or place of residence within a State.[64]

The rights to speak and vote are the two most fundamental ways in which citizens can influence their government. Yet there is a deep contradiction between the ways the Court has treated one right as against the other. The right to vote follows stringent, traditional equality norms, whereas campaign speech follows stringent, traditional individualistic libertarian norms. One can rationalize these antithetical approaches by invoking the doctrine of precedent: the Warren Court decided the one person, one vote cases and subsequent Supreme Courts refused to reverse them. The Burger Court wrote the first of the campaign finance cases and subsequent Courts refused to reverse them. There are multiple problems with this argument. First, lines of Supreme Court cases should be consistent with each other no matter who decides them. Second, Courts subsequent to the Warren Court reversed—or fundamentally changed—a considerable swath of that Court's free speech jurisprudence in areas such as access to the public forum and access to the media. Third, in extending protection to commercial speech, the Court reversed long—standing precedent. Fourth, *Buckley* was inconsistent with the long-standing thrust of Supreme Court cases in the First Amendment area, which were overtly or implicitly concerned with the distribution of speech rights. A governing premise underlying both the public forum cases and the content neutrality principle was that all speech should access the marketplace of ideas. There were also company town,[65] shopping mall,[66] and media access cases[67] that articulated this view.

One could also distinguish the lines of cases based on the text of the Constitution, viz. the voting rights cases are based on the equal protection clause whereas the campaign finance cases are based on the concept of freedom or liberty in the First Amendment. For several reasons, this is a difficult argumentative tack to maintain. First, the Warren Court moved toward a more and more egalitarian, or at least inclusive or participatory, approach to the First Amendment. Several free speech cases even incorporated equal protection analysis.[68] To say that the Warren Court's approach was more and more egalitarian does not suggest that the approach either failed to advance liberty or exalted equality over liberty. The weak libertarian paradigm of free speech jurisprudence is quite real. So the Warren Court endeavored to serve both values—just like the Constitution does. Rawls's notion of equal liberty descriptively captioned that approach. A second problem with trying to strip the First Amendment of egalitarian values is, as I previously noted, the First Amendment was applied to the states through the Fourteenth Amendment, which is overtly egalitarian. Third, although the equal protection clause extended to race relations, it was to say the least not obvious when the one person, one vote cases were decided that the clause was intended to apply to equalize votes between persons in different electoral districts. Indeed, the equal protection clause mentions neither a right to vote nor a right to speak. The one person, one vote cases were quite controversial when the Court decided them. They also violated the pact of the Fourteenth Amendment that the new Amendment would respect local rule. The Court also violated this pact in the race cases but with a much stronger textual basis.[69]

Even if one thinks that the First Amendment comprehends no egalitarian values, the main argument of this book is that authentic liberty requires attention to the distribution of liberty. This is plain from the text of the First Amendment itself. It doesn't guarantee freedom of speech for some; it guarantees freedom of speech for all. Attempts to defend the gross disparities between voting rights and speech rights on autonomy grounds are thin at best. Your speech rights are just as important as mine. Any other position requires a claim that since my autonomy is so much more valuable than yours, my autonomy is entitled to so much protection that I can infringe on yours. Specifically, my claim would be that the First Amendment gives me, in my capacity as a candidate, voter, or even a donor, the right to drown out your voice with impunity in the constitutive area of elections, and also to distort listeners' rights of voter/decision-makers. One who takes autonomy seriously has difficulty taking these positions. The Constitution bestows rights on everyone. A core problem with traditional libertarian theories is that they focus on governmental infringements of autonomy. This is a critically important move. By focusing just on governmental infringements on autonomy, the traditional libertarian can sidestep, or at least obfuscate, the problem of not taking the autonomy of others seriously.

But if one values autonomy, one cannot just care about autonomy violations committed by governments. One must also take seriously autonomy infringements committed by private parties. The law certainly does as exemplified in the law of torts, which elsewhere I have argued is centrally concerned with protecting autonomy.[70] One could argue that constitutional law places autonomy infringements effected by the government on a different plane by recognizing governmental infringements, but not those committed by private individuals. Even assuming that such a distinction is broadly valid, surely it does not inhere when courts create constitutional rights that enable individuals to infringe on each other's autonomy. A Constitution focused on liberty and equality surely does not prohibit laws that advance these values. When the legislature creates laws nurturing autonomy, courts should not strike them down on autonomy grounds.

Voice and vote are natural partners in the democratic enterprise. Mill is in a long line of distinguished political theorists who required the ruler to operate on the basis of consent.[71] Inherent in the concept of consent is informed consent. This necessitates information, which Mill says is advanced by a diversity of opinions.[72] Voting requires information.

Voice and vote also share a common heritage that is less obvious. A basic doctrinal and pedagogical divide in constitutional law is that between government structure and individual rights. Commonly, constitutional law courses and course books treat voice and vote as individual rights. However, this demarcation is somewhat arbitrary because voice and vote clearly involve structure as well as rights: speaking and voting are the key processes by which we elect or structure the government.

In American constitutional theory, the Framers thought of structure as more important than rights. Tellingly, the Bill of Rights were amendments to the Constitution; the Framers did not consider them important enough to include in the original document. Instead, the states insisted on them as a precondition to ratifying the Constitution. The original document almost exclusively involves structure because the Framers thought that the correct structure would automatically function to guarantee rights.

As they are constitutive, foundational structural provisions can be far more difficult to alter. "[A]s Madison predicted, many of the institutional arrangements that make up the constitutional structure of government appear to be less susceptible to political revision or override than rights and other constitutional rules."[73]

It could take a generation to rectify the constitutive structural changes wrought by *Buckley* and its progeny. If the cases are reversed, it could take a long time for Congress and state legislatures to change the campaign finance rules that got them elected. Even then, with the high level of incumbency re-election, it could take many years to elect legislatures less influenced by the impact of great wealth. Of course, incumbents may also think differently once the law has changed incentivizing them to think more about their constituents and less about their donors. After that, it will take many more years for those new or differently incented legislators to change the many laws that have been enacted over forty years by legislatures elected to represent property interests more than their constituents. The "*Buckley* Constitution" will take a long time to fix.

Notes

1. ARISTOTLE, THE POLITICS, Book III, Part IX (Benjamin Jowett trans.) http://classics.mit.edu/Aristotle/politics.3.three.html; MICHAEL WALZER, SPHERES OF JUSTICE: A DEFENSE OF PLURALISM AND EQUALITY 79-80 (Basic Books, 1983).

2. WALZER, SPHERES, *supra* note 1, at 221.

3. *Id.* at 74.

4. *Id.* at 19, 30.

5. *Id.* at 22–23.

6. *Id.* at 80.

7. *Id.* at 101.

8. *Id.* at 121.

9. *Id.* at 304.

10. *Id.* at 319.

11. *Id.* at 305.

12. *Id.* at 308.

13. *Id.* at 320–21.

14. *Id.* at 310–11.

15. *Id.* at 92.

16. John Cassidy, *American Inequality and Six Charts*, NEW YORKER (Nov. 18, 2013) http://www.newyorker.com/news/john-cassidy/american-inequality-in-six-charts. See also Daryl Levinson, *Parchment and Politics: The Positive Puzzle of Constitutional Commitment*, 124 HARV. L. REV. 657, 714–15 (2011) (constitutional system dramatically affects "the formation, composition, and political power and influence of various groups"); Joseph Fishkin & Heather K. Gerken, *The Party's Over: McCutcheon, Shadow Parties, and the Future of the Party System*, 2014 SUP. CT. REV. 175, 202 (positing an elite-driven model in which "parties are like firms, donors are like shareholders, and ordinary voters are like consumers choosing between the two parties' offerings").

17. United States v. O'Brien, 390 U.S. 367 (1968).

18. *Id.* at 377.

19. Kovacs v. Cooper, 336 U.S. 77, 87–89 (1948).

20. Public forums include but are not limited to public parks, streets, and sidewalks. For example, the Court has held a federal government charity drive in which government employees could give to various charities a limited public forum by governmental designation. Cornelius v. NAACP, 473 U.S. 788 (1985).

21. 336 U.S. 77, 97 (1949).

22. 395 U.S. 367, 392 (1969).

23. 47 C.F.R. 73 (1992).

24. 453 U.S. 367, 395–96 (1981).

25. 47 U.S.C. § 312(a)(7) (1934).

26. 453 U.S. 367, 395–96 (1981).

27. 326 U.S. 1 (1944).

28. 326 U.S. 1, 20 (1945). *See also* Indiana Farmer's Guide Pub. Co. v. Prairie Farmer Pub. Co., 293 U.S. 268 (1934) (applying triple damages against newspaper for monopolization).

29. 671 F.3d 174 (2d Cir. 2011) (Calabresi, J., concurring), *cert denied*, 567 U.S. 935 (2012).

30. *Id.* at 199.

31. *Id. See also* Landell v. Sorrell, 406 F.3d 159, 161 (2d Cir. 2005) (Calabresi, J., concurring in the denial of rehearing en banc), *rev'd sub nom.* Randall v. Sorrell, 548 U.S. 230 (2006).

32. Kenneth J. Arrow, Social Choice and Individual Values (Yale University Press, 1951); Duncan Black, The Theory of Committees and Elections (Cambridge University Press, 1958).

33. As the Acknowledgements suggest, Judge Calabresi is my teacher and mentor. I learned of his *Ognibene* concurrence well after the case was decided.

34. *Ognibene,* 671 F.3d at 200.

35. *See* Illinois ex rel. Madigan v. Telemarketing Ass'n, 538 U.S. 600 (2003).

36. *See* John Hart Ely, Democracy And Distrust: A Theory of Judicial Review 120 (Harvard University Press, 1980).

37. Editorial, *What's "Deplorable" About Presidential Campaigns*, N.Y. Times, Sept. 13, 2016, http://www.nytimes.com/2016/09/14/opinion/whats-deplorable-about-presidential-campaigns.html.

38. *See supra* text accompanying note 65, Chapter 5.

39. *See* note 58, Chapter 11.

40. For an argument disconnecting spending money and speaking in campaign finance, see Deborah Hellman, *Money Talks but It Isn't Speech*, 95 Minn. L. Rev. 953 (2011).

41. *See* Burt Neuborne, One Dollar-One Vote: A Preface to Debating Campaign Finance Reform, 37 Washburn L.J. 1, 21–22, 26–27, 30 (1997).

42. Walter Hickey, *Candidates Who Spent More Money Won Their Elections 95% of the Time*, Bus. Insider (Nov. 9, 2012), http://www.businessinsider.com/congress-election-money-2012-11.

43. OpenSecrets.org, Center for Responsive Politics, *Incumbent Advantage* https://www.opensecrets.org/overview/incumbs.php?cycle=2012 (website last visited on Nov. 4, 2017).

44. Bruce Ackerman & Ian Ayres, Voting with Dollars: A New Paradigm for Campaign Finance (Yale University Press, 2002). Each voter may contribute up to $25 "Patriot Dollars" to the presidential campaign, $15 to the Senate campaign, and $10 to House campaigns.

Id. at 76–77. Richard Hasen proposes that people would receive vouchers of $100 per two-year federal election cycle. RICHARD L. HASEN, PLUTOCRATS UNITED: CAMPAIGN MONEY, THE SUPREME COURT, AND THE DISTORTION OF AMERICAN ELECTIONS 9–10 (Yale University Press, 2016). Under his proposal, an individual cannot spend more than $25,000 per federal election to support or oppose a candidate in that election. A person cannot contribute or spend more than $500,000 in total per election cycle on all election activity. HASEN, *supra*, at 94.

45. G. Edward White argues that post-*Lochner* theorists rested speech protection on advancing democracy, rejecting libertarian rationales until Thomas Emerson re-introduced them. G. Edward White, *The First Amendment Comes of Age: The Emergence of Free Speech in Twentieth-Century America*, 95 MICH. L. REV. 299, 316–17, 325–26 (1996). *See* text accompanying notes 26–27, Chapter 5.

46. THOMAS I. EMERSON, THE SYSTEM OF FREEDOM OF EXPRESSION 6–7 (Random House, 1970); Thomas I. Emerson, *Toward a General Theory of the First Amendment*, 72 YALE L.J. 677 (1963).

47. Meiklejohn was a philosopher who received the Medal of Freedom from President Lyndon Johnson.

48. *See supra* text accompanying notes 31–32, Chapter 4.

49. JOHN RAWLS, A THEORY OF JUSTICE 464–79 (Harvard University Press, 1971, rev. ed. 1999).

50. *See* U.S. CONST. amend. V.

51. *See supra* text accompanying notes 76–90, Chapter 4.

52. Thomas Emerson, *Legal Foundations of the Right to Know*, 1976 WASH. U. L.Q. 1, 13 & n.19. [hereinafter Emerson, *Foundations*]. Several years earlier, in his highly influential book *The System of Freedom of Expression*, Emerson had hinted that he would allow the state to equalize campaign expenditures by candidates and also allow forced disclosure of candidate financing. In his earlier writing, he supported these measures as anticorruption ones. However, government could only regulate candidates during election seasons. In contrast, he would allow no regulations, not even disclosure, of the election spending or other activities of noncandidates. EMERSON, SYSTEM, *supra* note 46, at 639–40. Apparently his views changed six years later when he voiced support for *Buckley*.

53. *See generally* Emerson, *Foundations*, *supra* note 52, at 14–20.

54. United States v. Stevens, 559 U.S. 460 (2010) (affording constitutional protection to depictions of animal cruelty); Brown v. Entm't Merchs. Ass'n, 564 U.S. 786 (2011) (affording free speech protection to video games—even ones that involve rape, racism, and murder). In his opinion concurring in the *Brown* case, Justice Alito depicted the grizzly games thusly:

> There are games in which a player can take on the identity and reenact the killings carried out by the perpetrators of the murders at Columbine High School and Virginia Tech. The objective of one game is to rape a mother and her daughters; in another, the goal is to rape Native American women. There is a game in which players engage in "ethnic cleansing" and can choose to gun down African-Americans, Latinos, or Jews. In still another game, players attempt to fire a rifle shot into the head of President Kennedy as his motorcade passes by the Texas School Book Depository.

Id. at 818.

55. There may be some exceptions as, for example, the case of the candidate from the minority party whom the majority does not want to hear.

56. Jeremy Waldron propounds a helpful and compelling rationale for democratic decision-making based on a somewhat different set of considerations:

> [M]ajority-decision respects individuals whose votes it aggregates. It does so in two ways. First, it respects their differences of opinion about justice and the common good: it does not require anyone's sincerely held view to be played down or hushed up because of the fancied importance of consensus. Second, it embodies the principle of respect for each person in the processes by which we settle on a view to be adopted as *ours* even in the face of disagreement.

JEREMY WALDRON, LAW AND DISAGREEMENT 109 (Oxford University Press, 1999). *See also id.* at 111, 114–15. His idea of "respect for each person in the processes" of democratic decision-making resonates with distributive autonomy.

57. *See* Reynolds v. Sims, 377 U.S. 533 (1963). John P. Sarbanes & Raymond O'Mara, *Foreword*, 8 HARV. L. & POL'Y REV. 1 (2014). Congressman Sarbanes and Mr. O'Mara bring together voter districting and campaign financing cases, viewing them as part of the "two basic imperatives of a healthy democracy—the right to vote and the right to have your vote *mean something.*" *Id.* at 1.

58. *See supra* text accompanying notes 5–31, Chapter 1.

59. See Adam B. Cox, *The Temporal Dimension Of Voting Rights*, 93 VA. L. REV. 361 (2007); Richard Pildes, *Response: What Kind of Right Is "The Right To Vote"?* 93 VA. L. REV. 45 (2007).

60. *See supra* text accompanying notes 28–55, Chapter 4.

61. 377 U.S. 533 (1964) (citations omitted).

62. *Reynolds,* 377 U.S. at 555. Daryl Levinson argues that "in many contexts it may be more illuminating to view [rights and votes] as alternative tools for accomplishing similar functional goals." Daryl Levinson, *Rights and Votes*, 121 YALE L.J. 1286, 1361 (2012). Levinson thinks that this complementarity increases "in settings in which certain rights are necessary to the effective exercise of political power." *Id.* at 1353.

63. *Reynolds,* 377 U.S. at 557 (quoting Gray v. Sanders, 372 U.S. 368, 379–80 (1963).

64. *Id.* at 560–61 (quoting Wesberry v. Sanders, 376 U.S. 1 (1964)).

65. Marsh v. Alabama, 326 U.S. 501 (1945).

66. Amalgamated Food Emps. Union v. Logan Valley Plaza, 391 U.S. 308 (1968).

67. Red Lion Broadcasting Co. v. FCC, 395 U.S. 367 (1969).

68. Niemotko v. Maryland, 340 U.S. 268 (1951); Police Department of Chicago v. Mosley, 408 U.S. 92 (1972); Young v. Am. Mini Theatres, 427 U.S. 50 (1976); Carey v. Brown, 447 U.S. 455 (1980); Perry Educ. Ass'n v. Perry Local Educators' Ass'n, 460 U.S. 37 (1983).

69. *See supra* text accompanying notes 28–29, Chapter 4.

70. John Attanasio, *The Principle of Aggregate Autonomy and the Calabresian Approach to Products Liability*, 74 VA. L. REV. 677 (1988).

71. THE BASIC WRITINGS OF JOHN STUART MILL, ON LIBERTY; THE SUBJECTION OF WOMEN & UTILITARIANISM 4 (The Modern Library, 2002).

72. *See* text accompanying notes 31–32, Chapter 8.

73. *See* Levinson, *Commitment, supra* note 16, at 716.

V Distributive Autonomy: Capital and Politics

Where some people are very wealthy and others have nothing,
the result will be either extreme democracy or absolute oligarchy,
or despotism will come from either of those excesses.
Aristotle, *The Politics*, Book 4

Thus it is manifest that the best political community is formed by citizens of the middle class, and that those states are likely to be well-administered in which the middle class is large, and stronger if possible than both the other classes.
Aristotle, *The Politics*, Book 4

10 Distributive Autonomy, Democracy, and Capital

A. Disparate Voice in Elections Has Ballooned Economic Disparities

1. Post-Buckley Changes in Concentrations of Income and Wealth

Whether it is coincidental or not, at about the same time that the Court strengthened protection for property interests, some commentators noted a sharp increase in the concentration of income and wealth. The Congressional Joint Economic Committee, the Commerce Department, and the Census Bureau all documented that income disparities widened during the 1980s in a way that strongly favored the wealthiest members of society over the poor and middle classes.[1] In 1969, 1 percent of the population possessed 24.9 percent of the wealth of the United States. By 1987, 1 percent of the population possessed nearly 36 percent of the wealth of the United States, an increase of 44.5 percent just ten years after *Buckley*.[2] According to the Census Bureau, "the percent of income received by the three lowest fifths was the smallest since this information has been collected (1947). Conversely, the share received by the top fifth was the highest ever recorded."[3]

Lester Thurow, then dean of M.I.T. Business School, summarized the developments this way:

In the decade of the 1980s, the real income of the most affluent five percent rose from $120,253 to $148,438, while the income of the bottom 20 percent dropped from $9,990 to $9,431. While the top 20 percent was gaining, each of the bottom

Politics and Capital. John Attanasio.
© John Attanasio 2018. Published 2018 by Oxford University Press.

four quintiles lost income share: the lower the quintile, the bigger the decline. At the end of the decade, the top 20 percent of the American population had the largest share of total income, and the bottom 60 percent, the lowest share ever recorded.[4]

In 1980, the CEO's "average paycheck was a mere $624,996—forty-two times the pay of the ordinary factory worker. By last year [1995], the multiple had grown to 141."[5] The number of millionaires climbed from 180,000 in 1972 to 574,000 in 1980 and to 1.3 million in 1988. From 1981 to 1988, the number of billionaires rose from twenty-six to fifty-two[6] and the net worth of the richest 400 Americans tripled.[7]

These phenomena continued during the 1990s. From 1984 to 1994, average real household income rose less than 1 percent.[8] While the income of the bottom 20 percent rose 0.1 percent, that of the top 20 percent rose 20 percent.[9] University of Pennsylvania sociologist Douglas Massey claimed in 1996 that for the first time on record the richest fifth of Americans had more wealth than the middle three-fifths.[10] These growing disparities were confirmed by the Gini coefficient, which shows the overall income distribution in society. A Gini coefficient of 0 indicates a perfectly equal distribution of income. A Gini coefficient of 1 means that all of the income goes to a single individual or household, and no one else has any. In modern industrial societies, the Gini coefficient never approaches these hypothetical extremes. But when the Gini coefficient increases, income distribution becomes less equal. The U.S. Gini coefficient rose dramatically from .394 in 1970 to .456 in 1994.[11] According to the U.S. Census Bureau, the number rose to 0.479 by 2015.[12] Some put the number higher.[13]

Wealth differentials are also astonishing. The 2015 Credit Suisse *Global Wealth Databook* found that 75 percent of American wealth was held by the top 10 percent of Americans, and 35.5 percent was held by the top 1 percent. Both figures represent the highest concentration of wealth of any country they report on.[14] A 2016 report of the Allianz Bank puts the wealth Gini coefficient of the United States at 0.81, tops among the countries they report on based on 2015 numbers. Bear in mind that a Gini coefficient of 1 signifies that 1 person has all the wealth of a country.[15] In the Allianz Report, the United States ranked second largest in net per capita assets (160,949 Euros) just behind Switzerland (170,589 Euros). Great Britain was third (95,600 Euros).[16]

Discourse about wealth inequality has become global and mainstream. A continual, core theme at the World Economic Forum in Davos for a number of years has been growing income inequality.[17] But as we shall continue to see, the United States is special: it has the worst disparities of any advanced economy.

2. Dose Response Correlations between the Case Law and Increases in Campaign Funding

It is, of course, impossible to prove the extent to which changes in free speech doctrine caused these disparities, but the coincident rise of these immense income and wealth disparities, with these dramatic changes in free speech case law, suggests a possible causal relationship. The precise and repeated time correlations between these two developments are uncanny. Some might be skeptical that these time correlations suggest any causality. Instead, the uncanny correlations could be attributable to other variables. However, if other variables help to account for these disparities, a fair political process that produced actual constituent representation rather than radical misalignments would likely have adjusted for them. Instead, the heavily skewed "representational" system only enables or exacerbates the disparities it or other potential variables have created.

For example, to the extent that globalization has caused some of these disparities in income and wealth, the profits from globalization could have been spread more equitably among the population. To the extent that technology caused some of these disparities, then similarly, a political process fashioned with distributive autonomy in mind would likely have distributed the increased resources more equitably as well. For instance, workers could have been paid more for fewer hours while profit margins might have been somewhat less.

Even if one doesn't care about these disparities ethically, the chickens will come home to roost in the economic medium-to-long run. As Chapter 11 explains, these disparities have systematically weakened the demand curve, which has already led to more frequent and bigger financial crises.

Predictably, those few who were permitted to capture (or purchase) the political process have reaped enormous rewards from phenomena such as globalization and technology while multiplying the undue constrictions on the autonomy of the vast majority of the population. I am not claiming that technology or globalization is bad. Both are positive economic phenomena that increase the economic pie. The problem instead is distributional; a fair political process would have insured a more equitable distribution of these vast increases in societal wealth. Nor am I claiming that property interests have intentionally violated the rights of the less fortunate. Some may have; many haven't. As I have argued previously, a violation of distributive autonomy does not require this. Consequently, distributive autonomy can remain agnostic as to whether property interests are somehow to blame for this situation. Moral theory, however, requires that distributive autonomy infringements suffered by the vast majority of the population be redressed. Although I admit that other culprits may be involved beyond the campaign finance cases, let us see if we can further isolate this variable to substantiate the claim that it is the chief culprit.

There is a theory begun in risk analysis in medical pathology studies and now applied to other sciences that is called the dose-response relationship. It suggests that if repeated correlations continue to occur when a stimulus changes, then there is powerful evidence of causality. In other words, if a variable continues to change in a correlated way in response to larger doses or exposures to the same stimulus, there is strong evidence of a causal relationship.[18] The dose-response relationship also has been applied to environmental science to calculate the damage from toxins.[19]

As Chapter 1 suggests, the amount spent on political campaigns has grown by a factor of eleven to over $7 billion between 1992 and 2012. Although big money was always part of

American political life, these amounts are historically discontinuous. In a premier historical study of campaign finance, Robert Mutch recounts, "money was given and spent in the 2012 election on a scale that would have astonished even Jay Gould, Thomas Fortune Ryan, and J.P. Morgan."[20]

The numbers document two kinds of repeated dose-requirement correlations: one between key campaign finance cases getting decided and campaign donations increasing; another between key campaign finance decisions getting decided and increases in income, particularly focusing on the absolute top earners in the society.

Mutch states that: "after *Citizens United*: total outside spending in 2012 elections was more than $1 billion, almost triple the amount spent in 2008. Super PACs accounted for 60 percent of this spending, but one-fourth of it came from 501(c)s,"[21] specifically 501(c)(4)s which are nonprofit social welfare organizations under the tax laws.

In 1980 the richest .01 percent contributed approximately 15 percent of all campaign contributions. That number doubled to 30 percent in 2010. *Citizens United* was decided January 21, 2010. In the two years following *Citizens United*, the number continued upward to 40 percent and appeared to be still on the rise into 2015.[22] The number of PACs also highly correlates with *Buckley* and *Citizens United*. Mutch describes the 7,500 PACs that existed at the beginning of the 2015–2016 election cycle as having been produced by two "growth spurts." The first was in the late 1970s following *Buckley,* and the second was following *Citizens United*.[23]

As Chapter 6 documents, donations by the top 0.01 percent in presidential races increased over 65 percent just eleven months after *Citizens United* was decided, even though that number had held relatively constant during the previous three presidential election cycles.[24]

Moreover, *Citizens United* produces another important time correlation in the amount of giving to PACs and 501(c)(4) organizations. Much of the increase in 501 donations went to the 501(c)(4)s. In 2007, the Federal Election Commission ruled that these social welfare organizations only had to disclose "contributions that were 'made for the purpose of furthering electioneering communications.'" So if the organization does not disclose this purpose to a donor, it may now keep its donor list secret.[25] After *Citizens United*, donations to these 501(c)(4) nonprofit corporations almost tripled. The nondisclosure has given rise to the term "'dark money.'" This is basically money whose influence cannot be traced.[26]

The concentration of giving by property interests intensified in the 2016 election. Reinforcing figures detailed in Chapter 1, *Politico* reported that by February 2016, the top 100 donors "spent $195 million trying to influence the presidential election—more than the $155 million spent by the 2 million smallest donors combined."[27] This number is all the more remarkable, considering most people don't give at all.

So considerable data, from a variety of sources, correlates some extremely wealthy individuals dramatically increasing their campaign contributions shortly after changes in the caselaw. Dose-response relationships appear to exist. The first dose is the *Buckley* case; it almost immediately gives rise to a dramatic increase in electoral giving by the top 0.01 percent in particular and also by other wealthy strata. When *Citizens United* administered another major dose of campaign financing deregulation, almost immediately the top 0.01 percent dramatically increased their electoral giving.

A third jump occurs after *McCutcheon*. *McCutcheon* was decided on April 2, 2014. The number of $500,000-plus donors for the November 2014 election increased by 857 percent, eight-and-a-half-fold from the previous election. The number of million-dollar plus donors increased 687 percent.[28] As recounted in Chapter 6, donations among the top 0.01 percent increased an amazing 45 percent between the 2012 *presidential* election and the 2014 *midterm* election.[29]

3. Donations Lead to Access

Cogent evidence indicates that donations lead to access. A 2013 field study shows how differently congressional offices treat constituents from donors. Two political science graduate students, from Yale and Berkeley—with the help of a political group, CREDO Action—contacted the offices of 191 members of Congress by email to request a meeting. The study used two different form letters: the first specified that those requesting the meeting were "active political donors"; the second removed all donor references and simply said "local constituents" wished to meet the member of Congress. Both letters asked to meet the most senior staffer if the member of Congress was unavailable. The form emails were randomly assigned, and about two-thirds received the constituents' request and one-third received the donors' request.

When the proposed meeting would have been with "local constituents," 2.4 percent responded positively by making the member of Congress or chief of staff available; for the meeting with "active political donors," the positive response rate was 12.5 percent. Additionally, 18.8 percent of the "donors" requests received access to a senior staffer; only 5.5 percent of the "constituents" received the same level of access.

These differences were especially revealing as the email did not specify who the donors were, how much they had contributed in the past, or even if they had contributed to that particular member of Congress. The study had been sparked by the idea put forward in *Citizens United* that lawmakers are not influenced by political money that is not contributed directly to their own campaigns. It demonstrates that donors have a much higher probability of access to members of Congress.[30]

And well they might respond. In the 2012 election, House candidates who outspent their opponents won 95 percent of the time; of the thirty-three Senate candidates who ran, Senate candidates who outspent their opponents won 80 percent of the time. For the House, superior spending even outstripped incumbency as a predictor of victory as House incumbents won 85 percent of their elections.[31] Moreover, the average House seat winner spent three times as much as the average runner—up in the race.[32] As we shall see in Chapter 11, victory in the 2016 congressional elections was even more highly correlated with fundraising.

In a story aired on April 24, 2016, *60 Minutes* interviewed Republican and Democratic congresspersons about their pressure to fundraise. The Republican Party leadership told a Florida congressman "And your job, new member of Congress, is to raise $18,000 a day." A Democrat congressman from Minnesota said that "both parties have told newly elected members of the Congress that they should spend 30 hours a week in the Republican and Democratic call centers across the street from the Congress, dialing for dollars." A model daily schedule given to new Democratic members of Congress at an orientation meeting recommended they spend four hours a day soliciting funds and two hours a day on their work in Congress.[33]

Fresh Air, broadcast on National Public Radio, presented a show about a program for state and federal legislators sponsored by the American Legislative Exchange Council and funded by large Republican donors. It teaches legislators how to draft bills; it will also draft bills for them.[34]

As for the executive branch, Joseph Stiglitz, chair of the President's Council of Economic Advisers under President Clinton, remarked: "[i]n some administrations, the head of the campaign becomes the U.S. trade representative, making it very clear the link between raising money and trade policy. Not that the particular individual did anything wrong, but the optics are very clear that our trade policy is shaped to a very large extent by corporate interests."[35] (Recall the discussion earlier about how income disparities might be mitigated if the largess of globalization and technology was widely shared.)

A 2016 article in the *New Republic* detailed the tremendous influence that Wall Street had over the Obama appointments process and also, over key Obama policies regarding the financial sector, including the "light-touch" approach to the banks. The article further described the same process that took place within Secretary Clinton's campaign with its economic policy team being staffed by former treasury secretaries Timothy Geitner and Lawrence Summers and members of the Blackstone firm.[36]

As indicated, these fundraising activities have all taken away time from the governmental process. Former congressman Dan Glickman observed:

The sad truth is that given the frenetic search for money in federal congressional elections, there simply isn't enough time in the day to stay competitive in campaign finance and do the actual job of policy making... I remember when I was first elected to Congress, I and many other House members would often go down to the floor of the House of Representatives and just listen to the debate. I may not have had an amendment to the bill or a particular interest in the issue but I always felt that watching policy discussions and witnessing the crafting of laws was an important part of my day. It gave me the chance to educate myself and interact with members of Congress on both sides of the aisle. Today most lawmakers would tell you that any free moment not used raising dollars is time wasted.[37]

Lawrence Lessig says that from 1983 to 1997 the number of non-appropriations House Oversight Committee meetings fell from 782 to 297; the Senate drop was from 429 to 175. Between 1975 (just before *Buckley* was decided) and 2008, total congressional sub-committee meetings fell from around 8,000 to around 2,000, and number of days in session fell about 20 percent. The cause was time spent fundraising.[38] Some property interests may consider this a favorable development as they want less taxes, a smaller government, shrunk social welfare programs, and less regulation.

The legislative process is complex and time-consuming. So is the art of compromise. Time spent fundraising robs time from these time-intensive legislative duties. This might help to account for why there is so much bickering in Congress today and why Congress gets a lot less done because bills stall for failure to compromise. Of course, another possible reason for this divisiveness could be bimodal distribution of the donors, which has translated into a bimodal distribution of members of Congress. Obviously, both major donors being at the political extremes and members of Congress being at the political extremes does not induce domestic tranquility or compromise.[39] In any case, Congress does not spend as much time doing legislative work nowadays unless one counts meeting with the donors, many of whom aren't even constituents from their districts. If anything, trying to bridge the larger political divides would require more time, not less.

4. Access Leads to Influence and to Law

Predictably, this access has led to influence, and that influence has been "transacted" into law. Some of this story has already been recounted in Chapter 6. Most money comes from donors outside the constituency—mostly from out-of-state. Related and unsurprising, legislators' policy views are misaligned with the views of their constituents. One commentator summarizes the results of the alignment studies thusly: "[T]here is near consensus in the empirical literature that politicians' positions more accurately reflect the views of their donors than those of their constituents."[40] This is a remarkable statement in light of the fact that the core commitment that the Framers vividly etched in their Constitution was representative democracy, further refined by federalism. These ideas advanced their overarching goal of dividing power.[41]

As Chapter 6 discusses, the alignment studies correlate the bimodal voting patterns of legislators with the bimodal policy preferences of wealthy donors rather than the more normal, moderate distribution of policy views prevailing among the general public. My key question is different: Has *Buckley* and its progeny permitted property interests to enact a systematic legislative agenda that favors their economic self-interests, as elementary economic theory and public choice theory would project? Both could coexist. Campaign donors might have dramatically differing agendas on social issues that turn out to be bimodal. However, the same people could share similar agendas on issues of common economic interests—for example, opposing regulation and taxation both of which strongly affect their wealth positions.

The first step in determining this must be to ascertain whether property interests even have what amounts to a distinctive policy agenda. After all, if donors are politically bimodal, does a common agenda exist? Substantial evidence suggests that it does. But beyond a rudimentary understanding of general goals, the project here is not to ascertain precisely what that agenda might be. The limited purpose is to ascertain whether some distinctive agenda exists in order to correlate *Buckley* with the enactment of such an agenda. This will further uncover the scope of the infringements that *Buckley* has inflicted on distributive autonomy and democracy.

One study conducted by professors at the University of Chicago, Princeton University, and Northwestern University gives some content regarding what views the top 1 percent share. Predictably, these correlate around their economic self-interest and really around two ideas: less government in the way of social welfare programs and regulation, and less tax. The study found significant correlation among the views of the top 1 percent of Chicagoans in contrast with the general public. Some of the top 1 percent of Chicagoans' responses were compared with the general public of Chicago, and others with the national general public.[42] At least when it comes to economic interests, there is considerable correlation of the views of the top 1 percent on a number of issues, and these views contrasted sharply with the views of the general public.[43]

The data does have some limitations especially its localized nature, but the disparities between the top 1 percent of Chicagoans and the general population are so large that they suggest very real differences. So does the high correlation of issues the top 1 percent agree on. Some congruence of views on certain issues among the top 1 percent would probably be predictable from the common economic incentives that their wealth positions would galvanize. Some of their shared policy goals seek less government and regulation, less taxation, and no redistribution.

There are very high correlations in attitude among the top 1 percent of Chicagoans particularly when it comes to cutting the deficit by cutting government spending rather than increasing taxes and in reliance on private enterprise and the market rather than on government programs. There was also strong support for cutting government social welfare programs including Social Security and Medicare. Moreover, the policy goals of the top 1 percent differed sharply from the general public. Notably, 83 percent of the top 1 percent were against higher taxes on the wealthy to be used for redistribution whereas 53 percent of the general public favored heavier taxation of the wealthy for redistributive purposes.[44]

Remarkably, even within this top 1 percent, attitudes tended to grow more antiregulatory the greater one's wealth. Moreover, when one explored the effect of other variables, they did not affect the person's political attitudes, suggesting that wealth was the controlling variable.[45]

Although the Chicago study is interesting in giving a detailed idea of what agenda the wealthiest cohort of U.S. society might have, it is unfortunately limited to data from one city. Moreover, it was taken during the Obama administration when the president was from Chicago. Even if this and other evidence adduced below suggests a common agenda, do these differences in access and policy goals actually translate into differences in what political scientists and journalists call government policy, and what lawyers call law?

The reason I insist on using the word *law* is because that term clarifies that what we are talking about here is autonomy infringements and enhancements, not intellectual policy discussions. Policy discussions are for academic forums; laws have teeth. Laws affect people's autonomy. Sometimes they bite to constrict it and sometimes they enhance it. Many laws do both at once: they constrict the autonomy of some while enhancing the autonomy of others. In the parlance of the First Amendment, laws are action, not speech. Few people fear policy. So even if certain attitudes of the top 1 percent differ from others, and they spend lots of money trying to legalize them, do these attitudes actually become law?

Three categories of other evidence substantiate the Chicago study's conclusion that property interests have pursued the very legislative agenda that their economic self-interest would project and that predictably, they have been quite successful in codifying their agenda into law. Each of these three categories presents additional evidence of dose-response relationships and also of what risk management scholars call "biological plausibility."

Biological plausibility is "a method of reasoning used to establish a cause-and-effect relationship between a biologic factor and a particular disease."[46] Another way of thinking about this causal concept is: "The fact that a hypothesis and the relationship that it proposes are in harmony with existing scientific information."[47] There are many examples of large campaign expenditures having generated legal changes. Consequently, biological, or in this case political, plausibility is possible to demonstrate.

Biological plausibility and dose-response relationships are related. They comprise two of the principal seven factors in establishing causality posited in the classic paper by Sir Austin Bradford Hill. The factors are: (1) "the strength of the observed association," which Hill regards as the single most important factor; (2) "the consistency of the observed association"; (3) "the specificity of the Association," which can't be overemphasized because one variable, such as milk, could cause myriad diseases, not just one; (4) "the temporal relationship of the association"; (5) the presence of a "dose response curve"; (6) biological plausibility; and (7) coherence in the sense that the interpretation of the data should not conflict with generally known facts.[48]

Myriad examples demonstrate that campaign and related expenditures produce legislation that is advantageous to the person making them. These examples are consistent, specific, temporarily correlated, and cohere with the assumption that financial expenditures influence behavior. The success of these efforts documented by many studies also vividly demonstrates biological plausibility.

So what are these three categories of evidence further manifesting a distinctive agenda for property interests? First, there is statistical evidence of a larger policy/legal agenda. Second, there is extensive anecdotal evidence of ad hoc legislative policy agendas reflecting predictable economic self-interest in shrinking regulation and government largess and in other parts of the actual legislative agendas found by the Chicago study. Third, Section B of this chapter recounts the overwhelming success that property interests have enjoyed in a key part of their agenda—reducing taxation. Inevitably, in a deficit situation, reducing taxation will also lead toward reducing regulations and social welfare programs.

One study has received enormous attention. Martin Gilens of Princeton and Benjamin Page of Northwestern measured how much impact economic elites and groups representing business interests had, as contrasted with average citizens and mass-based interest groups.[49] They reviewed 1,779 national policy surveys from 1981 to 2002 in which a survey of the general public was asked a "favor/oppose" question about a policy change.

The study found that average citizens, measured as the fiftieth income percentile, had little to no impact on government policy. [50] Even the policy preferences of the top 30 percent had little impact. On the other hand, the views of high wealth individuals (measured as ninetieth income percentile) correlated very closely with the eventual government policy decision.

Gilens and Page think that using the ninetieth income percentile as a proxy for high wealth individuals *underestimates* the voice that economic elites have in government policymaking.[51] Given their findings, Gilens and Page state it is reasonable to infer that the "truly wealthy" (measured as the top 1 or 2 percent) have an even larger impact on policy, and presumeably law, than the top 10 percent.

Of even greater interest, Gilens and Page demonstrate that as the divergence in wealth widens, political preferences diverge more significantly.[52] Thus, the policy preferences of economic elites become more and more different from those of the average citizen, making the political clout of the top 1 percent that much more opposed to the interests of the bottom 99 percent and especially, to the bottom 90 percent.

As compared with the views of lobbying groups and other advocacy groups representing business interests and other economic elites within the top 10 percent of Americans—the policy preferences of ordinary citizens are virtually not taken into account.[53] In fact Gilens and Page's findings demonstrate there is a direct correlation between wealth and the ability to impact policy. Simply put, the more wealth an individual has, the more likely she will be able to prevail in a policy decision, or law, even if the vast majority of average Americans have a different policy preference. Gilens and Page conclude that as policymaking decisions continue to be dominated by a small number of affluent Americans, the United States "claims to being a democratic society are seriously threatened."[54]

Other extensive empirical literature indicates that donor preferences have tremendously impacted policy. Some studies correlate the votes of the Senate and House of Representatives with the preferences of their donors. In addition to voting records, studies correlate actual policy outcomes at the federal and state levels.[55] So giving gets results. If this were not the case, a lot of people are wasting their money. These results establish biological plausibility: the stimulus of money has actually achieved the predicted results.

Reinforcing biological plausibility are the many narratives in which campaign expenditures have had a direct influence on congressional legislation. Lawrence Lessig has chronicled a number of studies that document such instances: the areas include regulation of derivatives, the Dodd-Frank Act, the Prescription Drug Act, environmental legislation, and deregulation relating to the financial system, including the repeal of the Glass-Stegall Act that had split up commercial and investment banking since the Great Depression.[56]

Joseph Stiglitz recounts a number of other instances including tremendous benefits for companies in the financial sector, oil and coal companies, and drug companies.[57] Some of these individual stories that Stiglitz recounts are immensely impactful. For example, some involved the deregulation of banks and of derivatives, which helped to ignite the Great Recession of 2008.

Lessig and Richard Hasen also contextualize campaign expenditures as part of a larger picture of influence that includes lobbying. While the Dodd-Frank financial reform bill—the key legislation affecting banks after the financial crisis of 2008—was being drafted in 2009, financial institutions were being represented by 1,537 registered lobbyists. This amounted to twenty-five times more lobbyists than the registered lobbyists representing the groups advocating strong reform, such as unions and consumer groups.[58]

Lobbying expenditures have also paid off in reducing corporate taxes. For example, during the drafting of the national healthcare legislation proposed by President Obama, lobbyists for the medical device trade association successfully persuaded the drafters of the bill to reduce a tax on device-makers from $40 billion to $20 billion. A number of those lobbyists were former congressional aides, many of whom had worked for leaders in Congress or for some of the committees that were involved in drafting the bill.[59]

During the drafting of the American Jobs Creation Act of 2004, ninety-three companies hired lobbyists to successfully advocate for a tax holiday on repatriated earnings. A study of the economic consequences of this provision found that the companies spent $282.7 million for the lobbying and garnered $62.5 billion in tax savings.[60] This story portrays the kind of monetary rewards that electoral investing offers. Few investments can compete with these continual enormous, short-term monetary returns. Perhaps the single most stunning marker of the success of property interests in the political process has been the drops in the progressivity of the tax system.[61]

At the other end of the economic spectrum, the poor have lost out. Examples include welfare reform,[62] the cutbacks imposed on the Legal Services Corporation,[63] the general fraying of the so-called safety net for the poor,[64] diminishing and inadequate unemployment insurance both in terms of amount and lack of coverage,[65] and the three strikes you're out rule.[66] There even has been a return to imprisoning people who cannot pay certain debts. Those unable to pay fines for such minor infractions as unpaid traffic tickets, failure to maintain property, " 'sagging pants,' " and court fees are sometimes incarcerated.[67]

It is unsurprising that the electorate is indifferent to the interests of the poor. Distorting the marketplace of ideas in favor of wealth gives all voters a tremendously skewed picture of societal needs and interests upon which to predicate their policy choices.

Clearly, major donors are pursuing their legislative interests, exploiting the rules of the game to their advantage.[68] *Buckley* and its progeny radically changed the rules of politics. Inevitably, a free market democracy will allow property interests a somewhat greater ability to advance their interests by using their resources in the political process through lobbying, for example. Still, constitutional law should not dramatically magnify already extant huge advantages in influence.

B. *Buckley* and Piketty: The Astonishing Temporal Correlations

1. The Income and Wealth Correlations

To this point, we have explored several very different correlations between the *Buckley* case law and changes in laws. The previous section focuses on the various increases in donations and access following specific Supreme Court decisions, particularly *Buckley*, *Citizens United*, and *McCutcheon*. It temporally correlates increases in donations with specific cases. Section A also introduced considerable evidence of another dose-response relationship between the cases and specific legislative results. There were two kinds of evidence, statistical and anecdotal. A skeptic could still respond that the same things used to happen before *Buckley*; that is, the wealthy exerted the same kind of influence over public policy.

The analysis has already shown repeated, tremendous rises in campaign donations correlated with various cases.[69] This section demonstrates another dose—response correlation. Specifically, it shows a highly correlated, temporal relationship between the campaign finance cases and skyrocketing disparities in the distributions of income and wealth in the United States, which are unprecedented at least since before the Great Depression. As was done with donations, the analysis temporally correlates particular Supreme Court cases with rises in income and wealth disparities chronicled in the work of Thomas Piketty and others.

In his celebrated *Capital in the Twenty-First Century*, economist Piketty uses tax statistics to measure inequality arguing that the period from 1914 through the mid-1970s was a historical outlier caused by historical circumstances (in particular the tumult from 1914 to 1945 of two World Wars and the Great Depression) in which both income inequality and wealth inequality declined colossally.[70]

Yet since the mid-1970s, wealth and income gaps have been rising again rapidly. After a decline during much of the twentieth century, U.S. income of the top 1 percent boomeranged to its early twentieth century level. At times, Piketty argues that the inequality the Western world is now experiencing is in the nature of the free market, which increases economic disparities. Yet the rise of inequality that Piketty painstakingly details—starting in the late 1970s and continuing through today—coincides remarkably with the increase in constitutional protection for property interests in *Buckley*, which was decided in 1976.[71]

The correlations are uncanny. The disparity in income begins a slow rise in the late 1970s and dramatically ascends in 1980, after the first presidential election following the

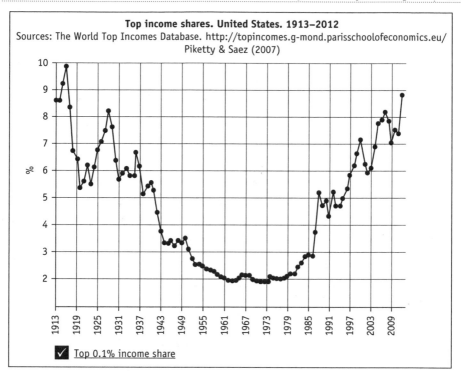

FIGURE 10.1, SOURCE: "Top income shares. United States. 1913–2012." The World Top Incomes Database. http://topincomes.g-mond.parisschoolofeconomics.eu/ Piketty & Saez (2007).

1976 decision of *Buckley v. Valeo* and *First National Bank of Boston v. Bellotti,*[72] decided in 1978. As discussed below, the income and estate tax systems also get changed in 1980 and 1988 to favor property interests. Contemporaneously, government regulation is attacked.

Tellingly, the graph in Figure 10.1 shows a dose-response relationship with the campaign financing cases. The first response is absolutely clear. The incomes of the top 0.1 percent begin a sustained increase just before 1980, several years after *Buckley,* and then rise dramatically through the mid-1980s. Although there are pauses, sustained dramatic increases really have continued on ever since. There are two declines that correlate with economic downturns occurring around 2001 with the.com bubble and the 2007–2009 Great Recession.

Again, evidencing a possible repeat dose-response relationship, Piketty's income chart in Figure 10.1 above shows another uncanny time correlation in response to the *Citizens United* case. *Citizens United* was decided in 2010. The graph shows another dramatic rise in income share of the 0.1 percent between 2010 and 2012.

In his review of Piketty's book, Nobel laureate Paul Krugman remarks:

> In America in particular the share of national income going to the top one percent has followed a great U-shaped arc. Before World War I the one percent received around a fifth of total income in both Britain and the United States. By 1950 that share had

been cut by more than half. But since 1980 the one percent has seen its income share surge again—and in the United States it's back to what it was a century ago.[73]

A 2011 report of the Organization for Economic Cooperation and Development (OECD) noted that inequality began a sharp rise in the United States in the late 1970s and early 1980s.[74] The Economic Policy Institute relates that from 1979 to 2006, wages of the top 0.1 percent grew by 324 percent; of the top 1 percent by 144 percent, and of the bottom 90 percent by about 15 percent.[75]

Moreover, starting in the 1980s, CEO income at the largest 350 U.S. businesses "increased from $1.5 million in 1978 to $16.3 million in 2014, or 997 percent" while workers' income remained relatively flat.[76] Concomitantly, "annual compensation, adjusted for inflation, of the average private-sector production and nonsupervisory worker (comprising 82 percent of total payroll employment) rose from $48,000 in 1978 to just $53,200 in 2014, an increase of only 10.9 percent":[77] Over the 35 year period, this would amount to 0.3 percent per year.

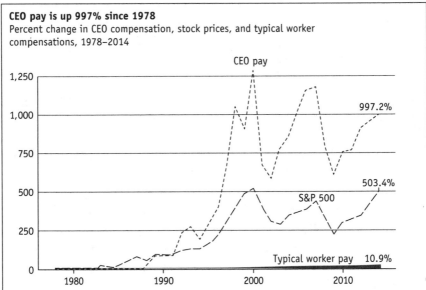

CEO pay is up 997% since 1978
Percent change in CEO compensation, stock prices, and typical worker compensations, 1978–2014

Source: Economic Policy Institute analysis of data from Compustat's ExecuComp database, Federal Reserve Economic Data (FRED) from the Federal Reserve Bank of St. Louis, the Current Employment Statistics program, and the Bureau of Economic Analysis NIPA tables, as seen in *Top CEOs Make 300 Times More than Typical Workers*.

FIGURE 10.2, SOURCE: "CEO pay is up 997% since 1978." Economic Policy Institute. Percent change in CEO compensation, stock prices and typical worker compensations, 1978-2014. Economic Policy Institute analysis of data from Compustat's ExecuComp database, Federal Reserve Economic Data (FRED) from the Federal Reserve Bank of St. Louis, the Current Employment Statistics program, and the Bureau of Economic Analysis NIPA tables, as seen in **Top CEOs Make 300 Times More Than Typical Workers**.

As shown in Figure 10.3, during the same time period, income inequality in Piketty's native France did not grow nearly as much. Moreover the French chart represents the top 1 percent; the American one, the top 0.1 percent:[78]

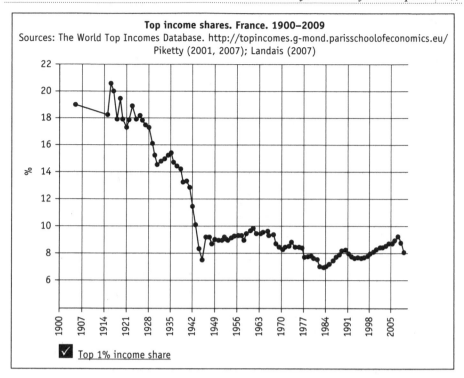

FIGURE 10.3, SOURCE: "Top income shares. France. 1900–2009," The World Top Incomes Database. http://topincomes.g-mond.parisschoolofeconomics.eu/ Piketty (2001, 2007); Landais (2007).

France is not an anomalous in this respect. Top-paid American CEOs are paid four times more than their German counterparts.[79] What accounts for these differences? France and Germany also have market systems.

Nobel Laureate Joseph Stiglitz, former chief economist of the World Bank, chronicles extensive data showing that the United States is an outlier around the world: we have the unenviable position of leading the "advanced industrialized countries" in inequality by a very substantial margin. Stiglitz says that we are approaching the inequality levels of countries such as Iran, Jamaica, Uganda, and the Philippines.[80]

Summarizing his U.S. analysis in *Capital in the Twenty-First Century*, Piketty states that the share of income earned by the top 10 percent increased from 30 percent to 35 percent in the 1970s to 45–50 percent in the 2000s. Most of this increase since the 1970s has benefited the top 1 percent.[81] Specifically, three-quarters of this increase went to the top 1 percent, and half of the total increase went to the top 0.1 percent.[82]

Predictably, wealth disparities in the United States tell a similar story. A recent survey of the Federal Reserve Bank indicates that the top 10 percent of Americans own 72 percent of U.S. wealth (the top 1 percent own 35 percent) while the bottom 50 percent own only 2 percent.[83] As a result, the top 1/10,000th of the population garners 70–80 percent (depending on the year) of the income produced by capital.[84] Unequal wealth is greater today in the United States than at the beginning of the twentieth century. While the wealth share of the top 1 percent and the top 10 percent start to increase in about 1980, the increase is much less than the increase in their share of income, in part because they already possessed an immensely disproportionate share of the wealth.[85]

2. Tax and Other Policy Changes

Is the problem capitalism, or is it the skewing of the democratic process? Suggesting the former, Piketty's copious research indicates that the historic return on capital has systematically far outstripped the historic growth rate, thus over time building these massive inequalities.[86] However, he frankly admits that the wealth, and particularly the income, disparities in the United States far outstrip those anywhere else in the world.

He chronicles the larger income disparities of the Anglo-Saxon countries but then singles out the United States, saying that from 1980 to 2010, the income of the top 1 percent increased twice as much in the United States as in Britain and Canada, and three times as much as in Australia and New Zealand.[87] The top 1/1000th of American earners forged an unparalleled increase in their income share from a 2 percent share of the total to a 10 percent share.[88] Although he speculates extensively about the uniqueness of the American distribution, he cannot account for the difference.[89]

Piketty admits that "[a] quick glance at the curves describing income and wealth inequality or the capital/income ratio is enough to show that politics is ubiquitous and that economic and political changes are inextricably intertwined,"[90] so much so that Piketty describes himself as a traditional political economist.

He emphasizes that the decreases in inequality that occur in France and the United States in the middle of the twentieth century were the product of public policy[91]—particularly the progressive income and inheritance taxes imposed on the wealthy.[92] Piketty says that marginal income tax rates have been closely related to the share of national income of the top 1 percent since 1980. He maintains that marginal taxation and income are "perfectly correlated: the countries with the largest decreases in their top tax rates are also the countries where the top earners' share of national income has increased the most."[93]

Nowhere did tax policy change more than in the United States, going from one of the most progressive tax systems on earth to one of the least progressive in very short order. In particular, Piketty details the change in the U.S. income and estate taxes in 1980 and 1988 respectively. The marginal income tax rates in the United States fell from 80–90 percent from 1930 to 1980, to 30–40 percent from 1980 to 2010, with a low of 28 percent in 1988. It plunged from 90 percent until the mid-1960s, to 70 percent early in the 1980s, to 35 percent in 2013. The top U.S. marginal income tax rate had averaged 81 percent from 1932 to 1980.[94]

At the time *Buckley* was decided, the capital gains tax rate was nearly 40 percent. It declined to 20 percent by 1982 and remained there for most of the Reagan and Clinton administrations. During the administration of George W. Bush, it bottomed at 15 percent. More than half of capital gains go to the top 0.1 percent.[95] The Dow Jones Industrials closed at: 905.11 on December 29, 1967; 875.00 on December 31, 1981; 8,776.39 on December 31, 2008; and 18,123.80 on September 16, 2016. It passed 23,000 late in 2017.

Similarly, the U.S. marginal estate tax rate had been 70–80 percent from the 1930s to the 1980s. Income tax rates for the highest marginal bracket first declined four years after *Buckley*, and then plunged to 28 percent (the lowest since 1920) twelve years after *Buckley*. The time correlation is all the more striking by the fact that the United States pioneered high marginal income and estate taxes. Prior to the 1980s, those rates had almost always far exceeded those in Europe.[96] Now the positions have reversed.

Other economists agree that the rising disparities in income illustrated by the rising share of the top 0.1 percent coincide with large tax cuts, financial deregulation, and less clout for labor unions.[97] In 2009, the 400 top income earners in the country paid an average total tax of 19.9 percent.[98] An article in the December 29, 2015, *New York Times* estimates that "the top 400 earners [each] took home, on average, about $336 million in 2012," and paid 17.6 percent in taxes. In contrast, the top 1 percent paid over 24 percent.[99]

The following chart in Figure 10.4 suggests that the United States does not have the greatest income disparities. But when one overlays the taxation systems, it rises to No. 1 among a fairly diverse group of high income countries.[100]

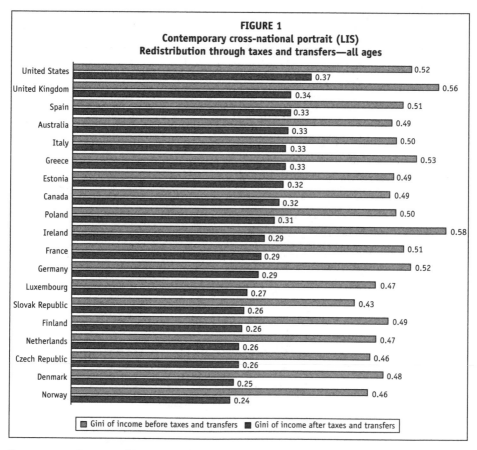

FIGURE 10.4, SOURCE: "Contemporary cross-national portrait (LIS), Redistribution through taxes and transfers—all ages," Luxembourg Income Study Center.

So as the *New York Times* suggests, the variable making the United States the country with the most disparate income distribution is public policy, especially tax policy.

Piketty gives this arresting view:

> what primarily characterizes the United States at the moment is a record level of inequality of income from labor (probably higher than in any other society at any time in the past, anywhere in the world, including societies in which skill disparities were extremely large) together with a level of inequality of wealth less extreme than the levels observed in traditional societies or in Europe in the period 1900–1910.[101]

He elaborates that the top 10 percent claims 50 percent of the national income, with the top 1 percent garnering 20 percent of the total national income.[102]

Piketty does offer evidence of current regressivity in overall taxes (including taxes on consumption and income) paid in Europe, which he thinks also exists in the United States.[103] These and all other tax decisions are for the legislature, but one fairly elected with equitable participation. This maximizes the chance that every individual is fairly represented in the body which makes laws that constrict or enhance his or her individual autonomy.

In an article published in December 2016, Professors Piketty, Emmanuel Saez, and Gabriel Zucman explore new U.S. data sets that further illuminate the dramatic rise in U.S. income inequality. These data sets enable the authors to contrast pre-tax and post-tax incomes, including how government transfers have increased some post-tax incomes. The authors focus exclusively on the United States, promising future articles on other countries. Taking into account taxation and government transfers slightly qualifies, but mostly reinforces, Piketty's conclusions.

In their 2016 U.S. working paper, Piketty, Saez, and Zucman summarize their first two overarching conclusions thusly. First, their data shows a much slower growth rate for the bottom 50 percent than the rest of the economy. From 1980 to 2014, pre-tax income for the bottom 50 percent has remained around $16,000 per adult expressed in constant 2014 dollars. During the same time, average national income grew 60 percent. As a result, the bottom 50 percent income share of the overall economy nearly halved (-40 percent). In the meantime, the average pre-tax income of top 1 percent adults tripled. The bottom 50 percent divided only 20 percent of total national income in 1980, which collapsed to a mere 12 percent by 2014. In the mirror opposite, from 1980 to 2014, the average pre-tax income of the top 1 percent increased from $420,000 to over $1.3 million, again expressed in constant 2014 dollars. Remarkably, the income shares of the top 1 percent and the bottom 50 percent switched positions to form an "upside down pyramid" with the top 1 percent having far more income (67 percent more income) than the *entire* bottom 50 percent. The upshot: "In 1980, top 1% individuals earned on average 27 times more than bottom 50% individuals before tax while they earn 81 times more today [2014]."[104]

The authors' second major conclusion was that government tax and transfer programs have only slightly mitigated the sharply increased differentials in pre-tax incomes: "Even after taxes and transfers, there has been close to zero growth for working-age adults in the bottom 50% of the distribution since 1980." Government transfer payments have largely benefited the elderly and individuals in the top 10–50 percent rather than the bottom 50 percent. Government transfer payments "to the bottom 50% have not been large enough to lift income significantly."[105] These conclusions reinforce the view that 1980 is a watershed for change in the distribution of income, particularly with respect to the amount earned by those at the top end.

Piketty, Saez, and Zucman illuminate the stark picture in the following Table 10.1:[106]

TABLE 10.1, SOURCE: "The Distribution of National Income in the United States in 2014," Piketty, Saez and Zucman.

Table 1: The Distribution of National Income in the United States in 2014					
		Pre-tax Income		Post-tax Income	
Income Group	Number of Adults	Average Income	Income Share	Average Income	Income Share
Full Population	234,400,000	$64,600	100%	$64,600	100%
Bottom 50%	117,200,000	$16,200	12.5%	$25,000	19.4%
Middle 40%	93,760,000	$65,400	40.5%	$67,200	41.6%
Top 10%	23,440,000	$304,000	47.0%	$252,000	39.0%
Top 1%	2,344,000	$1,300,000	20.2%	$1,010,000	15.6%
Top 0.1%	234,400	$6,000,000	9.3%	$4,400,000	6.8%
Top 0.01%	23,440	$28,100,000	4.4%	$20,300,000	3.1%
Top 0.001%	2,344	$122,000,000	1.9%	$88,700,000	1.4%

Notes: This table reports statistics on the income distribution in the United States in 2014. Pre-tax and post-tax income match national income. The unit is the adult individual (aged 20 or above). Income is split equally among spouses. Fractiles are defined relative to the total number of adults in the population. Pre-tax fractiles are ranked by pre-tax income and post-tax fractiles are ranked by post-tax income (and hence do not represent exactly the same groups individuals due to re-ranking).

Punctuating the importance of 1980, Piketty, Saez, and Zucman note:

From 1946 to 1980, real macroeconomic growth per adult was strong (+95%) and equally distributed—in fact, it was slightly equalizing, as bottom 90% grew faster than top 10% incomes. In the next 34 years period, from 1980 to 2014, aggregate growth slowed down (+60%) and became extremely uneven.[107]

For the bottom 50 percent, income grew from $16,000 in 1980 (calculated in 2014 dollars) to $16,200 by 2014. Pre-tax income growth in what they refer to as the *"middle class"* (the tenth to fiftieth percentile) was 42 percent over the same period, or a meager 0.8 percent per year. However, average pre-tax income doubled for the top 10 percent of earners and tripled for the top 1 percent. It increased by a factor of six for the top 0.001 percent—"ten times the macroeconomic growth rate."[108]

Government redistribution only slightly mitigated the tremendous inequalities in growth. After taxes and transfer payments such as food stamps and Medicare, "the

bottom 50% only grew +21% since 1980 (0.6% a year)." Growth among the bottom
50 percent approached 0 percent before government intervention. "Taxes did not ham-
per the upsurge of income at the top: after taxes and transfers the top 1% nearly doubled,
the top 0.1% nearly tripled, the top 0.001% grew 617%, almost as much as pre-tax."[109]

Again Piketty, Saez, and Zucman nicely summarize the dramatic shift with the following Table 10.2:

TABLE 10.2, SOURCE: "The Growth of National Income in the United States since World
War II," Piketty, Saez and Zucman.

Table 2: The Growth of National Income in the United States since World War II				
	Pre-tax Income Growth		Post-tax Income Growth	
Income Group	1980–2014	1946–1980	1980–2014	1946–1980
Full Population	61%	95%	61%	95%
Bottom 50%	1%	102%	21%	130%
Middle 40%	42%	105%	49%	98%
Top 10%	121%	79%	113%	69%
Top 1%	205%	47%	194%	58%
Top 0.1%	321%	54%	299%	104%
Top 0.01%	454%	75%	424%	201%
Top 0.001%	636%	57%	617%	163%

Notes: The table displays the cumulative real growth rates of pre-tax and post-tax national income per adult over two
34 years period: 1980 to 2014 and 1946 to 1980. Pre-tax and post-tax income match national income. The unit is the
adult individual (aged 20 or above). Fractiles are defined relative to the total number of adults in the population.
Income is split equally among spouses.

Just compare the striking differences in the pre-tax and post-tax income growth between
1946 and 1980, and pre-tax and post-tax income growth between 1980 and 2014. Most
starkly pre-tax income growth for the bottom 50 percent declined from 102 percent
in the period before *Buckley* to 1 percent in the period after *Buckley*. In sharp contrast, pre-tax income growth for the top 0.001 percent skyrocketed, increasing from
57 percent before *Buckley* to 636 percent after *Buckley*. The tax system ameliorated the
problem a bit so that the post-tax income growth of the bottom 50 percent declined
from 130 percent before *Buckley* to 21 percent after *Buckley* and the top .001 percent
increased from 163 percent before *Buckley* to 617 percent after *Buckley*. These incred-
ible swings hold for both pre-tax and post-tax growth.[110] The numbers reflected in
Figure 10.5 below encapsulate the enormous decline in the progressivity of the tax
system.

Piketty, Saez, and Zucman clearly capture 1980 as the inflection point. The graphs in
Figure 10.5 below also vividly depict the reversal of fortunes between the top 1 percent
and the bottom 50 percent that occurs in the first presidential election after *Buckley* and
continues (with some brief downswings) unabated thereafter:[111]

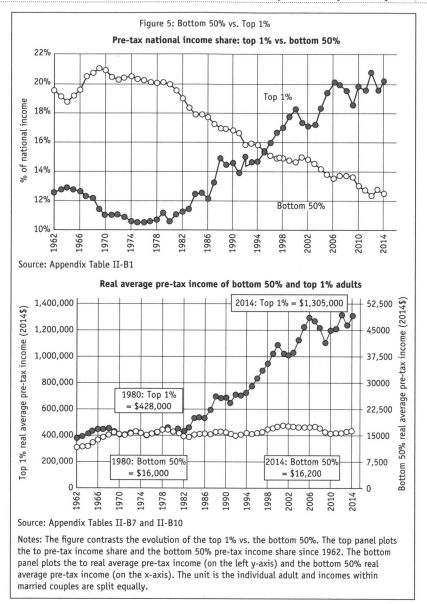

Figure 5: Bottom 50% vs. Top 1%

Pre-tax national income share: top 1% vs. bottom 50%

Source: Appendix Table II-B1

Real average pre-tax income of bottom 50% and top 1% adults

2014: Top 1% = $1,305,000

1980: Top 1% = $428,000

1980: Bottom 50% = $16,000

2014: Bottom 50% = $16,200

Source: Appendix Tables II-B7 and II-B10

Notes: The figure contrasts the evolution of the top 1% vs. the bottom 50%. The top panel plots the to pre-tax income share and the bottom 50% pre-tax income share since 1962. The bottom panel plots the to real average pre-tax income (on the left y-axis) and the bottom 50% real average pre-tax income (on the x-axis). The unit is the individual adult and incomes within married couples are split equally.

FIGURE 10.5, SOURCE: "Figure 5: Bottom 50% vs. Top 1%," Piketty, Saez, and Zucman.

The bottom 50 percent of adults (117 million people not counting their children) earn pre-tax $16,200 per year and receive 12.5 percent of national income. Illustrating the depth of the problem, Piketty, Saez, and Zucman classify as "middle class" those whose annual earnings lie between the tenth and fiftieth percentiles. This 40 percent of the adult population had a pre-tax income share of 40 percent of national income. As one moves up the ladder, the top 10 percent have 47 percent of national income; the top 1 percent, about 20 percent; and the top 0.1 percent received nearly 10 percent of the total income share. So pre-tax the top 1/10th of 1 percent has nearly as much income share as the bottom 50 percent. The top 1 percent has much more. Government transfers and progressive taxation soften the inequalities somewhat. After taxes, the income share of the top 0.01 percent increased somewhat less, 39 percent rather than 47 percent.[112]

The following chart in Figure 10.6 illustrates the impact that some progressivity in the tax system has had on the income share of the top 10 percent and the top 1 percent. The chart captures the 2013 Obama increases in the progressivity of taxes, which have driven the post-tax incomes of these top groups a bit downward.[113]

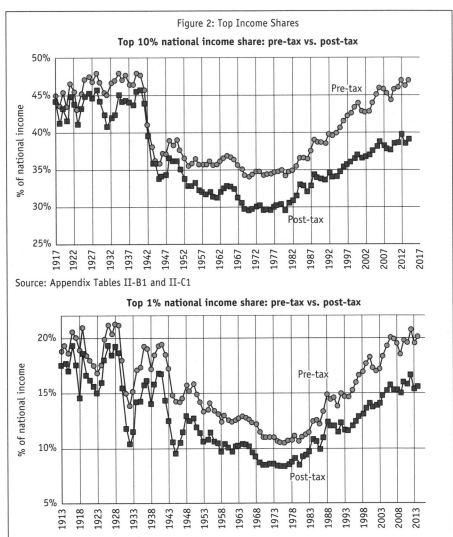

Source: Appendix Tables II-B1 and II-C1

Notes: The figure displays the share of national income pre-tax and post-tax going to the top 10% adults from 1917 to 2014 (top panel) and to the top 1% adults from 1913 to 2014 (bottom panel). Adults are all US residents aged 20 and above. Incomes within married couples are equally split. Pre-tax income is factor income after the operation of the public and private pension systems and unemployment insurance system. Post-tax national income is defined as pre-tax income minus all taxes plus all government transfers and spending (federal, state, and local).

FIGURE 10.6, SOURCE: "Figure 2: Top Income Shares," Piketty, Saez, and Zucman.

However, as the following chart in Figure 10.7 illustrates, the tax system has had a limited impact in blunting these expanding inequalities. The reason is reduced progressivity.

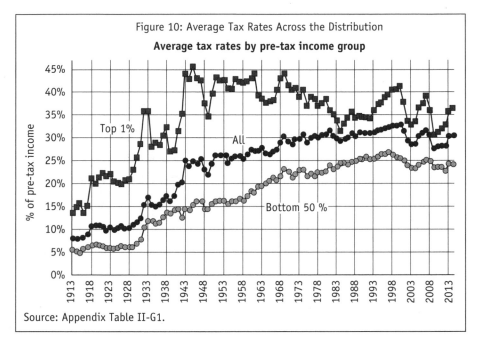

Figure 10: Average Tax Rates Across the Distribution

Average tax rates by pre-tax income group

Source: Appendix Table II-G1.

FIGURE 10.7, SOURCE: "Figure 10: Average Tax Rates Across the Distribution".

Again, 1980 appears to be an inflection point.[114] In a 2017 collection of articles celebrating his book, Piketty's concluding response invites political explanations for this amazing reversal of fortunes he and his collaborators chronicle: "I have tried to show that changes in representations and belief systems involve both the short and the long term, but my analysis of political change would without a doubt benefit from further exploration."[115]

The *New York Times* observed that in 2014, an average adult in the top 1 percent earned eighty-one times more than an average adult in the bottom 50 percent. The *New York Times* reported that this ratio "'is similar to the gap between the average income in the United States and the average income in the world's poorest countries, the war-torn Democratic Republic of Congo, Central African Republic, and Burundi.'"[116]

Moreover, increasingly, the route to extreme wealth is capital investment, but that requires having the capital to invest. Heather Boushey an economist from the Washington Center for Equitable Growth, suggested that this could have long-term effects. Increasingly, the path to wealth is having a stockpile of cash to invest by inheritance or otherwise rather than the traditional path of education and hard work.[117]

If this is the case, the long-term effects here could be to establish a kind of American aristocracy in which the very classicist system that the Framers of the American Constitution doggedly resisted would be established in the United States. Such a system would have a strong adverse effect on growth and creativity; innovation, education, and hard work have been the very stimuli that made the United States the most vibrant economy in the world.

To show the depth of feeling that the Framers had on this issue, the original Constitution featured a prohibition against titles of nobility. This was a radical innovation at that time and one of the few overtly egalitarian provisions in the original Constitution. The equal protection clause was added after the Civil War as were the prohibitions against slavery and against racial discrimination in voting.[118] In addition to being egalitarian, the prohibition against titles of nobility was utilitarian because it made possible advancement based on merit and hard work, which would benefit the entire society, rather than family ties. In explaining the exploding inequalities in the distribution of income, Piketty's book and subsequent article with Saez and Zucman emphasize the dramatic reduction in tax rates, specifically in the income and inheritance taxes. The best evidence of biological plausibility lies in the many correlations between and among *Buckley* and its progeny, Piketty's economic data, and the highly successful actual electoral, congressional, and presidential efforts to abate or eliminate the progressivity of the tax system. *Buckley* occurs in January 1976, *Bellotti* in 1978. Large cuts in the income and inheritance tax begin to occur in 1980 and 1988.

These correlations evidence additional dose-response relationships. Recall that a dose-response relationship represents repeated correlations between a particular subject and a given stimulus. If the subject repeatedly reacts in the same way to the stimulus, that is powerful evidence of correlation or even causality, that is, that the stimulus is causing a particular response from the subject. In simple terms, a dose-response relationship is basically a stimulus-response relationship. As extensively chronicled in the previous subsection, the repeated correlations between the Supreme Court's campaign finance decisions, tax cuts, and the shifts in the distributions of wealth, and particularly income, demonstrate repeated strong, temporally correlated, dose-response relationships.

These large cuts also evidence biological plausibility. If the data bear out a causal hypothesis—that is, if the hypothesis actually comes true—that too is powerful evidence of an actual causal relationship.[119] Tremendous evidence of biological plausibility lies in the many correlations between Piketty's economic data demonstrating tremendous growth in the disparity of income, and the relentless, highly successful efforts to abate the progressivity of the tax system.

The political stories behind both of these examples are related in great detail by Michael Graetz[120] and Ian Shapiro in their book *Death by a Thousand Cuts: The Fight over Taxing Inherited Wealth*.[121] They see the efforts to repeal the inheritance tax as part of a larger, highly organized effort to eliminate progressivity in the tax system in general. Like Piketty, they trace these efforts to approximately 1976, and then to the Reagan presidency in the 1980s. President Reagan was enormously effective in dramatically reducing both estate and income taxes. However, the movement to repeal the estate tax did not gather force until the Republican Party won the House of Representatives in 1994.[122]

Graetz and Shapiro calculate that changing the income tax would reap a dire budgetary picture as approximately one-half of all federal revenues come from the income tax.[123] The tax rebellion has had two objectives: one has been to eliminate the progressivity of the tax system and the other has been to starve the government. According to Graetz and Shapiro, the aim is to greatly shrink, "the government, including the New Deal and Great Society programs like Social Security and Medicare, for revenue. In that case, we might really become two Americas: one quite well-to-do, the other impoverished. We could become Brazil."[124]

Notes

1. *See, e.g.,* Jerry Kloby, *The Growing Divide: Class Polarization in the 1980s*, MONTHLY REVIEW 39, no. 4(Sept. 1987), pp. 1–8. (reporting Census Bureau data & U.S. Congress Joint Economic Committee Report); see also James Risen, *Fed Says '80s Boom Mostly Aided the Rich*, L.A. TIMES, Jan. 7, 1992, at A1 (reporting Federal Reserve Board Study); Lester C. Thurow, *A Surge in Inequality*, SCI. AM., May 1987, at 30; Lawrence Mishel & David M. Frankel, THE STATE OF WORKING AMERICA (M.E. Sharpe, 1991). John Attanasio, *Personal Rights and Economic Liberties: American Judicial Policy*, in GERMANY AND ITS BASIC LAW, 14 Series Dräger Foundation 241 (Paul Kirchoff & Donald Kommers eds., Nomos Verlagsgesellschaft 1993) (outlining evidence of increased economic disparities not long after the dramatic increase in disproportionate access to the marketplace of ideas); *Workers in Poverty Increasing Report Calls Numbers on Wages "Astounding"*, ST. LOUIS POST-DISPATCH, Mar. 31, 1994, at 1 (citing Commerce Department Report).

2. Mark L. Goldstein, *The End of the American Dream*, INDUSTRY WEEK 77, 80 (Apr. 4, 1988).

3. Kloby, *supra* note 1, at 2.

4. LESTER C. THUROW, HEAD TO HEAD 164 (1992). His colleague at M.I.T., Nobel laureate Robert Solow, made virtually the same remark about the increase in income disparities:

> [A]bout 40 percent of families . . . had moderate gains between 1977 and 1992, but only the upper 20 percent of families gained big time. We had a substantial increase in national income during those 15 years . . . less than nothing of it went to the lowest 20 percent of families [whose real incomes declined] more than all of it went to the upper 50 or 60 percent of families.

Remarks of Robert Solow, Nobel Laureate, MIT, to the Economic Conference, Little Rock Arkansas, Dec. 14, 1992, PRESIDENT CLINTON'S NEW BEGINNING 12(FEDERAL NEWS SERVICE, 1992). *See also* RICHARD B. DUBOFF, ACCUMULATION & POWER 131–32 (M.E. Sharpe, Inc., 1989). One study conducted for the congressional Joint Economic Committee showed that "the rate of growth in low-paying jobs during the period from 1979 to 1985 was twice as high as it had been from 1963 to 1979." Kloby, *supra* note 1.

5. John Byrne, *How High Can CEO Pay Go?* BLOOMBERG, Apr. 22, 1996.

6. KEVIN PHILLIPS, THE POLITICS OF RICH AND POOR 10 (Harper Collins, 1990).

7. *Id.* at 166. The share of total American wealth of the top 0.5 percent of Americans went from 21.9 percent in 1972, to 14.4 percent in 1976, to 26.9 percent in 1983. *Id.* at 241.

8. *Id.* at 1.

9. Elia Kacapyr, *Are You Middle Class?*, 18 AM. DEMOGRAPHICS, Oct. 1, 1996, at 30.

10. David J. Lynch, *Rich Poor World*, USA TODAY, Sept. 20, 1996, at B1.

11. Kacapyr, *supra* note 9, at 30.

12. Bernadette D. Proctor, Jessica L. Semega, & Melissa A. Kollar, U.S. Census Bureau, Current Population Reports, P60-256(RV), *Income and Poverty in the United States: 2015*, at 8 (Sept. 2016) https://www.census.gov/content/dam/Census/library/publications/2016/demo/p60-256.pdf. The 2015 Gini coefficient was actually slightly lower than the 2014 number of .480. *See* Carmen DeNavas-Walt & Bernadette D. Proctor, *Income and Poverty in the United States: 2014*, U.S. Census Bureau, Current Population Reports, P60-252, 8 (Sept. 2015). This may have been owing to the tax increases of the Obama administration. http://www.census.gov/content/dam/Census/library/publications/2015/demo/p60-252.pdf. But the change was statistically insignificant.

13. For example, Figure 10.4 puts the number at 0.37 based on 2010 *after-tax* data. In any case, all agree that the numbers are staggering and have climbed.

14. CREDIT SUISSE GLOBAL WEALTH DATABOOK 2015, at 15 (table I-5) http://publications.credit-suisse.com/tasks/render/file/index.cfm?fileid=AD6F2B43-B17B-345E-E20A1A254A3E24A5.

See also Bailey Bischoff, *As America's Middle Class Disappears, the Upper Middle Class Thrives*, CHRISTIAN SCI. MONITOR, June 21, 2016, http://www.csmonitor.com/Business/new-economy/2016/0621/As-America-s-middle-class-disappears-the-upper-middle-class-thrives.

15. ALLIANZ GLOBAL WEALTH REPORT 2016, at 121, https://www.allianz.com/v_1474281539000/media/economic_research/publications/specials/en/AGWR2016e.pdf.

16. *Id.* at 123. The 2015 Credit Suisse report put the U.S. fourth. CREDIT SUISSE, *supra* note 14, at 18–21 (table 2-1).

17. Ben Hirschler & Noah Barkin, *A World Divided: Elites Descend on Swiss Alps amid Rising Inequality*, REUTERS, Jan. 19, 2016, http://www.reuters.com/article/us-davos-meeting-divisions-idUSKCN0UW007; Mark Hanrahan, *Davos 2016: Experts Say Inequality Is Key Threat to Global Economy*, INT'L BUS. TIMES, Jan. 21, 2016, http://www.ibtimes.com/davos-2016-experts-say-inequality-key-threat-global-economy-2274650; World Economic Forum, *Outlook on the Global Agenda 2015* (Nov 7, 2014) ("Deepening Income Inequality" listed first), http://reports.weforum.org/outlook-global-agenda-2015/top-10-trends-of-2015/1-deepening-income-inequality/; World Economic Forum, *Top 10 Trends of 2014* ("Widening income disparities" listed second). http://reports.weforum.org/outlook-14/top-ten-trends-category-page/.

18. For these points about the dose-response relationship, I am deeply indebted to my teacher E. Donald Elliott. The *Encyclopedia Britannica* gives the following definition of the dose-response relationship focused on medicine and more specifically toxicology, which is where the theory was first developed:

> **Dose-response relationship**, effect on an organism or, more specifically, on the risk of a defined outcome produced by a given amount of an agent or a level of exposure. A dose-response relationship is one in which increasing levels of exposure are associated with either an increasing or a decreasing risk of the outcome. Demonstration of a dose-response relationship is considered strong evidence for a causal relationship between the exposure and the outcome.

https://www.britannica.com/topic/dose-response-relationship. For a catalog of toxicity dose-response relationships, see http://qmrawiki.canr.msu.edu/index.php/Dose_Response.

19. Environmental Protection Agency, *Dose-Response Assessment for Assessing Health Risks Associated with Exposure to Hazardous Air Pollutants* https://www.epa.gov/fera/dose-response-assessment-assessing-health-risks-associated-exposure-hazardous-air-pollutants; W.H. FREEMAN & SCIENTIFIC AMERICAN, ENVIRONMENTAL SCIENCE FOR A CHANGING WORLD 48–50 (2013).

20. ROBERT E. MUTCH, BUYING THE VOTE: A HISTORY OF CAMPAIGN FINANCE REFORM 162 (Oxford University Press, 2014).

21. *See* MUTCH, BUYING THE VOTE, *supra* note 20, at 177.

22. ROBERT E. MUTCH, CAMPAIGN FINANCE: WHAT EVERYONE NEEDS TO KNOW 89 (Oxford University Press, 2016).

23. *Id.* at 61.

24. *See supra* text accompanying notes 110–111, Chapter 6.

25. MUTCH, BUYING THE VOTE, *supra* note 20, at 174.

26. *Id.* at 177–78.

27. KENNETH P. VOGEL & ISAAC ARNSDORF 02/08/16 *The POLITICO 100: Billionaires Dominate 2016*, http://www.politico.com/story/2016/02/100-billionaires-2016-campaign-finance-218862.

28. *See supra* text accompanying notes 123–25, Chapter 6.

29. *See infra* text accompanying notes 124–25, Chapter 6.

30. Joshua L. Kalla & David E. Broockman, *Congressional Officials Grant Access due to Campaign Contributions: A Randomized Field Experiment*—Working Paper 2015, https://www.scribd.com/document/217686561/Kalla-Broockman-Donor-Access-Field-Experiment.

31. Walter Hickey, *Candidates Who Spent More Money Won Their Elections 95% of the Time*, BUS. INSIDER (Nov. 9, 2012), http://www.businessinsider.com/congress-election-money-2012-11.

32. OpenSecrets.org, Center for Responsive Politics, *Election Trends* https://www.opensecrets.org/overview/election-trends.php?cycle=2012 (website last visited on Nov. 4, 2017).

33. *Are Members of Congress Becoming Telemarketers?*, 60 MINUTES, Apr. 24, 2016, http://www.cbsnews.com/news/60-minutes-are-members-of-congress-becoming-telemarketers/.

34. *Who's Really Writing States' Legislation?*, FRESH AIR, National Public Radio, July 21, 2011, http://www.npr.org/2011/07/21/138537515/how-alec-shapes-state-politics-behind-the-scenes; *Fresh Air* also interviewed the National Chairman of the American Legislative Exchange Council, http://www.npr.org/2011/07/21/138575665/national-chairman-of-alec-responds-to-report.

35. David Brancaccio, *Is the Euro to Blame for Europe's Problems?*, MARKETPLACE, Aug. 18, 2016, http://www.marketplace.org/2016/08/17/economy/stiglitz-euro-globalization-trade.

36. David Dayen, *The Most Important WikiLeaks Revelation Isn't About Hillary Clinton*, NEW REPUBLIC, Oct. 14, 2016, https://newrepublic.com/article/137798/important-wikileaks-revelation-isnt-hillary-clinton.

37. Nick Penniman & Wendell Potter, *Nation on the Take: Dialing for Dollars in "D.C.'s Sweatshops,"* HUFFPOST, Apr. 28, 2017, www.huffingtonpost.com/nick-penniman/nation-on-the-take-dialin_b_9787106.html.

38. *See* LAWRENCE LESSIG, REPUBLIC, LOST: VERSION 2.0, at 125–29 (Twelve, 2015). The number of days that Congress was in session fell from around 306 in 1975 just before *Buckley* to around 258 in 2008, thirty-three years later. *Id.* at 125.

39. *See infra* text accompanying notes 58-59, Chapter 11.

40. Nicholas O. Stephanopoulos, *Elections and Alignment*, 114 COLUM. L. REV. 283, 341 (2014).

41. THE FEDERALIST NO. 51 (James Madison), http://avalon.law.yale.edu/18th_century/fed51.asp.

42. Benjamin I. Page, Larry M. Bartels & Jason Seawright, *Democracy and the Policy Preferences of Wealthy Americans*, 11 PERSP. ON POL. 51 (2013). Because of the difficulty of obtaining wealth-correlated data, the researchers from the University of Chicago, Princeton, and Northwestern could only obtain such data about local Chicagoans. The data was the result of personal surveys. The researchers had 83 usable interviews from 222 surveys. The researchers consider the response rate of 37 percent exceptional for an extremely wealthy cohort who generally are punctilious about their privacy. The surveys conducted by the researchers and their team were fairly extensive with each one lasting around forty-five minutes.

The comparison with the general public's views was based on three sources. Some of the national comparison was derived from a CBS News poll taken around the same time as the Chicago top 1 percent surveys were done. Most of the data was taken from a comparably worded questionnaire done by the Chicago Council on Global Affairs. A third source was a national questionnaire taken by the Pew Research Center and the American Association for the Advancement of Sciences (AAAS). *See id.* at 51–53, 55–56.

43. *See generally id.* at 56, table 4 (showing that the general public and the top 1 percent agree with their respective cohort groups but are far apart from each other).

44. *Id.* at 54–64.

45. *Id.* at 54–65.

46. MOSBY'S MEDICAL DICTIONARY (Elsevier 9th ed., 2009), http://medical-dictionary.thefreedictionary.com/biologic+plausibility.

47. MEDICAL DICTIONARY FOR THE HEALTH PROFESSIONS AND NURSING (Farlex 2012), http://medical-dictionary.thefreedictionary.com/biologic+plausibility.

48. Austin Bradford Hill, *The Environment and Disease: Association or Causation?*, 58 PROCEEDINGS OF THE ROYAL SOCIETY OF MEDICINE 295 (1965). https://www.edwardtufte.com/tufte/hill. Occasionally, there can be reliance on experimental evidence or analogous evidence. But Hill does not view these factors as being as important as the others already listed.

49. Gilens and Page state that they considered the four theoretical traditions of American democracy: "Majoritarian Electoral Democracy," "Economic-Elite Domination," "Majoritarian (Interest-Group) Pluralism," and "Biased Pluralism." They tested these traditions using empirical data to measure the impact of economic elites and business interests on public policy. Martin Gilens & Benjamin I. Page, *Testing Theories of American Politics: Elites, Interest Groups, and Average Citizens*, 12 PERSPECTIVES ON POLITICS 564, 564 (Sept. 2014).

50. *Id.* at 572.

51. *Id.* at 569.

52. *Id.* at 573.

53. *Id.* at 572–75.

54. *Id.* at 577.

55. Stephanopoulos, *Elections*, *supra* note 40, at 341–42.

56. LESSIG, REPUBLIC LOST, *supra* note 38.

57. JOSEPH E. STIGLITZ, THE PRICE OF INEQUALITY, *Preface*, 95–101, 166–72, 238–89 (W.W. Norton & Co., 2012).

58. *Id.* at 133.

59. *See* HASEN, *supra* note 57, Chapter 6, at 52.

60. *See* MICHAEL J. GRAETZ & IAN A. SHAPIRO, DEATH BY A THOUSAND CUTS: THE FIGHT OVER TAXING INHERITED WEALTH (Princeton University Press, 2005); HASEN, *supra* note 57, Chapter 6, at 6. Timothy Kuhner also describes the vast sums of money spent on political campaigns and how this has led to a dysfunctional democracy and, in turn, corrupted capitalism leading to discontinuities in the market. *See* TIMOTHY KUHNER, CAPITALISM V. DEMOCRACY (Stanford University Press, 2014).

61. Martin J. McMahon, Jr., *Individual Tax Reform for Fairness and Simplicity: Let Economic Growth Fend for Itself,* 50 WASH. & LEE L. REV. 459, 462–63 (1993); *see also* JOSEPH A. PECHMAN, WHO PAID THE TAXES 1966–85 (Brookings Institute Press, 1985).

62. *See generally* JOEL F. HANDLER, THE POVERTY OF WELFARE REFORM (1995); MARK ROBERT RANK, LIVING ON THE EDGE: THE REALITIES OF WELFARE IN AMERICA (1994); Peter Edelman, *The Worst Thing Bill Clinton Has Done,* ATLANTIC MONTHLY, Mar. 1997, at 43. https://www.theatlantic.com/magazine/archive/1997/03/the-worst-thing-bill-clinton-has-done/376797/.

63. MARK KESSLER, LEGAL SERVICES FOR THE POOR: A COMPARATIVE AND CONTEMPORARY ANALYSIS OF INTERORGANIZATIONAL POLITICS (Greenwood Press, 1987); NAN ARON, LIBERTY AND JUSTICE FOR ALL: PUBLIC INTEREST IN THE 1980S AND BEYOND (Westview Press, 1989) "The decline in funding for legal services in recent years has been dramatic." ARON, *supra* at 65; *see* Don Van Natta, *Lawyers Split on Impact of Ruling on Suits for the Poor,* N.Y. TIMES, Dec. 29, 1996, at 27.

64. One possible macabre indicator of the plight of the poor is that state-financed burials in Massachusetts increased from 2,094 in 1991 to 2,835 in 1996. Beth Daley, *Anonymous, Even in Death,* BOSTON GLOBE, Oct. 13, 1996, at 1.

65. JOSEPH STIGLITZ, INEQUALITY, *supra* note 57, at 242.

66. Federal law enacted in 1994 requires a mandatory life sentence for any "'serious violent felony'" conviction in federal court that carries more than a ten-year sentence and has some element of violence if the defendant has two or more prior convictions, at least one of which must be a serious violent felony. 18 U.S.C. § 3559(c) https://www.justice.gov/usam/criminal-resource-manual-1032-sentencing-enhancement-three-strikes-law. In *Johnson v. United States,* 135 S. Ct. 2551 (2015), the Supreme Court, (8-1) in an opinion written by Justice Scalia, struck down a key part of a related statute on vagueness grounds, saying it invited "arbitrary enforcement." *Id.* at 2556–57.

67. Whitney Benns & Blake Strode, *Debtors' Prison in 21st-Century America,* ATLANTIC, Feb. 23, 2016, http://www.theatlantic.com/business/archive/2016/02/debtors-prison/462378/.

68. *See* KENNETH J. ARROW, SOCIAL CHOICE AND INDIVIDUAL VALUES (Yale University Press, 1951); DUNCAN BLACK, THE THEORY OF COMMITTEES AND ELECTIONS, (Cambridge University Press, 1958); DANIEL FARBER & PHILIP FRICKEY, LAW AND PUBLIC CHOICE: A CRITICAL INTRODUCTION (University of Chicago Press, 1991).

69. *See supra* text accompanying notes 115–27, Chapter 6.

70. THOMAS PIKETTY, CAPITAL IN THE TWENTY-FIRST CENTURY (Harvard University Press, 2014).

71. E. Andrews, *The Economics of Inequality: Emmanuel Saez and Laura Tyson* https://businesssocialimpact.wordpress.com/2014/10/28/the-economics-of-inequality-emmanuel-saez-and-laura-tyson/. As previously mentioned, several other lines of cases involving free speech

decided by the Supreme Court in the mid-1970s had the effect of protecting property interests. *See supra* text accompanying notes 15–31, chapter 1 and notes 90–95 chapter 4. There were also other cases protecting property interests—for example narrowing the concept of state action under the U.S. Constitution. They enabled government to privatize many of its functions and avoid constitutional scrutiny for itself or the private entity. *See, e.g.*, Blum v. Yaretsky, 457 U.S. 991 (1982); Rendell-Baker v. Kohn, 457 U. S. 830, 457 U. S. 838 (1982); Lugar v. Edmondson Oil Co., 457 U. S. 922, 457 U. S. 928-935 (1982). While these and other cases nurtured the minimalist, libertarian state, they don't exhibit the remarkable time correlations with Piketty's curves. They may well have exacerbated the problems.

72. 435 U.S. 765, 784 (1978).

73. Paul Krugman, *Why We're in a New Gilded Age*, N.Y. Rev. Books (May 8, 2014) (very positive review of Capital in the Twenty-First Century).

74. The OECD also cited Great Britain. Joseph Stiglitz, The Great Divide 120 (W.W Norton & Co., 2015). Piketty statistics indicate that, U.S. inequality dwarfs that of Great Britain.

75. Stiglitz, Inequality, *supra* note 57, at 8 & n. 27.

76. Lawrence Mishel & Alyssa Davis, *CEO Pay Has Grown 90 Times Faster than Typical Worker Pay Since 1978*, Economic Policy Institute, July 1, 2015, http://www.epi.org/publication/ceo-pay-has-grown-90-times-faster-than-typical-worker-pay-since-1978/.

77. *Id.* This number is taken from the 2014 Census Bureau report describing the 2014 numbers. *See* DeNavas-Walt & Proctor, *Income and Poverty*, *supra* note 12, at 5.

78. Andrews, *supra* note 71. Oxfam released a report on January 18, 2016, stating that the wealthiest 1 percent in the world possessed more wealth than the rest of the world combined. 210 Oxfam Briefing Paper, *An Economy for the 1%*, Jan. 18, 2016, at 1, https://www.oxfam.org/sites/www.oxfam.org/files/file_attachments/bp210-economy-one-percent-tax-havens-180116-en_0.pdf. The Oxfam Report also said that in 2015, the wealth of the sixty-two richest individuals in the world equaled the combined wealth of 3.6 billion people. *Id.* at 2. However, in 2017, eight of the top ten, fourteen of the top twenty, nineteen of the top thirty, and twenty-seven of the sixty-two were Americans. There are large differences in wealth at the top, particularly the top twenty. The top person's wealth equaled that of around eighty members of the list who had around $1 billion. Kerry A. Dolan, *Forbes 2017 Billionaires List: Meet the Richest People on the Planet*, Forbes (Mar. 20, 2017), https://www.forbes.com/sites/kerryadolan/2017/03/20/forbes-2017-billionaires-list-meet-the-richest-people-on-the-planet/#74b5ec5062ff. So the disparities again seem largest in the United States.

79. Christoph Lakner, *Global Inequality* in After Piketty 274 (Heather Boushey, J. Bradford Delong & Marshall Steinbaum eds., Harvard University Press, 2017).

80. Joseph Stiglitz, Inequality, *supra* note 57, at 21–24, 55.

81. Piketty, *supra* note 70, at 294–95.

82. *Id.* at 296.

83. *Id.* at 257.

84. *Id.* at 283.

85. *Id.* at 349–50.

86. *Id.* at 571–72. A 5 percent return on capital has prevailed with a historical economic growth rate of 1-1.5 percent. *Id.* at 53, 68–69.

87. *Id.* at 316–17, 323.

88. *Id.* at 319.

89. See PIKETTY, *supra* note 70; Thomas Piketty, *Toward a Reconciliation Between Economics and Social Sciences: Lessons from Capital in the Twenty-First Century, in* AFTER PIKETTY, *supra* note 79, at 543, 558, 563–64.

90. PIKETTY, *supra* note 70, at 577.

91. *Id.* at 308–09.

92. *Id.* at 373.

93. *Id.* at 509.

94. *Id.* at 505–08.

95. *Id.* at 301–02.

96. Id. at 507–08.

97. PAUL KRUGMAN, END THIS DEPRESSION NOW! 81(W.W. Norton & Co., 2013, paperback edition); David Singh Grewal, *The Laws of Capitalism*, CAPITAL IN THE TWENTY-FIRST CENTURY, BY THOMAS PIKETTY, 128 HARV. L. REV. 626, 652-61 (2014) (book review).

98. JOSEPH E. STIGLITZ, THE PRICE OF INEQUALITY (paperback ed.) (W.W. Norton & Co., 2013) *Preface*, xxxi; http://forbestadvice.com/Money/Taxes/Federal-Tax-Rates/Historical_ Federal_Capital_Gains_Tax_Rates_History.html.

99. Noam Scheiber & Patricia Cohen, *For the Wealthiest, a Private Tax System That Saves Them Billions*, N.Y. TIMES, Dec. 29, 2015, https://www.nytimes.com/2015/12/30/business/economy/ for-the-wealthiest-private-tax-system-saves-them-billions.html.

100. Janet C. Gornick & Branko Milanovic, *Income Inequality in the United States in Cross-National Perspective: Redistribution Revisited* 2 (Luxembourg Income Study Center May 4, 2015) (based on 2010 data), https://www.gc.cuny.edu/CUNY_GC/media/CUNY-Graduate-Center/ PDF/Centers/LIS/LIS-Center-Research-Brief-1-2015.pdf.

101. PIKETTY, *supra* note 70, at 265.

102. *Id.* at 295–96.

103. *Id.* at 496.

104. Thomas Piketty, Emmanuel Saez & Gabriel Zucman, *Distributional National Accounts: Methods and Estimates for the United States* (Washington Center for Equitable Growth, Working Paper 3, Dec. 2016), http://cdn.equitablegrowth.org/wp-content/uploads/2017/02/ 24163023/120716-WP-distributional-national-accounts.pdf.

105. *Id.*

106. *Id.* at 37, Appendix.

107. *Id.* at 18.

108. *Id.*

109. *Id.* at 18–19.

110. *Id.* at 38, Appendix.

111. *Id.* at 43, Appendix.

112. *Id.* at 16–17.

113. *Id.* at 40, Appendix.

114. *Id.* at 48, Appendix.

115. Piketty, *Toward a Reconciliation*, *supra* note 89, at 562.

116. Patricia Cohen, *A Bigger Economic Pie, but a Smaller Slice for Half of the U.S.*, N.Y. TIMES (Dec. 6, 2016), http://www.nytimes.com/2016/12/06/business/economy/a-bigger-economic-pie-but-a-smaller-slice-for-half-of-the-us.html?_r=0.

117. *Id.*

118. *See* U.S. CONST. amends. 13, 14 &15.

119. "The fact that a hypothesis and the relationship that it proposes are in harmony with existing scientific information." MEDICAL DICTIONARY FOR THE HEALTH PROFESSIONS AND NURSING (Farlex 2012), http://medical-dictionary.thefreedictionary.com/biologic+plausibility. For further discussion of biological plausibility, *see* text accompanying note 47.

120. Graetz served in several high-ranking positions in the U.S. Treasury involving tax policy from 1990-92.

121. GRAETZ & SHAPIRO, A 1000 CUTS, *supra* note 60.

122. *Id.* at 4, 14.

123. *Id.* at 271. Only 1 percent to 2 percent of federal government revenue comes from the estate tax. *Id.*

124. *Id.* at 288.

11 Income and Wealth Disparities, and the Demand Curve

A. The Shrinking, Anemic Middle Class

Far from being the inevitable product of a market-based economy, the radical inequalities detailed in Chapter 10 afflict the market. I call them radical because if democracy is the baseline, these inequalities in political power signal oligarchy, and because these inequalities in economic power characterize oligopolies. Characteristic of oligopoly, some evidence exists that large income disparities adversely affect overall prosperity. For example, they decrease productivity because of such factors as deficient educations and atrophying skill sets, let alone illness, broken families, crime, etc.[1] Economic oligopoly and political oligarchy also have adversely affected the demand curve, as democracy is economically efficient.

Joseph Stiglitz details how the current levels of inequality have eviscerated the demand curve. *The Economist* agrees that the levels of inequality can hinder both growth and efficiency. Stiglitz and *the Economist* have recommended higher rates of progressive taxation.[2] The International Monetary Fund has similarly concluded that "'longer growth spells are robustly associated with more equality in the income distribution.'"[3]

Stiglitz details a number of ways in which the high levels of inequality have adversely impacted the economy. These include diminished public investment, laws that are highly inefficient and favor the most wealthy,[4] and lessened productivity and worker morale. Stiglitz sees the housing bubble as "the culmination of a three-decade stretch spent careening from one crisis to another without learning some very obvious lessons along the way."[5]

Politics and Capital. John Attanasio.
© John Attanasio 2018. Published 2018 by Oxford University Press.

As the housing crisis occurred in 2008, the time correlation between 1978 (the beginning of Stiglitz's "three-decade stretch") and *Buckley* is once again remarkable. Stiglitz sees the way forward as behaving more like a community rather than according to individual self-interest.[6]

Fellow Nobel Laureate Paul Krugman also sees 1980 as the watershed date for income inequality with median family income growing much less after 1980 than before. In contrast, the income of the top 1 percent quadrupled between 1980 and 2012. Deregulation of the financial markets also occurs at that time, which helped to account for why growth after 1980 slows as compared with growth before 1980. Krugman says that the deregulation sparked extraordinarily high and disparate rewards for a few who don't generate much productive value for society.[7] Diminished growth since 1980, correlated with expanding inequality, is a continual theme echoed by many including Krugman, Stiglitz, Piketty, Saez, and Zucman.

At the bottom, muting the voices of the poor may also account for phenomena such as the underclass. The underclass marks a cycle of hopelessness, and chronic poverty that sharply contradicts the American (or any other) dream.[8] Their suffering adversely affects productivity. Not addressing the problems of the poor and the middle class can also endanger everyone by sparking instability.[9]

The Pew Foundation has documented the dramatic decline in the middle class. From 1970 to 2014, the percentage of income of the upper class rose from 29 percent to 49 percent. The share of income for middle-income households declined from 62 percent in 1970, to 43 percent in 2014. As illustrated in Figure 11.1, between 1970 and 2015, the population cohort comprising the middle class shrank from 61 percent to 50 percent. The percentages in the top and bottom classes increased dramatically.[10]

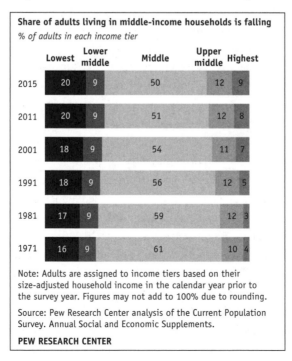

FIGURE 11.1, SOURCE: "Share of adults living in middle-income households is falling" Pew Research Center analysis of the Current Population Survey. Annual Social and Economic Supplements.

More disquieting is the Federal Reserve Bank's *Report on the Economic Well-Being of U.S. Households in 2015*, issued in May 20, 2016. Illustrating the weakness of the demand curve, the Fed reports: "Forty-six percent of adults say they either could not cover an emergency expense costing $400, or would cover it by selling something or borrowing money"; and "31 percent, or approximately 76 million adults, are either 'struggling to get by' or are 'just getting by.'"[11] "Twenty-one percent of those who borrowed to attend a for-profit institution are behind on their loan payments." "Thirty percent of respondents report that their income in the last 12 months was less than $25,000." "Thirty-one percent of non-retired respondents report that they have no retirement savings or pension at all, including 27 percent of non-retired respondents age 60 or older."[12] Moreover, "42 percent report that their income was under $40,000." The Fed stated that "median family income is in the range between $40,000 and $49,999."[13]

In its annual survey of income and properties issued in September 2016, the Census Bureau reported median household income increased 5.2 percent to $56,516. The Census Bureau went on to state: "This is the first annual increase in median household income since 2007."[14]

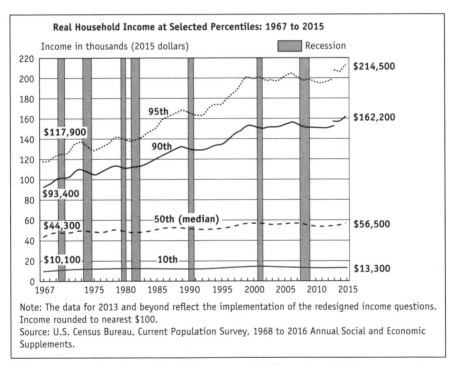

FIGURE 11.2, SOURCE: "Real Household Income at Selected Percentiles: 1967 to 2015," U.S. Census Bureau, Current Population Survey, 1968 to 2016 Annual Social and Economic Supplements.

Even with the Bureau's optimistic number, the above Figure 11.2 captures that median income has been essentially flat since the late 1990s. Figure 11.2 also shows that the largest increases came in the top 10 percent and top 5 percent. Again, one can trace these increases since *Buckley* in 1976.

Figure 11.2 does demonstrate that the largest percentage increase—from $10,100–$13,300—was to the lowest 10 percent, which most will agree is wonderful. However, without government subsidies such as food stamps the poverty level would be substantially higher, particularly with "the absence of stronger wage growth for low and middle-income workers." [15] Even with this dramatic increase and with the 5.2 percent overall household income increase reported by the Census Bureau, the Bureau reported that the 2015 Gini coefficient is "not statistically different from 2014. Changes in inequality between 2014 and 2015 were not significant as measured by the shares of aggregate household income by quintiles."[16] The Census Bureau may be more optimistically inclined. [17] In its analysis of the September 2016 Census Bureau numbers, the *New York Times* reported that the increase is largely accounted for by the increase in the employment number more than by the increase in the median salary.[18] In 2015, the Fed compared side-by-side several statistics based on 2014 data produced by the Fed, the Census Bureau, and several other sources. The Fed reported 5.3 percent unemployed and looking for a job, while the Census Bureau reported 3.9 percent unemployed and looking for a job.[19] At this same time, the *New York Times* also reported that 37 percent of Americans thought the economy was getting better, but 57 percent thought it was getting worse. This was based on a Gallup Poll taken around the same time that the Census Bureau reported its 5.3 percent wage increase. The same poll stated that 26 percent of Americans thought the economy was excellent or good, while 30 percent thought it was poor.[20]

Moreover, the Census Bureau's 2015 median household income number is still 1.6 percent behind the 2007 number, and 2.4 percent behind the peak of the median household income number, which occurred in 1999. Elise Gould of the Economic Policy Institute maintains that since 2013, the Census Bureau has changed the way it asked people about their income, which makes comparisons with previous years look better than they actually are. The Economic Policy Institute estimates that median income for Americans in the middle range remains 4.6 percent below the peak reached in 2007 and 5.4 percent below the peak reached in 1999. Moreover for several decades, it has been taking Americans much longer to catch up to wage levels reached at the beginning of a recession—three years for the recession of 1969, seven for the back-to-back recessions in 1981 and 1982, and not by late 2016 for either the recession of 2001 or the Great Recession of 2008.[21]

Perhaps the most disconcerting statistic about the middle class is that Piketty, Saez, and Zucman classify it as the tenth to the fiftieth percentile because this 40 percent of the population earns 40 percent of the income. The *Oxford English Dictionary* does not define the word *middle* that way.

B. Sellers Need Buyers and Buyers Need Sellers (Employers)

An unforeseen consequence is just a fancy way of saying, "I didn't see it coming." Many have discussed the unequal political power that the *Buckley* Constitution has produced.

Some have discussed its adverse impact on the economy in the way of pork barreling for property interests or lack of productivity due to poor education. But few saw coming the shot on the demand curve. That is surprising, because the subtitle of this section is tautological. Sellers need to sell things, and to do that, they need buyers. Buyers need money, and to get it, they need employers (sellers).

For those who do not care about first-order rights, compelling efficiency reasons urge correcting this system failure in our highly successful and cherished democratic-capitalist order. Bolstering the demand curve through a more balanced, broad distribution of resources may be necessary to avert sustained paltry growth, ballooning debt, or catastrophic downturns.

Nobel laureate Paul Krugman has written insightfully about financial crises and how much financial crises have inflicted long-term damage on the economy, not to mention the terrible toll they have taken on people's lives through unemployment.[22] He describes the financial crisis of 2008 as a demand-driven crisis the scale of which has not been witnessed since the Great Depression.[23] "For during an economic slump, especially a severe one, supply seems to be everywhere and demand nowhere."[24] Krugman maintains that it is consensus among economists that the Great Depression was demand driven.[25] "Once again, the question of how to create enough demand to make use of the economy's capacity has become crucial. Depression economics is back."[26] People with diminished incomes sometimes consume beyond their means, leading to excessive debt.[27] Then the debt bubble bursts, the more well-to-do panic and balloon savings while shrinking consumption. For example, once the 2008 crisis struck, the savings rate increased from $200 billion to over $1 trillion because people were reluctant to spend.[28] These related phenomena savage the demand curve. Illustrating the importance of income distribution to the demand curve, Angus Deaton won the 2015 Nobel Prize in economics for his studies of demand, welfare, and poverty. He developed a way of measuring demand based on individual incomes. As the Nobel Committee stated, one of Deaton's ideas "sum up how individuals adapt their own consumption to their individual income, which fluctuates in a very different way to aggregate income. This research clearly demonstrated why the analysis of individual data is key to untangling the patterns we see in aggregate data."[29]

In his magisterial work, *The General Theory of Employment, Interest, and Money*, John Maynard Keynes considered demand the product of interdependent choices by all individuals in an economy based on their relative decisions of saving and consumption, which in turn were based on their relative income and wealth positions.[30]

I regard the price level as a whole as being determined in precisely the same way as individual prices; that is to say, under the influence of supply and demand. Technical conditions, the level of wages, the extent of unused capacity of plant and labour, and the state of markets and competition determine the supply conditions of individual products and of products as a whole. The decisions of entrepreneurs, which provide the incomes of individual producers and the decisions of those individuals as to the disposition of such incomes determine the demand conditions.[31]

Keynes talks repeatedly about demand for goods being derived in part from the levels of employment and income and the propensity to consume and to invest. Keynes saw the Great Depression as a tremendous disequilibrium.

Before *Buckley*, greater distributive autonomy characterized the U.S. political system.[32] Voters and their representatives fashioned tax and other policies that tolerated considerable inequalities of wealth and income. Interestingly, Keynes thought that some inequalities lead to capital formation, which has frequently driven great leaps in innovation that broadly improved living standards.[33]

Adam Smith stresses that the absence of concentrated economic power favors economic liberty. The absence of such concentrations also intensifies competition, which was so important to efficiency in Smith's thinking.[34]

Merchants and master manufacturers are, in this order, the two classes of people who commonly employ the largest capitals, and who by their wealth draw to themselves the greatest share of the public consideration. . . . The interest of the dealers, however, in any particular branch of trade or manufactures, is always in some respects different from, and even opposite to, that of the public. To widen the market and to narrow the competition, is always the interest of the dealers. To widen the market may frequently be agreeable enough to the interest of the public; but to narrow the competition must always be against it, and can serve only to enable the dealers, by raising their profits above what they naturally would be, to levy, for their own benefit, an absurd tax upon the rest of their fellow-citizens. The proposal of any new law or regulation of commerce which comes from this order ought always be listened to with great precaution, and ought never to be adopted till after having been long and carefully examined, not only with the most scrupulous, but with the most suspicious attention. It comes from an order of men, whose interest is never exactly the same with that of the public, who have generally an interest to deceive and even to oppress the public, and who accordingly have, upon many occasions, both deceived and oppressed it.[35]

Inherently, democracies are strongly pro demand curve. Elected officials win or lose based on whether they can put a chicken in every pot. Assuming all voters vote their interests, voters will cast their ballots primarily to protect their incomes, which drive their individual abilities to consume. This protects the demand curve. Market economics is reciprocal, resulting in many mutual (but disparate) successes or failures. A participatory democratic process ensures that all interests are represented. This helps to ensure a robust demand curve. Bolstering the demand curve helps everyone. Former labor secretary Robert Reich has recounted that this breakdown in the demand curve has been fueled by the breakdown in wage increases. Because wealth and wage growth has been so concentrated in the upper class, and they can only consume so much, the economy has crawled. Reich says that in 2011–2012, corporate profits had risen to constitute their largest share of the economy since 1929, the beginning of the Great Depression. In those days, American wage-starved households made ends meet by borrowing. The Depression was sparked when the debt bubble burst.[36]

Reich traces stalled wage increases back about three decades. Meanwhile, during the three decades after the Second World War, the wages of workers approximately doubled. Three decades after the Second World War would be 1975. Again, the time correlation with *Buckley*, a 1976 decision, and its progeny is astonishing.[37] Like Reich, Piketty maintains that these inequalities adversely affect purchasing power and consequently, the demand curve. Indeed, Piketty claims that from 1977 to 2007, the bottom 90 percent of Americans had income growth of less than 0.5 percent per year.[38] Moreover, to try to mitigate the situation, the wealthy offered increasingly perilous credit to shore up the demand curve. Just before the Great Recession, the bottom 80 percent of earners was spending approximately 110 percent of their income.[39]

Piketty maintains that these disparities have produced much more tepid U.S. growth compared with previous decades.[40] Moreover, the United States is on a path that by 2030 would see the top 10 percent earn twice as much as the bottom 50 percent.[41] How the demand curve would survive such disparities tests the imagination. In their December 2016 article, Piketty, Saez, and Zucman say that increases in Medicare and Medicaid accounted for virtually all of the extremely mediocre post-tax economic growth of the bottom 50 percent since the late 1970s. A significant amount of this is attributable to the rise in price of healthcare services. Very little of this deterioration for the bottom 50 percent is attributable to age. Normally, the aging process reduces income because people earn much less on pensions than they did in wages. However, the average pre-tax income of retirees in the bottom 50 percent has actually increased compared to that of the average pre-tax income of those who are in the bottom 50 percent who are in the workforce. Among the bottom 50 percent, the average pre-tax income of those in the workforce actually declined rather than simply stagnated. Moreover, the retirement of the baby boomers will further soften the demand curve as people in retirement spend less.

Piketty, Saez, and Zucman depict the pre-tax and post-tax income stagnation of the bottom 50 percent with the following charts in Figure 11.3.[42]

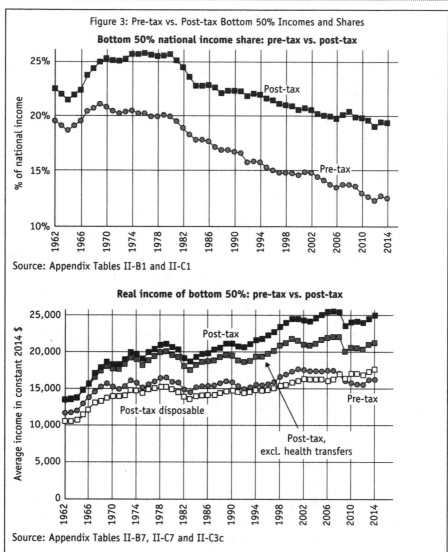

Figure 3: Pre-tax vs. Post-tax Bottom 50% Incomes and Shares

Bottom 50% national income share: pre-tax vs. post-tax

Source: Appendix Tables II-B1 and II-C1

Real income of bottom 50%: pre-tax vs. post-tax

Source: Appendix Tables II-B7, II-C7 and II-C3c

Notes: The top panel figure depicts the bottom 50% adult income shares pre-tax and post-tax since 1962. The unit is the individual adult and incomes within married couples are split equally. The bottom panel depicts the bottom 50% average real income per adult for four income definitions: (a) pre-tax national income, (b) post-tax disposable income (subtracting taxes, adding cash transfers but not in-kind transfers and collective public expenditures), (c) post-tax national income (adding all transfers and collective public expenditures minus the government deficit), (d) post-tax national income but excluding Medicare and Medicaid benefits.

FIGURE 11.3, SOURCE: "Figure 3: Pre-tax vs. Post-tax Bottom 50% Incomes and Shares." Piketty, Saez, and Zucman.

The income curve for the tenth–fiftieth percentile hasn't been much stronger. Piketty, Saez, and Zucman found "an overall U-shaped for pre-tax and post-tax income concentration over the century." This is very much like the curve reproduced in Chapter 10. Piketty, Saez, and Zucman further conclude, "Since 1980, growth in real incomes for the bottom 90% adults has been only about half of the national average on pre-tax basis and about two-thirds on a post-tax basis. Median pre-tax incomes have hardly grown since 1980."[43]

These increases in inequality are unsustainable. In *Capital*, Piketty claims that the 46 percent of national income (excluding capital gains) going to the top 10 percent is at a level higher than the concentration that prevailed just before the 2007 financial crisis.[44] The only time this happened in the United States was in 1928. In their December 2016 working paper, Piketty, Saez, and Zucman say that pre-tax income shares for the top 10 percent are "almost at the same level today as they were at their peak in the late 1920s just before the Great Depression." However, government transfer payments and progressive taxation have kept post-tax income inequality very high but further away from that level.[45]

Although wage increases became much more disparate in relative terms, absolute wage growth also markedly slowed as did absolute growth. Total wages increased 95 percent from 1946 to 1980, but only 61 percent from 1980 to 2014.[46] Even if this was attributable to other factors such as globalization or technology, the effect on the demand curve would be the same. Thus we have an anemic middle class, an increase in retirements, and a dramatic slowing in wage increases all adversely impacting the demand curve.

C. The 2016 Election

As Chapter 1 suggests, the 2016 presidential election cycle got off to a dynamic start of high-end fundraising.[47] There are anomalies such as the mismatch between Jeb Bush's fundraising amounts and his vote totals. Nevertheless, Hillary Clinton raised the most in both the primaries and the general election[48] and she ran against Donald Trump, a billionaire who made enormous contributions to his own campaign and received fantastic amounts of free publicity from the media.

The 2016 election is in many ways the culmination of the trends discussed in this book. Central to the campaigns of Donald Trump and Bernie Sanders were their critiques of the campaign finance system, characterizing it as garden-variety political corruption. The success of their critiques also evidences *Buckley* trends coming to a boiling point. There is a populist rebellion by the many losers in this skewed game. The protest vote—that is, those voting against traditional candidates—was huge. It was also genuinely bipartisan. If one adds the votes garnered by Trump, Sanders, and Cruz in the primaries, the sum represents an overwhelming majority of the voting electorate.

The general presidential election was contested between two candidates who are in the top 0.1 percent. Although candidate Clinton raised the most money in the campaign, candidate Trump raised immense amounts of money. As of December 31, 2016, the *Washington Post* reported that Hillary Clinton had raised $1.4 billion; Donald Trump, $957.6 million including $7.6 million of debt.[49] This included money raised by groups outside their respective campaigns. The campaign tracking organization Open Secrets reported that the

Trump campaign itself spent $398 million; the Clinton Campaign, $768 million.[50] Barack Obama spent $721 million and Mitt Romney spent $449.5 million in 2012.[51]

But most people missed the secret sauce. MediaQuant estimated that in the twelve months leading up to the election, President Trump received $4.96 billion of free media coverage whereas Secretary Clinton received $3.24 billion.[52] This amount put him easily past her in total spending. Donald Trump "received $ 5.6 billion throughout the entirety of his campaign, more than Hillary Clinton, Bernie Sanders, Ted Cruz, Paul Ryan and Marco Rubio combined."[53]

The top 0.01 percent gave $1.6 billion in the 2012 election. But in the 2016 election, this cohort's giving increased 45 percent, to $2.3 billion, while its size only increased 3 percent.[54] This is another dose-response relationship as *McCutcheon* was decided in 2014, right in the middle of the two elections.

Meanwhile, small donations of less than $200 declined by 3.4 percent despite a vast number garnered by Senator Sanders and a large (but smaller) number garnered by Mr. Trump.[55]

Soft money contributions more than doubled. Most of that increase went to super PACs, 501(c)(4) social welfare organizations, and other outside groups.[56] This is yet another example of a dose-response relationship. *Speechnow.org v. FEC* invalidated limits on contributions to outside organizations in March 2010. The FEC followed with myriad decisions in 2010–2012 allowing unlimited contributions to PACs and enabling them to coordinate fairly closely with candidate campaigns. These developments gave rise to super PACs and also to so-called dark pools in 501(c)(4)s in which campaign donors are not disclosed.[57]

Even within the top 0.01 percent, political contributions have been increasingly given by the very top of the pyramid. In 2012, the top fifty donors among the top 0.01 percent contributed 19 percent of its total; by 2016, their share jumped to 30 percent of the total of the top 0.01 percent. The top 0.01 percent *of donors* comprise about 200 persons. This donor subset spent nearly $948 million in 2016, an increase of 143 percent over the 2012 election cycle.[58] This is another dose-response reaction to *McCutcheon*.

Open Secrets recounted:

"On a lot of issues, it's really a shoot-out between these billionaires who are picking favorites," said Richard Painter, former chief White House ethics lawyer for President George W. Bush, professor of corporate law at the University of Minnesota Law School and a board chair of the liberal watchdog group Citizens for Responsibility and Ethics in Washington.

Painter said that wealthy donors often push their agendas to the detriment of society at large. "It's always hard for a broadly dispersed group to counter a very narrow interest," he said. "So the money tends to pursue very narrow agendas that are very selfish, and very destructive to the rest of society from the very top to the very bottom. It becomes chaotic; you have irrational policy positions." Million-dollar donors tend to vie for their own interests, whether those involve causes like gun rights or something more directly related to their business concerns. . . .[59]

In the 2016 congressional races, big money ruled, but unfortunately for challengers, it didn't hedge. In the Senate races, the average incumbent raised $12,708,000 whereas the average challenger raised $1,599,714. In the House races, the average incumbent raised $1,590,607 and the average challenger $231,727. Senate incumbents won 90 percent of their races; House incumbents won 97 percent. So contrary to some pundits, money still talks.[60]

Again, far from contradicting trends, Mr. Trump's election embodies the culmination of *Buckley* and its progeny—government by a group drawn considerably from property interests. This eclipses the direct judicial protection afforded by *Lochner.* President Trump's cabinet and other key advisers are widely reported to be the richest administration in American history.[61] Although more were officially or informally vetted, eventually, there were two billionaires and a dozen millionaires. Professor Brooke Harrington maintained the "collective wealth of Trump's team dwarfs that of any other in history."[62] President Reagan also had many wealthy (but not as wealthy) advisers who became key members of his government.

Candidate Trump did campaign on the inability of money to influence him. More importantly, he severely criticized the tremendous influence that money exerts over the political process, initially refusing to take campaign donations. Moreover, he explicitly campaigned on getting rid of super PACs.

Pointing to the effects of "horrible" super-PACs, Republican presidential front-runner Donald Trump on Sunday said America needs to come up with a solution to keep big money out of politics.

"Well, I think you need it, because I think PACs are a horrible thing," Trump said on CNN's "State of the Union" when asked if he would pursue campaign finance reform.[63]

Although Trump criticized money in politics throughout his campaign, particularly in the primaries and frequently in debates, critics were disillusioned by his appointment as White House Counsel of someone who has been criticized as working against campaign finance reform when he recently chaired the Federal Election Commission, and who then worked for a foundation that spends large amounts on political campaigns.[64]

D. The Tax Cuts and the National Debt

Another way in which President Trump's election marks a culmination of long-standing post-*Buckley* trends involves the tax cuts he proposed during his campaign. While Secretary Clinton outspent President Trump, he proposed large tax cuts while she proposed tax increases; both focused on the top 1 percent.[65]

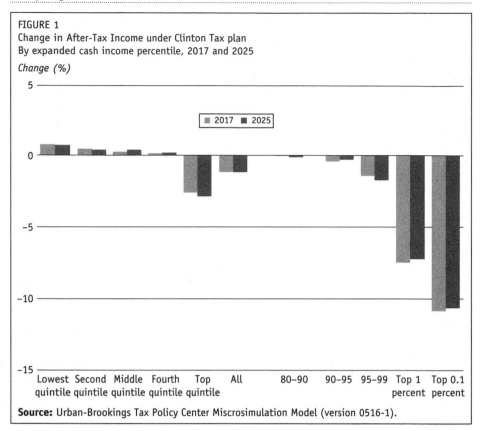

FIGURE 1
Change in After-Tax Income under Clinton Tax plan
By expanded cash income percentile, 2017 and 2025

Change (%)

■ 2017 ■ 2025

Lowest Second Middle Fourth Top   All   80–90 90–95 95–99 Top 1 Top 0.1
quintile quintile quintile quintile quintile   percent percent

Source: Urban-Brookings Tax Policy Center Microsimulation Model (version 0516-1).

FIGURE 11.4, SOURCE: Richard C. Auxier, Leonard E. Burman, James R. Nunns, and Jeffrey Rohaly, "An Updated Analysis of Hillary Clinton's Tax Proposals," Urban-Brookings Tax Policy Center, Washington, DC, October 2016, figure 1.

During the campaign, the candidates grew farther apart in their tax proposals. Under candidate Trump's initial proposal, the top 1 percent realized 35 percent of the tax cut. Under his revised proposal, which he introduced in August 2016, the top 1 percent receive 47 percent of the tax cut. In sharp contrast, candidate Clinton would have raised taxes, with 92 percent of the increase being paid by the top 1 percent. Moreover, candidate Trump campaigned on a top tax rate for business income. Some feared this would lead many highly paid corporate employees to convert salary, which had a proposed top marginal tax rate of 33 percent, into business income, which had a flat tax of 15 percent. He also proposed terminating the inheritance tax, which only affects high-end taxpayers. It is important to note that the analysis here treats only candidate proposals, as the book focuses on campaign finance and elections.

Candidate Trump's proposed campaign tax cuts at the top end would only make the Piketty curves jump off the scale. For the top bracket, the 33 percent rate is the same as the proposed Bush tax cut. According to the Tax Policy Institute, "the highest-income taxpayers (0.1 percent of the population, or those with incomes over $3.7 million in 2016 dollars) would experience an average tax cut of nearly $1.1 million, over 14 percent of after-tax income. Households in the middle fifth of the income distribution would receive an average tax cut of $1,010, or 1.8 percent of after-tax income, while the poorest fifth of households would see their taxes go down an average of $110, or 0.8 percent of their after-tax income."[66]

Figure 11.5 illustrates whom the Trump campaign proposals disproportionately benefited:[67]

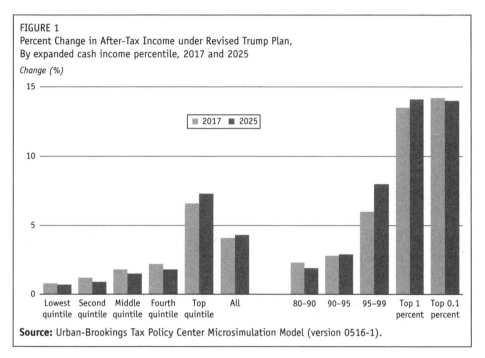

FIGURE 1
Percent Change in After-Tax Income under Revised Trump Plan,
By expanded cash income percentile, 2017 and 2025

Change (%)

Source: Urban-Brookings Tax Policy Center Microsimulation Model (version 0516-1).

FIGURE 11.5, SOURCE: Jim Nunns, Len Burman, Ben Page, Jeff Rohaly, and Joe Rosenberg, "An Analysis of Donald Trump's Revised Tax Plan," Urban-Brookings Tax Policy Center, Washington, DC, October 2016, figure 1.

Like President Reagan, candidate Trump professed a theory of trickle-down economics. We now know that not much wealth trickled down during the Reagan administration, or since. Nobel laureate Joseph Stiglitz maintains that the "median income . . . of a full-time male worker in the United States is lower than it was 42 years ago."[68] Conversely, we know without doubt that whatever wealth trickled down, much more gushed up. Piketty's statistics chronicle the dramatic rise in income inequality that began during the Reagan administration—shortly after *Buckley*—and has continued to this day.

Moreover, cuts in income, inheritance, and corporate taxes will exacerbate an already serious public debt problem unless drastic cuts occur in various government programs,[69] many of which benefit the middle and lower classes. Figure 11.6 relates tax reductions and budget deficits *before* candidate Trump's proposals:[70]

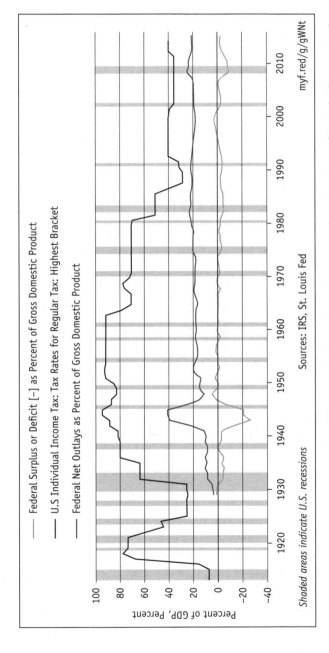

FIGURE 11.6, SOURCE: Figure was produced by the author by overlaying three graphs from the website of the Federal Reserve Bank of St. Louis. The sources for the three graphs are: the Federal Reserve Bank of St. Louis; the U.S. Office of Management and Budget; and the U.S. Department of the Treasury.

The Congressional Budget Office estimates that U.S. national debt will reach 75 percent of GDP by the end of 2016, 86 percent of GDP by the end of 2026, and 106 percent of GDP by the end of 2036 (surpassing the peak recorded at the end of World War II), and 141 percent of GDP by 2046. These percentages are computed *before* the massive additions to the debt driven by the tax cuts and spending proposals of candidate Trump.

Even before the tax cuts proposed by candidate Trump, the Congressional Budget Office warned of dangerous consequences of the already mounting national debt:

> CBO's extended baseline projections show a substantial imbalance in the federal budget beyond the next 10 years, with revenues falling short of spending by steadily increasing amounts. As a result, federal debt as a share of GDP would reach unprecedented levels if current laws generally remain unchanged. Such high and rising debt would have serious consequences for the nation's budget and economy.[71]

Figure 11.7, a chart generated by the CBO, puts the debt into an unflattering historical perspective.[72]

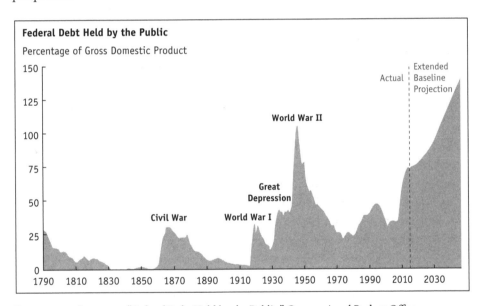

FIGURE 11.7, SOURCE: "Federal Debt Held by the Public," Congressional Budget Office.

The chart tracks debt as a *percentage of GDP* rather than in absolute dollars. So it automatically holds inflation constant. The chart also sheds further light on the tremendous impact of *Buckley*. In another remarkable temporal correlation, the dramatic increase in the national debt occurs shortly after *Buckley*. Moreover, we have only avoided economic catastrophe thus far with extreme measures such as accumulating massive public debt, and near-zero interest rates which may be causing asset bubbles and misallocation of resources. During this volatile time, Nobel laureate Joseph Siglitz says that economic downturns have been more frequent and more fierce.[73] Stiglitz has taken this position since 1993 and unfortunately, has been right. Between downturns, the debt will still stifle growth as evidenced by the experiences of many countries over a long period of time.[74] Astonishingly (but predictably under political and economic theory), the appearance or rise of *Buckley* and the campaign finance cases, of massive tax cuts for property interests, of inequality in wealth and particularly income, of public debt, and of the size and speed of downturns all occur around the same time and appear highly temporally correlated.

E: Epilogue: Distributive Autonomy, Libertarianism, and Democracy

Nobel laureate economist Milton Friedman thought that capitalism was necessary for freedom. By freedom, Friedman meant narrow individualistic libertarianism. The logical implication of this work is that democracy may be necessary to do, or at least to sustain, capitalism.[75] If political power becomes concentrated in the hands of a few, then it is highly predictable that economic power will become concentrated in the hands of a few. That is, oligarchy will lead to oligopoly. This is only natural as those in political power will deploy that power to increase their wealth and other resources. It also turns out that the resulting maldistribution of income and wealth is deleterious for capitalism in general because of the adverse impact on the demand curve and also because of diminished productivity of workers who have deficient skills and life setbacks. In this environment, economic power can also be cashed in for political power, which can then be used to acquire even greater economic power. The statistics recounted in this book suggest that this spiral of concentrated economic and political power has occurred and continues.

In a *Financial Times* column during the 2016 election cycle, Martin Wolfe cautioned: "Above all, if the legitimacy of our democratic political systems is to be maintained, economic policy must be orientated towards promoting the interests of the many not the few." If not, he worried that the tricky marriage between capitalism and democracy will end and that demagoguery and authoritarianism will burgeon in eruptions of populist rage.[76]

A core claim of this work is that distributive autonomy is necessary to do democracy. Another conclusion is that democracy may be necessary for long-term capitalism. If democracy is necessary to accomplish sustained capitalism, and if distributive autonomy is necessary to do democracy, it would appear that distributive autonomy is necessary to do long-term, successful capitalism. The concept of distributive autonomy contrasts sharply with the individualistic libertarian approach to autonomy that Milton Friedman espoused. However, if the analysis here is correct, freedom is necessary to do capitalism, but the kind of freedom entailed is very different from the kind that Friedman advocated. Distributive autonomy will provide more robust, perhaps essential, sustenance to both capitalism and democracy.

The participatory democracy paradigm of *Carolene Products* takes autonomy seriously in a way that the strong libertarian paradigm does not. Importantly, the participatory democracy paradigm is difficult to defend as an end in itself. Participatory democracy can be defended as a means to the end of effectuating individual autonomy in self-governance. As such, participatory democracy inherently involves distributive autonomy, as the essence of participatory democracy requires broad-based participation in fashioning the distribution of resources. Such is the case with constitutional protection for the right to vote; the opposite is the case with regard to constitutional protection for the right to speak to influence elections and, therefore, public policy.

One cannot equalize free speech rights like one can equalize votes. For example, one cannot strictly equalize the economic capacity to speak without draconian infringements on autonomy. But that is not what the principle of distributive autonomy requires. To be authentic and even coherent, any philosophical principle that takes autonomy seriously must be concerned with some minimal autonomy for all, not just unfettered autonomy for a few to drown out and then legislate away the autonomy of everyone else. Otherwise, the concern for autonomy becomes muddled and disingenuous, if not hypocritical.

If one does not take the autonomy of all seriously, citizens have little choice in how they are governed. Moreover, the autonomy violations are leveraged: autonomy and elections can then be abused by some to pass laws that further subjugate the autonomy of others. To the extent that autonomy ranks among the most fundamental rights, the incoherence of the libertarian position grows only more glaring. Specifically, one must support protecting virtually limitless individual autonomy for some, even if it enables massive autonomy deprivations for everyone else. The great paradox revealed by this work is that highly individualistic libertarianism encourages oligarchy and oligopoly that diminish the autonomy of the vast majority of citizens. That is a corollary to the positive synergystic relationship between distributive autonomy, democracy, and capitalism.

The participatory democracy paradigm of free speech jurisprudence respects the autonomy of all, whereas the strong libertarian paradigm empowers some to severely constrict the autonomy of others.

The principle of distributive autonomy exposes tensions between absolutist conceptions of liberty, as epitomized by modern libertarianism, and achieving democracy. It also reveals the deep tensions between extreme forms of liberty and the value of equality. Ironically, and perhaps most tellingly, the analysis glimpses the difficulties that extremely individualistic conceptions of liberty cause for both the autonomy and liberty of most citizens. Extremes of any philosophical theory further illuminate the timeless wisdom of Aristotle's golden mean.

In a haunting passage, Tocqueville cautions vigilance against an aristocratic challenge to American democracy:

> All things considered, I believe that the manufacturing aristocracy that we see rising before our eyes is one of the harshest that has ever existed on earth. But it is also one of the most limited and least dangerous. Nevertheless, friends of democracy must keep an anxious eye peeled in this direction at all times. For if permanent inequality of conditions and aristocracy are ever to appear in the world anew, it is safe to predict that this is the gate by which they will enter.[77]

Tocqueville had experienced the terror of the French Revolution. He traveled throughout the United States after that tragedy. *Democracy in America* was written as an optimistic foil to the horrors his beloved France had been suffering. Tocqueville subsequently depicted that dread in *The Old Régime and the Revolution*.[78]

My challenges are distinctly conservative.[79] In respecting the autonomy of others, the principle of distributive autonomy will conserve autonomy, prosperity, stability, and our commitment to participatory democracy. I end at the beginning. In his classic *Democracy in America*, Tocqueville eloquently describes the participatory democracy aspirations of the founding American generation:

> ... the principle of the sovereignty of the people governs the whole political system of the Anglo Americans. Every page of this book will afford new applications of that same doctrine. In the nations by which the sovereignty of the people is recognized, every individual has an equal share of power, and participates equally in the government of the state.[80]

In his classic, *The Politics*, Aristotle adjudged broad participation the ethos of democracy:

> For if liberty and equality, as is thought by some, are chiefly to be found in democracy, they will be best attained when all persons alike share in the government to the utmost.[81]

Elections matter. . . . Once we *elect* to have a democracy, the type of electoral systems that we fashion will shape our governments, laws, economies, psyches, and values.

Notes

1. *Cf.* Aaron Bernstein, *Inequality: How the Growing Gap Between Rich and Poor in America Hurts the Economy*, Bus. Week, Aug. 15, 1994, www.bloomberg.com/news/articles/1994-08-14/inequality

> [I]nequality may brake growth so much that even the rich lose out over 5 to 10 years, calculates Massachusetts Institute of Technology economist Roland Benabou . . . . "If you move to a rich suburb, it will improve your children's education," he says. "But if their co-workers still in the city are left sufficiently deficient in their education, it will more than offset the advantages your children gained," because productivity and growth suffer. *Id.*

2. Joseph E. Stiglitz, The Price of Inequality, at xv–xvi (paperback ed.) (W.W. Norton & Co., 2013).

3. *Id.* at 91.

4. *Id.* at 92.

5. *Id.* at 89.

6. *Id.* at xxi.

7. Paul Krugman, End This Depression Now! 73–82 (paperback edition)(W.W. Norton & Co., 2013).

8. For descriptions of this phenomenon, *see* William J. Wilson, The Truly Disadvantaged (University of Chicago Press, 1987); Christopher Jencks & Paul E. Peterson, The Urban Underclass (Brookings Institution Press, 1990). As labor secretary, Robert Reich expressed this view. David J. Lynch, *Rich Poor World*, USA Today, Sept. 20, 1996, at B1.

9. *See, e.g.*, Daniel Bell, The Cultural Contradictions of Capitalism 251 (Basic Books, 1976); Stephen L. Carter, *The Constitution, the Uniqueness Puzzle, and the Economic Conditions of Democracy*, 56 Geo. Wash. L. Rev. 136 (1987).

10. Pew Research Center, *The American Middle Class Is Losing Ground* (Dec. 9, 2015), http://www.pewsocialtrends.org/2015/12/09/the-american-middle-class-is-losing-ground/. The Pew study considered middle income to be households of three earning $42,000 to $126,000 in 2014, or households of five earning $54,000 to $162,000.

11. Federal Reserve Bank, Report on the Economic Well-Being of U.S. Households in 2015, at 1 (May 2016).

12. *Id.* at 2–3, 15.

13. *Id.* at 15.

14. Bernadette D. Proctor, Jessica L. Semega, & Melissa A. Kollar, U.S. Census Bureau, Current Population Reports, P60-256(RV), *Income and Poverty in the United States: 2015*, at 1 (Sept. 2016), https://www.census.gov/content/dam/Census/library/publications/2016/demo/p60-256.pdf; David G. Waddington, U.S. Census Bureau, *Income, Poverty, and Health Insurance Coverage: 2015* (Sept. 2016) (PowerPoint presentation) https://www.census.gov/content/dam/Census/newsroom/press-kits/2016/20160913_iphi_slides.pdf (website last visited Dec. 4, 2017).

15. http://www.epi.org/blog/poverty-declined-in-2015-by-all-measures-government-programs-once-again-kept-millions-above-the-poverty-line/, Editorial Board, *The Failure to Talk Frankly About Poverty*, N.Y. Times, Sept. 13, 2016, http://www.nytimes.com/2016/09/14/opinion/not-yet-talking-about-the-poor.html?_r=0.

16. Proctor, Semega & Kollar, *Income and Poverty: 2015*, *supra* note 14, at 8. The Fed has noted that the Census Bureau uses either Pareto interpolation or linear interpolation, whereas the Fed uses linear interpolation, and the Census Bureau's approach makes a difference in the results at the high end, which could account for some of the differences. Federal Reserve Bank of St. Louis, *Real Median Household Income in the United States*, FRED Economic Research, https://fred.stlouisfed.org/series/MEHOINUSA672N. The Census Bureau made this change to Pareto interpolation in 1977. U.S. Census Bureau, Money Income in 1976 of Persons and Families in the United States, at 18, 20, 274. http://www2.census.gov/prod2/popscan/p60-114.pdf.

17. One commentator attributed the rise reported by the Census Bureau to a fairly large increase in withdrawals from retirement accounts.www.shadowstats.com. (Sept. 18, 2016).

18. Binyamin Appelbaum, Patricia Cohen & Jack Healy, *A Rebounding Economy Remains Fragile for Many*, N.Y. Times, Sept. 14, 2016, http://www.nytimes.com/2016/09/15/business/economy/census-poverty-income-donald-trump.html.

19. Jeff Larrimore, Maximilian Schmeiser & Sebastian Devlin-Foltz, *Should You Trust Things You Hear Online? Comparing SHED and Census Bureau Survey Results*, FEDS Notes, Oct. 15, 2015, Table 2, http://www.federalreserve.gov/econresdata/notes/feds-notes/2015/comparing-shed-and-census-bureau-survey-results-20151015.html. The Fed also reported that 34.7 percent of the adult population were not in the labor force, whereas the Census Bureau reported 35.6 percent. The difference appears to be in the number of "students, homemakers, or not looking for work." In this category, the Fed reported 10.8 percent, whereas the Census Bureau reported 12.2 percent.

20. Appelbaum, Cohen & Healy, *Rebounding Economy*, *supra* note 18.

21. Eduardo Porter, *America's Inequality Problem: Real Income Gains Are Brief and Hard to Find*, N.Y. Times, Sept. 13, 2016, http://www.nytimes.com/2016/09/14/business/economy/americas-inequality-problem-real-income-gains-are-brief-and-hard-to-find.html?_r=0.

22. *See generally* Krugman, End Depression, *supra* note 7, *esp.* 210–11; Paul Krugman, THE RETURN OF DEPRESSION ECONOMICS AND THE CRISIS OF 2008, at 28 (W.W. Norton & Co., 2009).

23. KRUGMAN, END DEPRESSION, *supra* note 7, *Preface to the Paperback Edition*; KRUGMAN, DEPRESSION ECONOMICS, *supra* note 22, at 181–83.

24. KRUGMAN, DEPRESSION ECONOMICS, *supra* note 22, at 16.

25. *Id.* at 20.

26. *Id.* at 184.

27. KRUGMAN, END DEPRESSION, *supra* note 7, at 83–84.

28. *Id.* at 136–37, 145.

29. Nobel Prize Organization, *Consumption, Great and Small*, Oct. 12, 2015, https://www.nobelprize.org/nobel_prizes/economic-sciences/laureates/2015/press.html.

30. JOHN MAYNARD KEYNES, THE GENERAL THEORY OF EMPLOYMENT, INTEREST, AND MONEY 4 (1935) (Harcourt, 1964 ed.).

31. *Preface to the French Edition* (1939), JOHN MAYNARD KEYNES, THE GENERAL THEORY OF EMPLOYMENT, INTEREST, AND MONEY (1935), https://ebooks.adelaide.edu.au/k/keynes/john_maynard/k44g/preface4.html.

32. Beyond rising differentials in campaign finance, interference in voting and redistricting are increasing. *See, generally*, Nicholas O. Stephanopoulos, *Elections and Alignment*, 114 COLUM. L. REV. 283, 341 (2014).

33. JOHN MAYNARD KEYNES, THE ECONOMIC CONSEQUENCES OF THE PEACE 67–70 (1919, Prometheus Books, 2004).

34. ADAM SMITH, LECTURES ON JURISPRUDENCE 83–84, 363–64, 471–72, 497–98, 529 (R.L. Meek, D.D. Raphael & P.G. Stein eds., Oxford University Press, 1978); ADAM SMITH, THE WEALTH OF NATIONS (Edwin Cannan ed., Methuen & Co., 1950, 6th ed.). *See generally* Deborah Boucoyannis, *The Equalizing Hand: Why Adam Smith Thought the Market Should Produce Wealth Without Steep Inequality*, 11 PERSPECTIVES ON POLITICS 1051 (2013). DOI:10.1017/S153759271300282X.

35. SMITH, WEALTH, *supra* note 34, at 278.

36. Robert S. Reich, BEYOND OUTRAGE: EXPANDED EDITION: WHAT HAS GONE WRONG WITH OUR ECONOMY AND OUR DEMOCRACY, AND HOW TO FIX IT 69 (Vintage Books, 2012).

37. *Id.* at 43–48. *See also* ROBERT S. REICH, SAVING CAPITALISM: FOR THE MANY, NOT THE FEW (Vintage Books, 2016).

38. THOMAS PIKETTY, CAPITAL IN THE TWENTY-FIRST CENTURY 297 (Harvard University Press, 2014).

39. STIGLITZ, INEQUALITY, *supra* note 2, at 13.

40. PIKETTY, *supra* note 38, at 297.

41. *Id.* at 256.

42. Thomas Piketty, Emmanuel Saez & Gabriel Zucman, *Distributional National Accounts: Methods and Estimates for the United States* (Washington Center for Equitable Growth, Working Paper 3, at 41, Appendix I, Dec. 2016), http://cdn.equitablegrowth.org/wp-content/uploads/2017/02/24163023/120716-WP-distributional-national-accounts.pdf.

43. *Id.* at 32.

44. PIKETTY, *supra* note 38, at 295.

45. Piketty, Saez & Zucman, *supra* note 42, at 17–18.

46. *See supra* Figure 11.3.

47. *See* text accompanying note 27, Chapter 1.

48. An editorial in the *Wall Street Journal* suggested that money did not play a large role in the 2016 presidential election. *See* Editorial, *The Super Pac Bust*, WALL ST. J., Feb. 20–21, 2016, A10. Candidate Trump, a billionaire, could spend large amounts on his own campaign. Moreover, at the time this editorial was written, Secretary Clinton had raised more money than any other candidate on either side. As of February 22, 2016, she had raised $188 million. Second was Jeb Bush at $157.6 million; third was Ted Cruz at $104.2 million. Secretary Clinton had also doubled Senator Sanders's $96.3 million. By June, vote totals were fairly in line with funding with the exceptions of candidates Trump and Bush. Candidate Trump is addressed in the text. *Which Presidential Candidates Are Winning the Money Race*, N.Y. TIMES, updated June, 22, 2016, http://www.nytimes.com/interactive/2016/us/elections/election-2016-campaign-money-race.html?_r=0.

To the extent that money and votes didn't correlate, it could be evidence of a populist rebellion, continuing trends that go at least as far back as the Tea Party.

49. *Election 2016: Money Raised as of Dec. 31*, WASH. POST, Feb. 1, 2017, https://www.washingtonpost.com/graphics/politics/2016-election/campaign-finance/.

50. Niv Sultan, *Election 2016: Trump's Free Media Helped Keep Cost Down, But Fewer Donors Provided More of the Cash*, OPEN SECRETS, Apr. 13, 2017, https://www.opensecrets.org/news/2017/04/election-2016-trump-fewer-donors-provided-more-of-the-cash/.

51. OPEN SECRETS, *2012 Presidential Race*, https://www.opensecrets.org/pres12/.

52. Mary Harris, *A Media Post-Mortem on the 2016 Presidential Election*, MEDIAQUANT, Nov. 14, 2016, https://www.mediaquant.net/tag/donald-trump/.

53. https://www.thestreet.com/story/13896916/1/donald-trump-rode-5-billion-in-free-media-to-the-white-house.html.

54. Sultan, *supra* note 50.

55. *Id.*

56. *Id.*

57. *See generally* Richard Briffault, *Super PACs*, 96 MINN. L. REV. 1644 (2012). For a detailed narrative on the role of dark money, *see* JANE MAYER, DARK MONEY (Doubleday 2016).

58. Although their donations increased 143 percent between the 2012 and 2016 election cycles, the population of the top 0.01 percent of donors only increased 3 percent. Sultan, *supra* note 50.

59. *Id.*

60. https://www.opensecrets.org/overview/incumbs.php; https://www.opensecrets.org/overview/reelect.php.

61. Nina Burleigh, *Meet the Billionaires Who Run Trump's Government*, NEWSWEEK, Apr. 5, 2017, http://www.newsweek.com/2017/04/14/donald-trump-cabinet-billionaires-washington-579084.html; Rebecca Ballhaus, *Financial Holdings of Some Donald Trump Nominees Complicate Approval Process*, WALL ST. J., Dec. 27, 2016, http://www.wsj.com/articles/some-donald-trump-nominees-face-stiff-and-costly-confirmation-battles-1482753602; *Trump's $6 Billion Cabinet: Mostly Men, Mostly White and Not Much Government Experience*, BLOOMBERG NEWS, Mar. 27, 2017, https://www.bloomberg.com/graphics/2016-trump-cabinet/.

62. Brooke Harrington, *Yes, Trump's Cabinet Is Super Rich. That's Not Why We Should Be Worried*, WASH. POST, Jan. 19, 2017, https://www.washingtonpost.com/posteverything/wp/2017/01/19/trump-rich-cabinet/?utm_term=.2b9257294153.

63. Bradford Richardson, *Trump Open to Campaign Finance Reform*, THE HILL, Jan. 17, 2016, http://thehill.com/blogs/ballot-box/presidential-races/266189-trump-open-to-campaign-finance-reform.

64. Charles Tiefer, *McGahn Is Troubling Pick for White House Counsel Given Trump's Conflict-of-Interest Issues*, FORBES, Nov. 25, 2016, https://www.forbes.com/sites/charlestiefer/

2016/11/25/new-trump-white-house-counsel-donald-mcgahn-is-a-partisan-politico-consiglieri/#245684ab374f;

Marty Kaplan, *Like Kryptonite to Campaign Finance Reform*, MOYERS & CO., Dec. 2, 2016, http://billmoyers.com/story/like-kryptonite-campaign-finance-reform/.

65. Richard Auxier, Len Berman, Jim Nunns, Ben Page, and Jeffrey Halley, *An Updated Analysis of Hillary Clinton's Tax Proposals*, Tax Policy Ctr., October 18, 2016, at 12, Figure 1, http://www.taxpolicycenter.org/publications/updated-analysis-hillary-clintons-tax-proposals/full.

66. James R. Nunns, Leonard E. Burman, Ben Page, Jeffrey Rohaly & Joseph Rosenberg, *An Analysis of Donald Trump's Revised Tax Plan*, TAX POLICY CTR., Oct. 18, 2016, at 1.

67. *Id.* at 12.

68. http://www.marketplace.org/2016/08/17/economy/stiglitz-euro-globalization-trade.

69. Janet Novack, *Trump Tax Plan Gives 47% of Cuts to Richest 1%, New Analysis Finds*, FORBES, Oct. 11, 2016, http://www.forbes.com/sites/janetnovack/2016/10/11/trump-tax-plan-gives-47-of-cuts-to-richest-1-new-analysis-finds/#2929810659fc.

70. This graph was produced by the author by overlaying three graphs from the website of the Federal Reserve Bank of St. Louis. The three graphs are overlaid to illustrate the point that government deficits since 1980 correlate with declines in the highest tax rates much more than with government outlays. Federal Reserve Bank of St. Louis and U.S. Office of Management and Budget, Federal Surplus or Deficit [-] as Percent of Gross Domestic Product [FYFSGDA188S]; U.S. Department of the Treasury, Internal Revenue Service, U.S Individual Income Tax: Tax Rates for Regular Tax: Highest Bracket [IITTRHB]; Federal Reserve Bank of St. Louis and U.S. Office of Management and Budget, Federal Net Outlays as Percent of Gross Domestic Product [FYONGDA188S], retrieved from FRED, Federal Reserve Bank of St. Louis; https://fred.stlouisfed.org/series/, December 21, 2017.

71. CONGRESSIONAL BUDGET OFFICE, The 2016 Long-Term Budget Outlook, 7, https://www.cbo.gov/sites/default/files/114th-congress-2015-2016/reports/51580-LTBO.pdf.

72. *Id.*

73. JOSEPH STIGLITZ, THE GREAT DIVIDE 387–88 (W.W Norton & Co., 2015); COLIN HAY & ANTHONY PAYNE, CIVIC CAPITALISM 43–44 (Wiley Press, 2015). *See also* Mark Zandi, *What Does Rising Inequality Mean for the Macroeconomy?*, *in* AFTER PIKETTY 384, 402 (Heather Boushey, J. Bradford Delong & Marshall Steinbaum eds., Harvard University Press, 2017).

74. STIGLITZ, INEQUALITY, *supra* note 2, at 117.

75. MILTON FRIEDMAN, CAPITALISM AND FREEDOM (University of Chicago Press, 1962).

76. Martin Wolf, *Capitalism and Democracy: The Strain Is Showing*, FIN. TIMES, Aug. 30, 2016 https://www.ft.com/content/e46e8c00-6b72-11e6-ae5b-a7cc5dd5a28c.

77. ALEXIS DE TOCQUEVILLE, DEMOCRACY IN AMERICA 652 (Arthur Goldhammer trans., Library of America, 2004).

78. ALEXIS DE TOCQUEVILLE, THE OLD REGIME AND THE FRENCH REVOLUTION (Stuart Gilbert trans., Doubleday & Co., 1955).

79. As Justice Brandeis stated in his then-radical concurrence in *Whitney v. California*, "the path of safety lies in the opportunity to discuss freely supposed grievances and proposed remedies." 274 U.S. 357, 375 (1927) (Brandeis, J., concurring). For a wonderful elaboration of *Whitney*, see Robert M. Cover, *The Left, the Right, and the First Amendment 1918–1928*, 40 MD. L. REV. 349 (1981).

80. ALEXIS DE TOCQUEVILLE, DEMOCRACY IN AMERICA 80 (Francis Bowen ed., Cambridge University Press, 1863).

81. ARISTOTLE, THE POLITICS 98 (Stephen Everson ed., Cambridge University Press, 1996).

Index

Politics and Capital. John Attanasio.
© John Attanasio 2018. Published 2018 by Oxford University Press.